OLD MASTER

Field Marshal Jan Christian Smuts and President Roosevelt as they conferred in Cairo at the time of the Teheran Conference.

(*Photo by Press Assoc., Inc.*)

OLD MASTER,

The Life of
Jan Christian Smuts

RENÉ KRAUS

1944

E. P. DUTTON & CO., Inc.

New York

A WARTIME BOOK

THIS COMPLETE EDITION IS PRODUCED
IN FULL COMPLIANCE WITH THE GOVERN-
MENT'S REGULATIONS FOR CONSERVING
PAPER AND OTHER ESSENTIAL MATERIALS.

AMERICAN BOOK—STRATFORD PRESS, INC., NEW YORK

To

Audrey,

the inspiration,

in gratitude.

CONTENTS

Part One—STORM AND STRESS

Part Two—POWER

CONTENTS

Part Three—PHOENIX

OLD MASTER

NOTE

Field Marshal Smuts was christened Jan Christiaan. During his development which has made him an ardent Briton, while remaining a proud Boer, he dropped the second "a" from his second Christian name. The correct spelling is now Christian. The Old Master, however, signs his name merely J. C. Smuts.

During the period this book covers the Afrikander dropped the "d." Today he prefers to be called Afrikaner.

Defense is spelled with "c" when the word forms part of a name or title: Defence Force, or Minister for Defence. This is in South Africa the official spelling.

THE OLD MASTER IS A SON OF SOLITUDE. DESCENDED FROM THE early Boers who were so enamoured of loneliness that they seldom saw smoke rising from a neighbor's chimney, a delicate infant at the beginning, raised on a cattle and sheep ranch close to the Cape of Good Hope, he grew during the first seventy-four years of his life into that patriarchal loftiness that makes his people compare him to Table Mountain, the crest towering above the confluence of the Atlantic and the Indian oceans.

No other man in our times has devoted his life so entirely to bringing people and nations together, to making a whole out of parts, to co-operation, union, fusion, to the brotherhood of mankind. But his brothers leave him alone. Except for a model marriage, the effect of which has deeply influenced the fate of South Africa, and for his strong feeling for his family, another predominant trait of the Boers, his innermost self has remained solitary. He became the chief architect of a new country, the Union of South Africa, and of a new people, the South Africans. He suffered the birth pangs, yet seemed indifferent to the pain he endured. For half a century he steered his people through every storm. But the waves never succeeded in engulfing him. The Old Master remained untouched, secluded, very much himself.

The twenty-fourth of May, 1870, was joyously celebrated in

the old Cape Colony. So, of course, was every twenty-fourth of May, the birthday of the gracious Queen. The sturdy Dutch, the majority of the white people in the colony, were eager to prove their loyalty to their exalted sovereign. It was, to quote an old French proverb, a little love and a little faithfulness, and just a grain of falsehood admixed. Loudly proclaimed allegiance to the Queen was, first, an expression of a genuine personal feeling, and, secondly, a perfect excuse for the Dutch people's own national self-assertion, which, at about this time, began to show itself.

For a few years the Cape Colony, particularly the Western Province, the richer and more civilized part of it, had been in the throes of a religious revival. People prayed all night in the churches. Small wonder that they spent the night before the eventful birthday on their knees, praying God to save the Queen. In this general excitement local news lost much of its importance. Otherwise, the birth of the Father of the Fatherland, on the very birthday of Her Majesty, would not have passed all but unnoticed.

The newcomer at Bovenplaats, the farm outside the *dorp* Ribeek West, had certainly the right to claim local attention. Not only in the *dorp*, but even in the center of the district, the town of Malmesbury, nine miles to the south—and some thirty miles north of Cape Town—everyone knew and respected the Honorable Jacobus Abraham Smuts, for a time the representative of Malmesbury in the Legislative Assembly in Cape Town. He was a prosperous yeoman who worked his large *Zwartland* —black earth—farm wisely and profitably. Working is perhaps a slight overstatement. The dirty business of work was done exclusively by Kafirs. The Dutch farmers of this fertile soil, the land of the vine, the land of golden grain, alternately drenched with glorious sunshine and ample rainfall, were mere plantation owners. There had been no poverty among them. Jacobus Abraham Smuts, related to all the farmers in the neighborhood, was one of those fortunate people. His picture shows a massive, solid man, rather paunchy—the indispensable sign of prosperity—with well-trimmed whiskers and a short beard surrounding a shrewd but jovial face. He was famous for his sober judgment, his wise counsel, his instinct for the right word and the right thing. Steeped in his puritanical creed, which by no means entirely excluded a taste for the good things of life, deeply attached to his somber Calvinistic church, intelligent in a quiet way, traditionalist in much but believing in real progress, frugal, thrifty, patient and sometimes petty, a born man of law and a theologian, he was the typical, peaceful, cautious Dutch farmer of the colony. Men of his ilk never lost their greatest asset: their equanimity. When some of the more radical Boers followed the *Voortrekkers* to the harsh, poor, and inhospitable North, to live undisturbed by British magistrates and missionaries, neither of whom condoned slavery and the shameful abuse of the black man, men like Smuts *père* only shook their heads. They did not wish to be mixed up in other people's business, but they simply could not understand why anyone should prefer the wild, barren expanses north of the River Vaal, where man must lead a hard, semi-nomadic life and could at best only raise rickety cattle, to the rich, fecund soil of home.

Jacobus Abraham Smuts got along well with his English neighbors in the small towns. In his own house only *Taal*, today called *Afrikaans*, a sort of seventeenth-century Dutch, was spoken, but the English language, English customs and manners that slowly penetrated the colony did not in the least disturb him. Yet, the times were changing. In 1869, a year before the birth of his second son, the Suez Canal was opened, threatening to drain the commerce from the shipping lanes around the Cape of Good Hope. The new short cut might well replace Cape Town and its hinterland as the halfway house between England and India. The growing of wine was no longer as profitable. Now a *ligger*—or leaguer, a pipe containing a hundred and twenty-six gallons—sold for no more than three pounds, whereas a few years earlier it had netted the wine grower five to six pounds. South African vintages did not really get a fair chance in the motherland. London was completely unaware of the fact that the colonial *Great Drukenstein* compared favorably with better-known foreign wines.

But Jacobus Abraham Smuts took such reverses quietly, and was resigned to the will of God. One could always turn one's grapes into brandy, for which there were better chances of export and, above all, an insatiable market in Cape Town. "It's a beastly place," admitted an inhabitant of the colonial capital to an English visitor by the name of Anthony Trollope. "But we have enough to eat and drink, and manage to make out life very well. The girls are as pretty as they are anywhere else, and as kind—and brandy is plentiful."

The peace of the Western Province was not disturbed either by the constant Kafir scare disrupting the poorer and less progressive Eastern Province. In Bovenplaats, in particular, the relations between the white master and his family on one side and the colored labor on the other was patriarchal and idyllic. The Smuts children grew up with the native boys and girls, and listened to the tales of the black oldsters, all veterans of the innumerable Kafir and Zulu wars. While in the Eastern Province the maxim was generally accepted that the Kafir must be ruled with a rod of iron, since he was by nature a thief and obsessed by the sole idea of stealing cattle, the yeomanry of the Western Province, largely under the mellowing English influence, was much more liberal and tolerant. Although the Mohammedan Malays made the best laborers, the increasing Kafir element, with an ever thinning admixture of the vanishing Hottentot, was, if idle by instinct, neither as apathetic as savages, nor quite so indifferent as the Orientals. The Kafir, it was the general conviction, was not a bad fellow. He was not constitutionally cruel, he learned to work readily, and soon saved a little property for himself. The conditions under which his race lived had infinitely improved with the coming of the white man. But on the other hand the colonials did not doubt for an instant that if the Kafirs could choose whether the white man should be driven into the sea or allowed to remain in the country, the entire race would certainly decide for the white man's extermination.

14

The fear that the blacks, forming about four-fifths of the total population and increasing rapidly in numbers since the British administration had put a stop to their perennial fratricidal strife, and to their deeply ingrained habit of "eating each other up"—killing one another—would one day outvote or outfight the white man was the dark cloud overhanging the blue skies of the Cape Colony. Even now the cloud has not yet disappeared. The constant fear of losing his supremacy is the white man's nightmare in South Africa. This constant living in terror explains many anomalies which would otherwise appear inexplicable. It is a silent terror. Polite society does not speak of it. Society was much more polite in mid-Victorian times, in the Cape Colony as elsewhere. Mother Smuts, née Catherina Petronella de Vries, would certainly not have tolerated the slightest allusion to unmentionable topics of conversation in her well-established farmhouse.

Mrs. Smuts, by all accounts an energetic, strong-willed lady, was the grande dame of her rural society. Descended from an old French Huguenot family, many of whom have infused the blood of the old Boers with their pride and puritanism, she was strongly religious and traditionalist, but by the same token more resilient and worldly than the average Boer *vrou* of her day. She had received her education in Cape Town, which city had a famous public library, and a handsome museum, more noted for its precious collections of South African birds and butterflies, than for its two stuffed lions and its long-deceased elephant, not to mention an extremely shaky giraffe. Cape Town was the city of two beautiful cathedrals—most people found the Roman Catholic cathedral more impressive than the newer Anglican one, over which Bishop Jones at that time presided. Cape Town was also renowned for its botanical gardens where all the rich flora of South Africa flourished; for its castle, close to the sea; for its observatory, its hospitals and sailors' homes, and last but not least, for its latest institution: the lunatic asylum at Robben Island. But above all, Cape Town was a city of artistic and intellectual endeavour. Music and the French language were cultivated. Mademoiselle Catherina Petronella de Vries studied both. However, when she accepted Jacobus Abraham Smuts' proposal of marriage, she resolved to become a good Boer housewife. She brought her children up to fear God and no one else. Her second son, baptized Jan Christiaan, was her problem child. He had delicate health, and after his birth, seventy-four years ago, no one, not even his mother, thought he would live long.

Looking back into history, it seems to be more than a mere coincidence that little Jannie's natal year gave birth to the new South Africa as well. Two incidents ushered in the new times: the diamond rush had just started, and on September 1, in Durban, Natal, a tall, thin, sickly lad, fresh from England, disembarked to join his elder brother, a cotton grower, and to get rid under the southern sun of a bothersome cough, which might perhaps be tuberculosis. His name was Cecil John Rhodes.

These two events appeared quite unconnected. But they grew together. The discovery of diamonds tore South Africa from its century-long sleep. Fortune hunters from all over the world transformed the faraway land, literally overnight, into a more hectic than happy hunting ground. The luckiest of them, and certainly the most gifted, towering alike above competitors, foes, and friends, was the coughing lad, an English parson's son, who at sixteen came to South Africa to work as a farm hand, and died at forty-eight, the world's diamond and gold king; yet a scorner of money, which was to him only the shabby, if necessary, means of realizing his dream which he called the establishment of a power so strong as to make war impossible hereafter. The flag that should wave over this tremendous dream-building was, of course, the Union Jack.

The Boers did not care for the diamond-and-gold rush that set in. To their Old Testament rigidity—which, incidentally, never prevented them from being shrewd and pennywise bargainers—it was the dance around the golden calf; a nauseating spectacle in which they wished to have no part. They had much more important things on their minds. In 1872, the Imperial government granted the Cape Colony full self-government. For almost twenty years the elected lawmakers had learned the

16

craft of politics in a sort of shadow parliament that had only advisory functions. Now they themselves were the law. Under the gentle guidance of Mr. Molteno, the Prime Minister of the Cape Colony, who since he had occupied his seat from the creation of the first House of Assembly in 1854, handled power as to the manner born, the budding legislators took their first steps along the stony path of independence. One of their earliest acts was to forbid the extermination of the locust, since the plague was sent by God. Simultaneously, the right to use the Dutch language in the Cape Parliament was conceded. Mr. J. G. Luttig, the newly elected member for Beaufort West, made the first Dutch speech, and all the Boer members of the House felt better. Jacobus Abraham Smuts was now often absent from his farm. His new importance called him frequently to Cape Town. At home, his wife took little Jannie by the hand and taught him to walk. It was a difficult task. The child, listless and pale, showed no real inclination to put one small foot before the other. Nothing indicated the famous mountain climber in the making.

Jannie was not yet seven years old when an event, crashing like thunder, tore South Africa asunder. The Transvaal collapsed.

Chapter 2   TRANSVAAL INTERLUDE

TWENTY MILES NORTH OF NEWCASTLE, NATAL, THE WORLD OF civilization ended, and the realm of wilderness began. The few travelers who cared to cross the border noticed immediately that they had entered the territory of the South African Republic, generally called the Transvaal, although no barriers indicated the frontier. But from this point on the roads were almost impassable. The inns, exclusively run by straggling Englishmen or Germans, were primitive. The storekeepers along the dirt roads charged eighteen pence for a bundle of fodder for a horse, which they themselves had purchased for threepence from the farmer. A horse required six bundles per day. A trip to the Transvaal was an expensive pleasure for the visitor from Natal. When Sir Theophilus Shepstone undertook the trip, it became an expensive burden for the English taxpayer, and there was no pleasure in it at all.

Far from one another stood the Boers' farmhouses, very modest abodes. They usually contained two main rooms with a small lean-to: the sleeping place. The fireplace was in the living room. Outside the house, at some thirty or forty yards distance, a huge oven was built. Considering that most of the houses perched on uneven ground, and that none was floored, the huts, which in fact they were, appeared sufficiently solid and moderately clean. Two massive tables, not infrequently with a locker under them, made up the chief furniture. There were one or two chairs, never more. The objects in the house were rather dirty, and most of all the little Boerlings, who swarmed about in droves. The Boers are a prolific race. They marry early, lead wholesome, moral lives, and when they lose their mates, the widow or widower speedily finds another spouse. Thus it often happened that three or four families occupied the same two rooms. Yet when a foreigner arrived to stay the night, the bedroom, the sanctum—even in a very poor house usually equipped with a comfortable feather bed—was immediately cleared for him. These rough and ready Boers of the North did not forget their traditional kindly virtue: hospitality. More often than not they refused to accept any recompense offered for supper and bed, whereas the correct English settlers rarely forgot to present a modest bill. The Boers, it appears, were the more curious toward strangers. Every new face was welcome in their self-imposed isolation. But the welcome was seldom extended beyond a single night. At nine or ten in the morning, the hour at which the Transvaal Boer got up (the farmers in the Colony started their day at dawn), a hearty handshake indicated unmistakably that the moment of parting had come.

Only the Peruvians were allowed to remain a little longer. Peruvian was the courtesy name applied to the many Polish and Russian Jews who peddled their wares up and down the country. From them the Boer purchased the only thing on which he permitted himself to spend money, and very little money at that: his outfit. The process of haggling over the price of the accepted woolen clothing, the fabric mixed with calico, took the whole day. One could not dismiss the Peruvian before dusk, nor did one care to do so, since the Jewish peddlers were altogether popular. Were they not the descendants of the chosen people? To the Transvaal Boer, whose only reading matter was the Old Testament, they were, indeed. At least, as long as they came on foot, humbly, their backs bent under the weight of their packs, a docile smile on their sweating faces. Some years later, it is true, the Peruvians took to Cape Carts with well-fed horses, sleek and evidently well nourished themselves, and with smiles a little benign and a little insolent. It became also increasingly difficult to barter with them. And so that ferocious anti-Semitism sprang up in the country which still spurs the irreconcilables among the Boers.

The average Transvaal Boer of those times wore the same clothes every day. Still, this habit marked a considerable advance over the fashions of the previous generation. The children of the *Voortrekkers,* the generation of about the middle of the nineteenth century, were clad in hides. They lived upon the carcasses of the beasts they hunted, and what was a matter of necessity with them became a tradition with their grandchildren; to them it was a comfortable way of saving the expenses of food. Extreme penury was their predominant characteristic. They preferred to leave their large farms untilled and their pastures empty rather than pay the infinitesimally low wages for colored labor. The average Transvaal farm was the size of an English county. A man possessing less than six thousand acres of land was said to own only "half" or "a quarter" of a farm. But only the few acres surrounding the house were ploughed to provide the family with the bare necessities of life. This laziness was by no means inborn in the Boer, although, in the Transvaal it soon became second nature. It was due to desperate circumstances. What could he have done with his crop? There were no roads to transport it; the few dirt roads were unusable, a quagmire, since the contractors were never paid by the government. There was no market for one's products. Inside the Transvaal there were only two small towns; Pretoria and Heidelberg, both amply supplied by their surrounding neighborhood. Prohibitive duties obstructed any trade or traffic with the three other states of South Africa, the Orange Free State, a republic, and the two British colonies, the Cape and Natal. Above all, there was no money in the country. Only direct taxation was known, and the sturdy Transvaal Boer stubbornly refused to pay. For his neighbor, whom more often than not he loathed, did not pay either. Descendants of the fiercest fighting race, they even refused the call to arms when the savage tribes around them raided and ravaged the borderlands of the Transvaal.

Sullen, secluded, opposed to change and progress, the Transvaal Boer of 1870 lived a dreary life. His boorishness was the consequence of his isolation. He was excluded from all the amenities of social intercourse. The churches were too far away, as were the schools for his children. The small-town dances were reserved mostly for the English-speaking population. His days were drab. Only once in a lifetime there were a few days of lightness and brightness: when he went *vrying*. Looking for a wife, which came in early youth, the Boer lad employed an old established scheme. He began by riding around the country to see what young girls within his circle were available. When he had made his choice he put on his Sunday trousers, polished his saddle or borrowed a new one, stuck a feather in his cap, and went forth to conquer. He was further equipped with a bottle of sugarplums with which to propitiate his prospective mother-in-law, and a candle. As soon as he entered the house his purpose was known; it was fully explained by his clean trousers, and the candle. If any doubt remained in the mind of the mother of a marriageable daughter, the gift of the sugar-plums removed it the instant she received it. Without a word the candle was offered to the girl. If she refused it, the suitor left with no hard feelings. He simply rode on to the house of the next lady on his list. But if she accepted it, the candle was lighted. The mother stuck a pin into it and retired to leave the young people alone until the flame burned down as far as the pin. Tender mothers poured a little salt on to the flame so that it might flicker a little longer. The marriage took place the following day. And after a week the old dreariness of life began again.

President Burgers set out to conquer dreariness, the Transvaal disease. He was not one of the northern Boers himself and he had no tie with the *Voortrekkers*. He came from the Cape Colony, imbued with its liberal spirit. Originally a clergyman of the Dutch Reformed Church, he parted company with this intolerant sect devoted to the Old Testament God of wrath, gave up holy orders, left his country, and was, an eloquent and enthusiastic man, heartily welcomed in the Transvaal. Soon he was elected President, thus shouldering a burden that almost crushed him.

The country into which he came was bankrupt, its treasury empty, a paper currency, set afloat in 1865, greatly depreciated. Taxes could not be collected and quarrels with the far from subdued natives were incessant and perilous. Yet Mr. Burgers plunged into his task in high spirits. He succeeded in raising a loan, borrowing £60,000. He established a national flag, and had a gold coinage struck from the then budding gold output of the Transvaal: three hundred gold pieces, bearing his own likeness, and worth twenty shillings each. In order to build a railway from Pretoria, his capital, through the gold fields of the Transvaal down to Delagoa Bay in the Portuguese colony—indeed a prime necessity for the economic expansion of the country—he betook himself to Holland where he raised another loan, saddling his republic with a further debt of £100,000 for railway properties. To all this he added the boast that he would "liberate" all South Africa and become the George Washington south of the equator.

His interests, it must be admitted, were above all economic and cultural. He attempted to have the long neglected and entirely uncultivated public lands surveyed. But no one knew in the least what public lands there were, or how their boundaries ran. He issued a code of laws before he had either courts or judges to sit in them. His favorite plan was a high-flown scheme of education. However, he could only get five children all told to attend the one high school that was actually established. The parents paid £15 each for ten months' schooling. Hence the total income of the high school amounted to £75, whereas Mr. Burgers' budget allowed for a fixed salary of £400 a year for the headmaster. The district schools in the small towns and the rural ward schools failed equally miserably, as they were too expensive and pretentious. In the final year of the independent First South African Republic, two hundred and thirty-six pupils went to the district schools and sixty-five to the ward schools. Since the government was penniless for many months every year, the salaries were not paid and the schools sank into ruin.

They were as little popular among the Transvaal Boers as any of the apparently extravagant measures of reform progressive Mr. Burgers wished to introduce. The general welcome with which he had been received was wearing rapidly thinner. The obstruction of the state schools by the Boer people was a test case. Out of a total white population of 45,000 at least 10 per cent were of school age. But only three hundred pupils were sent to school. The average Boer found it enough education for his child if he could be made to read the *Bible* and learn sufficient of the ritual of the Dutch Reformed Church to pass the confirmation examination. Itinerant schoolmasters who had previously contributed a little to a primitive education could no longer continue in the exercise of their profession, since President Burgers stopped their meager allowances.

President Burgers, a well-meaning, if vain, man, was cursed

with the Midas touch in reverse. He floated loans which were astronomic in the depressed circumstances of his country, yet his administration constantly verged on the brink of bankruptcy. He introduced reforms, only to arouse and stiffen the bigoted prejudices of his people. He could not even guarantee the security and independence of the Republic, the only possession which the grossly materialistic Transvaal Boers prized more than life. The black man was lurking around the corner.

At the end of 1876, the natives from across the border invaded and ravaged forty square miles of the Transvaal, burning every house in the area. The Boers, indifferent in their seclusion, did not "saddle up" as was their proud tradition. There was no fight left in them. The natives got away. When the rainy season ended, Cetewayo, the great black chief, massed his forces in three groups on the borders of the Republic. According to a memorandum written by Colonel A. W. Durnford, "he would have undoubtedly swept the Transvaal, at least up to the Vaal River, if not to Pretoria itself." Twelve years after the South African Republic had begun its existence as an independent state, it had reached a condition of complete insolvency and defenselessness, with no way out of the perils of total ruin and chaos. The house was on fire and it seemed certain that the fire would spread all over South Africa.

It was under these circumstances that Sir Theophilus Shepstone arrived in Pretoria on January 22, 1877, accompanied by six other gentlemen from Natal, and a guard of twenty-five mounted policemen. Sir Theophilus, already an old man, had for many years been Minister for Native Affairs in Natal; he knew more about the colored problem than any other white man in South Africa. Moreover, he was held in especial respect by Cetewayo, the King of the Zulus, who was the torch if South Africa should, as British and Boer equally dreaded, ever be set on fire by the blacks. One of Sir Theophilus' first actions was to address a message to his friend Cetewayo, and to the Chief's lieutenant, Secocoeni, saying that the Transvaal, if attacked, would be defended by British troops. He received a reply in the quaint style of the natives which read: "I thank my father Somtseu (Shepstone) for his message. I am glad he has sent it, because the Dutch have tired me out, and I intended to fight them once, only once, and to drive them over the Vaal. Kabana, you see my impis (tribal chiefs) are gathered. It was to fight the Dutch I called them together. Now I will send them back to their houses."

Sir Theophilus settled down in Pretoria to wait quietly. He received hundreds of Transvaal petty politicians, listened to their suggestions and grievances, but did not disclose any ulterior motives of his own. He had come merely as a friend and an advisor, he emphasized, to see whether and how the Republic could be saved.

It was impossible to save the Republic from its own politicians. The English party had little reason to sympathize with President Burgers, who had made education in the English language almost impossible, and constantly proclaimed it his ambition to drive the "paramount power" out of South Africa. But whereas the Transvaal British adopted their inbred attitude of waiting and seeing, the Boer opposition persistently undermined the shaky system. The *Voortrekker* party, the radical wing of the Transvaal Boers, composed entirely of members of the fierce and fanatic Dopper sect, and led by Johannes Paulus Kruger, himself one of the last surviving *Voortrekkers*, and already a sort of sectarian saint (since as a lad in his teens he had participated in the extermination of Dingaan, the Zulu chief), approached the English with a suggestion to co-operate in bringing about the fall of Burgers. At the same time the saintly Kruger, ever a past master in the lower levels of politics, assured the President of his unwavering support. The *Volksraad*, the republican parliament, bragged, swaggered, and blustered, but was unanimous only in opposing any sound measure of reform. When its last session was adjourned, President Burgers commented: "The *Volksraad* has gone away having done nothing but harm."

The mass of the Boer population remained indifferent. Why should a man fight the accursed natives if his neighbor did not? Why should he cultivate his land, or more of it than he needed to feed himself? Why shear his sheep, if he could not sell his wool? Why pay taxes for a nonexistent government? The Transvaal Boer had sunk to this condition of not fighting, not working, not paying.

After ten weeks of watching and waiting in Pretoria, Sir Theophilus did the only possible thing. Without instructions from London, he annexed the Transvaal by a proclamation, issued at Pretoria on April 12, 1877, to restore peace and order, and bring the country back to normalcy. His proclamation had been read and approved by President Burgers, who had only insisted on two minor changes readily granted by Sir Theophilus. Contrariwise, the British Commissioner approved Burgers' message of farewell which contained a meek, face-saving appeal to the burghers never to weaken in their spirit of independence, but not to have recourse to acts of violence, at least not for a fortnight (within which time a sufficiently strong British garrison would have arrived from Natal). Heartbroken, Burgers returned to his native Cape Colony. The excitable, unstable, visionary, but truly enlightened and patriotic man left all of twelve shillings and sixpence behind him in the Treasury. His "bluebacks"—pound notes—sold for a shilling apiece. Yet Burgers had not drawn any salary while in office and in addition had expended all his modest private fortune on the State, and even incurred a heavy personal liability when money was urgently needed for the prosecution of the unsuccessful Secocoeni campaign. This debt hounded him for the rest of his life. However, unperturbed, Burgers resumed his social position in Cape Town, where he joined the ranks of the moderate, only slightly anti-British undercover opposition.

No one in the Transvaal shed a tear at his departure, no one grumbled over the annexation. The burghers and farmers had every reason to be thankful for their salvation. The price of land, until the annexation practically nil, soared as the British administration built roads and provided markets. The inflated currency was replaced by the most solid money in the world. The restive natives were quelled. No one disturbed the peace. Even Saint Paulus of the Boers took office under the Crown.

But he could not stomach his self-imposed subservience. He found an outlet for his dissatisfaction in repeatedly demanding an increase in his remuneration. When this was refused, he plunged headlong into the repeal of the annexation program. The English in Pretoria never doubted that he would have remained a loyal British subject, had the inducement he clamored for been forthcoming. History would have taken another turn. The South African war would never have claimed its toll of blood and bitterness.

The restless Transvaal, however, was not destined for security and tranquillity. With both hands the Boers grasped at whatever they could get. The country's debts, incurred by President Burgers, were settled out of the English taxpayers' pockets. The responsibility in the country rested on broader shoulders than before.

But with the revival of trade and the removal of burdens the old Boer habit of intransigence returned. The dangers and difficulties of the past were of small account now that they were indeed buried in the past. The benefits of annexation had been reaped. The pressing needs of the Boers had been relieved. Their debts had been paid; their credit restored; their black enemies subdued. Repeal would rob them of none of these advantages. They would, in short, have their cake and eat it too. The men who had silently, many of them cheerfully, accepted annexation, became vocal, in fact, noisy and clamorous. A wave of extreme nationalism ensued. Now that their stomachs were full and their worries removed, the time had come for what they called the spiritual things.

The tide of renewed Boer nationalism engulfed most of South Africa. In fact, not even the conservative and wealthy farmers of the Cape Colony had been as indifferent to their adventurous kinsmen in the North as prudence had advised them to appear. The Boers, a scattered handful of people at the utter extremity of the globe, would never have survived had it not been for their flamboyant nationalism which at times could be bridled, but never extinguished.

The repercussions of the rapidly mounting tide of Transvaal

nationalism were strongest in the Orange Free State. Now the only Boer republic left, the Free State saw its territory surrounded on all sides by the hated red color on the map. The Free State Boers had also fled from British rule. While the *Voortrekkers* had crossed the River Vaal, they, in turn, had crossed the Orange River. They were actuated by the same motives: by their disgust of the philanthropic English treatment of the natives, and the abolition of slavery by Her Majesty's magistrates.

New motives fanned their hatred. As soon as the diamonds of Kimberley were discovered, the English annexed the territory which had been in the possession of natives, but which closely bordered the Free State. Boer farmers who had estates in the vicinity of the sudden rush for diamonds were glad to sell their property at what seemed astronomical prices. They themselves had neither the resilience nor the ingenuity to work the mines. Nevertheless, they sat on their newly acquired moneybags and cursed the English, who had what it took to make millions out of the stones. Perhaps the strongest single factor arousing the Free State against the British was a German immigrant by the name of Borckenhagen. History has long forgotten this name, but without his incessant anti-British pamphleteering in his paper, the *Bloemfontein Daily Express*, feelings in the Free State would probably never have reached that white heat that made them side with the Transvaal, although they were by no means affected by the tragic conflict between the British Empire and the so-called South African Republic. Above all, they loathed this intruder Cecil Rhodes.

The "colossus"-in-the-making did not care. He was on the friendliest terms with the Afrikaner Bond, the organization of Dutch farmers in the Cape Colony, which mixed a then still slight and concealed sprinkling of Boer nationalism with a vivid sense for the protection of their agricultural interests. With their support, Cecil Rhodes entered the Cape Parliament in 1881. It was England's only success in the otherwise blackest year of her South African history. The Transvaal Boers had risen and defeated an insufficient and badly equipped number

of English soldiers, storming, at last, their stronghold, Majuba
Hill. It was an ignominious defeat of British arms. Fortunately
Sir Evelyn Wood secured adequate reinforcements and judged
his power sufficient to turn the tables, and to suppress the
revolt. But instead of establishing the Queen's authority, he
first asked for instructions from London. Mr. Gladstone was
Premier, and insisted on an immediate peace, peace at almost
any price. The Boers took Gladstone's pacifism, which was the
price he had to pay for his excessive promises to the voters in
his Midlothian campaign, for English weakness, and exulted
in their victory. The shamelessly abandoned Loyalists gathered
in Pretoria, and in tears they buried their own sacred flag, the
Union Jack.

All these events seemed entirely unconnected with the little
boy growing up on a quiet farm in the tranquil Western Province. It was no longer Bovenplaats, a family possession claimed
by an elder brother of Jacobus Abraham Smuts, who had established himself on a new farm; now it was *Klipfontein* (Stone
Fountain), a few miles farther to the north, when Jannie was
eight years of age, three years before the defeat of Majuba. The
black soil of the new farm was the best wheat land in all South
Africa. It demanded redoubled care and multiplied endeavour.
Another change had taken place. A dark cloud, the first, overshadowed the boy's life. His mother died. Smuts senior, true to
type, took a new wife, and two more infants arrived. Little
Jannie, by nature a shy and lonesome child, must have been
entirely preoccupied with his own changed life. He could not
know that the turbulent events in the distant outside world
were leading to the chaos which he would one day be called
upon to mould into shape. Was the little boy even aware of the
existence of such people as the English?

Evidently, he was.

After the tragedy of Majuba, beset, it seems, with doubts, he
asked Abraham whether the English were indeed the greatest
people in the world.

Abraham, a shriveled Hottentot of close to a hundred years

old, hesitated a moment. Then he declared: "The English? There is one people greater than they. A people coming from the high North. They call themselves Scots."

Chapter 3   SPRINGTIME IN STELLENBOSCH

IN CHILDHOOD ALREADY PERSISTENT, JANNIE WENT ON HIS WAY. Still a toddler, he became *touleier:* that is, he learned to hold a rope ahead of a team of draught animals. This was his apprenticeship. Soon he became a "goose girl." When he knew all about geese, he spent some time caring for the pigs. Goats succeeded pigs, to make way in turn for sheep. Finally he was entrusted with the stewardship of a small herd of cows and oxen. Now he had reached the top of the ladder. At the age of twelve he was an accomplished cattle farmer, and nothing beyond this achievement was to be expected of him. The fact that Jannie could neither read nor write did not unduly bother his father. The eldest Smuts boy received a careful education since he was slated to become a *predikant.* It was not necessary to have a second bookish son in the family.

But when Jannie was twelve his elder brother died of typhoid. Therefore it became his duty to prepare himself for the pulpit of the Dutch Reformed Church. He was, in consequence, sent to school in the village Ribeek West, where he lodged in the boarding house *De Ark,* run by the headmaster, Mr. T. C. Stoffberg.

The boy certainly did not relish the change in his circumstances. Described as an easily frightened child who used to run away, panic-stricken, when he saw people approaching, even those with whom he was well acquainted, he feared the big world of the hamlet of Ribeek West. On the *veld* the child had been independent and self-contained. Jannie had even done his own cooking. Now all that was left behind: the rolling hills of the Black Land, with its rich green grass and wild-flowers of every description; his favorite slope on whose summit he used to light his primitive stove; the few head of cattle which his father had given him as wages for his child labor.

Mr. Stoffberg had a difficult time in moulding into shape the high-strung, stubborn and self-centered country boy, to whom a tyranny prescribing proper clothes and regular hours was unbearable. "He behaves like a wild bird," the headmaster reported. The teacher-pupil conflict lasted throughout Jannie's first term, and far into the second.

Then, suddenly, a new passion overtook the boy, a passion which proved incurable, and which still possesses the Old Master: the passion for books. Mr. Stoffberg's library, in which Jannie was allowed to browse to his heart's content, opened to the lad the gates to a new world. His memory at this time was so unspoiled that he could, it was said, learn an entire book by heart in simply reading it over once. His mind was flooded by the onrush of ideas. Gradually, the youngster adjusted himself to his surroundings, which meant in the case of Jan Christian Smuts that he excelled all others. The belated tyro rapidly surpassed all the children of the neighboring farmers in his class, a success that, perhaps, did not make him over-popular with them. It is entirely possible that little Daniel François Malan, another small boy from Ribeek West, four years Jannie's junior, was already in his childhood imbued with that implacable hatred, born out of impotent jealousy, with which the present leader of the opposition in the South African House of Assembly persecutes and baits General Smuts to this very day.

But Jannie, it appears, still in elementary school, was as indifferent to hostility then as now. He did not play with the other boys, preferring to keep rigidly to himself. He devoured books throughout the night, even on his holidays at his father's farm. He took his first successes—moving up several classes in one term, and finishing the school with high marks in the headmaster's special scholarship class—with the same detachment which, for instance, he displayed when he was created a field marshal in the British Army on his seventy-first birthday. When he passed his final examination, he had certainly taught his headmaster an impressive lesson. Unfortunately, teachers seldom care to learn from their pupils. Almost thirty years later, in 1915, when South Africa shook in the convulsive aftermath of a revolution which General Smuts with difficulty suppressed, Mr. Stoffberg contested the parliamentary seat of Rustenberg against his former disciple. The teacher was once more bested.

Smuts' way to the pulpit was prescribed. The first step was Victoria College in Stellenbosch, an academic institution endowed with a famous theological seminary which within twenty-five years had won a country-wide reputation. The budding freshman laid his plans methodically. From his father's farm he wrote a letter to Professor Murray, informing him of his intention of coming to the college in a few weeks, and asking for the professor's kindly advice. A characteristic excerpt from this remarkable letter reads: "Such a place where a large puerile element exists, affords fair scope for moral, and, what is more important, religious temptation. . . . Of what use will a mind, enlarged and refined in all possible ways, be to me, if my religion be a deserted pilot, and morality a wreck? To avoid temptation and to make the proper use of my precious time, I purposely refuse entering a public boarding department, as that of Mr. de Kock, but I shall board privately (most likely at Mr. W. Ackermann's) which will, in addition, accord with my retired and reserved nature." This highly moral letter concludes with a few very practical questions as to tuition fees, school books, and examinations. Professor Murray preserved the innocent epistle as the early confession of a star-gazing realist.

The way to Stellenbosch was difficult. There was, once more, the dread of the great world, this time a charming old town with, at that period, a population of 2,000 souls. There was the necessity of providing for the tuition fees. Young Smuts solved this problem by selling the cattle he had earned as his father's farm hand. Last but not least, a knowledge of Greek was required. Greek had not been included in the curriculum of the village school. Moreover, no Greek tutor was available when the last moment for matriculation approached. Once more seclusion helped. Jannie retired to a farm, exactly one week before the beginning of the term, and stuffed the contents of a Greek grammar so completely into his head that he passed the examination first on the list. For relaxation during this week of grueling study he had equipped himself with a volume of Shelley. Another door was flung open to him. He had discovered poetry. A new sense for beauty awoke. It led him from Shelley to Keats and Milton, thence to Shakespeare (whose lack of religion he deplored), and finally to a young lady by the nickname of Isie. Sometimes, on his solitary Sunday walks he recited Shelley to the grass on the meadows. Yet it is questionable whether it was indeed the harmony of the rhymes that agitated him so deeply, or the lesson he learned from the poet's messages. Shelley's views on the rights of man influenced him profoundly. It was a little later that he fell helpless prey to another poet: Walt Whitman.

Still, he lived in complete solitude, engaged in hard study and the ascetic pleasures of loneliness. Except for joining the volunteers, where he acquired some military training, and for teaching a *Bible* class in a colored Sunday school, he remained by himself. He was an outsider in patrician Stellenbosch, then as today the most intensely Dutch town in the Cape, whose inhabitants disliked the loop line to the main railway because the train connected them with the vulgarity abroad. The town, one of the oldest in the country, had been founded in 1684, and a year later settled by Huguenot refugees, whose Puritan spirit still lingered. During the time of Smuts' study, Stellenbosch was markedly under the influence of Hofmeyr, the leader of the Afrikander Bond, whose new nationalist creed was mingled with the spirit of the old faith. The church service was the most important event in everyday life. The Scottish professors, who at that time almost monopolized Victoria College, encouraged regular church attendance and hard work, and not much else.

They were, however, not averse to co-education. Engagements between students were frequent, for people in South Africa marry early. Society, "much affected by widows," as contemporary gossip in near-by Cape Town put it, celebrated such events. It was quite an affair when a senior, though to tell the truth, a rather backward student by the name of James Barry Munnik Hertzog, became engaged to Mademoiselle Jacoba Wilhelmina Neethling, a young lady greatly interested in church matters. Nevertheless young Hertzog refused to continue his preparation for the pulpit, taking to the law instead.

The history of the Union of South Africa was, until Hertzog's death, in November 1942, the history of the running feud between the two schoolmates, Smuts and Hertzog. They resembled one another in but one respect. Jannie, too, during his years at Stellenbosch was beset with doubts whether he was meant to follow the theological calling. He certainly did not abandon his religious convictions. A perpetual student of the *Bible*, particularly of the *Old Testament*, the Boers' own Book of Books, he is the more deeply a convinced Christian for not loudly proclaiming faith. But he must have felt a premonition that worldly matters would demand his service, indeed, that one day the whole world would be his province. He abandoned the thought of theology; he read literature and science.

At home only *Taal*, the Boer language, had been spoken. Now, under the guidance of Professor Mansvelt, Smuts acquired a superb High Dutch, both in speaking and writing. One of his essays in the Dutch language bore the cumbersome title *The Commerce and Prosperity of the Netherlands during the Eighty-Years' War*. Professor Mansvelt was so deeply impressed with the opus that he showed it to Dr. Leyds, then the State Attorney of the Transvaal Republic, who also recognized promising talent, and noted the young author's name.

Throughout his time in Stellenbosch Smuts read and wrote. He did not stop with the English poets. He dove into Goethe and Schiller and the classic German lyricists. He was proud, he asserted in an article, of his Teutonic race. Some observers believed that he was simply going through a period of high-brow inclination toward the German spirit, not uncommon among intellectuals in English-speaking countries. But the fervor with which Smuts sided with Germany at the Versailles Conference and for many years after, permits at least some doubt whether his predilection was, indeed, only a passing phase.

In his nineteenth year a treatise of his, published in *Het Zuid–Afrikaanisch Tydschrift*, (*The South African Magazine*), caused considerable attention. The piece was entitled *Homo Sum*, and discussed the thorny problem of slavery, South Africa's major problem. The young author considered slavery as an ethical question that could not be, as was the custom, considered merely from the economic viewpoint. He did not refuse slavery entirely, but he contrasted the shining example of the Hebrews, who gave the slave an opportunity to regain his freedom after seven years, with the practice of "those nations," including his own, "whose slaves had to bid good-bye to all hope of freedom, and were thus bound to descend to the lowest depths of degradation and despair, sinking further and further in the scale of humanity. Moral elevation, the highest form of religion, is based on enthusiasm."

These few lines reveal three important elements in Smuts' make-up: the English influence, bent on giving the African natives freedom and equality within the scope of their civilization, admiration for the old Jews, whom he felt akin to his own old Boers, and whose country, Palestine, alone among all countries, he rates as beautiful as South Africa, and finally his confession of enthusiasm, a driving power he has never lost, although it froze, as it were, during the busy years.

Enthusiasm, indeed, truth, and other moral values were the *leitmotiv* of all his youthful writing. Even his articles on history and economics ever searched for moral causes. "If South Africa is to be great indeed, and not to be merely inflated with the wind of Johannesburg (then a boom city of gold diggers), its greatness will have to depend on its moral civilization," he wrote, early revealing the true aim of his life.

The citizens of Stellenbosch probably did not take the still painfully shy and nervous youth as seriously as he took himself. Their idle conversation, their social life with its well-tempered amusements, even their occasional evenings of dancing, at which he never assisted, seemed to him a waste of time. He retired deeper into his shell. He could be abrupt, anti-social, awkward. His colleagues took him for a prig.

He found but one colleague who, though only seven months his junior, understood his pathetic solitude: a co-ed, the above-mentioned Isie: Miss Sibylla Margareta Krige. By descent the two were not well met. Whereas Smuts had been imbued by his father with the spirit of inter-racial tolerance in South Africa, the Kriges were an old and politically influential family of un-reconstructed Boers and Britain-haters, who had left Cape Town to live in more congenial, and entirely Dutch, surroundings. Intellectually, however—and more than intellectually—they were destined for one another.

By all accounts Miss Krige was the most brilliant woman student of her day. She taught school in her spare time, and in addition, she, too, wrote articles for magazines, and even for the Cape Town newspapers. After a short acquaintance they both wrote poems, anxiously disguised under pen names or signed only with initials, lest the author of one should discover the confessions of the other. An early picture shows Miss Krige, now Mrs. Smuts and the much beloved *Ouma*—grandmother—of her country, as a young girl of medium stature. Her face is beautifully proportioned, unlined and untouched, at eighteen still a child's face, were it not for her enormous, searching dark eyes, arched by strong, almost masculine, brows. Her hair is trimmed in a boyish fashion. It is cut short and neither parted in the middle nor severely brushed back in the fashion of the pious Boer ladies. She wears a high-necked black dress with the merest and most innocent touch of coquetry, a white lace collar about her neck, and over her dress the white apron appropriate to a future housewife. The only jewel she displays is a double chain of semi-precious stones. But no one can overlook the heap of books piled up in front of the charming young girl who is gazing so seriously into the camera.

Young Smuts courted her in his own way. He translated

Schiller's *Das Ideal und das Leben,* and she took down the Dutch manuscript. He taught her Greek. When they occasionally "walked out" into the *veld* where she admired the flowers, which are, indeed, one of the particular beauties of the South African landscape, he told her the Latin name and the class of each plant and proved his knowledge of the various grasses, which has made Smuts one of the greatest of living botanists.

Of course there was more to their meeting than Schiller and Greek and the species of Andropogon, Panicum, and Digitaria, growing in the Themedra Triandria—to ordinary people the South African red grass. It was hero worship on her side, and on his a feeling of bliss. Perhaps life need not be spent on austere solitude. But it is doubtful whether many words were exchanged. The future of an incipient Bachelor of Arts seemed rather uncertain.

In fact, the future, at least the immediate future, of Jan Christiaan Smuts was pretty well assured after his eighteenth year. In this eventful year of 1888, Cecil Rhodes visited Victoria College. The "colossus" was at the peak of his success. A year before he had formed his gigantic Goldfields Company on the Rand, with the clear understanding that a large portion of the profits should be used for purposes entirely outside the commercial sphere—indeed, for furthering his imperial plans. In the very year he came to Victoria College he had further succeeded in combining all the diamond mines in Kimberley, practically the entire diamond output of South Africa, then the largest in the world. Had it not been for his premonition of an early death, due to his incurable heart disease, which prompted him to write one will after the other—he had just drafted his third testament—he would have come as the god in the clouds. In fact he came as the trusted ally of his friends in the Afrikander Bond, to inspect the model institution of Dutch education in the Cape Colony, whose Prime Minister he was about to become.

Cecil Rhodes addressed the students. Smuts was only one of the college juniors. Yet the principal had asked him to reply on behalf of the student body as academic custom demanded. Smuts spoke of the predestined greatness of South Africa, which, in her present stage, was comparable with Elizabethan England. He fell in completely with Cecil Rhodes' great and bold plan of a federated partnership of self-governing states under the British Crown. Mr. Merriman, an English-language politician who made his career on the Dutch side, a man feared for his biting wit, patted Jacobus Abraham Smuts' shoulder. The whole audience could hear him whisper to the proud father: "Your lad has done it!"

On the rostrum, the "colossus" shook hands with the lad. Jan Christiaan Smuts saw Cecil Rhodes only twice afterward. But on these occasions they did not exchange a single word. Both men were always in a hurry. Yet their meeting at Victoria College had important consequences. Cecil Rhodes marked down the young man as a future collaborator in his campaign for the brotherhood of English and Dutch. Smuts, conversely, was now ingrained with a conception of Rhodes as the maker of a greater British Empire, with South Africa having her due share of the glory.

A confirmed Rhodes man, his future path was now clearly marked out. He took his degree in literature and science with honors. He closed his Sunday school, presenting each of his colored pupils with a *Bible*. He wrote a poem *Love and Life (a Fragment)*, which subsequently appeared in the *Stellenbosch Students' Annual*, from which the following quatrain shall be quoted:

> Long are the coming years,
> Counted by lovers' tears,
> When, having lived together,
> Their parted days begin.

Now, having cleared the decks, his resolve was taken: he would read law in order to prepare for statesmanship, and nowhere else but at Cambridge.

IN 1891, SMUTS TOOK SHIP FOR ENGLAND. THIS SOUNDS EASY enough, but, as in everything he undertook in his youth, a tremendous effort underlay it. The perpetual obstacle had to be overcome: money worries. Fortunately Smuts received an Ebden Scholarship, named for a wealthy philanthropist in the Eastern Province, but unfortunately the sum was, due to a bank failure, reduced to £100 a year, all that the Ebden Trust had guaranteed, but only half the amount actually disbursed in previous years. To implement his meager assets he had to take out a life insurance policy which his friend and teacher, the Reverend Professor Marais, was willing to accept as security for a small loan. When the professor, five years later, sent a final account, he charged 5 per cent interest. Smuts replied: "Acknowledgment to Professor Marais of loan to be repaid at 6 per cent from September 1." His friends insist that the Old Master, at the summit of his wisdom, is still as little money-wise as he was as a Cambridge student.

At the time Smuts set sail for England, sensitive ears could discern the first distant thunder clap of the coming tempest in South Africa. Cecil Rhodes, who could handle almost anyone, did not succeed in coming to terms with President Kruger. Abortive negotiations over conditions in Johannesburg, the golden city that had sprung out of the reef five years before, now teemed with *uitlanders*—foreigners—predominantly Englishmen, ended with Oom Paul shaking his head: "This young man is getting dangerous." Rhodes stormed: "I meant to work with him, but not on my knees."

The noise was too far away. Smuts did not hear it. Confidently, and curiously, he embarked upon his studies at Christ's College, Cambridge. Again, he did not easily become a part of his surroundings. He was somewhat older in years, and definitely more mature in mind, than most of his new comrades. He spoke with that nasal twang that every South African instantly and joyfully recognizes as Malmesbury patois, but which sounds distinctly different from Cambridge English. He showed no interest in the college sports and games. When the other undergraduates were exercising, Smuts sat in the library "pale-faced and white-haired," as he was inaccurately described, since his hair was fair, so fair indeed that it was easily mistaken for white, particularly as it topped an ageless, unsmiling face. He no longer demonstratively retired into seclusion, yet he did not fit into the mould. The straightforward manners of the South African farms and villages in which he had been brought up were unlike the misleadingly easygoing appearance with which English people seek to disguise the sweat of their labor. No one would have reproached Smuts for his hard work. It was only the fact that he worked so openly and so unashamedly that seemed strange. Probably he had also to overcome a constant feeling of poverty. The lack of money "crippled" him, he wrote home. But it did not clip his wings.

Devouring law, Roman, British, and Colonial, he still found time to write his first book. It was a seventy thousand word essay, far away from paragraph and codex. Its title was *Walt Whitman: A Study in Evolution.* The book was by no means a biography. The American poet was in a way the test case for Smuts' philosophy of personality. Only a few people have ever read the manuscript. Some have maintained that the work contained the first seeds of psychoanalysis, the new science that, a few years later, at the turn of the century, carried Professor Sigmund Freud with his *Traumdeutung* to world fame. But in the late nineties London publishers were not interested in what appeared to be primarily a study of Whitman, who at that time was little known in England. One publisher wrote that had it been Goethe the manuscript would have been immediately accepted. Perhaps Walt Whitman's time will come, another ventured to prophesy. But at that moment his name did not mean much to the general public. The one magazine to which Smuts offered his opus also returned it regretfully. Miss Krige in far-away Stellenbosch had copied the seventy thousand words in

39

vain. In later years, when the author's name alone could have attracted international attention, Smuts stubbornly forbade the publication of what he termed his "boyish book."

He early learned to accept reverses as well as successes. He consoled himself with the thought that he had not been forgotten at home. In July, 1892, the *Zuid Afrikaan,* of Cape Town, mentioned ". . . Mr. Smuts who, having gained the Ebden Scholarship, thanks to his double B.A., passed first in Law at Cambridge." Yet it took two years and a half longer before the Council of Legal Education awarded to Smuts, J. C., Middle Temple, a special prize of £50 for the best examination in Constitutional Law and Legal History. A year before he had caused some stir by publishing a piece, *Law—A Liberal Study,* in the Christ's College magazine. On June 22, 1894, the *Cape Times* published a London contribution: "Smuts' success is unprecedented in Cambridge annals. He took both Parts I and II of the Law Tripos at the same time, was placed first in the first class of each, and has been awarded the George Long Prize in Roman Law and Jurisprudence; a prize only awarded in cases of especial merit. On referring to the Cambridge Calendar you will find that this is quite unparalleled." Years later the *Encyclopaedia Britannica* confirmed this opinion, stating that "his success was unprecedented."

For a short time Smuts read in chambers in London. He was offered a fellowship at Christ's College, Cambridge, but he declined it. Cambridge, the ancient seat of learning, had rather stimulated than entirely satisfied Smuts' intellectual hunger. He had not altogether cut himself off from the life of his fellow students, although he had not formed any close or lasting friendships with the undemonstrative young Englishmen he had met. England was more than ever a bright promise. But South Africa was the only country worth living in and living for. In the summer of 1895, he returned home.

The Cape Town newspapers welcomed the returned son in a friendly, if not enthusiastic manner. Advocate Smuts was admitted to the Cape bar. He went into chambers and began practicing at the supreme court. But in a very short time the moderate excitement over the brilliant Cambridge student of local origin abated considerably. Those who had predicted for him a brilliant future as a barrister were patently wrong. Everyone had heard that the young advocate was the best man for the most involved lawsuits, and that he took enormous pains in digging out hundred-and-fifty-year-old precedents to back up his cases. But he was not seen in the clubs and coffeehouses. He did not play whist. He did not slap backs, and would certainly have shuddered had anyone attempted to approach him in that fashion. He did not even use the tricks of the trade to soften the hearts of a jury. No briefs came.

The young man with the assured brilliant future had to look for minor jobs to keep himself afloat. His superb High Dutch came in handy. For a modest fee he examined in the Dutch language, a knowledge of which was required of those young men among the Cape Boers who sought positions in the Transvaal Republic. This occupation was nothing more than a stop gap. Journalism offered slightly better opportunities. Smuts began to write for both English and Dutch papers; soon he found a niche in the *Cape Times*. He reported the House of Assembly from the press gallery, he reviewed books, produced editorials on his favorite questions of moral and principle. Occasionally he earned as much as a pound apiece, but mostly it was considerably less. Probably his literary output in this autumn of 1895 was not worth much more. Today his yellowed pieces sound a little over-emphatic, and it seems as if the writer had occasionally lost his direction in the maze of metaphors. Yet some distinct traces of the man he was to become were already apparent in these months—the last before he found his ultimate vocation.

Discussing in the *Cape Times* the question why so many nations were anti-British, Smuts wrote: "The true explanation is not British Pharisaism, but British success. It is the success with which Great Britain is pursuing the policy of colonial expansion, and it is the comparative failure of the attempts of other peoples in the same direction which lies at the root of this international dislike of Great Britain."

Very soon afterward, however, Smuts traveled through the Transvaal, where the conflict between Johannesburg—the English residents—and Pretoria, the capital and stronghold of Paul Kruger, ever increased in sharpness. This time he wrote for a Dutch-language paper, *De Volksbode*. While he reported glowingly on Pretoria—"I was agreeably surprised by the aristocratic quiet pervading this handsome little town"—he scorned Johannesburg's "colossal materialism." And as to the conflict between Oom Paul and the *uitlanders,* he stated: "We can sympathize with the ideals of a farmer-president," although, already a believer in the Union of South Africa, he made no bones about his dislike of Kruger's high-tariff policy, intended to shut off his country from the neighboring British colonies. The contradiction of a eulogy on Great Britain and sympathy with her archenemy was by no means conditioned by his writing for two papers in different languages. It was undiluted Smuts, Smuts pure and simple: British by conviction, Boer by blood.

Altogether this autumn proved to be an unsatisfactory time. To be a briefless barrister and a prolific journalist, not much concerned with his own mediocre work was not undiluted Smuts. The call from Hofmeyr voiced his vocation: not the law, not the press—politics.

Hofmeyr was the Afrikaner Bond incarnate. Although he was called "the mole" on account of his notorious preference for burdening others with the show of leadership, it was he who, for thirty years, laid down the law. His support gave Cecil Rhodes his majority in the Cape Parliament. It was a marriage of convenience. Whereas Hofmeyr visualized a Dutch South Africa, Cecil Rhodes dreamed of a united South Africa, nay, Pan-Africa, under the British flag. But both were agreed that the union of the two colonies and the two republics was the prime necessity, and that South Africa, within or without the British Empire, must be self-governing. Their racial ambitions were diametrically opposed, but neither was a narrow-minded racialist. Personally, the great Imperialist liked the Dutch, and conversely the Dutch liked him.

Rhodes, a fisher of souls, was constantly on the lookout for young *Afrikanders,* as the Boers preferred to call themselves at that time. He had not forgotten the unusual youth from Victoria College. He had kept track of Smuts' extraordinary success at Cambridge, and when he was told that this chap was hanging about in Cape Town, marking time and becoming prematurely bitter, the "colossus" had a few words with Hofmeyr, perhaps during one of their habitual morning rides when South African history was made.

Kindly disposed himself toward the son of his old supporter Jacobus Abraham Smuts, Hofmeyr sent for Advocate Smuts, primed him thoroughly, and sent him, as his political debut, to the hottest spot along the firing line: Cecil Rhodes' own Kimberley.

In fact, Kimberley, where Rhodes had made his first handful of millions, was no longer quite his own. The diamond rush was over. Dr. Jameson, "Dr. Jim" to everyone, the most highly esteemed doctor in South Africa, the most popular character in town, and Rhodes' fanatically devoted right-hand man, had moved to Bechuanaland, where he served, without pay, as administrator of the Chartered Company's newly acquired territories. Instead, Olive Schreiner had moved in, a noted novelist, asthmatic and hence in need of the crisp air of lofty Kimberley, a German by descent, and once a most vocal admirer of Rhodes', but now his embittered foe. She and her insignificant husband formed a writing team under the pen name of Cronwright Schreiners. Under this trade-mark they published a furious attack on Rhodes in the *Diamond Fields Adventurer.* Rhodes wished this nuisance stopped. Hofmeyr obliged. Smuts was sent to recover Kimberley.

With the mayor of the town in the chair, young Advocate Smuts addressed a large audience in Kimberley Town Hall. *The De Beers' Political and Debating Society* sponsored the event. The day was Tuesday, the twenty-ninth of October, 1895. It was an eventful day for the youthful advocate. He sold himself to the devil. He pledged his allegiance to Rhodes. Untiringly, for hours, he defended his idol and all that the "colossus" stood for: from his conduct of affairs in the Cape Colony to his private annexation of Matabeleland; and, from his native policy, expressed in the catch phrase: "equal rights for all civilized men south of the Zambezi" to his determination to close the ranks between the two white peoples. Certainly, Cecil Rhodes was a great Imperialist. But so—tacitly understood, though plain to every listener—was he, Advocate Smuts. One could very well be an Imperialist and a passionate South African at one and the same time. Rhodes was both.

Rhodes was all in all to Smuts. He became obsessed with Rhodes. He lived Rhodes. He made Rhodes his hero and leader. A future under Rhodes was a great future. All this was not a youthful Rhodes-fixation. Smuts had opened his shy and secluded inwardness to the man whom he felt, although greater than himself, fundamentally akin. The very bigness of Rhodes' aims was the essence of Smuts' lifelong philosophy, which in later years he called "Holism," derived from: "Whole." What Rhodes used to call simply his "thoughts," became Smuts' mental life. And he did not care to live any life but one in the spiritual realm. He did not yet share Cecil Rhodes' deeply rooted devotion to the Union Jack. To Smuts it was a good flag, because it was Rhodes' flag.

He returned from his first oratorical triumph, which *Ons Land,* Cape Town's leading Dutch newspaper, ardently eulogized, filled with enthusiasm. He mellowed. He even resolved to visit his father's farm for Christmas. The family and the neighbors teased him a little for being unable to speak or think of anything but Rhodes. They were themselves loyal supporters of their Prime Minister, but primarily because the Afrikander Bond insisted on it. The Bond saw to their economic interests, it was their true protective power; they owed to their organization, and therefore to its chosen chief of government, their loyalty and allegiance. For the rest, they were not as excitable as Jannie, who had always been different from the rest. Well, it was good to have him at home again.

Jannie was lounging on the *stoep* of his father's farmhouse when the news came. To him, it was a scare rumor, one of the many poisonous stories that circulated as the tension between Kruger and the *uitlanders* increased. Smuts was sick of this rumor-mongering. It revolted his straightforward nature. Rhodes would never have allowed it!

An hour or two later the story was confirmed. Rhodes had not only allowed it; Rhodes had been behind it—behind the Jameson Raid, the blundering and abortive effort to unseat Kruger by an armed riot, or preferably by bluff. Old man Kruger had said long before: "I'll wait until the tortoise stretches forth her head. Then I'll cut it off." So now he cut it off. At Dornkoop, the handful of Jameson raiders were overpowered, and ignominiously arrested. To the Afrikander Bond it was an, perhaps not quite unwelcome, opportunity of getting rid of the English Prime Minister. Rhodes lost his parliamentary majority overnight. He was unseated.

But to Smuts it was the greatest betrayal since Judas' kiss. His idol was smashed. With his idol went his idea. The Cambridge man disappeared. In his place surged the male whose tribe had been injured. Smuts was no longer a dreamer of a South Africa; he felt a Boer of the Boers, and it is likely that his only spiritual companion, Miss Krige, at that time a pragmatic nationalist herself, encouraged this change. Smarting under the lash, Smuts condemned in print what he had praised at Kimberley. It was *Crucifige!* no longer *Hosanna!* He called Rhodes "the great racial stumbling block in South Africa." For a full year he did not dare to speak in public. He brooded endlessly over the matter. Was it Rhodes? Could it have been Rhodes? Rhodes alone? Did not people say that Joe Chamberlain had been involved in the conspiracy? And even the Prince of Wales?

Mr. Chamberlain and the Prince were none of Smuts' concern. To him it was Rhodes, the Englishman. "The English have set the *veld* on fire," he wrote. "We lift our voices in warning to England. If England sends Rhodes back to us, the responsibility will be hers. The blood be on England's own head!"

THE FULL TRUTH IN ALL ITS RAMIFICATIONS ABOUT THE JAMESON Raid will not be revealed until January 1, 1946, the fiftieth anniversary of this most spectacular blunder. Two sage old men decided not to revive the controversy which, after the event, aroused the whole world, until a time when the incident that many regarded as the first shot in the Boer War would be merely an historical anecdote.

In 1931, Sir Graham Bower, more than eighty-three years old, and on the point of death, sent a heavy parcel to General Smuts. It was the "complete history of the Jameson Raid as far as it was known to me" the accompanying letter stated, and the inside story must have, indeed, been very well known to Sir Graham, since he had been the British High Commissioner's secretary during the days of the raid. "The truth," his letter continued, "was rightly suppressed at the time, for had it been made public, a South African and a European war would have been inevitable." The dying man asked General Smuts to "take this long account, read it, seal it up, and deposit it with the Trustees of the South African Public Library, not to be opened until January 1946." Pathetically, he added that he hoped to live another week longer, and so might be able to "answer a questionnaire asking for information on any points that need clearing up after reading the papers."

General Smuts did as he had been requested. Whether he availed himself of the invitation to ask further questions is not on record. Probably he did not. The Jameson Raid, it may be surmised, is deeply and peacefully buried in his mind, although it once altered the course of his life. But General Smuts has lived several lives since.

Whether the raid was the signal fire, announcing the Three Years' War, or whether the incident, in fact, delayed the outbreak of hostilities, making the parties involved more cautious

46

and more careful in preparing first and shooting later, is an open question. There is, however, no question as to the fundamental cause of the conflict. The showdown became inevitable when Imperial Germany, muscling into Africa, decided to establish a great colonial realm from the east to the west coast, to include South Africa and its newly discovered treasure of gold. Bismarck had thrown overboard his old contempt for the acquisition of colonies. His phrase "The whole South Sea is not worth the bones of a single Pomeranian grenadier" no longer stood. In a desperate effort to come to terms with his adventurous "Young Master," he embarked upon trans-equatorial expansion. Personally, this venture was of no avail to him. Wilhelm II dropped him ignominiously. But while Bismarck's last, senile scheme was being planned, Cecil Rhodes' "thoughts" were gravely imperiled. He thought of a united, self-governing Africa, under the British flag, extending from the Cape to Cairo —a thought that General Smuts developed into his vision of the United States of Africa.

Bismarck was sure that he could use the, to him despicable, Transvaal Republic as a tool. Conversely, Paul Kruger, frequently called the Bismarck of the Bush, felt certain that he could outsmart anyone. According to the hallowed traditions of his race, he was determined to take while the taking was good, and particularly to pit the German menace against what he felt to be English aggression. Probably the old farmer-President would have refused German domination as stubbornly as British. He certainly did not plan a sellout; he was simply driving a bargain. But the absolute ruler of forty thousand shepherds and farmers in Africa overreached himself in trying to play two empires, one world-embracing, the other coveting world-domination, against one another. He negotiated so long and so intimately with the Germans that the British power was menaced at its very roots. This was one, and the most consequential cause of the following events in Africa. Actually, the first shot in the Boer War was fired when Bismarck took Dr. Leyds, Kruger's special emissary, by the arm—the scene was the Old Castle in Berlin—and, addressing the Dutch apprentice in diplomacy in Low German which sounds very much like Dutch, replied to a compliment in reference to the gluttonous dinner, that, together, they would devour much more. Compared with this playing with fire, the Jameson Raid was just the bursting of a soap bubble.

The other cause that finally led to the South African war was the impossible position in which Kruger kept the *uitlanders*. These foreigners, mostly Englishmen, but with a large admixture of Americans, Jews, and even Germans, were disfranchised and politically without rights, exposed to a hostile, corrupt, and backward administration, which worked perfectly among the antediluvian farmers on the *veld*, but built, as it were, a dam against the onrush of modern civilization. The foreigners contributed more than nine-tenths of the Transvaal Republic's revenues. On the funds extracted from them—frequently by brutal compulsion—the state thrived, and plunged into an armament race with England. Oom Paul himself, the son of a shepherd, acquired a formidable fortune. The *uitlanders* found themselves, as Sir Alfred, later Viscount, Milner rightly put it, in the position of helots. Yet they only wanted to reform the Transvaal, and merely asked for a fair share in its legislation. They had to endure the calculated ignominies and chicaneries imposed upon them, for long years, until their movement merged with Britain's decision not to be ousted from her paramount position in Africa.

A far greater nation than the *uitlanders* in the boom town of Johannesburg were once disgusted with taxation without representation. The explosion in South Africa, whose repercussions made Smuts the man he is, was a repeat performance on a smaller and less important, but just as thunderous scene.

After the Boers' triumph at Majuba Hill, made possible by Mr. Gladstone's hasty retreat, the new wave of Boer nationalism surged powerfully in the Transvaal. True to their *Old Testament* vision, the Transvaal farmers and burghers saw themselves as the chosen people. The Boers in the Orange Free State began asking whether their brethren in the North were not,

after all, right. Their conservatism matched very closely Oom
Paul's patriarchal system. Reluctantly, the Free Staters allowed
the newfangled idea of postage stamps inside the country.
When the first telegraph line was installed, it had but one customer: *The Friend,* the progressive newspaper. The radically
anti-British *Express,* supported by unanimous public opinion,
scorned the invention. Railways were considered detrimental to
the breeding and trading of horses. The Transvaal breeders,
incidentally, displayed a similar attitude. President Kruger
could only obtain their consent to build his strategical railway
to Portuguese Delagoa Bay by assuring a delegation that their
horses and donkeys would, in fact, find new employment: they
would be needed to pull the trains. This argument impressed
the Free Staters, too. Ever more keenly they took their cue
from the heroes of the Transvaal. To prove that they themselves were made of the same stern stuff, they forbade the speaking of English in markets and meetings; some members of the
Volksraad—diet—even wished to ban the English language altogether from the streets. President Brand had to threaten his resignation before he was permitted to accept a British knight-
hood. But as Sir John Brand he immediately lost his until then
firm hold on his people and died heartbroken, yielding his
place to a more severe Afrikander.

Even the Cape Colony was shaken by the first stirrings of the
Afrikander movement. True, the Afrikander Bond soon exercised some soothing influence. *Onze Jan*—Our Jan, meaning
Hofmeyr—decreed: "The present time is a time of transition.
Signs of fusion of the two white races are on every hand."
Most of the older Cape Dutchmen fell into line. But the
younger generation gazed spellbound at the heroes of the
North, where the conflict between Kruger and the *uitlanders,*
as well as the duel between the President and Rhodes—two developments still independent of one another—grew more and
more perilous.

The *uitlanders* complained bitterly about what they believed
to be London's callous indifference toward the fate of British

subjects as well as the future of South Africa. These complaints were only partly justified. The British Empire, indeed, was not built up by an irresistible expansion of an insular nation, but, as in the case of India, and South Africa, too, by the fanatic zeal of some great men far ahead of their times, among them Cecil Rhodes, who had to drag a reluctant Downing Street and Parliament behind them. After the self-imposed retreat following Majuba, Downing Street, conscious of having exercised supreme self-restraint and magnanimity, could well expect that some reciprocal justice would be shown. A man by the name of Andrew Marvell did not expect it. "The fault of the Dutch," he rhymed, "is giving too little and asking too much."

The Boers were not satisfied with the Convention of 1881. They claimed the removal of British suzerainty, the withdrawal of the clauses protecting the natives, and, above all, the restoration of the title South African Republic, which sounded more impressive than Transvaal State, the name to which their country had been reduced. Moreover, they demanded, although they hardly expected to receive it, complete freedom in regard to their international relations, and expansion of almost all their boundaries, which meant cancellation of the clause forbidding them to annex native territories. This last prohibition in particular made Kruger, then the Vice-President in the ruling triumvirate, see red. He bitterly complained that his country was being *kraal-walled,* and found a sly method of circumventing the text and spirit of the Convention. He embarked upon his time-honored method of expansion by trekking. It began with small hunting excursions into adjacent native territories. There the Boers grazed their own cattle, and thus established, according to old tradition, the right to consider the pastures as their possession. Frequently this "dry expansion" was promoted by fostering rivalries between the various native tribes. First one black clan extinguished another with the support of the Transvaal Boers. Then the conquerors were made to feel that they had acted on Kruger's behalf, but not really with his support. They themselves were exterminated.

This method was not only cruel, but the more superfluous as
the Transvaal itself contained immense stretches of uncultivated land, which the inhabitants were entirely unable to control, utilize, or administer. Their "land hunger" was insatiable.
The individual Boer, who did not cultivate more than twenty
acres, wanted to own 20,000. He coveted Swaziland, Zululand,
Bechuanaland, Matabeleland, Mashonaland, and Tongaland.
This greed involved a double threat: the natives were menaced
with extinction, and the British highways into the interior of
Africa were in danger of being cut off.

Kruger's expansionism was only moderately successful. After
his invasion of Zululand the English forced him to give back to
the natives two-thirds of his conquest, including the coastal region. Once more Kruger saw himself prevented from reaching
his anxiously desired goal: access to the sea. Cunningly, he in-
filtrated Swaziland, until he held the country firmly in his grip.
But it was a short-lived success. The Swazis shook off the yoke
of their *sjambok* (rhinoceros whip) lashing administrators from
the Transvaal during the Boer War. In Matabeleland Kruger's
raiders arrived too late. Alone and unarmed, Dr. Jameson,
Cecil Rhodes' right-hand man, met the Boer troops at Rhodes
drift, the border, and told them with truly English sang-froid
that they might kill him, but that this would mean the end of
the Transvaal. General Joubert's raiders returned. Matabeleland was soon a part of Rhodesia.

Kruger was kindled by the flame of fury. What did these
accursed English see wrong in the extermination of the natives?
Had not the blacks been a cruel and vicious enemy when the
Voortrekkers came to drive them away? Had he, Johannes Paulus Kruger, as a lad in his teens, not fought in the sanguinary
battle that crushed Dingaan, the great Zulu chief? And did the
Boers not carry out the Lord's word in exterminating the black
vermin? As surely as Kruger knew that the earth was flat, he
was convinced that there could be no harm in maltreating these
pagans, the Hottentots, whose women evidently carried the
mark which God had set upon Cain.

Times had changed, the English insisted. Elsewhere, maybe,

Kruger replied. But in South Africa, and not alone in his Transvaal, the mighty *baas* was determined to make time stand still. Was it 1894? He still lived in the year of the Lord 1855, the blessed year when he had participated in the destruction of Makapan's people in righteous revenge for their massacre of twelve Boer men and women.

But the shrewd old man knew that he was still too weak to provoke English power. He proceeded to London. With him went General Smit, the victor of Majuba, embodying the "or else," if Kruger's own stiff-necked persuasion should fail.

It did not fail. London was sick and tired of haggling and struggling over South Africa. Lord Derby was extremely annoyed. He granted Kruger a revision of the Convention. The new patchwork, the Treaty of 1894, failed even to mention British suzerainty. It was anybody's guess whether this privilege was abandoned, or considered self-evident. The *baas* of the Transvaal State returned as President of the Transvaal Republic. Instantly he interpreted this return to the high-sounding name of his country as a silent recognition of his claim to the whole of South Africa.

There was but one fly in the ointment: during the Boer negotiators' stay at the Albemarle Hotel their money gave out. They found themselves in the uncomfortable position of not being able to meet their hotel bill for the last few weeks. Finally the bill was paid by an un-named benefactor. Baron Grant, the well-known stock exchange speculator, received two concessions in return: the gold concession for the Lydenburg district, and His Honor's public assurance of good will, protection, and encouragement to British settlers in the Transvaal. Kruger, on behalf of the Republic, indeed, published in the London press a cordial invitation and welcome; he promised full rights and protection to all who would come.

This was how Kruger's promises were carried out: favoritism pure and simple decided the grant of concessions. Those willing to expend capital and energies in legitimate work could not compete. A test case was the dynamite concession, introduced under the guise of keeping the control of explosives and munitions in the hands of the state. The monopoly in dynamite cost the mining industry six hundred thousand pounds a year more than they would have had to pay for the better, imported article. Save for the administration's large share in the take, the beneficiary was Mr. Lippert, the concessionaire. He had a hard fight before the *Volksraad* agreed to his concession. One anti-British member in particular opposed stubbornly all trade and traffic with the English. Even Kruger was not able to bridle this adversary. But at the decisive division, this same man cast his vote in favor of the bill. He explained to the astonished House: "The voice of the Lord came to me in the night and told me to vote for Lippert."

The members of the Johannesburg Chamber of Mines strongly suspected that this voice might have borne some resemblance to Mr. Lippert's own. Indeed, some time later Lippert admitted that he had shouted God's message through the open window of his otherwise irreconcilable opponent.

It was not always as easy as that. The Hatherley Distillery turned out execrable spirits, labeled after well-known brands. The firm had the government's monopoly of liquor. Drinking became a scourge in the gigantic mining camp of Johannesburg. Particularly the natives were cursed with the habit. A third of them were constantly drunk. Their excesses made it impossible for the inhabitants to leave their houses after dark, or on Sundays. The police offered them no protection. On the contrary, the *Zarps*—Zuid Afrikaan Republican Police—were young brutes from the *platteland,* who relished their privilege of shoving *uitlanders* off the pavement, and gloried in their own brutality. The government did nothing to check the drinking plague. A dozen officials and Boer politicians were large shareholders in Hatherley's.

The *Volksraad,* it is true, frequently passed resolutions condemning the principle of monopolies. The oligarchy of Boer lawmakers, sable-clad, and exercising their parliamentary functions with the grave dignity of high priests, were bigoted but righteous minded. Only when it came to sharing the spoils they were not averse to taking. Twenty-one of the ruling body of twenty-five men were, in the case of the Selati Railway Company, publicly and circumstantially accused of accepting bribes, with full details of the bribes received; none of them sought to deny the accusation. According to a prominent Transvaal judge, himself a Boer of the old stamp, only one member of the *Volksraad* measured up to European standards of education. The handful of defiant opponents in the House, led by General Joubert, and inspired by a young, very successful cattle breeder and land speculator by the name of Louis Botha, did not exercise the slightest influence. Kruger, lording it over his herd, tolerated no criticism. His heavy, red fists thundered on the speaker's table, and the whole House was immediately cowed.

Kruger's high protective tariffs, introduced to emphasize his country's self-seclusion, deteriorated into mere burlesque. Smuggling was carried on openly. Mostly the customs officials "stood in" with the smugglers. It was easier than enforcing the law properly and relying on the share of the spoils the government would allot the watchdogs. The government, in fact, did not pay bonuses any more regularly than salaries. Hence, goods subject to heavy duties could be bought at any store at a price much lower than the original costs plus transport and duty. The customers loved it. The officials rubbed their hands. The administration, whose leading functionaries themselves did not receive their salaries for six months out of the year, looked the other way.

More profitable even than the trade of the customs officials was the business of the *veld-cornets*. In times of war the *veld-cornet* was the subaltern officer in the commando. In peacetime he acted as a district official, who collected taxes, was the petty justice, and was, above all, the authority with which each newcomer had to register. Since most of the *veld-cornets* were illiterate, they made a complete mess of the registration. Notwithstanding the bribes they habitually exacted, registrations were never correct, and never at hand, when, after a number of years, the *uitlander* needed his registration to claim his citizenship rights.

This was some of the pettifoggery that ruled Kruger's oligarchy. The big schemes were carried out by the President himself, who had come under the nefarious influence of a group of imported Hollanders. He came to rely more and more on them as the better elements of the Boer youth threatened to become impatient with the prevailing corruption. On April 16, 1884, Oom Paul, egged on by his Hollander advisors, granted to a group of Netherland and German capitalists a concession for all railways in the state. Immediately afterward Dr. Leyds arrived in the Transvaal. President Kruger had hired him as a State Attorney (Attorney General) on the recommendation of the Faculty of Law of the University of Utrecht. Dr. Leyds was a good-looking, well-bred young chap, endowed with pleasant manners, and obviously enthusiastic over his chance to lay down the law in the backwoods. His enthusiasm was well founded on solid facts: he represented the interests of the capitalists who had obtained the railway concession. Their representative, by the same token the State Attorney, had to supervise the complicated connection on behalf of the Republic to which he gladly swore allegiance. He quickly climbed the career ladder, and was soon entrusted by Kruger with secret negotiations in Berlin. But while in his new home, Pretoria, he saw to it that the Hollander promoters of the railways did not come to grief in their dealings with the Republic.

Dr. Leyds found his double position most amusing. In high good spirits he described, in a letter to a friend in Utrecht, his life among the savages, calling Kruger a "hairy old ape," and poking fun at General Joubert and other Boer dignitaries. The assiduous friend sent the letter back to a third friend in Pretoria, who, for his part, revealed it to the authorities. Joubert raised hell. But Kruger cut him short, defended Leyds as merely an irresponsible youngster, clung the closer to him, and forgave him even the personal insult. There is but one explanation for this unparalleled mildness in the old man's bearing:

he felt ever more isolated, even among his own people, and he desperately needed some younger man to rely on. During the two years State Attorney Leyds controlled the company's operations, the concessionaires failed to get their capital subscribed, they overcharged the government of the Republic, they asked excessive fares on the short routes they had, indeed, built, they violated vital conditions of the concession. The *Volksraad* was aroused. But the President stoutly defended his Hollanders. By his personal influence and the solid vote of his ignorant Dopper Party he completely blocked all legislation to control the company. He was dead set on getting his railway to Delagoa Bay, even at the expense of killing the goose that laid the golden eggs. Business in Johannesburg would not be able to function normally if the new railway, as was planned, should obtain a transport monopoly. What of it, if the *uitlanders* were crushed? Paul Kruger, himself drawing a salary of £7,000 plus large sums for entertainment into the bargain, owner of a number of prosperous farms, did not care for gold. All he cared about was the opportunity to make impotent the foreigners, who, by the sheer weight of their numbers alone—they were already twice as numerous as his own farmers and burghers— would wrest the power in the state from him, if they obtained the franchise.

He loathed these "dirty vultures" with a zealot's passion. To him they were the incarnation of the arch-evil: progress. They grew fat on the soil that belonged to his Boers. Did they want his state, too? "They can have it," Kruger grumbled. "But only over my dead body."

At a meeting on the Witwatersrand, to which a few *uitlanders* had come by courtesy, he addressed the audience with the words: "My friends, my people, and you *uitlanders*, murderers and thieves. . . ."

In vain the *uitlanders* petitioned him time and again. He refused to receive their delegations until one day he consented. Respectfully, the spokesman pointed out the inequities of the law: while every Boer lad of sixteen had the franchise, *uitlanders* were so restricted by law that they obtained the franchise only at the age of forty, provided they could prove fourteen years residence in the country—which due to the inefficient registration was next to impossible. Furthermore, their franchise was practically prevented by having a petition endorsed by the mostly hostile Boer neighborhood. Even then the President or the *Volksraad* could exercise the right of veto, which, indeed, they used to do with a vengeance.

There were other grievances as well: the *uitlanders* had no voice in the choice of officials. Entirely incapable functionaries controlled valuable interests in the most selfish manner. Once a Minister of Mines, on learning officially of some flaw in a mine's title, expropriated the mine and attempted to exploit it himself. They had no control over education. The Johannesburg Educational Council allotted one shilling and tenpence per head and year for the education of *uitlander* children, but eight pounds six shillings per head for Boer children—the *uitlanders,* as always, paying nine-tenths of the total amount. Municipal government in the English-speaking town was the privilege of the Boers. It was as corrupt and negligent as the administration of the Republic. *Uitlanders* could not even serve as members of a jury. Their press was throttled by censorship. Freedom of meeting was restricted by dictatorial laws.

Patiently, old man Kruger listened. Then he dismissed the delegation with the words: "This is my country. These are my laws. Anyone who does not like my laws is free to leave my country."

From London came no help.

So the *uitlanders* established a "Reform Committee," distributed all of 350 rifles, and decided to march to Pretoria, to force their demands upon the administration. They by no means intended a revolution. They wished to hoist the legitimate Transvaal flag on the government buildings—but upside down, to indicate the change.

They had but one ally: Cecil Rhodes, who had sent his trusted friend Dr. Jameson with two hundred and fifty of the Chartered Company's Bechuanaland Police and an equal number of hotheaded volunteers to Pitsani, allegedly to protect the construction of the railway line to Bechuanaland, in fact to join their slender force with the *uitlanders*.

Rhodes' heart was not in the venture. He knew that he was doing something he had never done: he took a short cut, the very method of proceeding against which he had always warned his friends. But he could not miss the opportunity of getting rid of the one great and immovable stumbling block on his way to Pan-Africa: Kruger, the mighty old gorilla. Kruger's influence was waning; Rhodes knew it. In a year or two he would be replaced by the Progressive Party in the Transvaal, people with whom one could deal fairly. But Cecil Rhodes feared that he no longer had a year or two to wait. He was growing stout, his face dark-red; he was shaken by interminable heart attacks. Death was upon him. Still he hesitated to flash the green light.

Dr. Jameson, nervous, overworked, restless, did not wait for the signal. On the twenty-ninth of December he crossed the frontier of the Transvaal. General Cronje, lying in wait for them, surrounded Jameson's soldiery, five hundred poorly armed men, and took them prisoner. Then Cronje marched to Johannesburg, where he rounded up the leaders of the Reformers. They were ill-treated in jail by their cruel warden, Du Plessis. One of the unfortunate men cut his throat while in prison. Their leaders were condemned to death. But soon they could buy their freedom by paying the astronomic sum of £25,000 each.

The German Club in Pretoria exulted. On January 27, 1895, the club had given a banquet in honor of the German Emperor's birthday, at which President Kruger had eulogized both the old and the present Emperor of Germany, as well as the loyalty of the Germans in the Transvaal. Kruger concluded with the words: "The latter I experienced once again at the time of the Kafir War. One day three or four Germans came to me and said: 'We are indeed not naturalized, we are still subjects of our Emperor in Germany, but we enjoy the advantages of this country, and are ready to defend it in accordance with its laws. If Your Excellency requires our services, we are willing to march out.' And they marched. That is the spirit I admire. They were under the laws, they worked under the laws, they obeyed the laws, and they fell in battle under the laws. All my subjects are not so minded. The English, for instance, although they behave themselves properly and are loyal to the state, always fall back upon England when it suits their purpose. Therefore, I shall ever promote the interests of Germany, though it be with the resources of a child, such as my land is considered. This child is now being trodden upon by a great power, and the natural consequence is that it seeks protection from another. The time has come to knit ties of the closest friendship between Germany and the South African Republic —ties such as are natural between father and child."

The young Emperor was perfectly willing to play father to the patriarchal child. After the Jameson Raid, Wilhelm II dispatched the historic Kruger telegram, congratulating the President on having repulsed foreign aggression without appealing for the help of friendly powers.

The earth trembled. But in the Transvaal, Kruger's shaken rule was perpetuated.

Chapter 6   MISTER STATE ATTORNEY

AT ANOTHER BANQUET, IN LONDON, ANOTHER GUEST OF HONOR ended his speech with the prophetic words: "In a cause in which one absolutely believes, even failure—personal failure, I mean, for the cause itself is not going to fail—would be preferable to an easy life of comfortable prosperity in another sphere." With these words Sir Alfred Milner bade farewell to his friends. He was about to embark upon a fatal mission. Appointed Governor of the Cape Colony and High Commissioner for South Africa, he was being sent to restore order in the fever-shaken country.

Smuts did not wait for the new man's arrival. He was out of politics, indeed, he had been ousted. His people did not accept his violent recantation of his association with Rhodes. To the suspicious Dutch it sounded too good to be true. To them it was English cant, acquired at Cambridge. Smuts was isolated, boycotted, excluded. His speech at Kimberley appeared inexplicable. Indeed, he could not himself give a satisfactory explanation. He had been cheated, betrayed by his idol. Yet he felt lost and lonely without Cecil Rhodes. Although his Boer nationalism burst into flames, he appeared to be helplessly compromised. He was still shy at that time, thin-skinned and easily hurt. He had fallen between two stools. He was disgusted by everything English. The rousing welcome the English majority in Cape Town gave Cecil Rhodes upon his return from England, where he had successfully defended himself against the "unctuous rectitude" of his critics, made Smuts sick. On the other hand there was no place for him in the Afrikaner Bond, which now methodically sought to obtain complete control of the Cape legislation with the aim of severing a united South Africa from the British "connection." The Bond fell back upon its original *Programme of Principles,* laid down at Graaf-Reinet in 1882, and demanded a Union of South Africa under her own flag. Even the anti-British gospel of the German Carl Brockenhagen, one of the founders of the Bond, was salvaged from the dustbin. The English became usurpers to be expelled. Their language was banned from school and home. Intermarriage with them was considered unpatriotic. English trade was boycotted, whereas Holland and Germany became the "domestic base" of overseas business. Every Afrikander was expected to provide himself with the best weapons available, and to practice marksmanship. Two compelling reasons for the "total excision" of the "British ulcer" were given: first, the English High Church was hardly distinguishable from the satanic Roman Catholic Church. Secondly, the English policy toward colored races was repugnant and dangerous. Both appeals to the Dutch bigotry and racial master-complex were well calculated to arouse the masses. In Pretoria, Dr. Leyds rubbed his hands. Now the influential Cape Colony would no longer remain indifferent to what happened in the Transvaal.

Smuts was left out in the cold. He found but one consolation: Miss Krige believed in him. She comforted him when he sought refuge in Stellenbosch. She helped him regain his strength and healed his spirit. He was wounded where youth is most vulnerable: in his pride. Her soothing influence gave him back his confidence.

In March, 1896, a few weeks before the *Norman Castle,* with Sir Alfred Milner aboard, anchored off Cape Town, Smuts went to Johannesburg, not because he loved the center of "gross materialism," but because the thriving town, which had already relegated Cape Town to second place, offered the best opportunities for a struggling young barrister. Spying out the land, he found the opportunities satisfactory, went back to Cape Town, closed his law office, dropped the British nationality with which he had been born, and returned to Johannesburg. In September, *Ons Land* announced that Advocate Smuts would seek admission to the Transvaal Bar, and commented: "it would be a cause for regret if the Cape were to lose one of its cleverest, most promising sons. No doubt Afrikaners would appreciate his sacrifice if he decided to remain in the Colony after all." Smuts had good reason to doubt the accuracy of this friendly prophecy. He was admitted to practice in Johannesburg. Ironically, Boer of the Boers, as he then felt himself, he was only a second-class burgher in the fatherland of his choice, an *uitlander,* coming from a British colony, and thus a man without franchise.

Nevertheless, he immediately proved a good Transvaal patriot. Within a few weeks of his arrival in Johannesburg he wrote some articles for the Cape Town press, urging strongly a more cordial understanding between the Colony and the Republics. Besides dabbling a little longer in journalism, he resumed his evening classes in law, and thus made sure that Johannesburg would provide an adequate living for two.

With his customary unyouthful caution, he did not return to the Colony before January, 1897. Mr. Gideon Krige met him at the train, and asked him to speak a few words—not in Stellenbosch itself, but, as a trial, in a political meeting to be held at Kuils River, near Stellenbosch. Smuts acquitted himself of his task by describing Cecil Rhodes as a permanent barrier between English and Dutch. Only a few listeners understood that their speaker was already, following his innermost and unshakable conviction, on the way to reconciliation and co-operation. He interpreted the difference between the two races as a conflict over an individual. All he demanded was the exclusion of a single man, the only man, it is true, whom he could not forget.

Once more he made a cautious effort to mend his fences. Toward the middle of January, he publicly uttered a warning, not in Cape Town itself, but at Philadelphia, a small town north of the colonial capital, that "if the same course were pursued (by the English), matters would become still more serious in the next years." Again it was a threat against England, but with an alternative: if the English would change their course, all would be right again. Mr. Merriman, the professional mediator in South African politics, referred to "Mr. Smuts' eloquent speech." But the *Kaffrarian Watchman* was not so easily appeased. The newspaper called Smuts a fire-eater and a political madman. This tactful insinuation accompanied him throughout his life.

At a Malmesbury meeting, with his father in the chair, he took his last shot at Cecil Rhodes. Accused by Mr. Louw, one of the few Dutchmen in politics who had remained faithful to the "colossus," of unfairness to an absent man, Smuts replied: "Mr. Rhodes had ample opportunity to account for his action in public without availing himself of it . . . I am no longer going to have anything to do with him." Smuts was twenty-seven years old when he thus buried his relation with his shattered idol. At the age of sixty he went to Oxford to deliver the Rhodes Memorial lecture, a grand address, and a confession of intellectual faith in the beloved enemy long in his grave.

There was one more thing to be done, one thing more important than anything else. On Friday the thirtieth of April, 1897, in the early morning, Smuts was back in Stellenbosch. No one was astonished to see him in formal black, since as a young man he rarely wore less ceremonial attire. He went to the Kriges' house where Isie was already waiting, perhaps a little impatiently, for she had, indeed, been waiting for twelve years. They were married by the Reverend Dr. Marais, the benefactor who had once lent undergraduate Smuts a little money on his life insurance. The hour for the ceremony was carefully chosen so that Miss Krige's younger brothers and sisters were safely in school. Only the bride's parents had been let into the secret. On the next morning the couple went off to conquer Johannesburg.

Johannesburg in 1897, eleven years after its foundation, was a town of excitement, energy and activity. Men and money from Kimberley had moved in. The old-timers brought, as it were, their accustomed surroundings with them. The Market Square in Johannesburg was an exact copy of the original in jolly, crazy, sweating Kimberley. The town was overcrowded. Although hotels were mushrooming, most newcomers had to sleep on floors. The streets were rutted tracks. Crossing Commissioner Street—the main street—one sank into the mud. Filthy buckets served for drains. Water had to be carted a couple of miles from the hills to the north, since the municipal administration, a body in which the *uitlanders* were not represented, refused to lay pipes. In times of drought this scarcity of water caused real hardship. But it was always a good excuse for replacing water with other liquids. However, in spite of orgies of drinking, in spite of hastily swallowed and irregular meals, in spite of dirt and discomfort, of the horrible sanitary conditions perpetuated by the unclean and unkempt Transvaal administrators, who turned Johannesburg, six thousand feet above sea level, a natural health resort, into the town with the most frightful child mortality—in spite of all these drawbacks, hope and enthusiasm ran riot.

The hope was noisy, the enthusiasm clamorous, the manners rough and ready. Yet the predominantly English settlement—

although having a strong admixture of Russian and German Jews, oily Portuguese, Hollander speculators, and even Turks and Armenians—craved the respectability of an English town. Soon Johannesburg was laid out in broad thoroughfares. Gum trees were planted in the residential districts where they grew with incredible speed. Houses were more the object of speculation in real estate than gems of architectural taste. Everyone was constantly moving; the city itself rapidly changed its face. The suburb of Doornfontein, where the young Smuts settled down, was at that time a respectable district. Later the natives swarmed over it.

The newcomers did not belong to the gay set of Johannesburg. They kept to their kin: to the other Dutch people who, also, after the Jameson Raid, had left the Cape Colony disillusioned. Most of them did not find their promised land in their chosen republic, either. When it came to appointments in the civil service, President Kruger preferred imported Hollanders, crafty and slick fellows, to his own young Boers. It was another aspect of his signal inability to come to terms with the new generation. Probably he felt the gulf himself, and did not relish it. But Oom Paul was now seventy-four years old, his painful and incurable eye disease—his eyelashes were growing inward, and constant medical attention could not relieve his terrible suffering—kept him in a state of permanent irritation. Besides, he became ever harder of hearing. Yet this wreck of a patriarch had, due to the Jameson Raid, become a saint and a symbol to most Boers over all South Africa. His greedy, possessive instinct was not sapped by his physical decay. He grew always more stubborn, autocratic, intractable, and lonesome. Sternly, he reserved all important decisions for himself. But his Hollander advisers were left to carry out the routine business. They were headed by Dr. Leyds, the Secretary of State, who, according to Milner, had won the confidence of Kruger by acting as a protagonist against England, and who was "largely the cause of recent troubles in South Africa by fomenting differences between Great Britain and the Transvaal."

Smuts' own attitude toward the Hollanders had been in his

best manner, conciliatory. While still in Cape Town he had written: "I am not pro-Hollander. But when the Transvaal struggled with poverty, when it was in sackcloth and ashes, our educated Cape men were not very eager to run after Cinderella. It was only from Holland that civil servants were to be obtained. It is but natural that those who stood by the country in those dark days should enjoy their share of the fat of the land, now prosperity has come. . . . Only in one way can the so-called Hollander question be solved. And that is by exemplary behavior on the part of the Colonial Afrikanders in the Transvaal. They are destined to bring about a slow, quiet revolution in this country."

What had been a program when he wrote those lines, became his practice now that he himself was a Colonial Afrikander in the Transvaal. His behavior was, indeed, exemplary, and he was bent on bringing about a very slow and quiet, almost inaudible revolution in the country.

His exemplary behavior, it is true, differed from the accepted standards in high-strung, hectic, convivial Johannesburg. Still a tight-lipped, square-chinned, lean young man, he was shadowed by personal tragedy. His twin daughters died in infancy, and the son who came in the second year of his marriage was also a weak child; he, too, was to die early, actually while his father was in the field. Yet personal tragedy did not break him. Perhaps he knew that his life would never be entirely his own. In his own words he was hard, confident, and successful as a young man. Friends were impressed by his "hungry, angry" eyes. "Well do I remember the Advocate Smuts of those days," a contemporary reminisced. "He was a familiar figure in Commissioner Street, and he did not resemble the later General Smuts at all. Imagine a pale-faced, tremendously serious young man, who appeared much taller than he really was, owing to his thinness; given to conversing with the pavement, absorbed in thoughts, and seemingly taking no notice of what went on around him; with high cheekbones, and the hungry look that betokens the man whose mind is grappling with many problems, prominent among which, no doubt, was the question why his energy could not find an adequate outlet."

Once more, but for the last time, Smuts was the lone wolf. None of the many causes célèbre among the quarrelsome populace of Johannesburg came his way. Yet he did fairly well. After a few months he could give up his law courses; he did not need the income on the side line any longer. The event was celebrated by a formal dinner in his honor. His hosts, a group of prominent lawyers, had tactfully ordered *Pudding Diplomat* by way of dessert.

The air was thick with rumors. President Kruger was about to reshuffle his cabinet. Dr. Leyds could perhaps better employ his outstanding qualities, amiability, civilized manners, the good looks of a blond young giant, in mobilizing the powers of continental Europe against the British menace. In addition to the Secretaryship of State, the office of State Attorney was also vacant. The *Young Afrikander Movement,* a clique of youthful Boers opposing the British as well as their Hollander counterparts in the Transvaal administration, would perhaps get a chance. The movement's uncontested leader was Advocate Smuts.

But a storm in a teacup outroared all political combinations and conspiracies. After many years of haggling with the administration the courts of justice were definitely fed up with Kruger's dictatorial habit of overriding their decisions simply by passing a *besluit*—resolution—which canceled judicial sentences in the docile *Volksraad.* The *grondwet*—constitution— had guaranteed judicial independence. Chief Justice Kotzé, an old antagonist of Kruger's, who had once been defeated by Oom Paul in a presidential election, decided a mining case against the government, compelling it to repay a sum of a few hundred thousand pounds. Conceivably, the already long punctured and abused constitution was not worth another £350,000 to Kruger. Moreover, he was aroused at another man's daring to be as pigheaded as he was himself. He passed a further resolution in the *Volksraad,* not only forbidding the courts to contest legislation, but threatening any judge who attempted to do so with instant dismissal. The High Court, in response, went on strike, demanding the re-establishment of their rights before legal business could be renewed in the Transvaal. The state of lawlessness in the Republic, already prevailing to a large degree, would thus have been openly advertised. This Kruger could not risk at a time when his emissary was appealing to European civilization for help against the threatening British "transgression of law." Kruger proved his cunning by promising that he would pass a suitable measure during the *Volksraad's* session.

The entire Transvaal debated whether the special or the regular session was meant. The High Court, backed by the whole of the legal profession, demanded its protective *besluit* from the special session, which was then in progress, whereas Kruger, evasive as ever, insisted that he had spoken of the forthcoming, ordinary session.

Advocate Smuts had his great opportunity. For the first time a cause célèbre came his way: He was briefed in a sensational murder case. But without batting an eye he forsook his chance. He perceived a greater one. Provoking the entire bar of the Transvaal, he came forth with a legal opinion, supporting the President. His paper was long and involved, based on a highly scientific interpretation of Roman-Dutch law in which no man was his peer, but it boiled down to the simple fact that the question *which* session Kruger had had in mind was open. Hence the President could make his own choice.

Undoubtedly, Smuts believed in what he said. He has never uttered a false word. But he disliked Chief Justice Kotzé's meddling in politics. A judge should keep out of it. Finally, he had made up his mind to throw in his lot with Kruger and the anti-English, perhaps in the hope that he could tame them and bring about that "silent and slow revolution" in the Transvaal whose necessity he had predicted.

His judgment, based on the authority of the generally recognized greatest expert in jurisprudence in the Republic—who, by a queer fate, happened to be a rather briefless barrister— struck like a thunderbolt.

The *Pretoria Volkstem,* President Kruger's own mouthpiece, suggested Mr. Smuts as a suitable candidate for the post of State Attorney, enthusiastically enumerating his qualities. A week later, the *Rand Post,* a conservative English-language paper, announced that Smuts, indeed, had been offered the post. "He is able and conscientious," the paper commented, "but though he may have all the precociousness of a Pitt, we still consider that twenty-eight years is rather too young an age for the State Attorney of the South African Republic." In his place, the newspaper suggested Mr. Krause, the Public Prosecutor in Johannesburg. Tactfully, the *Rand Post* had omitted Smuts' other evident disqualification: although siding with the ruling Boer oligarchy, the young advocate was technically an *uitlander* without franchise.

This fact, coupled with the drawback of his youth—he was two years too young to become a member of the executive—indeed prevented Kruger from making Smuts Secretary of State, as had been his strong desire. He was enamoured of Smuts, the very man for whom he had been looking: a young Boer who would be faithful to him. "Our relations were like those of father and son," Smuts expressed it later. But Kruger's uncanny knowledge of his farmers' and burghers' mood, prevented him from eliciting a showdown. Mr. Reitz, once President of the Free State, was appointed Secretary of State. Smuts had to content himself with the second job. It was still an absurd appointment. But there was only slight grumbling among the oligarchy. The old shepherds felt that a fresh wind was now sweeping over the green pastures of the Transvaal. Some suspicious members of the *Volksraad* comforted themselves with the thought that the intruder would only play second fiddle. Little did they realize that this was his innermost inclination. Smuts' creative urge was always greater than his personal ambition. The shy youngster developed into a modest man. Until he reached the fifties, he always contented himself with wielding the power "in close harmony" with a resplendent front man.

In June, 1898, Smuts arrived in Pretoria, and he had come to stay. The mellow capital of the Transvaal was already the Boers' holy town, although it had only been built some forty years before and sheltered an important English minority. The atmosphere was different from that of Johannesburg, not alone due to the fact that the altitude was some one thousand feet lower. Still, Pretoria lies on a high plateau, and is surrounded by gently sloping hills from which the town appears like a great park of tall, dark-green poplars showing glimpses of red roofs, the towers of public buildings shining above them.

From near by, however, Pretoria, toward the turn of the century, looked less ideal. City and suburb were strangely intermixed. Corrugated-iron shacks stood next to dignified bank buildings; the State Museum bordered the meat market. But everywhere trees and flowers grew, and the town was irrigated by the innumerable rivulets that flowed through the ditches. Among one-storied houses the spacious government buildings and the edifices belonging to banking and business interests stood out incongruously. Trolley lines ran through the principal streets, but the trams had frequently to stop: the farmers' oxcarts and trek wagons had the right of way.

Pretoria did not belong to its inhabitants, but to the President's own people. They *outspanned* on the public square when they came to town to partake of the *nagmaal,* holy communion, or to see Oom Paul. Kruger's house, a small whitewashed cottage, stood opposite the Dopper church, the sanctuary of the fiercest and most bigoted sect of the Dutch Reformed Church, where the President sometimes preached, intermingling his sermon with curses and loud outcries.

The President spent most of his day on the *stoep,* the verandah, of his house, ready to receive any of his burghers, smoking his pipe incessantly, using the pavement as a spittoon, and drinking, with his callers, innumerable cups of coffee throughout the day: the state allowed him £300 a year "coffee money" as part of his expenses for entertaining. On the *stoep* all business of state was negotiated. No records, no files were kept. Among all his new impressions, Smuts, punctiliously careful by inclination and habit, must have wondered at this form of gov-

69

ernment by word of mouth. But he rapidly accustomed himself
to his surrounding. Here he was not in Cape Town, not in Cambridge, not in Johannesburg. Here he was where he wanted to
belong.

Before six months had passed, the new State Attorney had
clamped down on corruption wherever he could stamp out the
evil without hurting the President's feelings. He was anxious
not to trespass on Oom Paul's own bailiwick, but he could
purge some of the evil in Johannesburg. An abstainer himself,
he was disgusted by the illicit liquor traffic. Instead of hunting
the small fry, he attacked the evil at its root. He dismissed the
chief of the corrupt detective service on the Rand. Philosophi-
cally, this worthy by the name of Bob Ferguson shrugged.
"Smuts says that I do not get at the big men," was his own
explanation. On the following day *The Standard and Digger's
News*, a Johannesburg paper, announced that the new State
Attorney would take over personally the whole detective service. "No one doubts the integrity and ability of Mr. Smuts," the
English paper commented. "He has it in him to make the law
respected."

A series of stern edicts ensued. They were promulgated by
the six oligarchs of the Executive Council—of which Smuts, due
to his absurd legal status, was not a member—and passed by
the *Volksraad*. But they had been drawn up by the State Attorney, some of the sterner ones undoubtedly at Kruger's behest.

Smuts was eager to serve his paternal friend. He saw in
Kruger the embodiment of the Boer character in all its higher
and larger aspects. He admired Oom Paul's iron will and tenac-
ity, and his mystic faith in another world. To him, Johannes
Paulus Kruger was the greatest man, both morally and intellectually, that the Boer race had produced. The existence of
such a personality was to him the safest guarantee that the
scattered, isolated, small tribe of the Boers, his own tribe,
would never go down. And that was all that mattered.

That they were opposite poles, Kruger and Smuts, the one
learned and scientific, a believer in pure intellect, an austere
thinker yet an enthusiastic idealist ever in search of a better

world; the other an illiterate, instinct-driven, pigheaded oldster, yet imbued with a glowing, if bigoted, creed, an intense feeling of pride and dignity, the last pillar of an obsolete microcosmic world . . . that they were opposite poles made no difference. North and South poles are a globe apart, and yet indistinguishable from one another.

Smuts, himself painfully correct, could not bring himself to stomach the corruption permeating the President's surrounding. Admitting Kruger's nepotism, he told Sir Percy Fitzpatrick, the head of the Johannesburg Reformers: "The President wants to do his best. But you have to remember that there are a number of hangers-on, people who have personal interests of which he knows nothing, and there are times when they make it difficult to carry out what we all know ought to be done." That old man Kruger should not have known anything of the personal interests of his own son-in-law, whom he had effectively helped to become a millionaire, was a charitable view. But Smuts followed his leader blindly. It was a repetition of the Rhodes-complex, this time within his own family circle.

In the very month of November, 1898, in which the detective force was put under Smuts' personal control, Kruger waged another of his favorite two-front wars: against a native tribe as well as against his despised *uitlanders*. He made the *Volksraad* decree that all white men living in the Transvaal were liable to military service in the *commandos*. His cause was righteous, nay, religious. The Lord had ordained his chosen people to enslave the Amorites and Canaanites. These strange names, of course, stood for the Zulus and the Matabele. But the *uitlanders* refused to fight for Kruger's Old-Testamentarian craze, which they rightly explained by his desire to have slave labor for his farmers.

Smuts, not representing a constituency, spoke in the *Volksraad* only when it was necessary to explain a legal matter. Now he spoke. He suggested a law compelling the *uitlanders* subject to foreign sovereignties to fight or pay.

Something in his instinct or his intellect, however—it is difficult to tell the difference, because Smuts is the rare case of a man in whom intellect and instinct are as closely wedded as is humanly possible—must have, at least occasionally, revolted against the uncompromising course to which he was now committed. On March 3, 1899, the British agent in Pretoria, a diplomat by the name of Sir Conyngham Greene, sent Milner an amazing report. He had been told by Sir Percy Fitzpatrick, the leader of the *uitlanders*, that Messieurs Leyds, who served a short term as Foreign Secretary before embarking on his mission to Europe, Reitz, the State Secretary, and Smuts, the State Attorney, had come forward with a conciliatory proposal, to which, they insisted, they were able to obtain Kruger's consent. The Transvaal Government would offer peace to the whole *uitlander* population. It would impose no new taxes without approval, appoint a European financier as auditor, and grant full citizenship rights to everyone after a residence of five years from the day the agreement was signed. The government would also offer to settle the vexed question of the dynamite concession by mutual consent. In return, the government demanded the support of the industry in the Chinese coolie question— which was to become a major headache to Smuts in later years —as well as in floating a loan; furthermore they insisted on the liquidation of the South African League, the foremost British patriotic organization in South Africa, and the ceasing of the press agitation both in the English papers in the Transvaal and in England.

However, Sir Conyngham added, Fitzpatrick had smelled a rat. Even if the offer were bona fide, the shrewd businessman believed, the *Volksraad* would not ratify any such agreement, whereas Kruger would have secured his dynamite—and probably not alone for industrial purposes. Smuts, according to Fitzpatrick, was the main agent. "He knows all about everything." Smuts insists he and Leyds had proposed and discussed the matter with Kruger, who for his part promised to suggest the compromise to the *Volksraad* and felt sure it would pass there. During the course of the negotiations Smuts offered further concessions. The coolie question should not be included publicly, and as to the franchise, the *uitlander's* waiting time could be restricted. "So altogether it looks genuine as far as Smuts is involved," Fitzpatrick concluded. "But who can believe that Kruger and Leyds have no ulterior aims? Smuts implored me as a fellow South African to try to get the proposal well received. It would be the real settlement of all our troubles, and the removal of the war cloud forever. The reason for hurry, he says, is that Kruger can't keep anything secret for any length of time. So Smuts wants to act now. While I believe that he means it, although he aims at a Republic of South Africa, I still mistrust the others."

A few days later Sir Conyngham Greene endorsed Fitzpatrick's confidence in Smuts, though he was beset by similar scruples concerning the others. "It is perfectly clear that Smuts and Reitz are genuine. But it is equally clear that the President and Dr. Leyds aim solely at safeguarding their dynamite and estranging the Dutch from the Imperial government."

Milner himself received the same impression, when, toward the end of March, Dr. Leyds called upon him for a farewell visit before leaving for Europe. Without mincing words, Milner warned him not to repeat his manoeuvre of two years before. If he again made fair promises to the government in London and to the English press, of which nothing more would be heard when the crisis was over, he would do irretrievable damage to the cause of peace. Dr. Leyds laughed off the warning, and did exactly as Milner had expected. He remained the stormy petrel of South African politics. His Dutch stubbornness wrecked Smuts' well meant peace plan.

Kruger went ahead with his proposed extension of the dynamite concession in clear violation of the London Convention. The High Commissioner protested. His objection was answered by State Attorney Smuts, who, in the shortest possible form, answered that the Transvaal Government would uphold its decision. Obviously he did not wish to stick his neck out again. Or perhaps he was embittered by the failure of his first peace effort. In his youth he was easily embittered. A telegram Sir Conyngham Greene sent Milner on May 15 testifies to Smuts' recurrent stubbornness: "The President is being urged, I am told, by influential old burghers to give way, and to recognize the legitimate rights of the *uitlanders* before pressure is brought to bear from outside. But Smuts and others from the Young Afrikander Movement, backed by the Hollander clique, are openly defiant. They believe the Imperial Government may threaten, but will not act."

On the same day, another signal fire flared up. The police in Johannesburg arrested eight persons on charges of high treason. Five were alleged to be British ex-officers, one of them the spy master for the War Office in London. The three others, it soon appeared, were stool pigeons, arrested on their own faked confessions, and planted in the cells to spy on their fellow prisoners.

The Johannesburg police was under Smuts' personal direction. The British agent rushed into the State Attorney's office, indignantly protesting against what was evidently a plot to poison the Transvaal's relations with England. Smuts washed his hands of the matter. The responsibility, he insisted, lay with the Public Prosecutor, Dr. Krause. Yet he assured Greene that any alleged intention to compromise Her Majesty's government would be suppressed. It is, indeed, unbelievable that, even in the heat of those explosive days, Smuts himself could have been involved in a scheme of that low order. However, the affair was the business of his department. Milner, rejecting Smuts' assurances, demanded a full and speedy investigation. The disgraceful conspiracy was finally exposed in court, and furnished one more proof of the methods used by the *Zarps* and by the *agents provocateurs* in the service of the Transvaal Government. No apology was extended to the Imperial government, nor did the innocent victims of the plot receive any form of compensation.

The dice were loaded. The situation became impossible for England, and was fraught with peril for the Transvaal. On May 13, Dr. Leyds cabled from London: "England has now everywhere a free hand. I doubt if anybody will do anything for us," and a fortnight later from Berlin: "Minister for Foreign Affairs says Germany still friendly to South African Republic, but cannot assist in war because England is master of the seas. Hopes government of SAR will concede as much as is consistent with independence. England has not asked Germany."

Milner, the new opponent of Kruger, was not an elementary force as Cecil Rhodes had been. If Rhodes and Kruger were both fighting demons, Sir Alfred Milner resembled Smuts very much more closely. Both were shy, reserved, and apparently haughty and unyielding, but both were warm-hearted idealists. They took, it is true, another twenty years before they discovered this similarity.

Milner had arrived in the middle of the extreme tension following the Jameson Raid. Under his soothing influence a degree of calm was achieved, at least in the Cape Colony. He made the leaders of the Bond understand that as British citizens they could not, without committing high treason, adopt the same extreme anti-British attitude that went unchecked in the Republics. Perhaps his argument was also made more intelligible to the Dutch master politicians by the dispatch of a small number of English troops to Durban, and by a minor naval demonstration; a few British vessels showed themselves off the coast of Natal. The Bond leaders understood. They were impressed by Milner's intensity, whereas he for his part immediately understood the fundamental unity of South Africa. The Cape Colony quieted down. Now Milner went at his next task: patching up the relations with the Transvaal. Joseph Chamberlain, the Colonial Secretary in London, had urged him to adopt a policy of patience. Milner was entirely agreed as to the wisdom of this course.

But one more incident occurred that again shook South Africa to its foundations. An *uitlander* in Johannesburg, an Englishman by the name of Edgar, involved in a street brawl, had been pursued by four of those brute Boer policemen into his house, and there shot down by one of them. The murderer was arrested, but charged only with manslaughter and released on bail of £200. Smuts immediately interfered. He ordered the rearrest of the policeman, and a renewed trial. The judge, a peasant's son from the *platteland,* and a fiery nationalist aged twenty-four, approved the verdict of the jury, entirely composed of Boers. The murderer was acquitted for the second time.

The *uitlanders* were in despair. They petitioned Queen Victoria to come to the assistance of subjects in the Transvaal "in which conditions had become well-nigh intolerable." Kruger regarded this petition signed by twenty-odd thousand British citizens to their own sovereign as treason toward the Transvaal. Smuts told Sir Percy Fitzpatrick with whom he had been negotiating on the most amicable terms: "I am morally certain that you are at the bottom of everything, and when I get proof of it, I will put it into you for all you are worth. . . ." All South Africa was in a state of unbearable suspense. To continue the endless and fruitless negotiations in which he had been involved ever since his arrival was useless, Milner understood. The question of the *uitlanders* had to be settled once and for all. Only one man could guarantee a settlement, President Kruger.

Milner availed himself of a standing offer by the government of the Free State, to bring him and Kruger together. He arrived in Bloemfontein, the capital of the Free State, on May 30, 1899, and was on the following day introduced to the President. Kruger had brought Smuts as his legal adviser.

Milner greeted the young man, whom he had long wished to meet personally, in the most courteous manner.

Smuts, who had so far only experienced the tempestuous "colossus," Cecil Rhodes, a man who did not fit into any frame, was now for the first time confronted with the power of the British Empire incarnate.

THE SCENE WAS SET. AN OFFICE IN THE RAILWAY DEPARTMENT, the newest building in Bloemfontein, had been freshly cleaned and got in order as a special sign of the neutral host's good will. The Free State had good reason to stress its neutral character. President Steyn had, half a year before the conference, on November 22, 1899, addressed a meeting of the Free State commandants from eighteen districts on the Caledon River with the words: "We must make necessary regulations against confusion in the event of a sudden call to arms." Among other measures it was resolved that at least 10,000 cartridges should be stocked in each magazine, and that each burgher should be provided with 100 cartridges.

Since Kruger's English was none too good, Mr. Abraham Fischer, Prime Minister of the Free State, acted as translator. Mr. Fischer took great pains to stress his impartiality. The fact was not revealed that he had just refused the Secretaryship of State in the Transvaal, and for a very sound reason: he could be of more help to Kruger in steering the allied Free State into the latter's camp if and when matters came to a showdown.

On one side of the conference table sat Sir Alfred Milner with his staff: Colonel Hanbury-Williams, his aide-de-camp, Lord Belgrave, his secretary, and three clerical assistants. On the other side Kruger was surrounded by his crew: Schalk-Burger, a member of the Executive Council with a certain liberal reputation, Wolmarans, another Transvaal politician, and the experts, among whom one lanky young man, more neatly clad than his companions, his face clean-shaven, lips tightly pressed together, steel-blue eyes fixed on his president, as if he wanted to imbue him with his own energy, caused some attention, primarily because he could not sit still. Repeatedly he jumped up to be nearer to Oom Paul, and to press scraps of paper into the old man's hand, although the invalid's red eyes could not decipher the scribbled words. However, the youthful State Attorney's restlessness was only a minor diversion. The general attention was concentrated on the two protagonists. They represented not only two countries, but two worlds.

Oom Paul in his tightly buttoned, stained frock coat, sat huddled in an armchair, a fringe of thick, unkempt hair surrounded his broad chin and his heavy animal face, marked by bushy brows and a cunning, stubborn expression. A strong will, it appeared, was once more pulling together his enormous mass of flesh. He obviously did not fear the duel in which he was now about to engage. It was not a new experience to him. Nothing was new to the patriarch. Why, had he not, three years earlier, triumphantly tricked Sir Hercules Robinson, another British High Commissioner? Moreover, the victory at Majuba Hill was still in his blood. He himself had not participated in the battle. But since that glorious day he was doubly sure that God in heaven and the Liberal Party in England would never desert him. Both blessed his determination to prevent foreigners from having a voice in his country. He breathed heavily. It sounded as if he were drawing his strength from the nation of shepherds for whom he stood; one of them, and yet their exalted leader. The recent elections had shown that not only the burghers but also the spokesmen of the *Young Afrikander Movement* were no less zealous and fanatic than he was himself. On the very eve of the conference the *Volksraad* had vetoed the franchise to some *uitlanders* who had acquired their right to citizenship by fourteen years of residence. This provocative gesture was clearly intended to stiffen their President for the forthcoming negotiations. The *Volksraad* would agree to no concessions, even if such were imposed on their President. While Kruger sat slumped in his armchair, shivering even in the warm South African autumn, his men on the *veld* were drilling; rifles were being distributed among them; *veld-cornets* galloped from farm to farm, instructing the burghers not to leave their homes, and to hold themselves ready. Paul Kruger grinned. It would please the Lord to let His most faithful believer see another, the crowning victory, either at this conference table or on the bat-

tlefield, before he closed his burning eyes. Whether by negotiation, or by the might of arms, the hated *rooineks*—rednecks—
would be driven into the sea.

Opposite the prophet sat Milner, tall, thin, with a strong face,
calm, immaculately attired, the prototype of clean, intelligent
efficiency. Equipped with all the learning of the schools, he was
wont to keep his strong emotions in leash to his reason. He was
reserved to the point of shyness. In manners and looks he appeared austere. Throughout all the trials that beset him he kept
his unshakable nerve, and his resolution of steel. Yet he was
far from nursing prejudices, or even rigid opinions. He had
come to Bloemfontein with his mind open to new suggestions
and ideas. But it was impossible to shake his ardent belief in
the civilizing influence of the British Empire. It was to this
cause that he devoted all his energies. He was not as cunning
as Kruger, but very much wiser. And he met the old fanatic's
pitchfork with the cold steel of his intellect.

The first meeting of the conference lasted but two hours. Already at half-past four in the afternoon, Kruger was becoming
tired. He had been rambling along all the time, his tone conciliatory, skilfully avoiding any concrete statement. He put in
a brief appearance at the evening reception given by President
Steyn of the Free State, and was just as evasive when the conference was resumed the following morning.

Kruger was biding his time. Time was all that counted. Time
for further armament. But, above all, time until the rains would
pour down. In the dry sub-tropical winter, with the *veld* a
desert, the Boer *commandos* were immobilized. Their horses
could find no forage. The men could not move. A man without
a horse was only half a man.

But he could not distract Milner. At the second session, Sir
Alfred decided to confine the proceedings to one clear issue:
would the President grant reasonable and immediate measures
of enfranchisement to the *uitlanders?* If such a measure was
promised, promised without ambiguity, the High Commissioner
was prepared to enter into consideration of other causes of
friction, but they must not obscure the main issue. Enfranchise-

ment was the vital question, and the acid test of Kruger's sincerity and good will.

Kruger fell back on obstinate, repetitious assertions that he could not sacrifice the independence of his country, a sacrifice which had never been suggested or asked of him. He grew visibly weary, hesitated in answering, his words lost in cumbersome, involved sentences. Whether he feigned fatigue, or escaped into it, was not clear.

It was then that Smuts jumped into the breach. Long before Fischer had finished translating Milner's replies, Smuts had already scribbled the answers on loose slips, pressing them into Kruger's hand, or, since the President could not make out the writing, handing them over to his fellow-delegates sitting next to Kruger. Smuts was as much a legalist as Milner. Moreover, he knew from his years at Cambridge how the English mind worked. Intuitively, he had the answer to every question, and his counter-demands were speedily prepared. Mr. Fischer, sensing that the position of the Transvaal delegation was improving slightly, dropped the last vestige of impartiality. Unabashed, he now aided Kruger's dilatory tactics, and did his best to soften Milner's slashing rapier thrusts.

Thus Kruger was able to offer plausible-sounding, but deceptive alternatives to Milner's franchise proposal. But soon he deviated from the central theme, throwing more monkey wrenches into the discussion. Now it was his turn to make demands: renunciation of British suzerainty, acceptance of "neutral arbitration" by the Imperial government, British cession of the whole of Swaziland in order to provide the Transvaal with the long desired access to the sea. These demands were so firmly entrenched in his mind that he could repeat them monotonously without visible signs of fatigue. He simply ruminated his stock-in-trade phrases. But to any question of a moderate and temporary reform he was more than hard of hearing. He was suddenly deaf. Full and honest franchise meant to him the inevitable subjection of his rule to the voting power of the inhabitants. It spelled the end of the system of fattening concessions and monopolies, of his dictatorial control of the judiciary, the end of corruption in the police, and of the cruel treatment of the natives; the end, above all, of his dream of Afrikanderdom's supremacy over all South Africa. "It is our country that you want," he burst out, bowing his head between his big, red hands, hot tears streaming down his bearded cheeks.

In a way he was justified. To him his system of corruption was, indeed, his country. But the English had no desire to wrest from the Boers the hard-won independence to which they clung so tenaciously. The conflict was greater. It was a clash between two civilizations. The stream of the new life, industrial, democratic, self-governing, surged against the barrier of a primitive oligarchy, corrupt by tradition, and still further deteriorated by wealth acquired overnight.

Milner tried to explain that His Honor was entirely wrong. Not only had Her Majesty's government not the slightest desire to infringe the independence of the South African republic, but actually less than full democracy was asked. The *uitlanders*, although outnumbering the burghers by two to one or better, would content themselves with eight seats in the *Volksraad*, thus acquiring a platform to vent their grievances, but only a small minority in the House of Assembly.

With flying fingers, Smuts wrote and wrote.

Embarrassed, Kruger stammered counter-proposals: he insisted on seven years of residence before enfranchisement, thus cutting down the old period by half. Milner listened attentively. He waited for the escape clauses. They came in abundance. The limitations and restrictions attached, rendered Kruger's compromise proposal a sham.

Patiently, Milner explained why he had to insist on five years before enfranchisement—not to gain two years but for the ". . . principle of legal continuity . . ." Smuts murmured with a faint smile, as if he were a mind reader.

Milner seemed to pay no attention to the interruption. But he was impressed by the "brilliant" State Attorney, as he called Smuts after the conference.

The principle of legal continuity, Milner argued untiringly, was established on those terms of enfranchisement in the Trans-

81

vaal which had been offered by the South African Republic itself in the "great deal" following Majuba. But more important, he added, were clear, simple formulas of admission, available to every duly qualified claimant.

Kruger tolerated no further interference on the part of his legal adviser. Precisely these conditions he rejected. With strong accents in his already broken voice he upheld the provisos enabling his government to elect potential electors, admitting supporters, excluding opponents.

The last three days of the conference were a cumbersome repeat performance. Kruger reiterated his parrot-cry of "my independence!" time and again. He adhered obstinately to his point. Yet he must have felt that, at last, he had to deal with an Englishman whose will was as strong as his own, and whose brains and power of argument were infinitely superior. His doggedness in the end made him look foolish and insincere.

This became painfully evident to Smuts. He was aware that the two republics had not a chance in the world against the might and power of Great Britain. If he felt a Boer of the old stamp, he had certainly inherited their predominant trait. He was a born negotiator. Something new, he understood, must be produced to save the conference; some alternative plan must be found.

One more afternoon was spent on a discussion of the scandal of the dynamite concession. Kruger gave a confused account, but he explained that he was considering a new agreement with the company. When asked to give a written statement about this new agreement, he disdainfully refused to comply. He was accustomed to government by word of mouth. Every deviation from this rule would endanger the independence of the Transvaal.

On the following day, the day before the last, Kruger insisted that concessions acceptable to the *uitlanders* would be "worse than annexation," and would "put an end to my indep . . ."

At this moment a telegram was delivered to Lord Belgrave. He read it, nodded, smiled, and passed it over to his chief.

Even the austere Milner smiled in turn, and handed the telegram around to his staff. Everyone seemed pleased. Finally the message was returned to Lord Belgrave, who folded it and put it into his pocket.

Milner apologized for the short interruption, and asked His Honor to proceed.

But Kruger was much too intrigued by what were evidently new and important instructions to the English delegation. He had lost his thread and repeated the precious words "my independence" several times before he dropped heavily back into his armchair.

Everyone awaited an important announcement from Milner. Instead, the High Commissioner merely suggested an adjournment. Now it was quite clear that some great event was in the making. Bloemfontein buzzed with rumors. The Intelligence Service of the South African Republic, a most efficient organization directed by the State Attorney, was set to trace various clues.

After a few days the full truth about the telegram filtered out. It read: "Flying Fox has won the Derby, Westminster." Flying Fox belonged to the Duke of Westminster, Lord Belgrave's father.

But this was the single ray of light illuminating a somber scene. Kruger sprang a few more conjurer's tricks, all of which miscarried. On the last day of the conference, Monday June 5, Kruger declared: "I am not ready to hand over my country to strangers . . . I understand from His Excellency's arguments that if I do not really give the whole management of my land and government to the strangers, there is nothing to be done."

Jumping up, Milner protested that he had proposed nothing that would have any such effect.

The final meeting was in the afternoon. Kruger stated formally in a grave voice, having recovered his patriarchal dignity, that his own franchise proposal went as far as it was possible to go. He would submit it to the *Volksraad,* as a step in the right direction, even if His Excellency did not fully agree with it, provided that His Excellency would recommend arbitration on future differences.

To Milner it was a clumsy trap. He saw both loopholes. The *Volksraad* could just as well disagree, and arbitration could only mean indefinite prolongation of the quarrel without further progress. The High Commissioner summed up: "Since the parties have found themselves unable to agree on the principal topic of discussion, the status quo ante is restored. I am not authorized to discuss the question of arbitration. But any definite proposal which His Honor might make at any time will be submitted to the consideration of Her Majesty's government."

After an elaborate exchange of compliments the conference broke up. Kruger said: "Milner is a hard man to tackle." He felt himself misunderstood. In a way the High Commissioner had, indeed, misunderstood him. Kruger had not the slightest wish to prolong the quarrel indefinitely. He only wanted to keep negotiations alive until the rains came. With a sigh of resigned righteousness he looked up to his Lord. He could not discern even the tiniest cloud in the sky. He sighed once more. Then he looked at Smuts, at this nice boy at his side, this confirmed pacifist. His Honor smiled.

Oom Paul had good reason to smile. He was as sure of his case as he felt justified in his cause. Imperial Germany stood behind him. Already, Sir Edward Malet, British ambassador in Berlin, had protested against Germany's encouragement of the Boers in their hostile attitude toward England. Sir Edward had pointed out that this might lead to serious complications. But Baron Marschall Biberstein refused the warning. It was, he insisted, based on unfounded rumors. Joseph Chamberlain himself felt the necessity to substantiate the English complaint. "It appears from information in the possession of the Intelligence Department," he told the House of Commons, "that during the last nine months the Boers have already imported 50 field guns, 26 maxims, 45,000 rifles, more than 20,000 rounds of large and 30,000,000 pounds of rifle ammunition from a foreign power.

There is no reason to believe that such purchases are not going on."

Backed up by his young emperor, Baron Marschall replied from Berlin that Germany insisted on her right to support President Kruger. Any retreat from this position would spread a storm of indignation throughout the Reich. Wilhelm II, for his part, scribbled one of his famous marginal notes to Marschall's report on the Transvaal affair: "We must vigorously make capital out of this affair for eventual naval increases to protect our growing trade."

When Baron Marschall's diary was published, Wilhelm II's final folly was disclosed. The diary contains the following entry:

January 3—At ten o'clock conference with His Majesty, at which Hollmann, Knorr, and Senden also present. His Majesty developed rather amazing plans. He proposed the establishment of a German Protectorate over the Transvaal, an idea from which I dissuaded him right away. Then the young master demanded mobilization of the Marine, and dispatch of German troops to the Transvaal. On my objection that this would be war with England, His Majesty said: "Yes, but only on land."

In the end the Emperor contented himself with sending Fuerst Hatzfeld, his ambassador in London, with an insolent oral ultimatum to Downing Street. Shrewdly, the aged diplomat presented himself at an hour when he knew Lord Salisbury would be absent. Thus he was unable to carry out his mission.

Kruger was perfectly informed about events in Berlin and London. Dr. Leyds constantly commuted between the two capitals. He had been received in audience by Wilhelm II an hour before the latter had despatched the Kruger telegram which turned the "All Highest" into the Dr. Jameson of the world.

Moreover, the German Consul General in Pretoria, Herr von Herff, sat daily on Kruger's *stoep*. He obtained the President's permission to send 5,000 German settlers of military age into the Transvaal. But when he alluded to the possibility of a German Protectorate, Oom Paul insisted that arms came first and diplomatic niceties later. So the stream of German arms floating in through Delagoa Bay flowed ever broader.

According to Portuguese harbor statistics, the turnover of war material in the port of Lourenço Marques had more than quadrupled in the year 1897. It had jumped in value from £61,903 to £256,291. Over a million and a half pounds were expended on the fortifications around Johannesburg. In February, 1898, they were equipped with heavy Krupp guns. German artillery officers, still in the Emperor's uniform, were placed in command. In the same month Kruger reported to his executive council that he had just acquired a very large consignment of rifles, field guns, and ammunition. However, he did not even entrust his six colleagues in the government with exact figures. The loquacious President well knew that garrulousness was the Boers' cardinal sin. The other was a complete lack of discipline. But that the autocrat did not learn for a year longer.

He had enrolled ten thousand volunteers. Seventy thousand pounds a year was allotted to the Secret Service, operating primarily in the British colonies, more money than the British Intelligence Service had ever seen. A naturalized British citizen of German descent furnished Milner a list of nineteen prominent journalists, officials, and civil servants in the Cape Colony who were bribed by the Transvaal Government. An Irish journalist, back from Pretoria, reported: "A member of the *Volksraad* asked me whether the Queen would send down all her army to be 'eaten up' "—the Kafir expression—"or whether she would content herself with sending the boys."

In fact, the great white Queen across the seas sent no soldiers at all. Joseph Chamberlain, backed by almost the entire government of his day, particularly by Lord Salisbury, the Prime Minister, exercised all his remote influence to save the peace. A war, he insisted, would be most unpopular among the English people. South Africa was too far away.

Milner was on the spot. After Bloemfontein he knew that either a show of power or Britain's ignominious retreat from all South Africa was inevitable. He was depressed by the indifference he encountered at home, and aroused by the defeatist attitude of Sir William Butler, his commander in chief, who refused to take any precautionary measures, or indeed to budge, as long as he had not received orders from the War Office. Butler even refused to recruit volunteers, for which, Milner insisted, "the material was plentiful and excellent." Butler would make no strategic preparations. "The General's heart," Milner wrote to Chamberlain, "is on the other side."

There was no half-heartedness whatsoever on the side of the Boers. For five years the Transvaal had spent more than half its revenues for armament. After Bloemfontein, money was no longer a consideration. Why, the English in Johannesburg were paying all. Pretoria was now as well fortified as Johannesburg. A ring of forts was built on the hills surrounding the capital. Large consignments of arms of all sorts in cases marked "Agricultural Implements" and "Mining Machinery" were smuggled into the Transvaal through the British ports of Cape Town and Durban. Soldiers of fortune congregated from all over the world. The soldiers' pay in the smallest republic was the highest in the world. But only the foreign *condottieri*, French and German instructors, penniless Russian aristocrats, Balkan *komitatschi*, and last but not least a group of Irishmen from Chicago, disguised as an ambulance corps and abusing the Red Cross, drew money. The burghers were prepared to fight for love, and for their hatred of the British.

Pretoria was an armed camp. Commandos from the *platteland* marched through the streets on their way to the border of British Natal. Batteries of artillery paraded before Kruger. Thousands of men exercised in all night rifle practice. Indeed, the President had to hold back his people who were spoiling for a fight. It was still too early. The *veld* was still bone dry. Yet a mere week after the breakup of the conference at Bloemfontein, Kruger introduced a draft law in the *Volksraad*, haranguing his lawmakers: "I don't want war, but I will not give anything further away."

Cables from Leyds, who covered Europe at top speed, encouraged the President and his advisers to stand firm. To yield would endanger the independence of the Republic and lower its prestige in the eyes of friendly nations, Dr. Leyds advised.

On July 2, he cabled from Paris a summing up of his London experience. "According to Labouchere"—the leftist Radical—"neither the Prime Minister nor his colleagues are desirous of war. The cabinet is against Chamberlain. The House of Commons is only waiting for the next step of SAR government to bring an honorable solution. Scott (*Manchester Guardian*) proposes President Kruger should take an extraordinary census in order to determine the number of *uitlanders,* and how many of them desire franchise. This would cause delay. Scott says that gaining time is gaining everything."

That was exactly what Kruger thought. He no longer listened to his foreign emissary. Indeed, he heeded no one's advice. Retired amid the turmoil around him, he gazed at the sky. Sometimes he shook his head. Even from Johannesburg, which was deluged by rain in and out of season, came no report of the slightest drizzle. How he hated Johannesburg!

Was there no peace party among the Boers? Louis Botha, one of the youngest members of the *Raad,* was against any adventure. He loved his fatherland, above all its green pastures, which a war, a senseless war at that, an impossible war, would seriously damage. But the opinion of the junior member did not count. General Joubert, the expert and presumptive commander in chief, was against the war. But since he had once unsuccessfully contested Kruger's presidency, his advice would only drive the stubborn old man further into his madness. General De la Rey, the most Christian soldier, a quiet, retired patriot without any worldly ambition, raised his voice in warning. He was laughed down in the *Volksraad,* and shrugged: "All right. Go ahead. I will be with you. And I will still be in the fight, when all of you are fugitives!" He was resigned to the will of God.

Smuts was the only one who was not resigned, never resigned. To all outward appearance he was one of the most fiery leaders of the war party. The English-language press warned of him. Indeed, he backed Kruger in every way. As State Attorney he was responsible for maintaining internal order in case of war. He introduced a new franchise law that looked harmless enough, but was so full of traps and snares that it virtually strangled every possible move of the foreigners. He worked out a great plan for infesting Ireland, India, and the British possessions and colonies with a network of seditious agitators to undermine the Empire from within. The plan aroused general amusement when some of its details filtered out. India, of course, was the country whence these disagreeable brown competitors had moved into Natal. But where, for God's sake, was Ireland? How long would it take to trek there by oxcart? Smuts, though lacking any military experience, even submitted to Kruger a plan of grand strategy, suggesting a double-pronged attack on English territory. He kept Kruger busy, while he was busying himself.

On July 12, he visited the British agent in Pretoria at the latter's house. A long conversation ensued. Sir Conyngham Greene used the opportunity once more to press for a guarantee concerning the franchise law. Smuts, in grave earnest, replied that the Republic could not admit the right of Her Majesty's government to any guarantee unless Great Britain agreed to some reasonable scheme of arbitration. He did not wish to drive a Kafir bargain—an expression Milner had used at Bloemfontein— but something in return would be expected.

The personal negotiations between the two men dragged on until the end of August. Greene was all the time under the impression that the State Attorney was bargaining on behalf of his government. In fact, Smuts had embarked upon a one-man crusade to prevent war. This fact was clearly revealed when Secretary of State Reitz became involved. His was a different tune. He wrote a note, dated August 19, which was entirely unsatisfactory. Greene remonstrated. But Smuts' peace plan had obviously been upset by the Transvaal Executive Council. Stiffly, its disillusioned author had to answer: "The terms of a settlement as embodied in a formal note of this government dated August 19 were very carefully considered. I do not believe there is the slightest chance that those terms would be altered or amplified. Your decision will therefore have to be arrived at on those terms as they stand."

Imperturbably, Sir Conyngham Greene replied: "I take it that the negotiations are meant to be off."

Smuts had gained a few precious weeks for Kruger. Unwittingly, his single-handed peace crusade had played into the bellicose President's hands.

Now only did the government in London understand that war was upon them. Reinforcements from India, those reinforcements Milner had been urging and pressing for in vain, were finally sent. Although they had a smooth voyage under the brilliant September sun, they arrived too late.

In the first days of October the rains fell. Violent downpours, accompanied by hailstorms, thunder and lightning, caused much damage. The earth trembled. But the grass burst forth. Overnight the desert was Jehovah's green garden. The horses in their ramshackle stables stamped their hooves impatiently. They did not fear the tempest. Neighing, they trotted out of the suddenly opened doors. Few of them ever returned to their stables.

Praising the Lord who sent the rains, every October anew, to make the land of his chosen people fertile, to feed man and beast, on October 9, Kruger dispatched an insolent ultimatum to the English. It demanded the instant withdrawal of all troops from the borders of the Transvaal and from British soil, and the re-embarkation of all units which had landed in South Africa during the last years.

The ultimatum expired within forty-eight hours. To the wild melody of the downpour a hesitating man, General Joubert, on October 12, 1899, crossed the border of Natal, invading British territory.

| *Chapter 8* | PRETORIA—PRIDE AND FALL |

THE FIRST VOLLEY IN THE THREE YEARS' WAR, AS WELL AS THE last shot, were fired by the same man: the amazing Mr. Smuts. The first volley was in the nature of a propaganda barrage. During the three days that elapsed between Kruger's ultimatum and the actual aggression against British territory by the commandos under General Piet Joubert, the *Review of Reviews,* a leftist London magazine, edited by Mr. Stead, then the official spokesman of the pro-Boer party, published a pamphlet *A Century of Wrong.* The co-ordination between Pretoria and the praetorians in London, it appears, was not entirely faultless. *A Century of Wrong* had been released rather hastily. The Dutch original *Een Eeuw van Onrecht,* a Transvaal Government publication, limped a few days behind. The authorship of the hymn of hatred was attributed to Mr. F. W. Reitz, the Secretary of State of the South African Republic, who had studied at the University of Edinburgh, and practised as a barrister at the Inner Temple, London, before returning to his native *kraal.* Conceivably, a man with so thorough an English background could know where his attacks would hurt most. To him the English were a nation of pharisees: "Under the cloak of religion the British administration continued to display its hatred against our people and nationality, and to conceal its self-seeking aims under cover of the most exalted principles. The aid of religion was invoked to reinforce the policy of oppression. Emissaries of the London Missionary Societies slandered Boers. It seems there is no place for the God of Righteousness in English policy." More than half the pamphlet was given to the discussion of the English "capitalistic jingoism." A particularly virulent paragraph began: "The development of British policy in South Africa had hitherto been influenced at different times by the spirit of jingoism, and by the zeal for annexation which is so characteristic of the trading instinct of that race."

91

While this torrent of abuse went entirely unchecked among the English pharisees and jingoists, a good number of Dutchmen in the Cape Colony shook their heads. Who would have expected such unbridled language from the Honorable Mr. Reitz? It was the climax of the pamphlet itself that provided the answer to this question. It read: "The spirit of capitalism found its incarnation in Mr. Cecil Rhodes. Although he probably had no exceptional aptitude for politics, he was irresistibly drawn towards them by the stress of his interests. By means of his financial influence together with a double allowance of elasticity of conscience, he succeeded. . . ."

And now it was clear to everyone who the real author was. Only one man was capable of such vilification of Cecil Rhodes, who at that time, as the leader of the Progressive Party, played again a formidable role in Cape politics: Mr. Smuts. He had indeed written the pamphlet, or most of it, in his superb High Dutch. Mrs. Smuts, his partner in politics too, was responsible for the brilliant English translation.

The piece was written in the white heat of injured righteousness—characteristic, however, of the confusion of a young enthusiast's feelings, during the very days when the author was conducting most amiable negotiations with the British agent in Pretoria, and it left behind no trace in Smuts. Undoubtedly, he was soon willing to forget it. But his enemies never forgot it. Right now, while this war is on, the Zeesen transmitter, Dr. Goebbel's lie-factory, broadcasts the dusty, yellowed pamphlet regularly in its Afrikaans hour.

The din of the battle soon outroared the propaganda volley. Against 27,000 English soldiers south of the Limpopo, the river at South Africa's northern border, only 11,000 of whom were stationed in the Cape Colony, the Boers had mustered an overwhelming force. They numbered 90,000, and were equipped with 110 guns, mostly of German make. The Boer commandos were made up of men born on horseback, unexcelled in marksmanship, confident that the Lord of battles was protecting them. They were well-equipped, and excellently fed. In the

Free State contingent, which rushed to the help of the Transvaal and provided some of the toughest fighters, each burgher had brought along his riding horse, saddle and bridle, the *achterlaaier*—rifle—thirty cartridges, and half a pound of powder. He had to provision himself for eight days. His saddlebag bulged with meat, cut in strips, salted, peppered, or dried, with sausages and "Boer biscuits" (small loaves twice baked, with fermented raisins instead of yeast). The Boers had learned enough from their German friends to know the Prussian dictum: the fuller the belly, the better the army. They were sure that English soldiers, drawing nothing but their nauseating daily ration of *blikkiescos*, as the Boers contemptuously called the hallowed bully-beef, would prove easy prey.

According to General De Wet, the trouble that immediately started was over the distribution of meat, when the private supplies had given out. Now the *vleiskorporaal*—meat corporal—handed out portions of raw meat to the burghers. They differed in size and quality, and since the impartiality of many a *vleiskorporaal* was not above suspicion, the rule was made that he had while performing this duty to stand with his back toward the commando, pick out the nearest piece and, without looking around, give it to the next man in line. Those burghers who were not favored by fortune showed their dissatisfaction. Quarrels—according to the General—were frequent.

The burghers roasted their meat on a spit cut from the branches of trees. A skilful warrior was able to produce a *bomtspan*—a team of oxen not of the same color—by alternating pieces of fat and lean meat on his spit. To provide ample portions the commandos were forced to kill all the oxen and sheep in their terrain of operations, but they boasted of never wasting a bit. Sometimes the meat was sandwiched between biscuits of flour cooked in boiling fat and called *stormjaegers*, storm hunters, since they were so rapidly cooked, or *maagbomme*, stomach bombs, on account of their digestive effect.

Well-fed and God-fearing, the Free State Army began the war in grim earnest by attacking and capturing an English armored train at Kraaipan. General de la Rey was their victori-

ous *veggeneraal*—fighting general. His legal adviser, not really
involved in the thick of the fight, was the newly appointed
judge, James Barry Munnik Hertzog, son of a pub-owner in
Kimberley, grandson of a German immigrant, whose picture
the faithful young man carried in his breast pocket throughout
the campaign—and, who was within a few weeks, President
Steyn's right-hand man. Judge Hertzog was thirty-three years
of age when the Boer War broke out. He was a careful dresser.
With his well-trimmed black hair and short-cropped mustache, and his gold-rimmed spectacles he looked like a stranger
among the Boers from the *veld*. He won military fame by being the first to quit Bloemfontein when Lord Roberts was besieging the capital of the Free State. Under cover of night he
took his men across a bridge. The whole commando sang:
"Daisy, Daisy, give me your answer, do!" It was taken for a
British detachment and got away, unmolested. For this feat of
arms the Judge was promoted to general, and, for all practical
purposes, soon dropped out of the actual fighting.

Smuts, although spoiling for the fight, had serious duties that
kept him for the first months of the war in Pretoria. His was the
main task of organizing both the home front and the army in
the field. As often as he could, he visited the battle fronts to
render strategic assistance. Except for a short time in Stellenbosch, where he had been a member of the volunteers, he had
not the slightest military training or experience. Yet his plans
were respectfully listened to. The State Attorney's authority in
strategic affairs went unchallenged. Smuts had his own explanation for it. To him everything, botany or statecraft, general-
ship or philosophy, is simply a matter of straight thinking.

He expended much of his energy on demanding aggressive
prosecution of the war. The Boers should not content themselves with their initial successes. Time was against them. He
knew better than any other man the power of the Imperial
army, once it was fully mobilized. He implored General Joubert not to idle around besieging Ladysmith, but to bypass this
English stronghold, and thrust forward. The aged Commander

in Chief, however, was reluctant. He quoted the Biblical virtue
of patience, a strong argument among Boers. Louis Botha, still
a *veld-cornet* from the district of Vryheid, joined in Smuts'
pleading. General Joubert liked Louis Botha. Everyone liked
him. He had, it was generally agreed, a magic personality. But
to the aged Commander in Chief he was, at thirty-nine, still a
youngster. His advice, too, went unheeded. As both Smuts and
Botha had foreseen, Ladysmith gallantly, and at times desperately, defended by General White withstood the siege until the
town was relieved by English reinforcements. Boer strategy
had missed a great opportunity. But the loss was more than
compensated. Out of their unsuccessful joint pleading grew the
comradeship of Botha and Smuts, which entered—and made—
history.

Kimberley, too, was encircled. On the last train connecting
the town with the outside world, Cecil Rhodes arrived. Purple-
faced, bloated, gasping for breath, he was still the colossus.
Immediately upon his arrival he set up his autocratic rule. It
was a benevolent autocracy. "What do you want?" became his
famous question. All could have anything from him: money,
food, shelter. He even had a heavy gun manufactured in the
workshop of his company. It was a makeshift cannon, patched
together by a couple of engineers who had seen the design of
a howitzer in a technical magazine. But the monster could be
fired, and it kept the Boers at a respectful distance. Rhodes
opened the mines to the women and children of Kimberley for
protection. The gold mines became the model for the air-raid
shelters of a later day. He was less benign toward the English
officers and generals, whose progress was much too slow for his
own furious speed. After Kimberley had been besieged for two
months, Rhodes addressed a letter to Lord Roberts, advising
him ironically that there was a perfectly good, flat approach to
the town through the Spyfontein Hills. After a further two
months Kimberley was relieved.

Cecil Rhodes was not relieved until two years later when
that "good, clean death," death from heart failure, he had so

often spoken of, came to him. He died on March 26, 1902, at the age of forty-eight, two months before the end of the Boer War. History records his last words: "So much to do. So little done." On the tombstone of the lonely reformer of the world in the Matoppo Hills only these words are inscribed: "Here lie the remains of Cecil John Rhodes."

After five months of reverses and retreat, the government and the people of England suddenly realized that they were faced with a tremendous military task whose difficulties no one had foreseen. Overnight the nation pulled itself together. Great Britain's two great soldiers, Roberts as commander in chief, and Kitchener as his chief of staff, were dispatched to South Africa. An unending stream of men and equipment followed. Disregarding the secondary theatres of war, the new English leaders thrust right into the enemy's heart. They made for Johannesburg and Pretoria.

Some of the Boers tried to put up a stiff resistance. But it was always the same thirty or forty men in a commando averaging three or four hundred, who threw themselves at the enemy, harassed the British advance platoons, and, indeed, exacted heavy sacrifices. The great majority of the citizen-soldiery refused to budge when the bugles sounded for action. They were well within their rights. They could elect and dismiss their commandants, and if one of the higher-ups showed too combative a spirit, one word from the ranks was enough. The word was: *Loop!* It stands for: Scram!

The presence of women in the *laagers* was another constant hindrance. The energetic Boer ladies wished to keep even their fighting husbands under control. The government refused General De Wet's demand to call the womenfolk back. The President insisted, and rightly so, that such an order would cause open mutiny.

Even retreat with the *laagers* was a difficult job. The Kafir drivers alone mastered the complicated art of *inspanning*. But in the skirmishes most of the Kafirs were either mowed down, since their masters had not equipped them with weapons, or they deserted. Hence the burghers were left to do the dirty work themselves. Unfortunately, few farmers knew which oxen were to be placed in front and which behind. Every retreat was a melee of terrible confusion. The aft-oxen placed in front of the span and fore-oxen behind, were too bewildered to move.

In the Free State Army an epidemic of heart disease broke out. An old law provided that a burgher who could produce a medical certificate pronouncing him unfit for duty should immediately be exempted from service. The military doctors were swamped with cases of sudden and severe heart attacks. One of them on a single morning pronounced nineteen patients unfit. But when the twentieth approached him, his hand pressed to the left side of his breast, the doctor lost his patience and barked: "No more heart attacks today!" Then he softened: "Come again tomorrow!"

General De Wet found a way to check the disease. He obtained a government order forbidding the doctors to write certificates. Only those burghers to whose poor health three old women were willing to testify would from now on be released. The percentage of old women in the districts of Fauresmith and Jacobsdhal must have been high. All the burghers from these two districts returned home. Commandant Weilbach, entrusted with the defense of Bloemfontein, deserted without incommoding the old ladies of his town as soon as Roberts' troops approached. When even the mighty General Piet Cronje surrendered, most of the burghers lost heart. Panic set in. "The hands-uppers are our undoing!" De Wet said gloomily.

Personally, he was not undone. Nor were Botha, De la Rey, Beyers, and a few other Boer commanders in the field. When all seemed lost, they formed that tightly knit brotherhood of generals that carried on the hopeless war, already lost within seven months, for another two years. Smuts even went them a couple of months better.

Unable to delegate even a part of his crushing burden to others—an inability which has marked General Smuts throughout his life, and explains why he always holds three or four posts at a time—the State Attorney, indeed, ran the government in wartime Pretoria. The duties of his own office required enough attention. Questions of internal rule and international law, the activities of the police and the secret service, the treatment of English subjects, supervision of the mines, problems like the legal position of the inhabitants in parts of the country that rapidly changed from hand to hand, "annexed" by Boer raiders, and again occupied by the English—all these and innumerable similar tasks were a full-time occupation.

It was, incidentally, in his capacity as State Attorney that Smuts met Winston Churchill for the first time, although it was not a personal meeting. South Africa, today, still teems with old-timers boasting that they captured Churchill when the armored train in which the young newspaper correspondent rode was held up near Chieveley. Every Boer general who visited London after the war let it drop that he had been the hero of the day, and Mr. Churchill pleasantly acknowledged every individual feat. Thus the legend arose that Smuts had taken him prisoner.

The facts, however, are these: after the first month of the war, to be exact, on November 14, 1899, Winston was captured between Chieveley and Frere, when the Boers trapped an armored train which the correspondent of the *Morning Post* was accompanying. Having left his revolver behind in the train when he ventured into the *veld*, he threw up his hands when he saw himself held up by a group of bearded Boers. It was the only thing to do. The fate of the world might otherwise have taken a different turn, and not for the better.

The prisoner was dispatched to Pretoria. On his way he was constantly surrounded by Boers curious to see "the greatest and the latest correspondent of the day," to quote a contemporary ditty. They displayed no hard feelings. Cordially they repeated time and again: "You know it's those damned capitalists and Jews who have caused the war . . . God is on our side . . . Every man has a stake in the fight for liberty." This last assertion was well founded: one had paid no taxes for four years, another was a friend of the *veld-cornet*. The ticket collector

98

drew absurdly high wages: "No British government for me!" he said determinedly. "Is it right," they asked their prisoner in a most friendly manner, "that a dirty Kafir should walk on the pavement—without a pass, either? That's what they do in your British colonies."

In Pretoria he was taken to the prison for British officers, installed in the State Model School in the fashionable suburb of Sunnyside. It was a long, low red-brick building, standing on a sandy avenue, lined with detached white houses. The prisoners had ample opportunity to watch the gay boulevard of suburban Pretoria from their windows. Winston found the spectacle petty and contemptible. He disliked the ugly women with their bright parasols, the fat burghers, the arrogant, white-helmeted policemen, the slimy, sleek officials of every nationality promenading during office hours. Most of all he detested the red-faced, snub-nosed Hollanders, and the oily Portuguese half-castes, prevalent among the bureaucrats.

One of these oily Portuguese was M. de Souza, who occupied the lucrative position of Secretary of War. *Landrost* Opperman, a "Peruvian," was in charge of the prison since, although he was a commandant, he was too fat to fight. Both these officials refused to listen to Churchill's well-founded complaints. As a noncombatant war correspondent his detention in a military prison was so much the less justified as the Boers had made it a rule to release all British civilians. The upkeep of the many firemen, telegraphists, and railway workers, who had been captured was too expensive. Winston had not fired a shot; indeed he had been captured unarmed. He tried to get in touch with Mr. Macrum, the American consul in Pretoria, representing the "protective power." But this gentleman was so fanatically pro-Boer that he refused to interfere; in fact he found it difficult to discharge his diplomatic duties, and was soon replaced by Mr. Adelbert S. Hay, a young and resourceful diplomat who did much good during the fall of Pretoria.

A batch of other civilians, railway men, were just about to be sent home. Winston wrote two letters, addressing them to the Secretary of War and to the Commander in Chief, General Piet

Joubert. He explained his legal position, and demanded to be released with his fellow English civilians. Receiving no answer within a few days, he lost his patience and made good his escape. On the next day, incidentally, a young lady of the best Pretoria society—and the Pretorians prided themselves that their best society was very good—was arrested for having aided and abetted the escape of a noted English war correspondent. Winston Churchill has always been too tactful to acknowledge such help, if, indeed, he did receive it. He left the prison one day before the State Attorney's answer was delivered. . . . The generals had referred Winston's letter to him. The gist of Smuts' reply was: "Winston Churchill a noncombatant? Impossible!"

Winston Churchill's flamboyant reports on the war were, of course, known to Smuts who acted as his own press chief, and as a most resourceful one. For the first time the Transvaal saw a propaganda campaign on a world-wide scale, not the least important part of which was the planting of misleading rumors in the South African and English press. By the same token Smuts was also "chief of information"—spy master—Kruger's handy man, steering the old man between the rocks of spelling and grammar as the author of Presidential decrees and messages, and finally in charge of supplying the fighting forces. He himself supervised the dispatch of the guns from the Pretoria forts to the battle lines. The German officers in command of the Boer artillery made this job a little difficult. But Smuts overrode the "technical difficulties" which they pleaded.

He worked incessantly as was his habit, but quietly as ever. His sovereign calm affected the capital. As the British columns approached Johannesburg, Pretoria was already awaiting its doom, but in quiet dignity. Kruger still spent his days on the *stoep* of his cottage, smoking, spitting, gulping down innumerable cups of coffee. His burghers copied the example of Kruger and Smuts. They were completely shut off from the world, both by Smuts' rigid censorship and by the fighting armies around them, but this isolation was exactly what they had always longed for. A few turbulent sessions in the *Volksraad* evoked local interest. The fact that an enemy army of some 150,000 men was slowly but steadily approaching left them undisturbed.

The men in command racked their brains to find a way out of the perilous situation. Should they blow up the gold mines in Johannesburg? The mine owners, after all, the Jews and capitalists, were guilty of all the trouble. If they saw their millions vanishing, they would be quick to bring pressure on the British government to conclude peace, peace at any price, in order to rebuild the mines and resume business as usual.

Botha was against it, and Smuts, after some hesitation, agreed with him. The Boers, after all, still held the Rand. If they caused wanton damage they would compromise their moral position in the world. Nevertheless, in Johannesburg, Judge Kock, the same who had presided over the Edgar trial, tried a little dynamiting of his own. Botha, who meanwhile had advanced to the rank of military commander in chief, ordered the mischief-maker arrested.

After the capture of Johannesburg by the English the situation changed. Now Smuts himself, in an attack of fury, sent a force of dynamiters to the Rand. He did not reckon with the local commandant, Dr. Krause. Twice in their running feud the State Attorney had bested the Public Prosecutor. First, when Smuts got the government job for which Dr. Krause had been the preferred candidate, secondly, when Smuts left his antagonist holding the bag after the abortive attempt to construct a sensational spy case. Now Dr. Krause's time for revenge had come. He arrested Smuts' dynamiters. Since the Pretoria government no longer exercised any authority in occupied Johannesburg, Dr. Krause, later to become a reputed K.C., was in a position to save the Rand.

The fate of Pretoria was decided by the fall of Johannesburg. Kruger fled to Machadodorp, a village on a hill near the Portuguese border, and set up government in a few railway cars on a siding. Botha decided to defend every step of the way to Portuguese East Africa, the last unoccupied part of the

Transvaal. Smuts remained in town. His was the hardest job: the definite liquidation.

With a handful of adherents, he tried a few abortive sorties against the onrolling British Army. But this was more of a foolhardy gesture than grand strategy. He had to comfort his conscience. When this was done, he went at his real task. He had to extract the government's treasure from the National Bank. The directors of the bank politely but determinedly refused to hand over the government funds to the State Attorney, who had no official legitimation for receiving them. To test their attitude, Smuts had originally only asked for the £400 in cash which formed a very small part of the entire hoard. When he did not get it, he called in his entire detective corps, and forced the directors at the point of fifty revolvers, to hand over to him everything: the £400 in cash, half a million in gold bullion, and £25,000 war funds, at the disposal of his friend Botha.

The gold hoard was immediately stowed away in the next train, which was the last one to the Portuguese border and which did, in fact, escape the shells from Lord Roberts' howitzers already pounding the railway line in an attempt to destroy it.

By that time Pretoria was in a state of chaos. Whatever authority remained was divided between the absent government's last representative, Smuts, and the self-constituted *Committee for Peace and Order*. But neither peace nor order could be maintained. Pretoria had lost its poise. While every burgher who could trekked out of town, men and women loaded like pack animals with their most precious belongings, some with household furniture, others with immense quantities of foodstuff, the great building near the railway station, the government storehouse, where food for the fighting forces was being kept, was looted. The State Attorney did nothing to prevent the looting. Indeed, Smuts had thrown open the doors of the storehouse. Rather than see his supplies fall into the hands of the British, he preferred to see his burghers helping themselves to the provisions. For hours the people of Pretoria, women and

children, Kafirs, burghers, shopkeepers, and ladies and gentlemen who were certainly not in need of food, mobbed the building, ripping apart the zinc walls, fighting for their loot, and
staggering away, loaded with everything they could carry. The
police looked on passively. The only restriction that was rigidly
enforced was the forbidding of snapshots. Such photographs
would not have made good propaganda. As the days went on,
the Jewish shops, unfortunately also located in the neighborhood of the railroad station, were broken into and emptied by
the crowd.

But Pretoria lost no time in tidying itself to receive the conquerors. The Pretoria Club, the center of the Boer notables,
was empty, whereas the English Club was the scene of a jubilant banquet. Shopkeepers suddenly displayed pictures of the
Queen, the Prince of Wales, Lord Roberts, and Joe Chamberlain. Mr. Hay, the new American consul, betook himself to the
prison for captured English officers, who, after Churchill's escape, had been removed from their comfortable abode in the
State Model School to a depressing quarter outside the town,
where they were now kept in fenced dark dungeons. Mr. Hay
besought the twenty imprisoned officers to accompany him to
Waterval, a camp where 5,000 British soldiers, prisoners, were
herded under atrocious conditions. The officers should keep
their men under control lest they get out of hand now that the
hour of liberation was rapidly approaching. The English prisoners behaved themselves perfectly. They cheered, when, on
June 4, the advance guard of Lord Roberts' forces entered
Pretoria: A hatless young civilian with that speed with which a
born journalist pursues a scoop, raced through the streets to
greet his old prisonmates. He was accompanied by his cousin,
the Duke of Marlborough.

Smuts escaped into the hills of Magaliesberg in the Western
Transvaal to join the remnants of De la Rey's forces. To him,
the fall of Pretoria was a blessing in disguise. The war was
practically over. But his fight was just beginning.

THE TRANSVAAL WAS ANNEXED BY LORD ROBERTS' PROCLAMATION
in the month of September, 1900, after less than eleven months
of war. Kruger, a fugitive on the Portuguese border, countered
the annexation with a manifesto of protest. With this last,
empty gesture of stubbornness the old man left South Africa.
He took a six months' vacation to promote the Boer cause in
Europe. After his departure on a Dutch vessel, the engine of
the government train got up steam, and the rolling refugee
government moved a few miles farther in the direction of the
Portuguese border.

Fuimus Troës: the Boers had been. But the last die-hards,
Steyn, the fugitive President of the Free State; De Wet, his
commander in chief; Botha, who still raided the Eastern Transvaal, and De la Rey with his new right-hand man Smuts, from
the Western Transvaal met at Cypherfontein, and swore they
would not give in. They determined that each should go his
own way. De Wet and Smuts should go into the Cape Colony
to arouse the Cape Dutch. From their revolution alone a revival of the shattered cause was still to be hoped for.

De Wet twice tried to cross the border of the Colony. Both
times the fire-eating martinet was ignominiously beaten back.
As for Smuts, the diary of Lord Milner contains the following
entry: "De Wet made his last incursion into the Cape Colony
in February 1901. Hunted for several weeks, he barely made
his escape. His mantle fell upon the worthy shoulders of Smuts,
who, after riding through the Orange River Colony, penetrated within a hundred miles of Cape Town itself. Constantly
hunted, but never caught by British columns, with extraordinary cunning and determination, he maintained himself in the
heart of the Colony until the end of the war."

It reads so easily. . . .

It was a pilgrimage through hell and high water, yet to

Smuts, as he recalled this tempestuous time in later years, it was the greatest "boyish" pleasure of his life. While it lasted, the joy of discovering his own physical fitness, his entire absence of fear, his resourcefulness in practical matters, above all the fact that he was a man of action and not only of thought—all these new sources of strength which he found in himself gave him a new lease on life. But they were overshadowed by his separation from his wife. Mrs. Smuts was sent to Maritzburg, though not to the detention camp which made the name of this little town ominous to the Boers, and to a great many English people as well. She could live with her children an undisturbed life in a house of her own, and it was there that she first met Miss Hobhouse, a middle-aged woman who had come from London to look after the unfortunate Boer women and children, and whose public life climaxed when she became a traitor to England as the First World War broke out.

Early in 1901, Smuts, now the chief of his own commando, took the Modderfontein Range from the English, and held it against repeated counterattacks. In fact, this was thus far the only success on the credit side of the Boer ledger. Everywhere else the last fighting Boers were harassed by English troops. Kitchener established his net of blockhouses which finally decided the war.

In May the Boer commandants met to review their perilous position in a secluded farm in the Transvaal. They decided to ask Kruger's advice. Chivalrously, the British allowed the outlaw Smuts to get into contact with his absentee President. The news from Europe was bad. Dr. Leyds had been cold-shouldered in Berlin. Wilhelm II received him with bad grace. He was obviously angry that the Transvaal had ordered some Creuzot guns. "We are the gun merchants of the world!" he said. What he did not say was that he had already made a complete volte-face, going so far as to send Lord Roberts a complete strategic master plan of how to conquer South Africa, a plan that duly landed in the British war lord's wastepaper basket. Kruger himself had been informed in his exile at Utrecht that he would be arrested the moment he tried to cross the German border. But even this humiliation at the hands of the Germans did not temper his spiteful hatred of the British. To the kibitzer, now watching the battle from the safe distance of 6,000 miles, no gamble was too high. He insisted on the continuing of the suicidal struggle "until the last means of resistance are exhausted."

On June 20, the spokesmen of the refugee government met again at Waterval. They discussed Kruger's order. The diehards, Steyn and De Wet, won out. Smuts was already back in the field. But President Steyn was able to produce a letter from him, stating that if the Boers had to give up at that moment it would be with the intention of resuming their fight as soon as England was in difficulties.

The men at Waterval, however, were determined to continue the struggle. Now the commandos concentrated on guerrilla warfare. Smuts took to it like a duck to water. It was a game of thinking and acting at once, truly a game after Smuts' heart. The guerrilla warfare of the commandos demanded a high degree of mobility, incessant surprise action, the harassing of the enemy without ever being trapped, destroying his means of communication, railroad lines, bridges, and telegraph wires, clamping down on isolated small bodies of English soldiers, being everywhere and nowhere; in fact, guerrilla warfare depended on ruses rather than on rules. Smuts could play his lifelong favorite game of matching his wits against any comer. But it was not the English alone that he had to fight against. The weather and the ground, rains, streams, hills, jungles, deserts, all were his enemies. He had to fight against starvation, thirst, tropical days and ice-cold nights, in which two men slept under one blanket, when indeed there were blankets, to steal a little warmth from one another's body. More often than not they fought in rags. Gradually they were reduced to stripping killed or captured Englishmen of their uniforms. They were forced to release their prisoners since they could neither feed nor transport them. Most of them were released naked, and most Boers, when captured, were found wearing English uniforms. This was a dangerous aspect of the game. In accordance with international law, Kitchener had decreed the capital penalty for those captured in English uniforms. Actually, however, the prisoners always escaped with their lives. The General understood the necessity; they must be clad in one way or another.

With a force of three hundred and fifty men, Smuts ventured into the Cape Colony. His main objectives were to detract some British troops from the North, to see whether a raid on a larger scale would be possible, and, above all, to arouse the Cape Dutch. In this supreme aim, however, he failed. He was able to collect some three thousand rebels who volunteered to join with his original handful of Transvaalers. Nine-tenths of them were British subjects, committing high treason. But the big upheaval failed completely. Although the Colonial Dutch sympathized with their brothers in the North, they were much too cautious and too phlegmatic to be lured into adventure, even by the now most renowned son of their own soil, the son of Jacobus Abraham Smuts.

Smuts showed his habitual indifference to the failure, although it spelled the complete breakdown of his only reasonable hope. He did not give in. Now he had three to four thousand men behind him; many of the newcomers had two horses at their disposal. And how many British and Colonial troops opposed this formidable body? About fifty thousand, if Smuts' spies reported the truth. And his intelligence service, relying on Kafirs, was rarely misinformed. He felt that the odds were even.

In forced marches, ascending steep mountains, crossing swollen rivers, relying on the horses' instinct when human ingenuity failed, always harassed by General French's columns, often by two or three of them in concerted action, constantly worried by the shortage of clothes and food, Smuts on the warpath pressed forward.

Early in September he entered the Colony east of Alival North, but he was already swinging southward when his pursuers arrived. Some of his men were ambushed at Dordrecht, but their leader was seen almost at the same time near Jamestown. Colonel Gorringe engaged and defeated him north of

Tarkastad. Smuts escaped and, in his turn, ambushed a detachment of the 17th Lancers. Only a few of the surprised men survived. Some of them reported that the guerrilla leader had personally behaved well, as a chivalrous soldier. But he had been unable to restrain his men from what an English understatement calls "unworthy acts."

Probably "Mannie" Maritz was at the head of those who committed the unworthy acts. A former Johannesburg policeman, famous for his unbridled cruelty even among the ill-reputed *Zarps,* he followed Smuts, the anti-English leader, with doglike faithfulness. But there must be now and then a little fun in guerrilla warfare, and Maritz, then as later, had his full share of it. Smuts had no objections. Toward the end of his campaign he promoted, on his own authority, the ex-policeman to the rank of general.

Smuts' chief lieutenant was van deVenter, later General Sir Jacobus van deVenter, and General Smuts' assistant in the East African campaign during the First World War. In their days in common as guerrilla leaders van deVenter was probably the only man with whom Smuts shared his plans. For the rest he remained inaccessible, even in this interlude of his life when for the first time he experienced real comradeship, hardship and shared danger, and an abiding sense of mutual trust.

He never disclosed his plans to his men. They were never allowed to know where the commandant would take them next or why they fought here and escaped there. Strangely, the Boers, the most stubborn individualists in the world, inbred scorners of any established authority, roughnecks among whom each insisted that he was as good as the next man, if not better —strangely, these Boers obeyed Smuts' every word without question. Probably they were impressed by his complete absence of fear. The commandant acted frequently as his own scout. When friendly Kafirs warned him not to venture in a direction where English patrols might be lying in wait for him, Smuts halted his men, and spied out the dangerous spot alone. Once he was poisoned by eating "Hottentot bread," an otherwise harmless fruit of the forest which was toxic in spring. The great botanist had forgotten this detail. He fell gravely ill and had to be carried or tied on to his horse. But the commandos marched on.

The refugee government promoted him Commandant General in supreme command of the Boer forces in the Cape. He took his new dignity in his stride. But when at last he became a first-class burgher of a non-existent Republic, endowed with the franchise for the non-existent *Volksraad*, his measure of happiness was full.

His last adventure led him through Namaqualand, the desert country in the far west of the Cape Colony. He was set on conquering the copper mining village of O'okiep, held by a small British garrison whose commander, Colonel Shelton, contemptuously refused Smuts' appeal to surrender. The defenders beat off two assaults by Smuts, carried out on April 6 and 12. The British, in turn, challenged their besiegers to a football match. The question whether to accept the invitation was hotly debated among the men of the commando. It took these loquacious soldiers a full fortnight of argument to arrive at no decision. On April 26, 1902, the question was suddenly dwarfed. Smuts received an invitation together with a safe conduct signed "D. Haig, Colonel" to join peace negotiations which had begun the very day he had for the last time hurled his men against O'okiep.

First he hesitated. He took a solitary walk in the *veld* to think over the new situation. He still had two thousand six hundred seasoned men under his command. The other commandos, he guessed, must for their part muster about seven hundred all told. With this formidable force the war might drag on indefinitely. His men would hate to hear that all must come to an end. This was the last boyish thought of Smuts' life.

He packed his saddlebag, not forgetting the *Greek Testament*, and a much thumbed volume of Kant's *Critique of Pure Reason*, his most faithful companions during the two glorious years of raids. Off he went to the peace conference. On his way, he visited the old farm near Malmesbury. His father, it is said, did not recognize him. The thin, lanky youngster with the haggard cheeks and hungry eyes was gone. So strong was the impact of the war on Smuts, although primarily an intellectual impact, that it transformed him physically as well, and completely. Now his chest was broad, his skin reddened; he held himself erect. A yellow beard covered his chin and he strode with a firm step. He was ready to shoulder untold responsibilities. He had left his youth behind.

| *Chapter 10* | *VEREENIGING* STANDS FOR UNION |

KITCHENER KNEW A GOOD SOLDIER WHEN HE SAW ONE. IN HIS gorgeous uniform as Commander in Chief in South Africa, mounted on a black charger, surrounded by his Pathan body-guard in their oriental splendor, he met Smuts' train at Kronstaad and continued the journey with him.

Smuts was not impressed by the display of imperial pomp. Emerging from a bitter campaign which he and his men had been forced to conduct mostly in the stolen uniforms of the killed or captured enemy, he found Kitchener's glamour rather misplaced. Moreover, he was suspicious. Surely, by showering him with honors, the British wanted to soften him up for the forthcoming negotiations. Why, otherwise, would they have dispatched a troopship to Port Nolloth to bring him to Cape Town with a military escort befitting his rank as Commandant General, when his army was barely still in existence? Why did they insist on putting a battleship, lying off Simon's Town, at his disposal as a residence during his one week stay in Cape Town? Why in God's name had Lord French, a notoriously tough customer, comported himself so mildly and so amiably when he appeared at Matjesfontein station to wish his foe of the day before bon voyage to Pretoria? Perhaps Smuts should not have let Lord French get away in his damned armored train, as he had once foolishly done in the days of battle.

Well, the battle was over. But not for Smuts. He peppered Kitchener with reproaches about his harsh conduct of the war as the two rode together through the barren land of the Transvaal, the curtains drawn over the windows of the compartment, lest the Commandant General should be disturbed by the crowds that gathered at every stop. Indeed, the victor had to defend his victory under the accusing finger of the vanquished. Only an English general would have taken this absurd situation with a smile. Kitchener did smile. He was anxious to get away from South Africa, the grave of so many military reputations; the war was over for all practical purposes, the peace must be signed, and that was all that counted. In fact, Kitchener had for a long time been trying to bring the war to a rapid and mutually honorable conclusion. At the end of March, 1902, while his army drove on relentlessly, he suggested to the government in London that it guarantee the Boers full self-government within two or three years, provided that they behaved themselves. He hated the idea of a dictated peace. He was anxious lest the ultimate reconciliation of the two white races in South Africa should be definitely precluded. Besides, he wanted peace before the approaching coronation of King Edward VII. But Natal, where people had had ample experience with their Boer fellow citizens, demanded an unconditional surrender of the foe as a prelude to any concessions, and other parts of the Empire, primarily Australia, who had made great sacrifices in the Boer War, backed up Natal.

Kitchener's actual negotiations with the Boers started on April 12. Smuts was six hundred miles away assaulting O'okiep on the very day that Schalk-Burger, Kruger's understudy, with a few other Boer leaders, graciously were received in Kitchener's house in Pretoria, to read the seven peace conditions. The gist of it was—although not expressed in so many words—that the Republics should remain independent, if they promised to reform. Regretfully, Kitchener saw no basis of negotiation in this proposal, nor could he commit himself to any particular time when the Boers should receive self-government. "Is there no means of ending this war without depriving us of our self-respect?" asked Steyn, who had a marked predilection for empty, great words. Tactfully, Kitchener assured him that men who had fought so well could not lose their self-respect by facing the inevitable. He carried his sympathy so far as not to use a strong bargaining argument. The day before he had received the information that General Ian Hamilton had smashed the bulk of De la Rey's forces under General Kemp at Roodeval. Kitchener felt certain that the Boers, maintaining excellent communications by heliograph, must already be aware of their grave setback.

On the next day, a Sunday, Milner arrived in Pretoria. He took up quarters in the Old Residency. His arrival gave the negotiations a new direction. He was firmly convinced that British sovereignty, founded on an acknowledged military conquest, could alone be the basis of peace negotiations. Already he had long-devised plans for resettlement, reconciliation, and reconstruction. But he required a certain length of time under a modified Crown Colony government until the political storm had blown over. He did not agree with the concessions Kitchener planned. He was not ready to sacrifice the British in South Africa, and still less the Dutch loyalists, in order to save the faces of the bitter-enders, who were now in a desperate plight. Each day their numbers diminished, each day their prestige dwindled. But each day, on the other hand, the strength of the National Scouts and the Boer volunteers on the English side increased. That was why Milner disliked Kitchener's vague promises and unnecessary concessions. The general's tendency to avoid awkward details would certainly compromise the accomplished victory, and render the task of peacemaking immeasurably more difficult.

On Monday, April 14, Milner occupied his seat at the conference table. He introduced himself by saying that, in spite of any rumors to the contrary, he was most anxious to see an end of the bloodshed, and a settlement honorable to all. It was a duty to humanity to repair the damage.

President Steyn, ever evasive, wanted new British proposals to submit to the burghers in the field, not to the entire Boer population. He would present them not as his own suggestion, but as the terms of the conqueror. However, on the same after-

noon he weakened and decided to ask for an armistice in order
to consult his own people, and for safe conduct for one of their
delegates from Europe; obviously the understudy wanted to
burden Kruger himself with the responsibility for swallowing
defeat. Even conciliatory Kitchener declared that an armistice was premature, and that the safe conduct had already been
refused by the government in London. However, he would invite the British Government to formulate new terms.

Milner had the measure of his opponents. On Wednesday he
sent a "secret, private, and personal" cable to Chamberlain, informing the Colonial Secretary that the result of the negotiations evidently depended more on personal considerations than
on the exact nature of the terms. "Three-quarters of the Boer
representatives," he wrote, "want to give in, but no one wants
to take the lead in doing so. Each is manoeuvring to put someone else in front, and if they finally decide to give way they will
try to make it appear that they are acting under pressure from
the burghers in the field. In fact these men will do exactly as
their leaders secretly desire. The Free Staters are much less
friendly than the Transvaalers. Judge Hertzog (whose name
appeared for the first time in an official document) is probably
quite irreconcilable; he is said to have great influence with
President Steyn. . . . But my greatest difficulty is Lord Kitchener," Milner continued. "He is extremely adroit in his management of negotiations, particularly as to what he gives away.
If he knew as an absolute certainty that His Majesty's government would not yield on certain points, no one would be more
skilful in steering the Boers away from these points, and guiding the discussions into directions in which some concessions
are possible. Lord Kitchener even suggests that a definite date
should be fixed for introduction of self-government, exactly
what Schalk-Burger demanded. But Lieutenant-Governor Major
Goold-Adams in the Orange Free State, and Lieutenant-Governor Fraser of Natal were horror stricken by that idea. They
warned me that Kitchener would wreck the whole result of the
war. Responsible government can only be given when all traces
of racial animosity will have disappeared."

The cleavage between Milner and Kitchener was politely concealed. But to Smuts it was plainly visible when he entered the negotiations. He was determined to carry them to a successful conclusion. He went right to the core of the matter. He brushed aside President Steyn, who was already annoying Milner with his incessant parrot cry of independence, just as Kruger had done three years earlier at Bloemfontein. He simply asked whether the Boers were expected to become British citizens. Milner and Kitchener referred to the terms of Middleburg, to a peace offer the London government had made a year before, and which had been rejected by the Boers without explanation. Milner pointed out that the British negotiators were not authorized to discuss on any other basis. Kitchener added that, a month previously, President Steyn had undertaken to consult the Boer people on the definite proposals of the British Government. If the Boers now refused to discuss those terms, His Majesty's government should be informed at once. Chamberlain, indeed, was informed, and he answered that the Middleburg terms still stood. The Boer delegates retired to consult their electors.

In Vereeniging Union, a little village on the Vaal River where Kitchener had ordered tents to be erected, the Boer delegations met: thirty men from the Transvaal, thirty from the Free State. The Free Staters were in a comparatively easy position. Their state was essentially Dutch. Whatever happened, it would not lose its national character. Matters in the Transvaal were different. Already the majority of the population, a short time before still the despised and disfranchised *uitlanders,* had taken over. They were assisted by the National Scouts, those Boers who had sided with the English during the war, and by the peace-minded part of the Boer people. If matters could not be settled, it might easily happen that the fighters on the *veld,* the stanchest of the Boers, the protagonists of independence, would become outlaws and be crushed piecemeal. Then, indeed, the Transvaal would be definitely lost. Hence the delegates from the Transvaal were not for surrender, but for a compromise.

115

Generals De la Rey, Beyers, and De Wet described conditions in their districts. Their reports were contradictory. De la Rey was not afraid of starvation, the gravest peril, since, in his opinion, he could get all the food he wanted from the enemy. Beyers admitted that in his section the Kafirs were in open revolt against the Boers. (The Boers invaded the native *kraals* and stole the food, since they believed that it was all right for the blacks to starve, but never for a white man.) De Wet was as cantankerous as ever.

Smuts gave a cautious, but on the whole pessimistic account of the state of affairs in the Cape Colony. The Colony, he asserted, would not rise. The ultimate outcome would be decided in the Republics.

Finally, F. W. Reitz, the Secretary of State in the defunct Transvaal government, made an appeal to reason. At his behest, three conditions were stipulated and next day proposed to Milner and Kitchener as peace terms: first, the Republics were prepared to surrender their independence in foreign relations. Secondly, they wished to retain internal self-government under British supervision. Third, they were willing to give up parts of their territory, meaning Swaziland, whose administration was costly and unprofitable, as well as accursed Johannesburg into the bargain. Moreover, they offered to enter into a defensive alliance with Great Britain.

The five men entrusted to offer these counter proposals to the British, the Generals Botha, De Wet, De la Rey, Hertzog, and Smuts, were perfectly aware that there was not the slightest chance of their half-baked suggestions being accepted. Accordingly, Smuts introduced them with the cautious explanation that they represented no definite new proposals, but only a new basis of discussion.

But even Kitchener, bent on achieving a rapid settlement, found the counter proposals impossible. "It would be much better to write down something practical," he suggested. Milner offered to refer the new proposals to his government, but he distinctly warned that they were likely to hamper, and not facilitate further negotiations.

Instantly Smuts pointed out part three: the offer to surrender parts of the Transvaal. Did that hamper negotiations? Milner coolly asked whether this offer meant that one part of the Transvaal should be a Crown Colony, the other a protected Republic. "Impossible," explained Kitchener. "Impossible on military grounds. We would be at war again in a year."

After the luncheon interval, the Boer lawyers, Milner recorded, fought for a forlorn hope with infinite ingenuity. Smuts fell back on Kitchener's suggestion: "We must have something practical to go on." The most practical thing would be his informal meeting with the English plenipotentiaries. Kitchener had frequently spoken with the Boer delegates outside the conference room, and off the record. Now they held a brief conference of three. No longer hampered by the presence of the bully De Wet and the snakelike assistant legal adviser, Hertzog, Smuts could make his English partners understand that the Boers did not expect acceptance of their proposals, but merely wished to find out how far the ultimate British concessions would go.

Milner and Kitchener drew up their final document. It involved unconditional surrender, but it included concessions partly of a sentimental nature, to soothe the pride of the Boer leaders, and partly of a financial character. This document was handed over to the Boer generals when they reappeared at four o'clock in the afternoon.

Another heated controversy ensued over the responsibility of the Boer signatories if their burghers should decline the agreement. De Wet, his face dark red, every unruly hair in his patriarch's beard trembling with indignation, his fist banging the table, refused to accept any responsibility whatsoever if he should not be backed up by his people. Kitchener once more proved his diplomacy. He suggested that the "military element" should withdraw from further discussion. Thus he excluded himself, but he also got De Wet out of the way. The civilians continued alone. On the side of the Boers were Smuts, a few weeks before still a fiery guerrilla leader, and his assistant Hertzog, who was also a general but had never been regarded as a military element.

Milner noted: "The next two days were spent in hard conflict with the Boer lawyers. They fought stoutly, though they won few concessions. At last an acceptable formula was found."

But before this formula was found, Smuts drove a hard bargain for every penny. Already the abortive Middleburg proposals, he insisted, had committed Great Britain to pay all debts, including war debts, of the two bankrupt Republics. The inference was that the amount of these sums to be paid by the British taxpayer for the war the Boers had conducted against them, should only be limited by the appetite of the claimants.

Both Kitchener, who was back in the conference, and Milner demanded to know the limit.

Smuts was mute.

"A million pounds?" Milner suggested.

Smuts sensed a bargain: "That . . . would . . . not . . . meet . . . the case."

Kitchener, smiling: "Will two million meet it?"

"It is not possible to gauge the amount," De Wet raged.

Milner showed distinct signs of boredom. The afternoon was dragging on. It was getting late, perhaps too late.

Kitchener, it seemed, visualized another year in South Africa, to be spent in mopping-up operations which he disdained. He whispered to Smuts: "Come out, come out for a while."

The two men paced up and down in front of the house through the dusk. Finally Kitchener spoke. He had a personal opinion to convey to Smuts. In two years, he believed, the English Liberals would come to power, and they would certainly grant South Africa a constitution—self-government.

"That is a very important pronouncement," replied Smuts thoughtfully. "If one could be sure. . . ."

No, Kitchener could give no assurance whatsoever. But he *did* honestly believe that this was in the cards.

Gladstone, the great Liberal, had retreated, panic-stricken, after Majuba. Mr. Campbell-Bannerman, the present Liberal leader, had publicly protested against the harsh treatment meted out to the Boers during the war. His lieutenant, young Mr. Lloyd George, had used still more burning eloquence to the same purpose. And there was this newcomer among the Liberals, Winston Churchill, who toured all England and the United States with a magic lantern illustrating a lecture praising in truly magic words the splendid resistance of the Boers, and demanding magnanimity in their treatment.

Kitchener and Smuts returned. Smuts appeared convinced. Still, he insisted upon three million and not a penny less, which the victor was to pay to the vanquished in order to repair the loser's ruined credit. Kitchener, eager to have the last word without Milner's interference, and still more keen to get away from it all, said: "You demand a large sum." But he nodded. He concluded that the extra two million could probably be deducted from the sum allowed for re-establishing farms. "But they did not mind this argument at all," he cabled to Mr. Broderick, the Secretary for War. "They only wished their receipts paid."

Finally, Milner, too, understood that the Boers' credit and honor depended on their being able to repay the worthless scraps of paper they called "receipts." An English statesman does not kick a dead dog. The peace of Vereeniging was drawn up.

Years later friends congratulated General Smuts on his foresight. It was great statesmanship to bank on Kitchener's necessarily irresponsible prediction, which had finally tipped the scales.

Had it, indeed, tipped the scales? General Smuts smiled. The conference had had to reach an agreement, Kitchener or no Kitchener.

The struggle was over but the battle was just beginning. Smuts had a terribly difficult time to make the agreement palatable to the sixty delegates, who met for the last time in their tents at Vereeniging, most of them sulking like Achilles in his tent. Their independence was gone. The loss was irretrievable.

But they would not omit the funeral orations at the grave of their Republic. For two days they debated. It was shadow boxing. Even the irreconcilables felt it. Yet De Wet repeated for the hundredth time that he was for continuing the war. The word *peace* simply did not fit into his bull head. Hertzog carried water on both shoulders. For the first time he delivered one of those: on the one hand . . . but on the other . . . perorations on the strength of which, and due to their mystic-sounding quality of unintelligibility, he subsequently rode to power. De la Rey, curt, intense, with subdued passion in his dark eyes, hated surrender. But since the end had come, an honorable end was better than a dishonorable one, the only alternative. He finished on his habitual Christian note: "Lord, *Thy* will not mine be done." Botha argued soundly and sensibly for accepting the compromise in order to save the nation.

Smuts carried the day. He hesitated to speak since he was only the legal expert, not a delegate. He would not even sign the peace he had extracted from the British. But he had to say this much: from the military point of view the war could be carried on. "But we represent the blood and tears of the entire nation. . . . Comrades, we decided to stand to the bitter end. Let us now, like men, admit that the end has come for us. . . . The result of that struggle we leave in God's hands. It is His will to lead the people of South Africa through defeat and humiliation and even the valley of the shadow of death to a better future and a brighter day." He had already, with all due deference to the Deity, made up his mind to help Providence in order to shorten the march through the valley of shadow and death.

One hour before Milner's ultimatum expired, the peace treaty was adopted by fifty-four votes to six. The grey beards wept.

Chapter 11 THE VALLEY OF THE SHADOW OF DEATH

THE VALLEY OF THE SHADOW OF DEATH PROVED THE MOST COM-
fortable, broad and bright road through which the Boers had
ever trekked. The period of reconstruction set in on the very
day the peace of Vereeniging was signed. Milner, now Viscount
Milner, High Commissioner of the Cape Colony, Governor of
the new Crown Colonies, threw himself into the herculean task
of, as he expressed it at a meeting in Johannesburg, "repairing
the ravages of war, and restarting the new Colonies on a higher
plan of civilization."

He began his work in an atmosphere of almost unbearable
tension. The Boers could not believe that their war was lost
and their independence gone. The commandos stubbornly insisted that they were unconquered in the field. Yet they had to
listen to their commandants, who, according to agreement, explained the situation to the ranks and supervised each man as
he stepped forward and handed over his rifle to a British
officer.

Botha, the ex-commander in chief, discharged this unpleasant task with his habitual nonchalance which concealed the
strong emotions of a highly sensitive man. The bulky, deeply
tanned six-footer, whom his friends called the Maharajah, did
not hesitate to shake hands with the British officer in charge.
He sent Lord Kitchener his compliments. Indeed, he was
strongly impressed by the hard-hitting, yet peace-minded English general. There was that inexplicable feeling between them:
sympathy.

De Wet, the martinet of the Free State, growled the prescribed address to his men. Then he left abruptly. He could
not witness the actual gesture of surrender.

Smuts could not bring himself even to return to his commando in the Cape Colony. It was impossible to tell the men
that the free life, the life of a bird of prey, was over. Neither

Milner nor Kitchener insisted on his complying with the proper formalities. Both understood that Smuts was very much a man in his own right.

Besides, the two British leaders had their hands full. Their gravest handicap was the complete breakdown of the railway system, caused by the war, and particularly by the guerrillas. Kitchener demanded military priority to get the troops out of the country as quickly as possible. Milner needed the few facilities left intact to distribute food and medicine among the desolate population. This was their last conflict. It was solved within three weeks after Vereeniging. In this surprisingly short time, the transport home of the troops was in full swing; the districts suffering the worst were relieved, and the surrender of the commandos was accomplished. A month before Milner had written to his friend Major Hanbury-Williams: "If Kitchener is going to make the bed let him lie in it, not me." But on the eve of the general's hurried departure, the High Commissioner paid Kitchener due tribute for his great achievement: "A great task thoroughly completed, a perfect piece of workmanship." They parted, however, without tears.

Some of the Boer leaders smiled. General Smuts smiled bitterly. He had an account to settle with Milner. He could not bear to see another working miracles while he, once more, was left out in the cold.

History has long acknowledged the miracle of South Africa's coming into being. The case of a victor reviving the loser immediately after his conquest, lavishing work, money, and care on the foe of yesterday, transforming him into an independent partner, giving him more freedom than he had ever had under his outworn system, and doing all in the face of sullen resentment, of a constitutional inability on the part of those being saved to fall into step with the new times, with modern civilization, economic development, democratic enlightenment, was unprecedented in the annals of human progress, and was, on the same scale and to the same degree, never again repeated. Lord Milner had chosen the toughest job there was toward, and after, the turn of the century. As he had predicted with visionary foresight: he failed personally. But his cause could not fail. He laid the foundations for the house that in the same spirit his archenemy, and later his friend, General Smuts, finally built.

Repatriation of the exiles, return of the refugees, restitution of the prisoners, transfer from military to civilian government, renascence of common law, revival of trade and industry, modernization of agriculture, reparation of the damages and losses of war, these were the foremost tasks with which Milner found himself confronted. He directed and supervised them all. In his superhuman task he was assisted by a group of young Oxford men, generally called his kindergarten, each of whom subsequently made a brilliant career. Among them were his private secretary, Geoffrey Dawson, later editor of the *London Times* for decades; John Buchan, the novelist and historian, who died as Lord Tweedsmuir, Governor General of Canada; Philip Kerr, who became the Marquess of Lothian, and ultimately British wartime ambassador in Washington; Patrick Duncan, who was to remain for half a generation in the Union government as Smuts' lieutenant; and F. B. Smith, the Nobel Prize winner, and famous professor of Agriculture at Cambridge.

Opposite them stood the Boers of the war and post-war generation. Their fathers had been excellent colonizers. The Boer of the old stamp had taken his wife and family and all his belongings into the wilderness. He had established his crude domesticity in the midst of savagery, tilled the land, and within a decade had become a part of the soil.

The sons were different. True, they preserved some of their inherited traits. They remained the most dogmatic individualists in the world. Their allegiance to the family, including their distant relatives, remained untouched, although it deteriorated into narrow clannishness. They maintained their faith in their somber version of sixteenth century Protestantism, the Dutch Reformed Church. But somehow, as John Buchan observed, they seemed to have missed civilization, and hit upon the vulgarity of its decline. Many sons of old peasant families left the soil, acquired a smattering of education, and migrated to the towns. Falsely they claimed the virtues which their fathers had, indeed, possessed without advertising them. Ignorant, swaggering, mentally and bodily underbred, they decided to live on politics. Much of the spurious nationalism that still prevails in South Africa, comes from this source.

Money meant everything to them; money without work. Why, even the Kafirs no longer wanted to work after the war. They had grabbed their share of the spoils. The liquidation of the British Army's stores left them with carts, horses, and oxen. Fat "like the Jews" the Kafirs drove through the *veld*, and only a few of them cared to sweat in the mines, although their wages had skyrocketed during the war. They had jumped from five shillings a week to three or four pounds. But the Kafirs knew that they had a monopoly on work under the ground. No white man would break his back that way. Why should the blacks not bask in the glory of being top dog for the first time in their wretched lives?

The Boers were outraged. The laziness and the ingrained showiness of the Kafirs would not have gone unchecked under Oom Paul. Under British rule one could, unfortunately, no longer horsewhip them without incurring a five shilling fine from His Majesty's magistrates. The world had gone mad.

Johannesburg was anxious over the future of the industry. Milner recognized the pressing importance of the mining problem, although he was fully aware that the gold would be exhausted within a generation or two, whereas agriculture, so far terribly neglected, would always be the mainstay of South Africa. But in his orderly mind first things came first. A few days after the conclusion of the peace he imposed a 10 per cent tax upon the profits of the mining industry. Thus he relieved business from doubts as to its fate in the future and procured a large and expanding revenue. Only the rapid recovery and expansion of the gold output of the Rand could provide the capital for his great schemes of irrigation, expert farming, improved transport, and could end the stagnation in which the Boer farmer in the Transvaal had been content to remain. The introduction of scientific agricultural methods into the new colonies, his greatest and most lasting achievement, was due to Milner's drive and inspiration. Although the blood of a soldier flowed in his veins, the spade was mightier to him than the sword: another striking similarity with Smuts, the war lord who spends his off time as South Africa's model farmer.

As soon as the pressing problems of transportation and transfer of stores were solved, a month after Vereeniging, Milner tackled the matter of reparations. *Article 10* of the peace treaty, for which Smuts had fought so valiantly, had placed three million pounds at the disposal of local commissions, including Boer representatives, to restore the homes of the people, supply their most pressing needs, and honor the receipts issued by the bankrupt Republics. As soon as the Boers smelled the distribution of cold cash, their apathy vanished. Their spokesmen protested violently against the decision that those among them who had taken the British side in the war should be included in the great relief work. On the other hand, fantastic claims were put forward. Even Louis Botha, whom, in spite of his political integrity, no one could accuse of not knowing on which side his bread was buttered, claimed almost £20,000 compensation for damage done to his farm, *Rusthof*—place of rest—near Varkenspruit, in the district of Standerton, now Smuts' own constituency. Most carefully the department investigated the plea of so important a claimant. He received a cheque for £900, which he immediately returned. Yet no one could say that the wolf was at his door. A few days later Louis Botha bought 10,000 acres of first-class ranching land in his district, and he acquired the habit of buying and selling large estates, preferably on the same day.

Smuts put forward no claim. His treasured library in his house in Pretoria had been destroyed. But the loss of a library cannot be compensated with money.

Milner once more decided to do first things first. He had the exiled Boers repatriated and their farms restored, leaving the claims for adjustment later. This step prevented widespread distress. It was, however, not an economic proposition. A Central Judiciary Commission went to work. After five years the commission had investigated 63,079 claims, many of them fantastic, and had distributed a round sum of £9,500,000, more than thrice the amount for which Smuts had haggled at Vereeniging. British residents were entirely excluded. Only ex-burghers of the two republics, whichever side they had fought on, were considered. Even claims by rich farmers and burghers, who certainly needed no government assistance, were accepted, provided they could prove war losses. Ultimately, all ex-burghers, again with the exception of the British residents, were granted the so-called "rebel-credit" up to £25 each. In addition to these free grants, loans totaling nearly £3,000,000 were made. The War Office handed over to the civil administration £4,500,000 for the settlement of claims against the army, based on goods requisitioned for receipts and promises to ex-burghers in return for assistance. Finally, an expenditure of over £6,500,000 for repatriation was incurred by the colonial government. Thus, at a total cost of some £16,500,000 the stupendous task of reinstating a whole nation was promptly and efficiently accomplished.

The Boers, however, were dissatisfied. They took the unprecedented British generosity as their due; indeed, they regarded the sums awarded as insufficient payments. They had, of course, never dealt in such fabulous sums. But the republican politicians, now out of a job, and a great number of *predikants* fanned the flames of discontent. Since they could not openly attack the government, they looked for whipping boys among the defenseless. "Bully the National Scouts until they repent!" preached the Reverend Bosman. Whereupon Milner, while refusing a suggestion that all National Scouts should be armed, decreed that arms should be equally distributed. Those friendly to the government should not have a smaller number than the irreconcilables. He also suppressed the resurging anti-Semitic wave. A number of Boers demanded that the Jews should become second-class citizens, on the pattern of Kruger's *uitlanders*. Very firmly Milner replied that he would not revive the "bigoted mediaeval tradition of the late Transvaal government. Whatever the conditions of naturalization," he added, "it is quite certain that they will not contain any discrimination against Jews."

On June 21, 1902, soon after Kitchener's departure and his replacement by General Lyttleton, Lord Milner moved in state to Pretoria to receive formally the oath of allegiance from all chief officials, and to take over the civil administration. He had luncheon with Botha and De la Rey. It was a pleasant meeting. Botha recognized that the best was being done to repair the damages of war. He welcomed the revival of legitimate business in anticipation of a great economic expansion in the new colonies. Indeed, in town and country land values were rising rapidly. Land speculations no longer involved much risk.

General De la Rey, himself a big landowner in the aristocratic district of Lichtenburg, was above material considerations. But he also stood ready to throw the great weight of his uncontested prestige into the scales of co-operation. He could, Milner suggested, render the cause valuable service. Many Boer prisoners in Bermuda and India refused to take the oath of fealty. The internees in Ceylon were the most stubborn group. Gladly, De la Rey agreed to travel all the way to Ceylon to soften and soothe his old soldiers. Due to his military fame—it was he who, by capturing Lord Methuen, had won the last important Boer victory—and to his well-known profound religiousness he was particularly well fitted for a mission of reconciliation. Its success was greater than was expected. The example of their fellow prisoners in Ceylon, whom De la Rey had won over, was followed by the group in India and even in the faraway West Indies. By March, 1903, all the prisoners were repatriated. Many of them returned with their families who had followed them into exile. All were laden with heavy bundles. The thrifty Boers took with them even the blankets from the prison camps. From Bermuda not a single family returned without a parrot in a spacious cage—all of which added to the terrible congestion of the scanty means of transportation available.

Instead of being grateful for their homecoming and for the

rebuilding of their farms, the repatriated Boers instantly became an unruly element. They celebrated their new freedom by organizing man hunts on "hands-uppers," those who had surrendered before the peace. Even in the Cape Colony Loyalists were boycotted. The Dutch Reformed Church used all its powerful influence to fan racial antagonism. Real British supremacy, the politicking *predikants* feared, would upset their spiritual monopoly. As for the wire-pullers, Milner expressed his suspicion in the words: "The Afrikander Nationalist Movement is being engineered in Cape Town. I am afraid that even Botha, De Wet, and De la Rey tumbled into it. A dead set is made against the National Scouts. Some of the Boer leaders even had the impudence to demand that they should be excluded from any share of the three million, and the mendacity to say that I agreed to this. The latter is the most thumping lie yet produced, even in South Africa. . . ."

Smuts was not on the list of those whom Milner suspected. He had, it appeared, dropped out of politics. He had already been conspicuously absent from the luncheon in Pretoria where the reconciled antagonists resumed social relations. He was, in fact, in hiding. After the conclusion of the war he returned to Pretoria, no longer the influential State Attorney, but once more a junior member of the bar. His law practice did fairly well. Pretoria was thriving on the spending of the numerous highly paid English officials. As soon as communications with the outside world were restored, business was in full swing. Now all South Africa was attached to the enormous market of the British Empire. The country sent huge quantities of livestock, slaughtered during the war, to Australia, receiving in return frozen beef.

Prices soared. Before the discovery of gold the Transvaal was the cheapest country in the world. After the war, the Colony was the most expensive. A sharp wind blew across the hills from Johannesburg to Pretoria. Legitimate business began for the ordinary merchant at 120 per cent profit, or thereabouts. Polish Jews and Indian storekeepers could make a good living throughout the country in which they were not popular by charging reasonable prices. The British administration itself lavished money on both productive and unproductive enterprises and kept, by the same token, customs, railway and freight rates, as well as taxation low, in order to bring forth the great hidden wealth of the country. It is true that a terrible drought in the second half of 1902 all but ruined the farmers. It was, as Milner put it, the "ogre in his nightmares." But this catastrophe affected only the *platteland*, and the government. The cities flourished. A Pretoria lawyer of Smuts' reputation had easy going.

The trouble with Smuts was, and still is, that he cannot bear easy going. Even in his formative years—he was thirty-two when the Boer War ended—he cared not a hoot about money. Indeed, in a letter written at this time he bitterly complained of the "atmosphere entirely devoid of culture, and frankly materialistic in the worst sense." It was unjust to call the atmosphere in which Milner and his kindergarten of young Oxonians moved an atmosphere devoid of culture. But theirs was not Smuts' world. While he was bursting with the repressed urge for activity, he had to live in the friendly suburb of Sunnyside and to content himself with entirely unproblematic law cases.

The English-language papers still accused him of being "one of the five men responsible for the Boer War." He felt the consequences of this war in his bones. So, and perhaps even more so, did Mrs. Smuts. She had returned from Maritzburg pale and haggard but unbroken in spirit, insisting stubbornly again and again "I am just a Boer woman, a Boer woman as my ancestors were."

Smuts brooded over the wrongs of fate. For his part, he really traversed the valley of the shadow of death. He was unsociable as before. When Botha, De la Rey, and the irrepressible De Wet went overseas to collect money for the Boer cause, he did not join them. Everywhere, and particularly in London, the three Boer generals were cheered and received as heroes. But in Germany, in Holland, and in France, they received nothing but the advice to settle their affairs with the Empire. The journey was unsuccessful except to General De Wet, who managed to sell the copyright of his war memoirs for a fabulous sum in London. He retired to Bloemfontein, and declared: "I am leaving politics severely alone. I am only occupied with looking after my business."

That was exactly what Smuts was unable to do.

His opportunity to return to the fray came with Joseph Chamberlain's arrival in South Africa. The journey caused a sensation. Never before had a Colonial Secretary bothered to visit such a distant outpost of the Empire, and a newly acquired one at that. As Chamberlain disembarked on December 26, 1902, the people of Durban, an English-speaking city, gave him a jubilant welcome. He was acclaimed all along the way to Pretoria. The Boers, who a year before had still called the war "Chamberlain's war," had in the meantime found ample reason for recognizing how gravely they had wronged the man, who, though a great Imperialist, had, after the Jameson Raid, done his best to put out the fires.

Smuts regretted that Chamberlain had not come five years earlier. The war, he believed, might have been averted if Chamberlain had seen for himself. But it was never too late. He came out of his self-imposed seclusion, and was, indeed, elected the spokesman of a large deputation representing the Dutch inhabitants who had obtained a hearing in the assembly hall of the old *Volksraad*. The fact that he was chosen was significant. In the Republic he had been an important official but never a political leader. Now he assumed the leadership. The way was clear for him. Most of the old Boer leaders had emerged from the war as ruined men. Their reputations and their fortunes were gone. They were entirely absorbed with making a new living. Almost alone Smuts and Botha had not fallen by the wayside. Shrewdly, they agreed to work together. Botha was cast in the role of charmer for which he was particularly well fitted, whereas Smuts adopted the part of the rock.

In his unbending attitude, fundamentally opposed to his conciliatory nature, he went so far as to address Mr. Chamberlain in Dutch. An interpreter had to translate, and, unfortunately, did not acquit himself too successfully. Smuts himself would have done the job much better. After handing to Chamberlain a petition which listed the Dutch population's wishes, Smuts spoke. "It is said," he observed, "that we do not wish to cooperate. That is not so. Our interests are so firmly tied to the country that we cannot stand aside. We must work together for the country's good. It is, however, our desire that this cooperation should rest on a proper basis—that of confidence and respect. Mutual disrespect has been the curse of South Africa." Referring to the first point on the list of grievances, the treatment of the Cape rebels, he said: "We do not wish to minimize the crime of these people. But we must admit the crime is ours." And he concluded: "A profound characteristic of the Boer is his loyalty to authority—not the loyalty that pays, but the loyalty that is true till death. We now come to our new government, and offer them that loyalty, but we ask them to think what we have been—that we have been a free people, the freest people on earth."

Mr. Chamberlain replied politely, but he pointed out that the Treaty of Vereeniging was the charter of the British nation. "You have every right to call on us to fulfill this in spirit and letter. But it is a little too early to try to go further than the terms thus concluded." Yet he welcomed Smuts' declaration, and concluded: "I believe that with consideration on both sides, with strict observance of agreements on both sides, with a readiness to give as well as to take, before many years are over, probably sooner than any of us can now anticipate, we shall be one free people under one flag."

Lord Milner nodded: "A most excellent and impressive speech."

As the two British statesmen left the *Raadzaal*, the Boers responded to Botha's call for a hearty round of cheers.

For the rest of Chamberlain's stay in South Africa the Boer leaders showed him much attention and politeness. Affably,

General Botha unbosomed himself to Chamberlain. He had returned from his journey to England deeply impressed by the greatness and the excellence of British institutions. There was no reason to withhold complete co-operation and mutual trust. Perhaps . . . well probably not . . . but, however . . . possibly Lord Milner might feel otherwise. . . .

It had worked with Kitchener. It did not work with Joe Chamberlain. His confidence in his proconsul was unshakable. Yet when he left he advised Milner to treat the Transvaal as if the people already had self-government.

Milner followed his suggestion. Barely a month after the Secretary's departure, on the thirteenth of February, he offered Generals Botha, Smuts, and De la Rey seats in the Legislative Council, which was to advise the administration.

The offer was promptly refused. In their opinion the time had not yet come for popular representation. They preferred to wait until the peace of the country was fully assured. The refusal was signed by De la Rey, but so obviously drafted by Smuts that the then leading newspaper in Johannesburg, the *Rand Daily Mail,* commented: "If they had been honest enough to say that they declined the great honor because they had no intention of associating their names and persons with British institutions, we could have believed them. In the circumstances, however, we must decline to do so, and take it that all their fair words about loyalty and co-operation are so many barren expressions. In view of the characteristic jesuitry of Mr. Smuts we are at an utter loss to conceive why he had been offered the honor at all."

Lord Milner accepted the snub with English imperturbability. He addressed a letter to De la Rey: "You may have seen in the papers that an unfavorable interpretation has been put upon your refusal to accept a seat in the Legislative Council. I only wish to say that, while I regret your decision, I did not and do not think that it was due to any wish to embarrass the government . . . I will only ask you to treat me with the same confidence, and not hesitate to let me know if you have anything which you wish brought to my notice. . . . You can write to me in Dutch, if that saves you trouble, as, though I speak and write that language with difficulty, I read it with perfect ease."

After this cordial reply, General Smuts, too, eased up a little. He explained that they had had no reasonable period of time to consult their people, on whose minds a curious impression might have been made, had they accepted the offer precipitately.

He was again in close touch with his people. In double harness with Botha he built *Het Volk,* as a central organization of those Dutchmen who were willing to co-operate loyally with Great Britain, but more or less on their own terms. He felt that his race needed guidance. They had lost their way in the valley of the shadow of death exactly as he had. But after two years of depression, he pulled himself together. The shadows were fading; the sky brightened.

An incident occurred that threw him again into the deepest despair. It was the fall from which he emerged to his full stature. But he did not foresee that. He could not know that the celestials, who suddenly swamped his land, were really heaven-sent.

Chapter 12   RECONCILIATION

"THE COUNTRY IS VERGING ON BANKRUPTCY. YOU KNOW THE CAUSE. Well, the cure is Chinese. . . ." Smuts wrote, in February 1903, to Miss Hobhouse. He could not have chosen a more unreliable recipient for his confession. Miss Hobhouse, who, during the war, had befriended the Boer women and children in Maritzburg, and who after the war had valiantly aided General Smuts

133

in taking care of destitute farmers, was a kindhearted, aging spinster. Invariably her kind heart went out to the enemies of her own country, England. She was the last woman to whom a man of Smuts' penetrating judgment and imperturbable reason would have unbosomed himself had not his enforced idleness during the English administration of his country upset his otherwise strongest characteristic: his balance. He was now thirty-four, in the prime of life, filled with the urge for activity, indispensable, he believed with good reason, to the reconstruction of his country, and the bigger task of uniting South Africa, and he was frustrated. He vented his bitterness by indulging in unmeasured exaggerations.

Thanks to the generous expenditure of Lord Milner's government, the Transvaal was saved from the bankruptcy in which Oom Paul's corrupt oligarchy had left the country. But there were almost insurmountable obstacles to contend with. Last winter the rains had not come before the end of December, the three preceding months of drought had ruined the crops. The Boers from the *backveld* attributed the catastrophe not to the Lord, who had tested them equally severely in many a previous year, but to the ungodly introduction of scientific agriculture by Mr. Smith, Lord Milner's expert.

The gold industry, on whose output the Transvaal virtually lived, was in bad shape. The cause was the shortage of labor. The Kafirs refused to work after the inflationary wages of the war and immediate post-war period had been reduced to reasonable levels. They now received thirty shillings weekly, instead of the twenty shillings their wages had averaged under the Boer regime. But they had expected the millennium from the British overlords, and since God's kingdom did not come, or had not come to stay, they sat out the period of reconstruction. Gone were the short-lived days in which they had driven in Cape carts, fattened on the large stores the British Army had left behind, and corrupted by equal rights which, in South Africa, were not yet applicable to them. They did not really care for equal rights, but neither did they care to return to the mines. They preferred to live on the poisonous berries and the

parched grass of the *veld*. They devoured the rotten carcasses
of dead animals. Their children were rickety and disease-
ridden. By the scores of thousands the Kafirs sank into hopeless misery.

Due to the labor shortage, many mines shut down. Others
had to reduce their output. In this crisis Mr. F. H. Creswell, the
manager of the Village Main Reef Mine, came forward to advocate a world-shaking innovation: the employment of white
manual labor below the surface. Captain Creswell was a well-
meaning man of good English descent. Born on the Rock of
Gibraltar, the son of the British Postmaster General there, educated in England as a mining engineer, but imbued with progressive ideas acquired during an apprenticeship in American
silver and lead mines, he dared a proposition which no one had
expected of a distinguished officer of the Imperial Light Horse,
a well-decorated veteran of the Boer War. Milner alone encouraged his efforts. Indeed, Mr. Creswell carried out his experiment with white labor in his own mine. Its success was
argued about and contested for twenty years. But the mine
owners protested instantly. They had two good reasons. First,
white labor was too expensive to make gold mining profitable.
Second, the mines could not wait until enough white emigrants
came, and were trained. An immediate solution was vital for
the further existence of the industry.

The few Kafirs willing to work were fully employed on railway and reconstruction projects. Lord Milner sought native
labor outside South Africa. But his search was of no avail. The
English colonial administrations in East and Central Africa
were themselves in need of black hands to open out their territories. Only the Imperial government in India had the necessary pool of fifty thousand men to draw upon. But the India
government's consideration for the welfare and prosperity of
their Indian wards was such that the mining industry in Johannesburg could not meet the demands of the British Raj. As
the situation on the Reef became more acute, indentured Chinese coolie labor was suggested. Milner was hesitant.

Before he had had time to make up his mind a storm of indignation swept the Boer people. Their touchiness on the color question was, and remains, almost hysterical. They lived, and still live, under the constant dread of being overpowered by the four-to-one majority the natives have over the white population. Moreover, they had already their domestic Indian problem. Not only in Natal, but even in the Transvaal, the Indians, who had come as farm hands, had established themselves as shopkeepers, money lenders, and finally as property owners. Should the coolies be invited to come and follow suit? White South Africa from the Cape to the Limpopo was in danger. Every man's job was threatened, although not even the *by-woners*—the squatters living rent free on farms—would have disgraced themselves by heavy manual labor. Lord Milner had done his best to solve the virtually insoluble problem of these poor whites. Now these people, themselves outcasts among the Boers, formed a solid front with the respectable farmers, burghers, *predikants,* and professional men (predominantly Afrikanders), to stave off the yellow peril.

Smuts was back in the fold. He was, with Botha, the leader of his nation, and he was by far the more vocal of the two. He felt that he represented a mighty if inarticulate power. But he could not use his own strength. Under the Peace Preservation Ordinance, introduced by Milner after the war, he might have been expelled from South Africa for advocating open resistance. The English-language papers were always at his heels. To them he was still one of the handful of men guilty of the war.

So Smuts found, at first, no other outlet for his high-strung emotions but the wretched letters he wrote to Miss Hobhouse. "The apathy of the Boers"—about which Lord Milner had complained in London—"ought to give him even greater pangs than the fiercest opposition," Smuts wrote. "For beneath this apathy there burns in the Boer mind a fierce indignation against the sacrilege of Chinese importation . . . against the folly, the criminality of it all. . . . We think that government must be for the greatest good of the greatest number; they think that the mining industry must be saved at all costs. And it cannot and will not be saved, for the major part of it is bogus, and a sham. . . ."

He wrote in the best tradition of Oom Paul and his henchmen, who had always cursed the heathen gold on which they
thrived without being able to produce it. Miss Hobhouse could
not, conceivably, understand this. To her Smuts' practice in
composition was not a mere relapse into unconsidered, long
outworn language, but a revelation. She hurried to a newspaper office. Smuts' letter was published on March 15, 1904.
A veritable thunderstorm was unloosed.

In England *Punch* published a poem by Sir Owen Seaman,
seven stanzas ending with the lines:

> Do you protest against imported labor
> And mention sacrifices made in vain
> Simply because you hope your Kafir neighbor
> Will, by and by, consent to work again?
> I may not plumb these deep forensic levels,
> But all my native common sense rebuts
> The bare idea that you're the lazy Devil's
> Advocate, Smuts!

In South Africa, too, the cartoonists went for Smuts. The cartoon is the indigenous weapon of the country. In his letters to
Miss Hobhouse Smuts had bitterly complained of having to
while away his time watering the oranges in his garden and
reading Kant's *Critique of Pure Reason*. The image of Smuts
with the watering can and Kant in his hand, sprang up in all
the gazettes. Every cartoonist derided the pushing, impatient
young politician. The Boer War, like all other wars, had swept
away the influence of the older generation. A new fellowship
was arising. Smuts was its personification. When he, at last, became the sage, he once admitted: "I was too pushful in my
youth. I was impatient because I wanted the good of my country." Undoubtedly, this confession referred to his tooth and
nail fight against Milner.

The real danger to Milner's importation of coolie labor, however, was the furious indignation in England. Milner had foreseen very clearly the time when the fluctuations of politics in
England would deprive him of the support necessary for carry-

ing his work of reconstruction to a successful conclusion. "My policy," he told Sir Clinton Dakins in one of his prophetic moments, "will not for any length of time commend itself to British opinion. I am convinced I am right, and I will not yield. But for me to be thrown over would be an almost irreparable misfortune to the British cause in Africa."

Clinging firmly to this conviction, and through sheer sense of duty, he refused Balfour's offer to make him Colonial Secretary, after Chamberlain had resigned. Milner insisted that he still needed a year or a year and a half to accomplish his task in Africa. He used a brief stay in London to sound his Liberal friends on the Chinese coolie question. Campbell-Bannerman and Sir Wilfrid Lawson were violently opposed to any measure which would offend the Boers. They also were against Milner's great schemes of land settlement and industrial development in South Africa. They would have best liked to hand back the country to the Boers. But Sir Edward Grey and Lord Haldane, the two right-wing Liberal leaders, promised Milner their support. On that understanding, and in agreement with the government, Milner returned to the colonies to carry out his program.

The Chamber of Mines, under Sir Lionel Phillips' guidance, created a highly efficient organization to avert any possible abuses in hiring labor in China. Men of unquestionable integrity were dispatched to supervise the transaction. Every coolie received an individual contract, at wages much higher than were customary in China. Every precaution was taken for the coolie's safety during the voyage. His living conditions in Johannesburg were much more sanitary and modern than anything he had ever known before. Health inspection was carried out regularly. The only occasion when force was necessary against some coolies arose when their contracts expired and they refused to return home. The celestials, it is true, were no saints. They added somewhat to the rise of the crime curve. But the Reef was no place for plaster saints anyway.

Certainly, the Chinese proved most useful as deep-level miners. They were thrifty, intelligent, tolerably clean, and on the whole law-abiding. Their example taught the Kafirs a new taste for work and earning money. Instead of replacing white labor the coolies, in fact, created new jobs for white men. The employment of 100,000 Chinese led to such an expansion of the industry that 20,000 additional white men found work. The influx of white artisans and mechanics, which had long been decreasing, rose rapidly and continuously after the celestials' arrival. Milner summed up the situation: "To say that Chinese labor is a substitute for white is quite simply a lie. But it has taken in thousands of people. The exact opposite is the truth: Without a substratum of colored labor, white labor cannot exist in South Africa. But when even the very rich mines are worked out, the country will return to its primitive barrenness—and to the Boers. That is the true inwardness of the whole business."

It was, indeed, the true inwardness, but only a part of it. The Boers hated the mines, and foolishly wished for their extinction. But they loathed the Chinese and not alone for keeping the mines going, and thus bringing new prosperity to the country under British administration. They feared that the importation of Asiatics would lead to their permanent immigration. Indeed, the Chinese is the world's born interloper. However careful the supervision, a Chinese population, feared more for their virtues than their vices, will grow and expand, "underliving" the white middle class in the cities. Hence a real conflict between a pressing economic need and a potential political danger arose. For this reason the importation of Asiatics was undertaken by Milner's administration with a very clear understanding and a distinct object: the ideal of white labor in the long run was to be preserved, although the Boers showed little inclination to live up to this ideal; and the way should not be barred to that industrialization of native races on which the future of South Africa ultimately depended. For this supreme reason the indentured Chinese were subject to certain restrictions. They were confined to segregated districts. They could not easily mingle with and disappear among the general population. Yet the celestials felt at home, in heaven, in Johannesburg.

Strangely, this very fact, the safeguarding of the Boer people and the natives, aroused the magnanimity, the compassion, indeed the passions of the English. They were not opposed to the fact that Chinese coolies were at work in the distant Transvaal. But they would not stand for what the Liberals successfully presented as "yellow slave labor within the British Empire."

The echo of aroused English righteousness resounded in the Transvaal. Smuts kept his ear to the ground. Intuitively he felt that his hour was coming. On the strength of the English reaction, misguided as it was by Liberal electioneering, the Boers, he anticipated, would return to power in their native land. He himself would be in power once more, directing, guiding, leading, in the center of things. He highly resolved that he, for his part, would not abuse the British confidence, from which he had good reason to expect self-government for the defunct Republics. He was about to win the Boer War. He, too, would be a magnanimous victor. His pact with the British, the foe of yesterday, the idol of the day before that, was concluded before he had spoken a word with the men in London. For the rest of his life he has abided by this pact.

While he hammered the Boers into shape, preparing them for independence and self-government, he strongly stressed that racial distrust was the arch-foe of South Africa. He pleaded for unity. In Lichtenburg, where General De la Rey was the local patron saint, Smuts advised the "bitter-enders" to be reconciled with the "hands-uppers." He was by no means unselfish, for his people he demanded "the whole egg, not half an egg." But he resented and rejected those who wanted to make the country a reservation for "pure Afrikanderdom." "Let us take the hand of brotherhood," he addressed an audience at Potchefstroom, a violently Dutch-feeling town. And at Klerksdorp, another stronghold of unreconciled Boers, he demanded that the "union of Boer and Briton should resemble that of England and Scotland—not of England and Ireland." Still, his innate caution was not quite extinct. "Do not let us either approve of or refuse anything until we have seen what it is proposed to confer upon us," he warned.

He trespassed upon the enemy's ground. With Botha and Beyers, he addressed a meeting at the Johannesburg Wanderer's Hall, speaking on behalf of *Het Volk*, his own party, to his opponents in the Progressive (English) Party. He called political parties "something of an evil," and almost excused the existence of *Het Volk* by pointing out that the Progressives had been first in the field. "They make very much of the British Flag. . . . The position of *Het Volk* was perfectly clear. They had signed their names to a document at Vereeniging, and as long as that document lasted they would keep their word."

The natural conciliator had found his vocation.

The sand in Milner's hourglass was running out. Like Cecil Rhodes he found that there was so much to do, so little done. In fact, he had done as much to revive and rebuild South Africa as any human in his position could possibly have achieved. He knew that his term would not be extended. He did not ask for it. But he entered upon the last year of his administration without allowing himself the slightest relaxation from his high-pressure. Regardless of his vanishing popularity, unmindful of his overtaxed strength, he accelerated his drive on men and measures.

Lord Milner was the spiritual father of some of the great reforms and changes that were accomplished under Smuts. Their visions were very much alike; their difference was one of tempo and temperament. Although Milner personally raced ahead, for the time allotted to him was measured, he believed in letting development ripen and mature, whereas Smuts, with the restlessness of youth, wanted quick results, speedy action, immediate achievement. Their beliefs were similar. Perhaps their conflict was also caused by the good reason that the one was in, the other out.

Both men were seriously concerned with the defense of the country. Milner told Colonel Sir Charles Crewe: "There is a very big question—that of the local armed forces of South

141

Africa. What I want to do is: first, to work towards their ultimate amalgamation under a federal government, secondly, to
develop some organic connection between them and the Imperial forces." Smuts did, indeed, found the Defence Force
under the Federal Government of the Union, and "some organic
connection" between this splendid force and the Imperial forces
was truly established in two world wars, ultimately in the heroic
achievements of the British Eighth Army, in which the South
African contingent has more than once formed the spearhead.

Above all, their common creed in the unity and, finally, the
self-government of South Africa, united the two men. To the
Bloemfontein Town Council, Lord Milner said: "My work has
been constantly directed to a great and distant end—the establishment in South Africa of a civilized and progressive community, one from Cape Town to the Zambezi, independent in the
management of its own affairs, but still remaining by its own
firm desire, a member of the great community of free nations
gathered together under the British flag. That has been the
object of all my efforts. It is my object still." It was *Holism* pure
and undiluted, expressed twenty years before Smuts incorporated the idea of bringing the whole together into a philosophic system.

Milner concluded, in his farewell speech, delivered in Johannesburg, on March 21, 1905, with the words: "British and Dutch
can, without loss of integrity, without any sacrifice of their
individual traditions, united in loyal devotion to an Empire-
State, in which Great Britain and South Africa would be partners, work loyally together for the good of South Africa as a
member of a greater whole. And so, you see, the true Imperialist
is also the best South African."

A flood of farewell letters showered Milner as he left. Perhaps not the most important, but certainly the most touching
came from the black King of Barotseland. It read: "Dear Lord,
I am sorry to hear that you are leaving to England from hear-
say, but when I hear that I was very, very sorry. When your
letter reached here which said now you leave the country then
another man will take your place, I was very sorry with all my

people. How shall that will suppose is only coming to look after the white people not to take care for the black people. I enclose my short letter with respectfully salutations. I beg to be your little friend Lewanika."

On April second, Milner's no longer unreconciled antagonist, General Smuts, wrote to the departing Governor:

Will you allow me to wish you *bon voyage* now that you are leaving South Africa forever? I am afraid you have not liked us. But I cherish the hope that, as our memories grow mellower, and the nobler features of our respective ideas become clearer, we shall more and more appreciate the contribution of each to the formation of the happier South Africa which is certainly coming, and judge more kindly of each other.

At any rate it is a consolation to think what is noble in our work will grow to larger issues than we foresaw, and that even our mistakes will be covered up ultimately, not only in merciful oblivion, but also in that unconscious forgiveness which seems to me to be an inherent feature of all historic growth. History writes the word "reconciliation" over all her quarrels, and will surely write it over the unhappy differences which have agitated us in the past. What is good in our work is not disposed of in the present, but can safely appeal to the ear of the future. Our respective contentions will reach a friendly settlement which no one foresees today.

Here spoke the philosopher Smuts. He was at peace with the man who was Great Britain incarnate. The two antagonists parted, to meet again as friends.

Chapter 13   EARLY TRIUMPH

THE VERY MOMENT LORD MILNER LEFT SOUTH AFRICA, THE LITTLE man in Bloemfontein put out his head. Now that the imperious Governor had gone, Hertzog saw his chance. The "General," as he stubbornly called himself, was already noted for his anti-

British machinations. Dissatisfied with the magnanimous settlement of grants for ex-burghers, he had demanded more money for his Free Staters, and the assurance of complete self-government at the earliest possible moment. Sir H. Goold-Adams, the Lieutenant-Governor of the Orange Free State, had invited Hertzog to discuss matters with him. But the little man refused. He was possessed by an insurmountable aversion against straight talk. He hid behind a resolution that no conversation or co-operation between Britisher and Boer was possible until his demands were satisfied.

Now he stabbed Botha—whom he had eulogized three years before at Vereeniging—and Smuts in the back. Hertzog founded the *Oranje Unie*, the Free State competitor of *Het Volk*, with the avowed purpose of making things difficult for the two conciliators.

Botha and Smuts remained undeterred. They spent the second half of 1905 in crisscrossing the country and campaigning for a genuine understanding with England. The team was well matched: Botha supplied the popular appeal, Smuts the driving force. Smuts was still reserved, and could only unbosom himself when he stood on a platform, addressing a multitude. His heart went out to all of them, but he was aloof even from the few. In public he had the habit of referring to the most insignificant local grandee as "my old friend John" or "my trusted friend Piet." But this was clearly a way of working off his self-seclusion. On the stump throughout the country, he kept more than ever to himself. Villagers and townspeople who had come to meet the speakers, had to content themselves with Botha's company. Smuts stood apart, wrapped in his heavy coat with upturned collar, his hat low over his forehead so that only his nose showed. Thus he waited for the horse-drawn bus, the usual means of conveyance on the *platteland*. People who called upon him found a man with a faraway look in his eyes, seeming still to ponder the book or document he had on his mind, while he spoke in precise terms straight to the point.

Louis Botha was the very opposite. He was, indeed, heir to the best and most engaging traditions of the old Boers. He was at once conservative and progressive. He relished the memory of Oom Paul, whom he had often attacked in the *Volksraad*. He had inherited the President's pipe, his habit of drinking coffee with all and sundry, he even went Kruger one better by patting innumerable shoulders. His hand had the magic touch. People felt that they mattered to him, and returned proud and satisfied from their interviews, even when the meeting had not brought forth any result. On the other hand he was a confirmed modernist: he was among the first to replace whist with bridge, and he became famous as South Africa's best bridge player long before he was South Africa's leading man. He was the only Boer to venture into the mining business. But he lost his shirt when he tried his hand with a speculation in Premier Diamond mining grounds. Undaunted, he immediately built a beautiful house in Sunnyside, Pretoria's fashionable suburb, near Smuts' cottage. He had borrowed the money from Abe (later Sir Abe) Bailey, the most spectacular character in South Africa, a country teeming with queer types.

Before Sir Abe was thirty years old all South Africa already called him Old Bailey, probably on account of his intimate acquaintance with police stations, where his unbroken chain of fisticuffs and brawls made him a frequent guest. The son of a Yorkshireman from the West Riding, who had made good in South Africa and even entered the Cape Legislative Assembly, young Bailey grew up as an all-round sportsman of distinction. He was amateur heavyweight boxing champion of South Africa, and a famous lion hunter. At the age of twenty-three he made and lost a fortune in the gold rush, whereupon, with ten pounds borrowed from a friend, he took out a broker's license. In front of the Stock Exchange of Barberton he accosted a rich Dutchman by the name of Van Reenen, a big holder of Republic shares, in the Dutch language. This was a quite unusual method of procedure since English was the accepted language in business. But this deviation from the prescribed way pleased the Dutch moneybag so much that Abe's future as a stockbroker was assured. From then on, although a fiery Imperialist at heart, he preferred speaking Dutch in South Africa.

One year after the birth of Johannesburg he arrived in what was then a mining camp, started as a broker, and obtained commissions from Breit, Barnato, and the rest of the Jewish gold kings. Later he entered the field of land speculation where he suddenly encountered an old friend.

"Old Bailey" and Louis Botha had met for the first time when the young commander from Vryheid helped in rounding up the Jameson raiders, in whose midst a young giant challenged all Boer heroes—in fact he used a different expression—to come on. But there were no hard feelings left. Their friendship lasted even when Old Bailey succeeded Cecil Rhodes in his constituency of Barkley-West, and became the spokesman of the Progressive—English—Party in the Cape Parliament.

Nevertheless, the Boer leaders were indebted to him. Already one of the richest speculators, he tided most of them over the lean years after the war. He was also the backer of almost the entire Afrikander press, which ill-concealed its anti-British feelings. Carrying water on both shoulders, he remained a rugged individualist, and was almost always "agin it." In London he was regarded as an eccentric colonial multimillionaire, but nevertheless his shrewd advice on South African matters was seriously listened to, and it was largely on his insistence that the English Liberals granted self-government to the defunct Republics. Needless to say, Old Bailey immediately opposed the government that was, at least in part, of his own making.

Botha had none of Smuts' visionary conception of a United South Africa within a great partnership: the British Empire. For his part he had liked Kitchener already when they agreed to disagree at Middleburg; he had been received with great ceremony in London, he was impressed by the strength and solidity, but also by the charm and courtesy of England. He knew that the City was always good for a loan running into six figures for the Transvaal; he was pro-British, pure and simple.

His sympathy increased when Lord Selborne succeeded Lord Milner as High Commissioner. Both men were immediately attracted to one another by their common love for, and knowledge of, agriculture. Lord Selborne was a quiet man with engaging manners. He showed strong sympathy for the Boer leader. In his first speech, the date of which coincided with Smuts' thirty-fifth birthday, the new Governor referred to "Mr. Smuts, the brilliant lawyer, the brilliant soldier."

At the unveiling of a monument to the memory of the victims of the war at Frederikstad, Smuts spoke in characteristic fashion. "At this spot we find the graves of rebels alongside those of burghers; Boers lie buried here next to British. My heart is full. My lips refuse to shape the words that alone would be adequate to convey my feelings. . . ."

While speaking incessantly, he listened across the sea. He heard the echo of a savage election campaign, conducted by the English Liberals against the Conservatives; those slave traders, those merchants of human flesh, the privileged who defamed the British Empire by introducing serfdom for the sole benefit of the moneyed class.

Early in December, 1905, the general elections upset the Conservative regime. Mr. Campbell-Bannerman with a rich assortment of full-fledged Liberals assumed office.

Smuts interrupted his own campaign. He went to Cape Town to wait for a ship. His visit to London was of a private nature, he insisted. He went simply for a change, which, indeed, he brought about.

He took up his quarters in a small hotel off the Strand, and refused to give any interviews. He only told the reporter of the *Evening Standard* that he was happy to be in England again, where he had studied. The *Pall Mall Gazette* welcomed him with the ominous lines: "British colonials have learned before to tremble at the thought of a Liberal government, and they may well prepare to face the worst. . . ." The *Daily Express* hailed him as the "Dutch Irreconcilables' agent in London." Reuters published an interview with a certain Mr. Hosken, a Johannesburg millionaire, who believed that General Smuts had come "to obscure the issue." The *Globe* referred to the visitor as "Mr. J. C. Smuts, sometimes known as General Smuts."

Only the *African World* gave him a fair deal. This weekly reprinted Lord Selborne's flattering characterization of Smuts, which, it hoped, would "serve to silence ill-bred sneers." Smuts was indifferent as ever to attacks. When he finally spoke for publication, he expressed to the Reuters man his "warm appreciation of the cordial reception extended to him in London."

He made a sentimental trip to Cambridge, a journey into youth, and then he visited methodically the Liberal leaders: Morley, Lord Elgin, Lloyd George, Campbell-Bannerman, and Winston Churchill, who held his first office of profit under the Crown as Under-Secretary for the Colonies. He had known none but Churchill personally, and it is questionable whether the acquaintance of the one-time State Attorney and his prisoner, based on nothing more than a letter that had arrived too late, could pass for a social relation.

Churchill asked Smuts if he had ever known of a conquered people governing themselves so soon after defeat. No, Smuts admitted frankly. But he insisted that they would not, and, indeed, could not govern themselves without England's assistance. This Winston Churchill understood.

Lord Morley, although pro-Boer during the war, proved reluctant toward Smuts' demands. Finally, Campbell-Bannerman listened to his argument with sympathy. He was the first to be convinced of the righteousness of the Boer cause.

On the next day in a Cabinet meeting, the new Prime Minister moved to grant the Boers responsible self-government. After a short discussion all his colleagues agreed. Their main reason, it was said, was their wish to rid themselves of the whole Transvaal business. They were well aware that the battle cry: "No Chinese slave labor in the Empire!" had done good service in the campaign, but that it had misled the people. They knew perfectly well the merits of the matter. Young Winston Churchill took the lead in disassociating himself from his party's slogan. Slave labor in the Empire, he admitted, had been a "terminological inexactitude."

Smuts left a memorandum in Downing Street, assuring that

the Boers no longer wished to raise the question of the annexation and of the British flag. Then he returned home.

Within a few weeks a Royal Commission arrived in Pretoria to work out the framework for responsible government. All that was left to do was to form governments in the two ex-republican, now self-governing colonies. In the Free State Mr. Abraham Fischer formed a cabinet, with Hertzog as Minister of Education, and De Wet as Minister for Agriculture. It was a strongly anti-British administration. In the Transvaal everyone expected that the Premiership would go to Smuts. But he refused. The honor should be Botha's. At first the Pretoria Club was astonished. Then, shrugging, they agreed to the latest inexplicable whim of the inexplicable General Smuts. Botha became Prime Minister, and proved an excellent choice. Smuts took the offices of Colonial Secretary (Minister of the Interior), and Minister of Education.

At the first banquet in Pretoria, given in honor of the first responsible government under the British flag, in March, 1907, the whole audience shouted "Smuts! Smuts!" when the ministers made their entry.

Smuts smiled: *"Myn takhare!"* (My die-hards!)

Now he was in his element. Although painfully aware that he had no parliamentary experience—nor, for that matter, had Botha or any other member of the government served any parliamentary apprenticeship—he wielded power as to the manner born. From the first day he was the undisputed master in the House that most Boers called *Praatfontein:* the talk shop.

Smuts did most of the talking. He led a substantial majority. Thirty-seven out of a total of sixty-nine seats were occupied by his followers from *Het Volk*, whereas the opposition only numbered twenty-nine Progressives—English—, and a handful of Laborites and Independents. The *Het Volk* members were in fact the commanders of the Boer War, feeling a little uncomfortable in their new civilian dignity, and grateful for guidance. The speaker was Christiaan Beyers, a minor Boer general, who had not played any particular role in the war, but was destined to come into the forefront a few years later.

Botha rarely attended the sessions. Although the great majority of the members were Boers, most of the discussion was in the English language. Botha, however, hard as he tried, could not hammer the complicated English language into his head. On the other hand he spoke excellent High Dutch and a racy *Taal*. He was a much admired speaker, and did not care to expose his linguistic deficiency. Moreover, his practical mind was set upon more important things than the babble in the talk shop. He was obsessed with the idea of setting up a land bank to further agricultural development, and largely to promote this scheme he went to London, after one month of his premiership. He attended the Imperial Conference, the meeting of Dominion premiers and the prime ministers of self-governing Colonies, and was again received with that English courtesy and hospitality that transforms converted foes into devoted friends.

Now Smuts had the run of the government bench. His first measure was an act of reconciliation. While in opposition, he had violently argued the case of the Christian National Education Movement which tried to exclude the English language from schools for Dutch children. Now a Minister of the Crown, Smuts set his face against an "education to separatism." He declared that the C.N.E.M. would receive no subsidies from the government, and demanded an end of the movement, while promising to take the Dutch private schools under State control.

The members of the movement, among them many *predikants* of the Dutch Reformed Church, were stunned. In a secret conclave they resolved not to yield to Smuts' decision. In fact, they still wrested a little money from sympathizers. But before many months had passed the schools were, indeed, taken over by the government, and the movement faded gradually.

Smuts declared the English language, the language of progress and business, obligatory in the schools, while Dutch was optional. He dealt the Dutch Reformed Church another blow by banning in the schools denominational religious education.

Bible classes taught Christian ethics; that was enough. The private schools and the churches could look after the rest. An outcry arose throughout the bigoted *platteland*. Smuts was denounced as a heathen. To dispel this hate-propaganda he sometimes opened his meetings with a prayer. But he stubbornly kept the *predikants* from his own educational system.

He did not care how many enemies he made. Many Transvaal Boers believed that self-government meant the revival of Oom Paul's golden days of nepotism and offices of profit without work. Although remaining throughout his life a faithful admirer of President Kruger, whom he called the greatest man the Boer race had ever produced, Smuts made it perfectly clear that job-hunters were pursuing a "blind alley." He was fully aware of, and frequently deplored, the Boers' ingrained laziness. Himself a "tiger for work," to use Milner's phrase, he saw, once more in never admitted harmony with Milner, that agriculture was his country's future.

At a meeting in the country an old man complained that something was wrong with the ground in the Transvaal: it was too low, one had to bend one's back to work. *"Baatje uittrek!"*— take off your coat!—Smuts replied. His phrase became a slogan.

Another word he popularized in South Africa, and perhaps in general use, was: steam roller. It referred to his strong majority in Parliament which, at his signal, rolled over the prostrate and flattened out opposition.

He was at that time constitutionally unable to bear resistance. He celebrated his thirty-seventh birthday by calling out two Imperial regiments, the Camerons and the Queen's Bays, to patrol the Reef against a short-lived miners' strike. Many of the miners shouted that they had served in the commandos against the same troops that were now pitted against them. But Smuts did not listen to this argument. He had learned, at long last, that, at least for his generation, the country lived on the output of the mines.

Gradually his relations with the English mine owners improved. Although the English party in the House of Assembly formed the opposition, which Sir George Farrar valiantly led, the industry understood that Smuts was the "necessary man." Sir Lionel Phillips, the President of the Chamber of Mines, took the first step to ease the tension between big business and the government. Sir Abe Bailey threw all his dynamic power into the scales. Some magnates looked askance at the effort. Messieurs Farrar, Chaplin, Fitzpatrick shook their heads. Sir Lionel, their good friend, was indeed incorrigible. He honestly believed that one could make Boers parlor-broke. He would not learn from his own experience. Remember that evening with Joubert?

Some years before the outbreak of the war, Christian Joubert, Minister of Mines of the South African Republic, had accepted Sir Lionel Phillips' invitation to the theater. It was a courageous gesture on both sides at a time when social intercourse between Oom Paul's oligarchy and the industry was taboo. Sir Lionel, however, was always an innovator, and the white-bearded Joubert, for his part, was rather curious to see a theater from inside. He had never been to a play. The dinner, preceding the show, went off swimmingly. His Excellency drank maraschino by the tumblerful, and was in high good spirits. Later, in the box, he refused to take off his huge "smasher"—silk hat—since this would have been undignified.

The experiment was not repeated for thirteen years. In 1907, Sir Lionel, in the face of widespread scepticism, gave another party for members of a Boer cabinet. Botha put in an appearance; he could not do otherwise. His bronzed face, illuminated by the most engaging smile, contrasted effectively with his immaculate, white stiff shirt. Smuts, in his habitual easy conversational tone, quoted liberally from Aristotle and Kant.

Smuts ventured rarely enough into polite society. He was entirely absorbed by his work. Work was his second nature. Since all his cabinet colleagues, with the exception of Botha, were mediocrities, he was soon recognized not only as an important member of the cabinet, but as the cabinet itself. In a series of articles entitled *Things They Say in Their Sleep*, the Johannesburg *Sunday Times* published a cartoon of Smuts, uttering the words: "To all intents and purposes, I am the

Ministry, 'the whole team and the little yaller dog under the wagon,' as I believe they say in the States." And the Johannesburg *Star* concluded a survey of the first session with the words: "Practically the whole of the Government business has fallen on Mr. Smuts, who dominates and overshadows his party. He obviously shares the complete control of the Cabinet with the Prime Minister, whose comparative effacement in Parliament is partly linguistic."

The inevitable cartoonist, Mr. A. W. Lloyd, later of *Punch* fame, drew a cabinet meeting of the six ministers, all bearing Smuts' face.

Chapter 14   GANDHI

THERE WAS BUT ONE MAN WHOM THE STEAM ROLLER COULD BEND and flatten, but never crush: a frail, emaciated, dwarfish gentleman by the name of Mohandas Karamchand Gandhi. Smuts' trouble with him started in the month of August, 1907. At that time Mr. Gandhi already had an almost fifteen years' old reputation as South Africa's nuisance number one.

Early in 1893 Gandhi, then Indian barrister, had arrived at the port of Durban, representing a big business house in Porbander with a branch in Pretoria, to conduct an important lawsuit in which many Indians in the Transvaal were involved. Mr. Gandhi came fresh from London. He had spent five years there reading law and learning, on the side, dancing, elocution, and the violin—three accomplishments, he believed, which were essential to the stock in trade of a gentleman. According to his own confession he had no ear for western music, yet, with an early display of perseverance, he continued to fiddle until, it was said, his neighbors in the Hotel Victoria complained.

In spite of his persistence, Mr. Gandhi was even at that date rather touchy by nature. Since the white world of the Hotel Victoria obviously wanted nothing of him, he retired to a very simple room in a cheap suburb, bought a stove, his only investment, he confessed, partly to protect himself against the London climate, partly for cooking his own porridge for breakfast and supper. He dined for sixpence in a vegetarian restaurant, and felt highly extravagant when, once in a blue moon, he had a shilling to pay for his bill. It was all by way of sheer virtue. His uncle, a wealthy merchant in India, footed his bills. Mr. Gandhi passed his examinations without winning any particular distinction. In due course he was called to the bar. This act of generosity, it seems, reconciled him with England. Much later he admitted that, next to India, he would rather live in London than any other place in the world.

Fate, that Jester, however, singled him out to spend his early life in the one country in which colored people were by no means treated with English tolerance, but with a heartfelt and unconcealed dislike. The people of South Africa made no fine difference between black, brown and yellow skins. To them Kafirs were the sons of Satan and Asiatics simply coolies. True, the English courts in the Crown Colony of Natal avoided anything like the color bar. When barrister Gandhi, on the second day of his arrival, appeared in court at Durban, he was received with the customary courtesy. The judge only discreetly suggested that the gentleman from India should remove his turban, as it was the custom in English courts to take off one's headgear. Deeply insulted, Mr. Gandhi left Durban, and betook himself by the night express to Pretoria. He had taken a first-class ticket, but in this fashion he only got as far as Pietermaritzburg. There a fellow traveler objected to the presence of a coolie and called a guard, who ordered Mr. Gandhi into the van. Gandhi preferred to get out. He shivered all night in the waiting room, but he was, as usual, undeterred. At dawn he took the coach to Johannesburg, but already in Paardeberg fate in the person of a conductor, a heavy-set Boer, approached him with the friendly invitation to vacate his corner seat. The conductor wished it for himself, in order to smoke his pipe in comfort. "Sammy," he said cordially, "you sit on this." Helpfully, he spread out a piece of cloth. Mr. Gandhi did not care to be called Sammy. He did not yet know the custom of the country, whereby Sammy was a friendly way of addressing an Indian or a Jew. It really only meant pal. "No!" he said. The bulky Boer immediately boxed his ears, whereupon Gandhi realized that he was in the independent Transvaal. At the next stop, Standerton, he changed into another coach, and had an uneventful journey as far as Johannesburg.

The Grand National Hotel, however, had no room free. Mr. Gandhi disappeared into a washroom, changed into frock coat and top hat, not to mention a white tie, to look impressive as he ventured forth, called upon the stationmaster, insisting on a first-class ticket to Pretoria, as befitted an Anglo-Indian gentleman. He arrived in Pretoria after hours—nine o'clock was curfew for all colored people without a pass—and since the policeman caught him strolling in front of President Kruger's house, he was kicked off the pavement, and arrested.

This reception did not endear the Transvaal to Mr. Gandhi. He spent a few months in Pretoria, attending to the law case with which he had been entrusted, and toward the end of the year returned to Durban on his way home. A large number of fellow Indians gave him a farewell party, which lasted until the morning. The morning paper was already on the streets. Mr. Gandhi read in the *Natal Mercury* that the government of the Colony was about to introduce a bill to disfranchise the Indians. It was a sheer measure of self-protection, a necessity if Natal wanted to remain predominantly white. The Colony was already swamped with Indians. More than forty years before they had come to work on the sugar plantations. Soon they became gardeners, indeed, they transformed Natal into a garden-colony. Then they spread out into trade and the professions. They undercharged and undersold the white middle class. Due to their fertility they were about to transform the British Crown Colony into an African dependency of India. A head tax of three pounds, imposed on them, did not disturb them. Prime

Minister Sir John Robinson's new government saw clearly that Natal would be submerged by the wave of Indians. Hence the disfranchisement bill.

After reading the paper, Mr. Gandhi immediately drew up a petition against the bill, insisted that his friends at the farewell party sign it, and entered upon his lifelong struggle. Despite his protest the bill was passed. But Sir John Robinson attached a few helpful amendments, and the English press in Natal showed sympathy for the "persecuted" Indians. Gandhi shrewdly gauged that his chances were good. He became what he has remained throughout his lifetime: Propa-Gandhi. He campaigned to instill into the hitherto apathetic, if rapidly spreading, Indian community a new self-consciousness. Soon, he formed a new power in colonial life.

He remained three years in Natal. Within this time he organized the Natal Indian Congress, the forerunner of the present Congress Party in India, and the Natal Indian Education Association. He was admitted to practice at the Supreme Court in Natal. While the administration of the Crown, faithful to the idea that all subjects of the British Empire had the same rights in every part of the Empire, allowed him to do as he pleased, the common people, even the English-speaking, saw their very livelihood threatened by the sudden Indian upsurge. The Boers, all over South Africa, expressed their indignation with their habitual violence. The decision never to accept English tutelage, with its system that shielded the colored people to the detriment of the whites, was immeasurably stiffened in the Republics. In fact, the leniency of the British towards Mr. Gandhi was a very real factor in inciting the great Dutch upheaval that exploded in Kruger's ultimatum and the subsequent war.

For his part Mr. Gandhi knew how to use the English instrument with great skill and cleverness. In India, to which he returned in 1895 to collect his wife and children and bring them to South Africa, the land of his adoption, he conducted a veritable atrocity campaign, abusing the credulity of Reuter's agency, the official British mouthpiece. In repeated interviews he told Reuter's that the Indians in Natal· were robbed and assaulted, treated like beasts, and totally unable to obtain any redress.

Indignation meetings in the Colony resulted. When Gandhi returned, the S. S. *Courland,* in which he had booked his passage, could not land for twelve days, since Gandhi feared he would be lynched if he disembarked. A committee of Durban citizens offered to pay his and his family's return expenses to India. The sturdy little man refused this offer. He demanded the protection of British troops during the disembarkation. The shipowners, no longer willing to pay the costs of the S. S. *Courland,* idle at anchor, got in touch with the authorities. While 3,300 infuriated people staged a riotous protest demonstration on the pier at Durban, determined to prevent Gandhi's landing by force, if necessary, the English Attorney General Captain Milne told the shipowners: "I want to inform your passengers that they are as safe under the laws of the Crown as if they were in their own native village."

Whereupon Mr. Gandhi, all of five feet and one inch tall, strode down the gangplank. An outcry of "Phoooey!" from 3,300 throats was all the damage he suffered. Thanks to British magnanimity, Mohandas Karamchand Gandhi crashed the gates of South Africa once more.

He was grateful to England. At the outbreak of the war he formed a corps of one thousand Indian stretcher-bearers, for whose employment he had drawn up a carefully worded contract. One of its provisions guaranteed to the Indians "immunity from the dangers of the firing line." He himself helped remove the dying General Woodgate from a field hospital to a base hospital. After the war, and the switch of the real power in South Africa to the Boers, which appeared paradoxical to some observers, Mr. Gandhi declared that his heart had always been with the Boers. "But every single subject of a state could not hope to enforce his private opinion," he admitted with becoming modesty.

After another visit to India, Gandhi returned once more to Pretoria. He arrived on New Year's Day, 1903. Chaotic confusion prevailed in the Transvaal, after its surrender. The country was destitute, the Boers ruined, the very existence of the mines menaced, the cattle gone, and the crops annihilated by the ravages of war. Milner and his staff had their hands full with the great task of reconstruction. To soothe the feelings of the Boer population was the first task. Conceivably, they would not tolerate an influx of the Indians who had already swamped Natal. How would the English care to be submerged in their own country by a nation of hundreds of millions which could export not hundreds of thousands, but millions of its people without, indeed, feeling the loss in numbers? It was a pertinent question; Lord Milner understood it. His Peace Preservation Proclamation closed the borders against any Asiatic immigrant without an individual permit. This measure alone precluded a new sanguinary revolt on the part of the Boers.

Gandhi was not a welcome visitor in Pretoria. The officials were unapproachable. The Assistant Colonial Secretary asked him to go back to Natal. He did so, but only to lead a deputation to waylay Joseph Chamberlain when the latter arrived in Durban. Then his Indian followers, intoxicated by the first taste of success, insisted that Gandhi should return to the Transvaal, their next field of expansion.

Upon his return to the capital of the Transvaal, he was generally considered a pest. Lord Milner, although admitting that civilized colored people ought to be able to obtain all rights, irrespective of their color, declared: "But in this case the Asiatics are strangers forcing themselves upon a community reluctant to receive them." Reluctant was an understatement.

The Indians were not to be got rid of. Although most of them who were prewar settlers in the Transvaal had left the country at the beginning of the war, other Indians, defying the Peace Preservation Proclamation, filtered in continuously.

Finally, Milner tried a compromise. He was willing to readmit prewar Indian residents, providing they would register in order to establish their right to admission. As a means of identification they had to have their right thumbs fingerprinted.

Mr. Gandhi was the first to be thumb-printed. Three months after Pretoria had cold-shouldered him, he enrolled as a duly qualified attorney at the Supreme Court in the Transvaal. This was not a happy ending, but only a new beginning. Many Indians had large financial interests in the Transvaal. To look after their business, to win absolute equality for them, relief from segregation, full citizenship, became Gandhi's next aim.

He could rely on the British Government, which had already protested on behalf of its Asiatic subjects against the restrictions imposed upon them by President Kruger. Now, however, the government in London was confronted not only by the opposition of an irreconcilable Boer system, but by a united colonial feeling. Joseph Chamberlain had rejected all restrictions imposed on "Asiatics" including the three pound tax; to him such measures were practically a continuance of the system of the South African Republic. Measures of restriction, he insisted, could only be justified on sanitary grounds.

In the first months of 1904 torrential rains drenched Johannesburg. The downpour lasted unabated for seventeen days. The Indian population could not stand it. In March, bubonic plague broke out among them. As it happened so frequently, the savage climate of South Africa decided a political issue. Chamberlain's "sanitary grounds" were fully met. Although British doctors and nurses brought the plague quickly under control, the plea for the restriction of the Indians was now irresistible.

Advocate Gandhi himself retired from the hot soil of Pretoria. He founded an Indian rural colony, named it "Phoenix," and started a community life after Tolstoy's pattern. In Phoenix he started, and edited, the *Indian Opinion,* a weekly that was later to become the mouthpiece of his passive resistance movement.

Only two years later, in June 1906, he found a new opportunity to display his usefulness. A minor Zulu war was in progress. Gandhi volunteered once more. He collected a platoon of twenty stretcher-bearers, entrusted the military command to a German sergeant-major, and himself toiled hard, as he declared later, for more than a month. This time his men did not like the toil. They were disgusted at having to carry the wounded Zulus as well. They resented being, in Gandhi's words, voluntary nurses to men not yet emerged from the most degraded state. Gandhi was disappointed at British humanity.

Yet he embarked upon a mission to London. He was most courteously received, but informed that the Transvaal would soon be self-governing. New Asiatic measures, such as Gandhi asked for, would have to be delayed until the independent constitutional government of the Transvaal could decide them.

Infuriated, Gandhi organized his first movement of passive resistance. It took practical form in July 1907, when he was joined by one thousand Chinese under the leadership of Leong Quinn. Hundreds of Gandhi's followers went to prison. Their leader emerged as "our true Karma Yogi."

It was here that General Smuts stepped in.

The Colonial Secretary was busy repatriating the Chinese coolies, who had brought him into power. He went slowly and cautiously to work, since he no longer wanted to damage the mines by a suddenly enforced removal of their most valuable labor. He was all the more impatient with the Indian lawbreakers, constituting a racial danger for white South Africa, much graver than the indentured labor of the modest celestials.

In August, 1907, Smuts wrote Advocate Gandhi an unmistakable letter, announcing that he would carry out the law, "and if the Indians resisted, they would only have themselves and their leaders to blame for the consequences."

Gandhi smiled enigmatically. But his smile concealed a terrible fear. He was rightly afraid that his resistance would arouse the Boer population before exhausting Smuts' already proverbial patience. In that case a change of government might come to pass, and Gandhi understood perfectly well that he would never again find as fair-minded opponents as the team of Botha-Smuts. "The East is not wanting to flood South Africa with Indians," he solemnly declared. "The resident Indians do not wish an influx of their brethren." He fought, he said, for only two points: for the repeal of the Asiatic Law Amendment, and for recognition of the status of educated Indians, of whom six, only six a year, should be allowed to enter.

Smuts replied with a counter offer: he would grant temporary permits. But this concession Advocate Gandhi refused "for reasons of self-respect." Passive resistance continued. To sit *dhurma,* he explained, was a right inherent in Indian philosophy.

He had caught Smuts where he was vulnerable. Smuts could not be out-philosophized by another man. Moreover, he respected Gandhi. To him this was a man who acted in a way he thought right in defiance of a whole nation's opposition. Yet Advocate Smuts made a fine difference between respecting and giving in. Gandhi considered his own people, and Smuts, too, had to consider his own. He introduced a severe Immigration Act in the first session of the new Transvaal Parliament, which passed without debate.

One of the stipulations of the new Act was that every registrant must have his fingerprints taken. In India this custom had long been established. It was used to guarantee the identity of the receivers of pensions and grants of every sort. Moreover, Mr. Gandhi himself, as well as a hundred thousand Indians in Natal and sixty thousand Chinese coolies, had been fingerprinted without recrimination, when Milner had demanded it.

Not *finger*prints but *thumb*-prints, Advocate Gandhi insisted, and at that, only the print of the *right* thumb. In India criminals were dishonored by having their left thumb printed. Besides, religion—about which Mr. Gandhi was otherwise vague—forbade the taking of all *ten* fingerprints. It was some sort of Indian religion, one of the eight hundred-odd denominations.

Everyone, including Advocate Gandhi, knew that one could buy fraudulent certificates, not to be verified by a simple thumbprint, in any Indian bazaar between Johannesburg and Calcutta. Yet, when November 30 came, the deadline for registration, he once more refused registration on behalf of his people, whose numbers in the Transvaal increased by all manners of means, while the controversy about a mere *point d'honneur*—as Gandhi slyly put it—went on.

The Indian Association picketed the government offices to prevent unfaithful co-nationals from complying with the registration order. But five hundred Indians slipped through the picket lines. Immediately the Association denounced those fellow Indians as men who had no right of residence. The others cheered their leader and were prepared to go to jail for him, to lose their trading licenses, and, if he so decreed, their homes and their very existence.

Gandhi marched ahead of his crowd right into the Pretoria jail. The martyr's crown sat firmly on his head. After his sentence to a one-year term he stated that he was delighted to have a full year's time for uninterrupted study and contemplation.

His contemplations, it is true, were frequently interrupted by more or less harmless incidents. In January, the hot South African winter month, a great many Indian prisoners fainted, which was perfectly within the limits of passive resistance. On another occasion they refused to eat their rice or corn prepared with animal fat, the habitual diet of the native prisoners. Their religion, this time a different one, was strictly vegetarian, forbidding the taking of animal fat. In complacent, English-run Johannesburg jails, the rice and the mealies were consequently cooked in butter. In stern, Calvinistic Pretoria, rice disappeared entirely from the prison menu. The Indians had to eat their corn without any fat whatsoever. Some of them actually fell ill. Gandhi alone thrived on mortification.

From his cell, he suggested an interview with Smuts. The prisoner was perfectly willing to give the Colonial Secretary a hearing. It might, he promised, remove some misunderstandings.

Smuts was not aware of any misunderstanding. He sent word that no useful purpose would be served by an interview.

Gandhi continued to plead. Even at the peril of losing some of his treasured self-respect, he wanted to meet the man in authority for a palaver.

Palaver means *indaba* in *Taal*. The Boer has not yet been born who would miss an *indaba*. Moreover, revengefulness is a word unknown in Smuts' vocabulary. He agreed to the meeting. Advocate Gandhi had used his meditations to draw up a scheme, carefully elaborated and ornamented with a few face-saving loopholes. The Indians would voluntarily register in a body within three months from their release from prison, if, on the other hand, the act would not be carried out during the time he needed to persuade his followers. The leaders, however, would be allowed to sign in writing; no more humiliating fingerprints for Mohandas Karamchand Gandhi.

Smuts pointed out that it was not possible to repeal the Asiatic Act, a legislative measure, while Parliament was not in session, but he promised he would introduce "the whole matter" to the House, and would guarantee that until then no Indian would be prosecuted under the act. He had another reason in addition to his permanent inclination for compromise. Botha was then in London, angling for a five-million-pound loan. The chances were good. But the English Government was visibly irritated over the harshness of the treatment meted out in the Transvaal to His Majesty's loyal Indians under faithful Mr. Gandhi.

Smuts admitted publicly that he had "climbed down," insisting that only narrow characters would not do so. The Indians registered "voluntarily." Even Gandhi's famous soul-force allowed him to give his fingerprints, despite the considerable loss of face.

At the next session, Smuts passed a law in the House, at once repealing the Asiatic Act and amending the Immigration Act. The certificates of all registrants were declared valid, but no further Asiatics would be permitted to enter the Transvaal.

Gandhi declared this to be a breach of Smuts' promise. Smuts denied the accusation. Gandhi spoke of a personal promise. Smuts, not unlike his behavior toward Sir Conyngham Greene immediately before the outbreak of the war, knew nothing of personal promises. Parliament was the authority, not he.

The Indian registrants, Gandhi at their head, burned their certificates. The trouble then made did not abate throughout the years. Gandhi came forward with a new demand: repeal of the three pound tax imposed on the permanent Indian settlers in Natal. By this time the Union of South Africa was already achieved. Smuts, now wielding country-wide authority, refused to be blackmailed. Provocatively, 3,000 Indians from

Natal under Gandhi's leadership crossed the provincial border of the Transvaal. They were promptly arrested, and once more imprisoned.

Smuts was worn out. Gandhi, too, seemed slightly fatigued by his exertions. Unhesitatingly, he added *Brahmarcharya*—the vow of chastity—to his already practiced *santygraha,* soul force. He was detained in the Bloemfontein prison. Now the Indians in India rose in his support. The English wanted no trouble in the Empire, as dark clouds were overshadowing the political horizon. They interfered discreetly with the Union government. Gandhi's sojourn in jail suddenly ended.

At a triumphal farewell banquet Gandhi and his wife drank one another's health in two glasses of water. *Brahmarcharya,* it appeared, was a rather rigid prescription. Then the couple slipped out of South Africa—two days before World War I started. Gandhi returned via London to India, where he practiced what he had learned in South Africa. Ever since he has paid his debt of gratitude to England in his own inimitable fashion.

Smuts was reconciled with the Indians when he watched the splendid performance of their troops during the First World War. But Indians, like other peoples, are not a nation of splendid soldiers alone. Some of them who remained in South Africa, a fat and increasingly rich lot, right now do their best, or their worst, to impede the Union's magnificent war-effort.

Chapter 15   UNION

CERTAINLY THE MOST SPECTACULAR, AND PROBABLY THE MOST consequential incident during the three years of the Botha-Smuts regime in the Transvaal was the story of the *Cullinan.*

On January 26, 1905, a tremendous diamond was found in the half-State-owned Premier mine. More than 50 per cent of its value belonged to the State. But no one could tell how much that would amount to in money. In fact, the giant gem, weighing 3,025 carats, was beyond estimate, since there was no market for a precious stone of this magnitude. It was insured for £250,000, but this sum represented only a fraction of its real, if immobile, worth.

The government of the Crown Colony was rather embarrassed by the find. What should be done with the *Cullinan?* In London, patriots suggested an Empire-wide collection to buy the miraculous stone as an offering to the King-Emperor. But before this collection materialized, Smuts had a brain wave. Why not present on behalf of the Transvaal the unique jewel, too precious to be worth anything, to King Edward VII? Smuts had good reasons to believe that the King was not a particular friend of the Boers. Edward VII still stressed his admiration for Cecil Rhodes, he treated with great distinction Viscount Milner, whom the Liberals had sent into the political wilderness, and he only thinly disguised his disapproval of Campbell-Bannerman's post-war policy in South Africa.

A truly majestic present seemed to General Smuts the best method of reconciling the King with his new colonies. Perhaps he also felt, in the exuberance of newly acquired power, a little flattered by the vision that he, Jan Christian Smuts, would present the world's greatest diamond to the King-Emperor, the world's greatest monarch. Smuts rarely indulged in even the most innocent vanity. This case may have been an exception.

Botha, both a little sentimental and very practical-minded, concurred wholeheartedly. He was very ready to oblige his king in the most grand-seignorial manner. Moreover, he still had the Transvaal Land Bank on his mind, for the establishment of which he needed a formidable English loan, perhaps five million pounds.

On August 16, 1907, the government suggested to the House to offer the *Cullinan* to His Majesty. An acrimonious debate began immediately, and lasted for two days. Strangely, the conservative Boers took no part in the discussion. They distrusted the Anglophilia of their ruling team. The couple Botha-Smuts, they found, had grown a little too big, too broadminded, and too magnanimous in their generosity toward England. But suspicious Boers are silent Boers.

The Progressive—English—Party was not silent. Their spokesmen, Sir George Farrar and Sir Percy Fitzpatrick, opposed the proposed gift as "inexpedient." In fact, they saw through the trick: they knew perfectly well that the Land Bank, breaking the English banking monopoly, was lurking around the corner, and they had no reason to wish the King to undergo a change of heart toward the Boers. The King's attitude, if constitutionally of no consequence, was yet the last rampart in the Transvaal, defending the English from being entirely brushed aside by a wholly Dutch government.

But the Progressive Party was split from top to bottom over the merits of the matter. Some of them could not swallow Smuts' biting sarcasm in the debate: "When I see the Knight Commanders and the D.S.O.'s rise and unblushingly oppose the motion, it shows me that although there may be great financial power behind them, there is little political insight." Sir Abe Bailey, a mere dilettante in politics, but a multimillionaire of his own making, could not tolerate such an insult. He was for the motion. Mr. Henry Lindsay backed him up. He saw in the motion for the disposal of the *Cullinan* diamond the materialization of the great event for which he had been waiting all his lifetime: an act that symbolized the junction of two races in their common allegiance. "The seed of a wider national sentiment, sown by Advocate Smuts at Kimberley in 1895, has germinated," he ended his contribution to the debate. His words were well chosen.What Smuts had considered the gravest political blunder of his life was vindicated. The wound was healed. He concluded the discussion by informing the House that word from London had just come through: By 199 to 62 votes the House of Commons had approved the guarantee of a loan of five million pounds to the Transvaal, a large slice of which was earmarked as capital for the Land Bank. Immediately the Transvaal House of Assembly agreed upon the gift by 42 to 19 votes. The unanimity of the resolution, Smuts pointed out, was only thwarted by the professional guardians of British prestige in South Africa.

The *Cullinan* as a whole could not be polished. The "cleaving" was undertaken on February 10, 1908. The process succeeded splendidly. The largest fragment weighed nearly 2,000 carats, the next over 1,000 carats. The remainder consisted of many small pieces. In November the parcel was delivered in London, to be dealt with by His Majesty's jewelers. Ultimately, *Cullinan I* weighed 516 carats, *Cullinan II* 309, the next heaviest, the *Nizam*, 277.

Early in January, 1909, Botha and Smuts went to London. They were summoned to Court to see the gem, and were not a little surprised to meet, on this occasion, Sir George Farrar and Sir Percy Fitzpatrick, the leaders of the opposition. There was a last little difficulty to overcome. The cleaving, polishing, and setting of the stones had cost £35,000. Since one could not well let the King pay for a present, the Transvaal Parliament voted the sum under the heading "unforeseen expenditure." This time the vote was unanimous. Smuts had made sure that no questions would be asked. The English opponents rubbed their hands. They were, after all, very pleased with the outcome. The unreconciled Boers jammed the counters of the newly opened Land Bank to grab their share of the credits.

The *Cullinan* affair had a twofold political consequence. The Progressive Party remained split, and its influence dwindled. A great many English voters, now convinced by the proved loyalty of Botha and Smuts, switched to *Het Volk*. On the other hand, *Het Volk* lost many of its old adherents to the dangerously surging Boer nationalist movement which found the donation an act of megalomania on the part of the two leaders, now clearly on the highroad to England, and which thrived on the appeal to the traditional Boer thriftiness. It can be assumed without exaggeration that the renewed and never-since-abated nationalist Afrikander movement originated in the *Cullinan* affair.

Smuts was gambling for high stakes. The *Cullinan* had removed the last English suspicion. The time had come for the fulfillment of his supreme idea: the Union of South Africa. True, the people still needed a little prodding. His approach had to be careful. South Africans were not high-flying idealists of his own mould. They must be brought to understand the problems that, varied as they were, all made Union necessity.

Once more Smuts toured the country. Now he had no enemies, or at least he did not recognize them as such. His innermost urge of human brotherhood overcame all barriers. To his own constituents in Pretoria he explained the advantages of his Education Act. It was bound to bring people together. In another ten or fifteen years there would no longer be any racial differences. A good kick had brought down the wall that had separated them thus far. After this appeal to the irreconcilable Boers he welcomed Sir Lionel Phillips on his return from England. It was no longer private parlor conversation. It was a frank, public welcome, unmindful of the fact that the English-language newspapers of the House of Eckstein, which Sir Lionel represented in Johannesburg, had incessantly attacked *Het Volk*. At the Johannesburg Debating Society Smuts mentioned Paul Kruger and Cecil Rhodes, in the same breath, both as great personalities.

To the farmers he spoke in their own language. To a Western Transvaal audience he gave practical advice on mealie—corn—growing, potato blight, the production of negro-head tobacco, the darkest and the richest, on sheepshearing, on the best methods of marketing.

He was now a prosperous farmer himself. Union was coming, he felt it in every drop of his blood, and he would have to stay for many months out of the year in Cape Town. So he bought the estate *Dornkloof* (Mimosa Gorge) near Irene, ten miles south of Pretoria, to give his family a permanent home. *Dornkloof* has remained General Smuts' favorite private residence, the abode of his famous library, and South Africa's model farm.

The Transvaal farmers listened patiently to all the good advice they had received from their exalted fellow husbandman. But what they wanted was more than advice. They clamored for protective tariffs to secure the home market against the competition of the incomparably more fertile Cape Colony. Internal tariffs, even the low ones then in existence, were the worst obstacle to Union. Smuts said he would not erect a fence around the Transvaal to exclude fellow South Africans. Isolationism, protectionism, separatism were the targets of his hard-hitting speeches. He interspersed them with just the proper dose of nationalism. Many of the Cape farmers had helped the Transvaal in the war. Were the Transvaalers now going to bite the hand that had drawn the sword in their defense? At a meeting at Christiania, where Smuts once more conjured up the memories of the Boer War, a listener shouted: "General de la Rey has promised all those fighting under him a good living afterwards!" "Nonsense!" replied Smuts, "what he promised you was certain death!"

He demanded intensified work on the *veld* to make good the destruction wrought by the war. "What do we need in addition to land and irrigation?" a heckler asked. "Seed!" said Smuts. "And then?" continued the stubborn Boer. "A plow!" "And then?" "A harrow!" "But most of all?" The fellow meant, of course, protection. Smuts replied: "Sweat!"

His dwelling on the Boer War did not prevent him from doing justice to the English. He wanted all and sundry in his fold. In Johannesburg he paid glowing tribute to Colonel Briggs, who had hounded his own commando through the Cape Colony. When the Imperial Light Horse, the English crack regiment, one of his most formidable foes in the war, was threatened with absorption in the Defence Force, then in the making, Smuts pushed through a cabinet resolution to retain the identity of the historic formation, and its name.

Again in Johannesburg he coined a word that became the battle cry of South African politics, and remained so ever since. Smuts pointed to Canada as a warning example. There English and French did not blend. They did not become one people.

They remained almost like two streams, flowing side by side. He wanted the flow and growth of a South African nation in one stream.

Unwittingly, he had given his foes their cue. Hertzog picked it up, and his successors repeated it incessantly to this very day. They call their policy of racial division and hatred: two-stream-policy.

Hertzog, thus far generally regarded as a troublesome and ungrateful Boer agitator of no particular importance, was now a Minister in the Orange Free State. Lacking any sort of parliamentary or governmental experience, he sought to attract attention as a violent anti-British racialist. He succeeded particularly well with the Boer women who exercised strong influence in the family and in social life. Although he himself spoke English with his children, he warned the mothers to confine their household speech strictly to *Taal*. They must never forget their sufferings in the camps during the war, and teach their children what he called "the truth of the matter." Pretending that he was only seeking Dutch equality, and that there should be nothing to suggest one race's superiority to the other, he embarked upon the doctrine and practice of violent anti-British prejudice. In fact, it was not his bias against Britain, but his insane jealousy of Smuts and Botha that shaped his course.

In the Transvaal the two races were approaching one another step by step. On the English side Sir Lionel Phillips, the mining magnate, was the protagonist of this rapprochement. His social relations with Botha and Smuts developed into confidential political intercourse. Sir Lionel made it his business to keep abreast of government proposals and often to point out in the most friendly manner defections or possible unforeseen consequences of impending legislation. Mostly he reached an agreement, and had dangerous bills amended and modified. When Smuts introduced his bilingual Education Act with the support of the English opposition in Parliament, Hertzog could not bear it any longer. He publicly accused Botha and Smuts of "weakening under the blandishments of the Empire builders," and was bent on proving that the Boers in the Orange

River Colony, as the Free State was then called, were better Boers. In his capacity as Minister of Education he introduced a pointedly anti-Smuts Education Bill of his own, a crude system that tended to exclude the English language from the schools in his colony. Under the pretext that they had not passed their examination in Dutch, he excluded several hundred teachers newly imported from England. Furthermore he dismissed the three English school inspectors. The Director of Education in Hertzog's own Free State resigned in protest. The three inspectors sued for wrongful dismissal, and obtained damages from the Court. But the *Oranje Unie,* Hertzog's henchmen, collected enough money to refund all expenses.

While the Boer chauvinists under ex-President Steyn's nominal leadership and Hertzog's actual guidance did their best to poison the relations between the Orange River Colony and the Transvaal, the English South Africans were foremost in supporting Smuts' idea of a Union of the whole country. In fact it was Cecil Rhodes' and Lord Milner's legacy, which General Smuts, mustering all his forceful idealism, was now carrying out. Dr. Jameson, of all men, the same Dr. Jim who eleven years before had organized the blundering raid, was now Prime Minister of the Cape Colony. His "misdeed" was forgotten and forgiven, particularly by Botha and Smuts. Dr. Jameson now addressed Lord Selborne, urging the Governor to pay attention to a series of articles in *Ons Land,* Smuts' own mouthpiece in Cape Town, which pointed out that the time had come for South African unification. Lord Selborne, himself deeply convinced of the necessity of Union, entrusted Messieurs Lionel Curtis and Philip Kerr (later the Marquess of Lothian), two members of Milner's Kindergarten, with a blueprint. This paper, to become famous as the Selborne memorandum, was published in January, 1907. The cornerstone of a united South Africa was laid.

Unceasingly, Smuts drove matters on. He had to overcome grave obstacles. The Transvaal Boers loved their old comrades in arms, the Boers from the Orange River Colony, but they were not willing to pay for the perennial deficiency in the Free

State's budget. Pretoria was the center of the protection movement, the natural antagonist of Union. Racial bias was fanned in the Free State. Mr. Merriman, by now the patriarch of South Africa, while eulogizing General Smuts as a great asset in the coming united South Africa, declared himself as a *pas-op*, a cautious, conservative man, unwilling to accelerate the speed of a natural but necessarily slow development.

Smuts replied to all criticism that he fully understood the temporary difficulties, but that he was building for the centuries, not for the moment. He was even unwilling to grant a general election on the subject. The Parliaments in the four States, he declared, had full powers to act. In June, 1907, the four Parliaments indeed passed resolutions favoring national union. Eleven months later an inter-colonial conference in Pretoria resolved that the permanent prosperity of South Africa could only be secured by an early Union, under the Crown of Great Britain, of the four self-governing Colonies. Smuts prepared a constitution, which, he foretold, would be more than a mere instrument of government. "It ought to be a grand pact of peace between the white people of South Africa," he demanded. "Do not let us have a Union of top-dog and under-dog. Let us have a union of brothers."

From the Free State came Hertzog's reply: "The Afrikander must be *baas* of all South Africa."

But Smuts was too busy to listen to criticism. He was entirely absorbed by the study of existing federal constitutions. The American Constitution occupied him above all. But he found its principles of States' rights and rather loose federation not applicable to young South Africa, where an iron hand was wanted to bring the divergent interests together. He later said that the Constitution was not a man's work, but "bore the impress of a Higher Hand." Undoubtedly, he had lent the Higher Hand his own right hand.

On the twelfth of October, 1908, exactly nine years after the beginning of the Boer War, a National Convention opened its session in Durban, to proceed later to Cape Town and finally to Bloemfontein. The debate was conducted with great deco-

rum and in an atmosphere of good will. Not a single word was
uttered about racialism. Fire and water were happily wedded.
The Rand mine owner and the Natal sugar planter, the Cape
wine farmer and the Free State ex-commander discussed matters as if they never had been at one another's throats. General Botha, the patriarch Merriman, Sir Percy Fitzpatrick, President Steyn and many other arch-foes spoke and acted like a
band of brothers. They were all in General Smuts' grip.

Smuts was accompanied by a staff of nineteen advisers and
experts, a larger staff than the delegations of all the three other
colonies together had brought along. He himself had made an
intensive study of the problem in all its details; there was no
question which he had not explored with all his customary
thoroughness. He surpassed himself both as a thinker and
speaker. He appealed to the convention not to pay too much
attention to material interests. The problems of the day were
not the problems of the future, for which alone they were working. He reconciled diverging interests and opposing views. He
settled the haggling between Pretoria and Cape Town about
which should be the Union capital by suggesting that Pretoria
should be the seat of the Executive, and Cape Town the seat of
the Legislative. He insisted on one supreme Parliament and
one Government. Yet he believed that the insoluble native
question—the problem about which the liberal Cape Colony on
one hand and the intolerant Transvaal and Free State on the
other could never agree—should remain a matter of the individual States. He promised the interior of the country its due
share of the development to avoid the example of Australia,
where almost the whole population was concentrated at the
coast, and he drew a glowing picture of the prosperity that
would accrue to the ports and the coastal regions by handling
the business of the Rand which would no longer be impaired
by internal customs. The clause concerning unification of the
railway system—another piece of Lord Milner's heritage—he
called "the Magna Charta of the Interior." But the *leitmotiv*
was, time and again, the blending of all free people in a common nation.

Alexander Hamilton was reborn.

Throughout the months of discussion everyone paid tribute to Smuts' wide and ambitious vision. The logic of his cut and dried plans, his arguments worked out to the minutest particular swayed the convention. Only one backbencher dissented. He did not speak a single word about the great idea of Union. Instead he harped incessantly on his two hobbies: the predominant right of the Dutch language, and the native franchise which should not be extended. The Natal delegation grew restless as Hertzog constantly assailed the use of English, and the representatives of the Cape were aroused by his attacks on their traditional liberalism toward the color question. Hertzog did not mind appearing as a strange and disturbing element. While the benches emptied rapidly, he produced a long and involved resolution, which was finally voted down. His insistence had made him the most unpopular member of the convention. Yet many of the delegates recognized that he was the one man who felt most strongly on his obsessions and that, in view of his following among the Dutch, some day they would have to heed his voice.

Smuts' draft constitution was accepted in Cape Town on February 9, 1909, and a few months later slightly amended in Bloemfontein. A large group of South African politicians carried the amended act to England, where it was embodied in an Imperial Bill, and subsequently ratified by the Parliaments of Westminster and South Africa.

On the fifteenth of April, 1909, a banquet was held in Johannesburg in honor of Lord Selborne, then on the eve of his departure from South Africa, since his term had expired. Smuts, still the Colonial Secretary, substituting for Prime Minister Botha, eulogized Lord Selborne as the "father of Union, who had first ventured into the open." But he left no doubt that the Union was now very much his own business. However, he had not the slightest ambition for the formal leadership. He did not wish to enter the scramble.

May 31, 1910 was the appointed day when the Union of South Africa should come into existence. It was the eighth birthday of Vereeniging. On this day a government had to be ready, strong enough to carry the elections which were to follow in September. There was not much time left to build a cabinet. Moreover, the battle of the spoils was marked by the most complicated intrigues. It was, indeed, difficult to find proper representation for the two white races and the four ex-colonies. Dr. Jameson suggested a best-men-ministry including the leaders of all parties and both races. But aged John X. Merriman, widely considered as the great impartial, sided with the irreconcilables from the Free State, with President Steyn and his chief adviser Hertzog, in rejecting the plan. Botha himself refused to head such a government. He would, he feared, lose all his influence with his people, if he wished to preside over an administration which included the English. The English leaders understood that the plan was premature. They formed a loyal opposition, but ultimately their exclusion, and the division along national lines, revived racialism.

The natural choice for the Premiership seemed to be Mr. Merriman, who cautiously announced his candidature, and was supported by Hertzog. However, after fifty years of work in Parliament and public he was denied the highest honor. Lord Selborne, shortly before his departure, had expressed his displeasure with the old man, who, for his part, had prevented the Governor-General from presiding over the National Convention. Besides, it was known that King Edward strongly disliked the English-born Boer leader. Ex-President Steyn's health failed so rapidly that he, too, was out of the race. Smuts produced Botha. The kingmakers agreed, but on one condition: Hertzog would have to be included in the Cabinet. Everyone, with the exception of his own Free Staters, despised him. But this delegation had seventeen men in the elected chamber, and to the last man they insisted on their spiritual leader. The bulk of the English voters was infuriated. Natal threatened to abstain from co-operation, if Hertzog in the Ministry was the price they would have to pay.

Once more Botha and Smuts had to calm the troubled waters. Botha, himself Natal-born, sent emissaries to the troublesome

Free State. Smuts suggested that Hertzog should come along
to welcome the new Governor-General, Lord Gladstone, the
son of the Grand Old Man, to whom the Boers owed their triumph after Majuba. Smuts' idea was to reconcile Hertzog with
the British. But it failed completely.

In a new conciliatory effort General Smuts visited Hertzog
on May 10, 1910, in the Mount Nelson Hotel in Cape Town.
Stubbornly Hertzog insisted that all the trouble around him
was due to political agitation from the Rand. Smuts suggested
that Hertzog should go to the Court of Appeal. Hertzog indignantly replied that he could not do so without playing false to
his people. Was he an inconvenience? he asked, smiling.

Pigheaded, he refused all further advances. Even the threat
that Dr. Jameson would be sent for, if Botha should not succeed
in forming a ministry, did not deter him. He preferred a hated
Englishman in office than a Boer government without himself.
In his diary he entered: "Botha's weakness and lack of principle was known to me and my friends before Union. So was
his half-heartedness about the language question. The days
before and during the National Convention gave me and my
friends a fair foretaste of what we had to expect from him as
our future leader. But this convinced me all the more that it is
my necessary duty to take my place beside him in the interest
of our people and country. Three things are now clear to me:
How sensitive 'people' [meaning Botha and Smuts] are to opposition. How eager 'people' are to satisfy criticism, but how
willing also to offer me up on the altar of another opposition."

Botha was finally convinced that he must accept Hertzog,
behind whom stood the whole Free State and all the irreconcilables throughout South Africa. He chose the lesser evil. Only
one week before the Union Cabinet had to be announced he
asked Hertzog, whom he had thus far personally avoided, to
see him in the Mount Nelson Hotel. Hertzog appeared, but instead of Botha, Smuts received him and notified Hertzog that
he would become Minister of Justice. Then both men went to
Botha's room. The Prime Minister-in-the-making did not utter
a single word in connection with the appointment. Hertzog

entered in his diary: "There was no mistaking with how much reluctance he accepted me as a colleague." But he had wormed his way into the Cabinet, and was perfectly satisfied.

On account of Hertzog's inclusion, the first Union Cabinet got a very bad press. The Johannesburg *Star*, then the most powerful organ in South Africa, complained that Botha's party had capitulated to the Orange Free State racialists.

There shone but one ray of hope. Smuts was in the government. He was very much in it. He held three portfolios simultaneously; the Interior, the Mines, and the Defense. In this latter capacity, as Minister of Defense, he was to enter history.

Ch. 16   THE RISE AND FALL OF GENERAL HERTZOG

IN THE ELECTORAL CAMPAIGN THAT FOLLOWED THE FORMATION of the first Union Government, Smuts strongly stressed the fact that he regarded the Defense Office as the predominant one among his portfolios. The year was 1910. "In England," Smuts declared to a Natal audience, "people live in a false sense of security, and it is difficult to get them to take an interest in defense. But we in South Africa have known war, and while the feeling of responsibility is still warm within us, we shall create a national defense system." While he dwelt on the subject, he warned against South Africa's building a "tin-can fleet" of her own. It would be better to increase their contribution to the Royal Navy guarding the South African shores.

His audience was deeply impressed. But immediately his cabinet colleague Hertzog raised his ugly head. Any money that was to be spent on the defense of the country's shores, he insisted, was to go toward the building of an independent

South African Navy. He entirely opposed an increased naval contribution to the Imperial Exchequer, about which General Botha was, in fact, already negotiating with London. The Cabinet was split, even before it had won approval from the electorate.

Smuts knew what he was speaking about. Among Cecil Rhodes' "thoughts" that he had inherited was the colossus' distrust of German penetration of Africa. Although he himself at that time was still a strong believer in the color bar, Smuts was aroused by the barbaric cruelty with which the German colonizers, neighbors, at that, treated the natives. When Germany took South West Africa in 1892 the Hereros owned one hundred and fifty thousand head of cattle, incidentally their only possession. By the end of 1905 they had not a single head left. Two years later a German law formally forbade them to own cattle. The Hereros themselves were annihilated like their cattle. Shortly after the building of the Union of South Africa the natives rose in rebellion against their systematic persecution by the German overlords. In 1877, according to the findings of a British commission, the Hereros had numbered eighty-five thousand. A few months after their revolt the Germans took a census of the population, and announced triumphantly that only 15,130 "savages" were left.

A few years before the outbreak of the First World War German colonial aspirations ran riot. Central Africa was considered an essential part of the *Vaterland's* living space. One argument was that at least a million black soldiers could be trained there. The other was that the country would supply inestimable raw materials. And last, but not least, German naval bases, coaling stations, munition dumps, and strongholds would interrupt, and, if the opportunity arose, sever Great Britain's vital lines of communication with India, the Pacific, and the Far East. The race for naval superiority, into which Wilhelm II plunged, had its immediate bearing on South Africa, the country situated at the confluence of the Atlantic and the Indian oceans.

Smuts was far away from the ever-darkening European

scene. But this very distance gave him a broad, world-wide outlook. He did not see the trees, he saw the woods. His first promise in the electoral campaign was that he would fortify the shores of South Africa. This pledge won him the confidence of many English-speaking voters.

On the other hand, Hertzog was just about to develop his creed, which, under the name of Hertzogism, was to permeate and poison South Africa. As it was evolved in 1910, Hertzogism was not so much anti-English as anti-British. He wished to leave the English-speaking South Africans in peace, if in an inferior position. His hatred was concentrated on the Empire. Viewing world problems from a narrow standpoint, acquired in the Orange Free State, an almost exclusively Dutch province in a parochial state of mind, he hated large units, the very goal of Smuts' life. The Britain-hatred that subsequently marked him began as bigoted, limited provincialism.

Hertzogism, vocally expounded, antagonized the English part of the electorate. Botha himself lost his seat in Pretoria to Sir Percy Fitzpatrick, on account of the Prime Minister's coalition with Hertzog. As a matter of precaution, the Prime Minister had also contested the Dutch agrarian constituency of Losberg which gave him an overwhelming majority. But Botha's pride was hurt, and he realized perfectly well that he owed his defeat to his colleague more than to his opponent.

Pretoria-West returned Smuts after a three-cornered contest. His rivals were Major Creswell, the leader of the newly founded Labor Party, once the whip of the British section of *Het Volk*, and the man who had introduced white labor under the surface, and the Unionist, Major Hopley, later to become Smuts' friend and follower. Smuts won his victory largely by disassociating himself from Hertzogism. The Unionists, successors to the Progressives, made much of this curse that found its particular expression in the educational system prevailing in the Free State. Smuts admitted that this system was non-germane to Union. However, he cautiously insisted that the abrogation of the educational laws of the Free State would be impossible without a revolution.

On the whole, *Het Volk* did well at the election. The Boer

Party won sixty-seven seats, the Unionists, led by Dr. Jameson, now Sir Starr Jameson, mustered thirty-nine, and the new Laborites four.

The Duke of Connaught went to South Africa formally to open the First Union Parliament. In a glowing address his Royal Highness dwelt on the fact that five self-governing nations were now willing to co-operate in Imperial affairs. Everyone applauded. Hertzog alone was visibly out of sympathy. He did not join in the three cheers led by Botha. He eyed the cheerleader with ill-concealed suspicion.

Botha, indeed, committed sin after sin. Particularly in educational matters he did not display the "right spirit." Two mining millionaires, Julius Wernler and Alfred Beit, had bequeathed half a million pounds to the University of Cape Town. The Unionist spokesmen, Sir Lionel Phillips and Sir Starr Jameson, pleaded for a worthy use of this sum. But almost unanimously the Boer members wanted to use the legacy for fostering the study of archaic, primitive *Taal,* not for purposes of educational excellence. Botha did not side strongly enough with them, they complained. Smuts' attitude seemed indiscernible, yet his heart was in Pretoria, not in Cape Town. At the founding of the Pretoria University, an *Afrikaans* language institute, he expressed the hope that this seat of learning would become the Oxford of South Africa. In educational matters, however, he stuck to his principle of compulsory English with Dutch optional, in the schools.

On November 24, 1910, a fiery debate over the Free State Education Act incensed the House of Assembly. The Unionists asserted that this act conflicted with the principles of freedom and equality. Hertzog riposted with a fighting speech. Botha finally decided that a select committee should inquire into the matter. The mere fact that an inquiry in his own domain was to be held increased Hertzog's hostility against Botha. The report of the Select Committee dealt Hertzog's school system a crushing blow. Now Botha was forced to act. He could not disappoint the Unionists too strongly. After all, it was still their industry that carried, almost alone, the burden of taxation, whereas the Boer farmers were practically tax-exempt. The English did not complain about this condition. They knew that any government that tried to impose even most modest levies upon agriculture would be swept away by irate *backveld* farmers. They had to put up with many things. The *platteland* constituencies were violently opposed to regulations for combating pests and diseases or for the scientific treatment of the many scourges of plant life and the eradication of poisonous varieties. All this would be against God's will. Many bearded representatives of the *backveld* in the House were just as intransigent on the color question. Smuts' new Constitution had made this problem a state affair, not a Federal one. Thus the men from the backwoods could still stick to the old Transvaal *grondwet* classifying the population as *mannen* (men), *vrouwen* (women), and *schepsels* (creatures). Only about the educational question, on the solution of which the future of their own children depended, the Unionists were unyielding. At their insistence, and based upon the findings of the Select Committee, General Botha asked the provinces to conform to certain principles in the management of their schools, in order to attain equality without compulsion. Although he had addressed his demand to all the four States, the Orange Free State alone was meant. The Free State complied. Its schools were purged of Hertzogism. The revolution that Smuts had foreseen did not break out immediately. But when it eventually came, the aroused parents of the Free States formed the most violent mob in the fray.

In April, 1911, Botha visited London once more, again to attend a conference of colonial prime ministers. This time the conference was called Imperial Conference, to soothe the sensitive feelings of the peoples in the Dominions. Hertzog, however, scented the Imperial devil. His suspicions were vindicated by a number of events in London. Botha was lionized. He was promoted honorary general in the British Army, an honor otherwise reserved for royalty. He became a Privy Councillor. At the King's levee he appeared in the prescribed knee breeches and silk stockings. His picture was taken in this attire. Smuts took good care that it should not be published or otherwise circulated at home. Yet the news that Botha wore silk stockings spread like wildfire throughout the *platteland*. Losberg, his own constituency, was perturbed. Some called him *Engelsman* —Englishman—a calculated insult.

The worst came to the worst. On the anniversary of Union Day Botha addressed a London audience, ending with the words: "No more loyal and wholehearted part of the Empire exists than the land where Dutch and English brethren live together in amity—the Union of South Africa."

At home, Hertzog replied with poisonous speeches. He complained that too much was said about the Empire and too little about South Africa. His hostility against his chief was now completely undisguised.

On May 7, the first census of united South Africa disclosed that the country, four times as big as Great Britain and Ireland together, had only 1,255,545 white inhabitants, against a colored majority of 4,621,531. The Unionists used this figure, which frightened the whole country, and most of all the conservative Boers, into demanding the encouragement of white immigration. Smuts agreed, and campaigned for the idea, with the proviso, however, that only the right type should be invited to come; no city loafers, no poor whites. Characteristically, he extended his welcome even to the persecuted Russian Jews, "the Maimonideses and Spinozas of the future South Africa." Botha, for his part, told the Eighty Club in London that his country was wide open to new English settlers.

Once more Hertzog bristled. The Empire-builders and Imperialists were influencing the *papbroek*—weaklings. He did not need to add that he meant Botha and Smuts. He poured contempt on the very idea of a new wave of immigration. At the height of his combative spirit he even ventured into Johannesburg. It was his first visit after thirteen months in office. Like Oom Paul before him, he loathed the foreign town. Johannesburg was heavily policed when the Minister of Justice arrived. Surrounded by a cavalcade of mounted police, Hertzog

drove right into the Dutch suburb of Turffontein. There he let
off steam. Referring to Botha's prolonged stay in England, he
declared: "In the ambitions of Europe we do not participate.
In its intrigues we do not share. With its quarrels we have no
concern. State-aided immigration would be a national crime."

Smuts found it high time for Botha to return home. The
Premier complied. Upon his arrival in Cape Town, he moved
into the Prime Minister's official residence, the Groote Schuur,
bequeathed by Cecil Rhodes. His first act was to unveil a memorial to the colossus. He eulogized the instigator of the Jameson
Raid. With Sir Starr Jameson, once the raider, now the leader
of the opposition in Parliament, Hertzog was on amiable terms.
It was characteristic for this man that he retained his courteous
manners and his *bonhomie* toward everyone, and particularly
toward English acquaintances. But when Botha uttered a few
appreciative words about Rhodes, Hertzog was outraged.

Smuts kept aloof in so far as he could from the domestic
quarrel. He had more important things on his mind, a variety
of things. As Minister of Mines he introduced a bill on an extremely difficult subject—miner's phthisis; his speech displayed
accurate medical knowledge. But the miners objected to his
proposals. Smuts insisted on the principle of contributions by
the miners themselves, in order to make them more careful
while at work. The miners were no longer old Cornishmen, but
mostly young Boers from the *platteland,* to whom a miner's
wage meant an almost incredible fortune. Yet they declined to
have contributions to a medical fund deducted. They found
strong support among the Boer politicians. Smuts was accused
of listening too carefully to Sir Lionel Phillips, who was now,
indeed, among his advisers. For the first time Smuts was called
"unsocial."

He made a few remarks which seemed to justify this label.
At Barkley-West, the diamond center of a Kimberley already
past its prime, the diggers asked for a Royal Commission to
inquire into their living conditions. Smuts answered that there
was a less expensive and more expeditious way of arriving at a

solution. They could safely leave matters in his hands. He meant every word. But the diggers only heard the refusal of their claims. Around the corner, in Kimberley itself, he was waylaid by Dutch inhabitants who complained about the poverty in the dying town. Perhaps things would be better if one ousted the English townspeople? "It appears to me that the rich are getting too rich, and the poor are getting too poor," Smuts replied. "But I do not wish to speak, because the older I get, the more I am convinced that speeches do greater harm than good." However, he refused the suggestion to oust the English. Only one policy, he asserted, had a chance of success —the policy of co-operation.

As Minister of Defence he introduced in the House, on March 1, 1911, his great scheme for building the Defence Force. Immediately General Beyers rose in opposition. He had been Speaker in the old Transvaal House of Legislation, but had lost this dignity in the Union Assembly. He bore Smuts and Botha a grudge, and displayed it by attacking the Defense Bill. Smuts did not answer. He had another plan. It was always his preferred method to reconcile his opponents. Now he offered the ex-commandant, who had played only an insignificant role in the Boer War, the post of Commander in Chief of the Union's Defence Force. Beyers snatched at it with both hands. Hertzog shook his head, and remained strangely silent. But *Die Week,* a young Pretoria newspaper, attacked the Defence Plan tooth and nail. It was "based on a foreign system," wrote the editor, Mr. Oost, who was mildly famous as the villain in many dramas staged by amateur theatrical societies. Only a few weeks later the fact filtered out that *Die Week* was owned by a group of capitalists who had entrusted Hertzog with its management.

Hertzog had good reason for once to keep out of the struggle. A cabinet reshuffle was under way, and the change might have involved his enforced retirement. He himself had already frequently threatened to leave the government. But such a menace was nothing but blackmail. He craved power, concealing this desire behind the reiterated statement that he owed it

to the Boer people to remain. He must control the inner workings of the Cabinet.

Now more power came to him. He emerged from the shuffle
as Minister of Native Affairs in addition to his post as Minister
of Justice. The appointment was only made in order to have
the troublesome Free Stater aligned as an associate, rather than
allowing him to run riot as a foe. Smuts dropped his two minor
jobs, and in exchange added the Ministry of Finance to the
Defence.

Hertzog was not placated. The tension in the House grew
when Sir Starr Jameson, who had acquired something of his
friend Cecil Rhodes' desire to co-operate with the Dutch, retired from the leadership of the Unionist Party, to be replaced
by Sir Thomas Smartt, a more energetic and combative man.
Under Sir Thomas' leadership the Unionists demanded that
South Africa's contribution to the Royal Navy should be in
proportion to the sea-borne trade of the Union, which was
entirely dependent on the British fleet. Sir Thomas pointed out
Canada, which contributed seven million pounds annually to
the Empire's naval defences, and the example of the tiny Straits
Settlements, which had just donated a Dreadnought to England. Much to Botha's and Smuts' regret the opposition motion
was defeated.

Hertzog was in his element. On October 5, 1912, in a speech
at Nylstroem, he burst out. He mixed rude personal attacks
against Sir Thomas Smartt and against Colonel Byron, a distinguished soldier and member of the Orange Free State Legislative Council, calling them "foreign adventurers," with a furious
statement that South Africa was sick of being governed by
aliens.

The speech exploded like a bombshell. The Cabinet was
deeply perturbed. Yet Smuts still made excuses for Hertzog.
He tried to explain some unsavory expressions used by his colleague such as "bastard sheep," and "caked dung adhering to
a kraal wall" as similes in the language used on the *veld*. Perhaps Hertzog would apologize for his forceful expressions. But
Hertzog replied: "I make no apologies—I have never done so!"

This was what made the essential difference between him and Smuts.

Social relations between Hertzog and the opposition members were instantly interrupted. The English members cold-shouldered him. Easily hurt, as Hertzog was, despite his own rudeness, this treatment drove him to a frenzy. On December 7 he produced another burst of eloquence. He addressed the villagers of De Wildt in the Transvaal district of Rustenburg: "South Africa should be governed by pure Afrikanders. . . . Had we chosen to heed certain voices, we would by now have presented Great Britain with twenty to thirty Dreadnoughts. . . . Imperialism interests me only as far as it benefits South Africa. . . . The main object is to keep the Dutch and the English separated." He was ready, he concluded, to stake his whole future on this thesis. And so he did.

For at least one of his cabinet colleagues, this was too much. Colonel Sir George Leuchars, a Minister from Natal, resigned immediately. He did not wish to serve with a man who wanted to squeeze the Empire and then throw it away like a sucked orange.

The Cabinet sustained a further blow. While Hertzog reveled in his mischief-making, in a faraway *dorp,* Botha appealed for conciliation in English-speaking Grahamstown, the center of the Eastern Province. But Hertzog's challenge disgusted the English voters. The candidate of the Unionist opposition was elected by an overwhelming majority. The Cape Colonials did not care for a government that spoke with two voices. Smuts' whole conception of racial reconciliation was shattered.

Hertzog rejoiced in Colonel Leuchars' resignation. "One of my colleagues was too weak to digest that fare," he grinned.

Botha sent him word that the entire Cabinet would appreciate it if Hertzog, too, would resign. Hertzog replied in a message to the whole Cabinet: "I have merely said what every good Afrikander is entitled to say." Tenaciously he clung to his office.

Even Abraham Fischer, his ex-premier and colleague from the Free State Cabinet, could not persuade him to sign a letter regretting his utterances at De Wildt and to promise no longer to speak about controversial matters without his prime minister's consent. Hertzog read the letter. "Smuts has drafted it," he said suspiciously. His suspicion was well founded. "Tell him to go into a lunatic asylum," was Hertzog's reply.

Saturday, December 14, 1912, at midday, Botha's private secretary informed ex-Minister Hertzog that the Prime Minister had resigned on behalf of the whole Cabinet. Silently, Hertzog closed his desk, and walked home.

A week later Botha announced his new cabinet. Both Leuchars and Hertzog were dropped.

In his fall Hertzog had risen to become the hero of the *platteland*. But the bulk of the Boers, shrewd politicians, refused to follow him into the wilderness. If they turned against the government they would lose pork and patronage. Some of them were guided by higher motives. Lord de Villiers, South Africa's most eminent jurist, himself a proud Afrikander, expressed a low opinion of Hertzog's statesmanlike qualities. Even Grandfather Abraham Fischer, throughout the past Hertzog's nominal leader, disassociated himself from the prodigal son. "He has made impossible personal demands," the old man explained to his constituents in Bethlehem. "He lost the support of the Free State members largely through his want of tact. He has the faults of his youth. There are members in the government who have done for the country ten times as much as he did. They don't deserve to be called traitors and men without principles."

The farmers of Bethlehem listened attentively. Then they resolved by 261 to 152 votes a motion of non-confidence—of non-confidence in their lifelong leader Fischer, who was leaving Hertzog in the lurch. Brokenhearted, the veteran Boer leader dropped out of politics. A few months later he died.

In the Park of Pretoria a poorly attended meeting was held, protesting against Hertzog's dismissal. Advocate Tielman Johannes de Villiers Roos, a promising young barrister, presided.

Around him five members of Parliament—five out of a hundred and twenty-one—were gathered. A few disgruntled professional politicians joined them. The population of the capital was conspicuously absent. The meeting appeared to be a flop. Yet it marked the beginning of the Afrikander crusade that eventually burst out in civil war, and repeatedly came close to it. The unholy crusade split South Africa from top to bottom. To this very day the split has not yet healed.

Chapter 17   PRELUDE TO CIVIL WAR

AFTER LOSING THE FIRST ROUND IN HIS QUARREL WITH BOTHA, Hertzog turned his guns against Smuts. This was the man whom he held responsible for his own abject dismissal. For once, Hertzog was right. Botha might perhaps have tried to patch together a new compromise. But Smuts, although himself a compromiser by natural inclination, knew where to draw a definite line. His inflexible determination had, indeed, been the principal factor in the Cabinet's decision of December, 1912, to resign collectively.

Few people knew the inside story. Parliament was not unduly disturbed. Hertzog himself remained in the government camp, then called the South African Party. But their uncanny instinct for politics—their strongest instinct, and, by the same token, their most comfortable means of livelihood—told the Boers that something was going wrong behind the scenes. They did not like the development. In their political perversion they found fault not with the hysteric troublemaker, but with the man of right, justice and order, the protagonist of co-operation.

Hertzog had just begun his crusade when Smuts found the

going difficult. A few days after the Cabinet reorganization he addressed the voters in Paardekraal. Making a virtue of necessity, he thanked Providence for having saved South Africa from the fate of many a country whose inhabitants led monotonous, drab lives. *Ex Africa semper aliquid novi* was at that time his favorite quotation. But it is doubtful whether the bearded *backvelders* from Paardekraal were strongly impressed by Pliny's unintelligible phrase. Smuts' sense of humor was never infectious. It certainly did not sweep Paardekraal. Hastily he fell back on his *leitmotiv:* the banishing of bitterness and recrimination, and the necessary unity between Briton and Boer, lest South African people should become the tools of other nations. He did not mention the increasing German peril, but an allusion to the Defense Act which would involve sacrifices, was unmistakable. He felt sure, he concluded, that the Transvaal, at least, would act as it had always acted, sensibly and circumspectly.

Here Smuts' lofty patriotism erred. The Transvaal had rarely acted sensibly and circumspectly. Paardekraal, the typical Transvaal Dutch *dorp,* was in an indifferent mood, when Smuts left. Two weeks later he addressed a meeting at Rustenburg, the center of the most nationalistic district in the Transvaal, where he met with open hostility. Before he could begin his speech, the local *predikant,* the Reverend Mr. Vorster, jumped up, and barked at the Minister to refrain from discussing the crisis; such a discussion would give offense. Shrewdly, Smuts decided to speak as the veteran Boer general and the famous guerrilla fighter rather than as the Union Minister. He spoke in ringing, nationalistic tones, yet he staunchly defended his and Botha's policy of conciliation, and concluded with a strong assertion that he, at any rate, would stand by it, firm as a rock. He burned his boats behind him. But he did not convince his audience, most of whom had listened to Hertzog's venomous outpourings in neighboring De Wildt, and were completely under the spell of the Fuehrer-in-the-making.

Smuts soon had another proof of what a profound impression Hertzog's expulsion from the Cabinet had made on the nation. In May, 1913, the voters of Pretoria West, his own constituents, adopted, in their member's absence, a motion censuring General Smuts for his attitude in the Hertzog dispute.

This motion of censure, an unparalleled act of ingratitude after all Smuts had done for Pretoria, was the direct result of the "gospel of Hertzogism," as an open letter, six newspaper columns long, which Hertzog had published in March, was called. In his habitual involved and cumbersome style Hertzog poured out atrocious accusations against Botha and Smuts, reviewing his running feud with them, which now entered the third year. He concluded with an appeal to the Boers, to approve his "creed."

The entire English-language press called the manifesto the confessions of a dangerous fanatic. The ruling South African Party Organization condemned him. In Parliament he still had only five adherents. Opposition, however, makes strange bedfellows. The Parliamentary session during the first half of 1913 witnessed an unmistakable rapprochement between the Britain-baiter Hertzog and Major Creswell, the leader of the handful of Labor members, a distinguished English gentleman with a social Messiah complex, looking and acting very much like a forerunner of Sir Stafford Cripps.

No couple was, both in spiritual make-up and in physical appearance, worse matched than the sudden team-mates Creswell and Hertzog. Major Frederick Hugh Page Creswell was a tall, tight-lipped, immaculately attired Englishman, imbued with a silent but profound patriotism, a peace-minded man, although his bushy eyebrows and his prominent nose indicated that he could also be a sturdy fighter. But his every movement, as well as his strong emotions, were rigidly controlled. He was a gentleman, and so he sided with the underdog.

Hertzog, on the other hand, was at that time a spare figure, with a narrow chest and elevated shoulders, his deep-set black eyes almost hidden behind his spectacles, gesticulating hysterically and histrionically, constantly losing the thread of his rambling, hair-splitting, repetitious speeches, a weakling consumed by the desire to be top dog. German by descent, he was a foreigner to the people. He had to out-Boer the Boers. His mind was confined to the narrow range of subjects understood by the *platteland*. His every thought was bitter, his every word acid. He thrived on the imaginary wrongs he and "his" people suffered. They had never lost the Boer War; they had been betrayed by the criminals of Vereeniging, the pact Hertzog himself had signed. Now they were a people scattered and oppressed, a nation trodden under foot. He could not speak less than three hours at a time. He was frequently laughed at, particularly by the Englishmen in the towns. They could not believe that a single man could succeed in upsetting the democratic system of the new Union. But Hertzog kindled the slow-burning *veld* fire. The flames spread, and in their glowing light his dark shadow lay heavily across the land.

Creswell disliked Smuts because he suspected him of a lack of social conscience. This suspicion was so strong that it led him to find associates wherever he could, to attack the government. He must have been appalled by Hertzog's parliamentary manners and language. He certainly saw through the hollowness and emptiness of Hertzog's harping on his old obsession, anti-Imperialism, and of his loudly proclaimed loyalty to never-defined principles. Creswell once interrupted a wild Hertzog oration with the question: "What are these principles?" "The party exists for its principles, and not the principles for the party!" was the answer. To Creswell it was the peak of platitude. But the Boer people preferred the thunder to the substance, and since they were in the majority, Creswell believed, he could use and direct them in line with his lofty social aims. From January 24 till June 16, 1913, Creswell and Hertzog were working together, unostentatiously, careful, united only in opposition to Smuts.

Hertzog was still a member of the South African Party. He never gave up a position before being forcibly driven out. He resolved to undermine the Botha-Smuts regime from the inside. He formed his cells; the "Vigilance Committee."

The gang was quickly assembled. Hertzog's right- and left-hand men were both British citizens by birth, sons of the Cape Colony. Neither of them had, like Smuts, given up his British citizenship. They were not honest foes, but insidious traitors during the Boer War. At the beginning it appeared that Advocate Roos of Pretoria would become Hertzog's number two man, and, indeed, he held this position for some time. Born in Cape Town, Roos had followed the nationalistic trek to Pretoria, where he emerged into the open as chairman at the protest meeting against Hertzog's dismissal. Political circles had known him already as the leader of the "Young Turks," the radical youngsters, always ready to egg on Botha and Smuts. At the age of thirty-four, when he came to the forefront, he was already pale, bald, and bloated; unhealthy to the marrow, but excelling by his biting tongue and his roaring voice. He became known as the "lion of the Transvaal," although his main qualities were more those of the hyena. He regarded politics as a game, he frankly confessed in Parliament, yet he played the game seriously, indefatigably traveling up and down the country to wrest the Transvaal from Botha and Smuts. On the side he was in charge of his movement's relations with the labor wing of the British population. The youth of South Africa, even some English-born, found him great fun. A most useful body of youthful admirers followed him everywhere. Among them was Advocate Hans Van Rensburg, already in his budding days regarded as South Africa's infant prodigy, who became Advocate Roos' private secretary as the first step to a remarkable career.

Tielman Roos and his opposite and rival, Dr. Daniel François Malan, had only one similarity. Each had, already in his early years, a sagging double chin. Since this was, like the paunch, a sign of affluence, it did not really matter. Otherwise they were complete antagonists. To noisy, boisterous, swaggering Roos, life was a riot. To pious, stern, never-smiling Malan it was a burden, to be borne with humility and respectability. True, under the cover of humbleness a consuming flame of envy burned. Its object was Smuts. Both had come from the same village, Riebeek West. Jannie was only four years older, but he was advancing in rapid strides, much beloved, much maligned, ever

in the center of talk and things, while Malan had to struggle as
an underpaid schoolteacher until he was ordained a *predikant*
in the Dutch Reformed Church. His first parish was the village
of Montagu in the Western Province. He did not endear himself to his happy-go-lucky parishioners, all prosperous wine
growers, in preaching temperance and even abstinence. He was
shifted to Graaff-Reinet, the original home of the Afrikander
Bond and the stronghold of Afrikanderdom in the Cape. Here
his somber sermons were listened to by bigoted Calvinists.
Only when he mingled carefully couched, but vitriolic anti-
English remarks with his monotonous litany, faint smiles lighted
the morose, sullen faces of the congregation.

Jannie was a Rhodes-man at that time. Young but unyouthful Dr. Malan felt sure he would catch up with him, and smash
him. He devoted himself to serious social work, with an early
premonition of vote-getting. But the Synod of the Dutch Reformed Church did not tolerate social work, suspecting leftish
tendencies. Unmistakably Dr. Malan was told that he could not
obtain the professorship in Stellenbosch he coveted.

Predikant Dr. Malan abandoned holy orders, but he could
never rid himself of the attitude and mask of the divine. His
small, restless eyes hid behind unrimmed glasses. His voice
sounded unctuous, and his every phrase allowed of three different interpretations.

Among the other henchmen of the gang was Beyers, whom
Botha had helped into politics in the old days and who had
subsequently become Speaker of the House and finally Commander in Chief of the Union Defence Force. He was an implacable racialist, yet intensely religious in a somber Calvinistic
way, superstitious like many Boer "generals," inordinately vain
of his personal appearance, a true megalomaniac. A similar
"general" was Jan Christoffel Greyling Kemp, the son of a
wealthy farmer, an illiterate until his eighteenth year, who had
during the Boer War become the right-hand man of the most
Christian General De La Rey, "Oom Koos" to the entire country. A born fighter, a true *velds* man, he deserted his chief at
Vereeniging, threw in his lot with the "bitter-enders," and

vowed to wrestle with Smuts for the rest of his life. He is still true to his vow.

Last, but not least, General Christiaan de Wet was one of the crowd. An irascible, uncouth-looking giant, reactionary to the core, his wrinkled face hidden behind a jungle of a beard à la Kruger, an irate foe of those British, who regarded the Kafirs as human, whereas everyone in the Free State knew that the natives were less than animals, he had a domineering personality. Strangely, he was slavishly devoted to one man, thirty years his junior, a weakling, entirely lacking in all military virtues. But when friends heckled de Wet about his clamorous allegiance to Hertzog, he used to answer: "The general is not a soldier. He is a lawyer." To the illiterate General de Wet, whose best-selling memoirs of the Boer War had been written by a staff of ghosts, a lawyer, even a shyster lawyer in the small town of Bloemfontein, was a higher being. The strong-featured man with protruding nose and thick eyebrows, always clad in a conservative, if amply stained frock coat with silk revers, had been the head of the Hertzog Demonstration Committee at Pretoria. He proved his allegiance again at the "Dungheap Demonstration," so-called for the aroma of the speeches, on December 28, 1912, when he noisily protested against Hertzog's expulsion. Deceitful even in his angry outburst, he reminded his audience that a few years after the Boer War he had been dragged by the hair into the Free State Cabinet—as Minister for Agriculture—but soon had left it, recognizing that there were more educated men who could profitably replace him. After Hertzog's fall he resigned also from the Defence Council presided over by Smuts. The martinet became a mere rabble-rouser.

The gang was assembled, and ready for action, when the attention of the country was diverted by an explosion in a different quarter.

Once again the miners in Johannesburg got out of hand. The lawabiding citizens were not astonished. They were accustomed to minor strikes that paralyzed their town for a few hours, or for a day or two. They took their habitual precautions. They filled their bathtubs to the brim, since the water supply would probably be cut. They had ample stores of candles; there would be no electric light. All meetings and appointments were suspended. It was not even necessary to call them off. No one ventured out of his house without a compelling reason.

This strike, they were sure, would be just another nuisance. The management of the Kleinfontein mine, a lesser one on the Rand, had extended the working hours for mechanics underground until half-past four in the afternoon, on Saturdays until one or one-thirty, to fit in with the mining shift. The order concerned only five men. But the Unions, banking on the general political unrest in the country, and having accumulated large unused funds, were spoiling for a fight. They called out their men. Bands of strikers marched through the streets. This happened on May 26.

Two leaders of the industry, Sir Lionel Phillips and Mr. Chaplin, asked for government protection. But neither Botha nor Smuts cared to side with big business against the youth of the *platteland* that now formed the large majority of white labor in the mines. Throughout the month of June the situation deteriorated. The strikers, emboldened by the government's attitude of wait and see, dragged out the men who wanted to remain at work. They felt in a safe strategic position. Only seven thousand men of the Imperial troops had remained in the country. The old commando force was disarmed, and Smuts' Defence Force was still in a formative stage.

Shivering, Johannesburg recognized that this was not a flare-up of the usual minor variety. The jobless and the poor whites, a large group in the town Smuts had frequently called the Mecca of hooliganism, could not miss their golden opportunity. The houses of "scabs" were stormed and burned down. Innocent bystanders, among them women and children, were killed. On Thursday, July 3, things took a dangerous turn. The huge Market Square was the scene of a large and unruly strikers' meeting, in which the whole mob of Johannesburg joined with a vengeance. Only at this moment, after keeping aloof for almost six uneasy weeks, Smuts, in his capacity as Minister of Defence, asked the Governor General Lord Gladstone for the intervention of Imperial troops.

London cabled in reply to Lord Gladstone's inquiry that the local Defence Forces should be used in preference to Imperial troops. The Empire had no reason to become involved in a purely domestic trouble of the self-governing Union. Imperial troops had only the task of watching the borders of South Africa against an enemy attack. In the summer of 1913 it was expected that the Germans might strike at any moment.

The local Police Force proved entirely inadequate. On Friday, the Fourth of July, an open revolt flared up in the center of Johannesburg. The offices of the *Star,* the leading English-language newspaper, were set on fire. The houses of the mine owners were surrounded by threatening crowds. The three thousand policemen as well as the entire detective corps were helpless. In this moment of emergency four thousand British regulars occupied the Market Square. They were under orders to use arms only in self-defense. So they confined themselves to pushing the mob here and there, but made no attempt to clear the square and establish the full authority of the law.

The law was a sham. The Union government had forbidden incendiary strike meetings. But no one paid any attention. Continuous squabbles between the police and the rabble flared up. General O'Brien, the Imperial officer in command, a fighting Irishman, wanted to get the situation under control. The High Commissioner, however, who had personally come to Johannesburg, still forbade the use of arms.

Large groups of strikers and sympathizers flooded Commissioner Street, lined with the huge office buildings of the mining companies. All offices were closed. The good people were hurrying home. The mob started upsetting their cars and cabs. At nightfall the Park Railway Station and the building of the Argus Printing and Publishing Company were burned down. Before midnight, the mob attacked Corner House, the seat of one of the largest corporations. At this moment the police opened fire. The mob was dispersed.

On the next morning, Saturday, the government became alarmed. Throughout the forenoon citizens were enrolled as special constables, and armed. In the meantime the crowd attempted to storm the Rand Club, the gathering place of the mine owners. A ferocious battle between Imperial troops, the police, and the rabble ensued. Again blood was spilled. Twenty-one people were killed, and almost fifty wounded.

But the worst was still to come. The natives in the mines, two hundred fifty thousand in all, adopted a threatening attitude. They were in no way connected with the strike, purely a matter between management and white labor. But a later investigation proved that Russian "syndicalists," as the pre-war Communists were called, had enticed the Kafirs to take a hand in the game.

Botha's and Smuts' arrival on Saturday morning prevented the worst. They drove through the riotous streets right to the Carlton Hotel, where they received four delegates from the Trade Unions led by a man called Bain. The Ministers were unescorted. They had literally taken their lives in their hands. They knew they must act. Another night of uproar would not have been a repetition of carnage and arson alone. The gold mines were no longer safe. So much dynamite had passed unchecked into the possession of the miners that they would easily have been able to blow up the mines.

Botha and Smuts were unarmed as well. The four delegates had heavy revolvers at their belts. While they presented their insolent demands, hell broke loose in front of the hotel. Thousands of hooligans were assembled, barely kept under control by Imperial troops. "The very moment the General commands fire, I will shoot him," said one man of the delegation, leaning out of the window. The other negotiators were satisfied that they had the two unarmed Ministers "covered." Neither Botha nor Smuts was aware that their lives were imperiled. But they knew of a graver peril: unless they were able to restore order, the mines would be ruined for good, the town would be robbed and plundered, and the Kafirs let loose on the wives and the children. Under the impact of this threat, the two generals surrendered unconditionally. They signed an agreement, granting all the strikers' demands.

In the evening, they visited the Orange Grove Hotel, three miles outside the city. On their way they were waylaid by an irate mob, threatening to shoot. "We are unarmed," Botha cried. "Shoot! But we are here to make peace for you, and if you kill us, all that is finished."

Smuts did not utter a word.

In this same hotel the Ministers were met by Sir Lionel Phillips and Sir George Farrar, the leaders of the mine owners. Botha explained the situation: "The military advisers told us that they were able to restore order in town, but that they could not guarantee the protection of the mines and the villages along the Reef. Besides," he added with a sharp touch, "I am not prepared to face a large expenditure of blood—neither of the rioters themselves nor of innocent spectators."

Smuts remained silent. Obviously, his complete capitulation had shaken him to the depths. All South Africa resounded with criticism. The "Bain Treaty" seemed a proof that the government had abdicated to let the gangsters run the country.

Work was resumed on the following Monday. But it was no longer regular work. The strike leaders were drunk with triumph. Discipline was gone. Many miners, particularly among the young Boers, were flagrantly indolent. The nationalistic wave among the Boers was coalescing with their social self-assertion. The atmosphere was electric. Victory had whetted fresh appetites. Sinister threats against directors were uttered at Union meetings. The tension lasted for half a year.

One day in December, as Sir Lionel Phillips was approaching the Rand Club for luncheon, he was assaulted. A man emerged from a shop, drew a double-barreled revolver, fired, and missed. Sir Lionel jumped at his assailant, advancing about eight paces, when a second bullet got him in the lung. Yet the undaunted elderly Englishman still applied a well-aimed left to his assailant's chin. The criminal fired three more shots. But in the struggle, he missed. Sir Lionel collapsed on the pavement, but pulled himself together again and renewed the fight. The fourth shot entered his neck.

At first the terrified bystanders bolted. Then they steadily crept up behind the criminal. Just as he fired for the fifth time they grabbed his gun. The last bullet missed wildly, hit a window, and landed in a room in the Corner House.

The assailant was later identified as a crank peddler by the name of Misnum, who had been thrown off the grounds of Sir Lionel's company. He seriously believed that since the strike there was open season on mining magnates. He bought a second-hand revolver, practiced the whole morning by shooting at trees, and cheerfully went to wait for his prey. He was sentenced to a term of fifteen years, which he spent in the asylum for criminal lunatics.

Toward the end of December General Smuts came to visit the convalescing patient in the hospital. He was glad to see that Sir Lionel, his old friend, was rapidly recovering. Casually he remarked that another strike, this time on a somewhat larger scale, was about to break out. He expected it on New Year's Day. But this time his government was prepared.

A grave depression throughout the country was the consequence of the miners' strike in Johannesburg and of the six ensuing months of incertitude on the Rand. Unemployment increased. Radical agitation set in. Hertzog sensed the decay on which he thrived. He wooed labor, not only, as before, the British section, but now primarily the Boer youth working in factories and mines. Maintaining close relations with some Dutch financiers and occasionally soliciting contributions for his cause, it is true, never for himself, he became, by the same token, the apologist of the poor whites. His dupes were the half-educated white-collar class who hated the exclusively English-run world of business; railway employees, petty civil servants, small shopkeepers who saw their livelihood endangered by the up-and-coming department stores. Hertzog never appealed to primitive greed for money. He simply promised the millennium when the Afrikander, the pure race—incidentally a mixture of Dutch, Huguenot, much German, and some Portuguese blood —would be the *baas* all over the country. His anti-Imperialism was tinged with a good admixture of lucrative promises.

The Empire Parliamentary Association came to visit Cape Town. Smuts received the gentlemen with a superb speech on the problems of South Africa, not concealing the difficulties of a young country, but proudly stressing the immense progress that had been made in the eleven years since the war. Lord Emmot, in reply, bore eloquent testimony to the "brilliant speech of General Smuts," and Lord Sheffield lauded it as "the most remarkable speech we have heard on our tour."

Two British lordships praising Smuts was too much for the suspiciously watching Hertzog. He was resolved to break away completely. The final split came on November 13 at a Party meeting. The South African Party was divided between adherents to the government, and followers of Hertzogism. General de Wet, in his highest combative spirit, launched the first attack. He proposed to elect ex-President Steyn leader of the party outside the Parliament with the power to nominate a Prime Minister.

A leader outside Parliament lording over a puppet-government was, in 1913, an innovation. It was clearly a ruse to do away with Botha and Smuts. All eyes were centered on Hertzog. "On personal grounds I would give Botha my hand!" he said amidst general cheers. "But on political grounds," he contradicted himself as usual, "I would be obliged to withdraw the hand at once!"

Botha won the division, but only by 131 to 90 votes. Hertzog and his followers rose silently, and left the hall. Only de Wet could not keep his mouth shut. "Adieu!" he shouted to those remaining behind. It was an open declaration of war. Immediately Hertzog started to organize his Nationalist Party. The union of brothers was definitely wrecked.

Another appeal for Botha's dismissal hurt Smuts much more deeply. Again his own constituents of Pretoria West attacked the government. They asked Smuts to interfere on behalf of Botha's resignation. Pretoria West was a quarter largely settled by railway employees. Rumors of impending cuts in their salaries, and mass dismissals had aroused their ire.

In fact, the general manager of the railways announced that he would have to discharge some hundreds of his men. The powerful Society of Railway and Harbor Servants took up the gantlet. Mr. Sauer, then Minister for Railways, tried to bring about a peaceful solution of the conflict. But the leader of the railway men refused his offer. This man, by the name of H. J. Poutsma, was the prototype of the power-drunk labor boss, who for five or six ensuing years tyrannized the Rand. He was an adventurous character. He had started upon his career with anarchistic "propaganda of the deed" in his native Holland, served a term of a few years, emigrated to South Africa, became a leader of the Free State contingent in the South African war, fled after the defeat, founded a short-lived Negro republic in Basutoland, returned to South Africa after self-government was introduced, became a Union agitator, and soon the recognized boss of Afrikaans labor, and ended, after having spent half his life in "syndicalism" and under the red flag, as a violent ultra-nationalist Hertzog man. At the time he decreed the railway strike he was sure that he could establish a proletarian dictatorship in the Union simply by choking all traffic in a country of such tremendous distances.

Precisely as Smuts had foreseen it, the strike began on New Year's Day 1914, exactly five minutes after Botha had returned on the last train to Pretoria. The railway men themselves were divided as to the wisdom of their Union's action. But Poutsma tolerated no opposition. "Scabs" were violently pulled from engines, and generally banned from railway premises. The life line of South African traffic, the route between Johannesburg and Pretoria, was paralyzed.

At this propitious moment the Rand Federation of Trades decided to declare a general strike in sympathy with their comrades from the railways. Again Johannesburg suffered two days of mob violence and terror. The Germiston Station at the East

Rand, the center of the railway system and the most important junction in South Africa, was attacked by strikers and the associated hoodlums. The General Strike Committee issued an order to the Trade Unions to transform their membership into commandos, to strengthen the "forces" behind the strike.

While the whole country was, for the second time within half a year, in convulsion, idyllic Bloemfontein, the capital of the Free State, alone maintained its dignified quiet. The danger was not far away. The natives employed in the diamond mines near the neighboring small town of Jagersfontein were running amuck. But the first Congress of the newly founded Nationalistic Party, in session at Bloemfontein, kept completely aloof from the disaster that had befallen the country. Hertzog indulged in vitriolic speeches against the government, and none of his henchmen uttered a single word about the social revolution, into which the general strike was rapidly degenerating.

True to the style of Oom Paul, whose memory the faithful disciple could never forget, General Smuts had waited until the tortoise had stuck out her head. But now he acted with energy and precision. He declared martial law along the Reef, and called out his burgher forces. He had, he later disclosed, got in touch with London. The Imperial government had uttered the gravest objections to another show of force. But London recognized that the Union government was at liberty to make its own decision.

The country, although torn by the strife engendered by Hertzog, responded on the whole favorably to the call to arms. Even in the restive Free State the people rallied round the government. The Wolmaranstad commando, in its full force of one thousand men, assembled twenty-four hours after Smuts' call had reached its commander. This occurred in a large and thinly populated district, which was generally regarded as Hertzog territory.

But as the burgher force was moving ahead, it proved that they were, above all, eager to show the English town of Johannesburg what a Boer commando could do. They were by no means marching to support Smuts and Botha. On the contrary, a majority of the men found this emergency an excellent opportunity to unseat the government, and to proclaim the Republic. True to their old traditions, the commandos interrupted their advance as they pleased, held meetings, and became intoxicated on mutinous speeches. In the meantime the rumor spread in Johannesburg that Hertzog with 2,500 Free Staters was coming to the aid of the strikers. It is possible that this rumor was deliberately spread; it was in line with Hertzog's wooing of labor. But it did not sound at all like him. General Hertzog, one of the first heroes to drop out of the Boer War, kept well away from any firing line for the rest of his life.

The Free State contingent that actually marched towards Johannesburg was led by Deneys Reitz. A few miles outside Johannesburg, General Beyers, Commander in Chief of the Defence Force, joined the commando. He appeared in full-dress uniform, and delivered a sanguinary speech, attacking Botha and Smuts. But he refrained from giving the final order to revolt. He only invited the Free Staters to follow him for a promenade through the streets of Johannesburg. The burghers' appetites were whetted. Cheerfully, with high hopes, they marched on.

Beyers had just returned from Germany. He had been Wilhelm II's personal guest at the Imperial manoeuvres, and had watched a frontal attack of massed German infantry against strong fortifications. Obviously, he was deeply impressed, although upon his return he gave an account of his experience according to which he had got the better of the Emperor. "You have seen a lot of campaigning, General," the Emperor allegedly said, "now tell me what you think of this." "In real warfare," Beyers prided himself to have said, "even against our small Boer rifles, Your Majesty would be sending those men to certain destruction." The Kaiser's repartee, as reported by Beyers, sounded genuine. " 'Not all of them,' His Majesty said laughing. 'Some would get through. And we only expect to use each soldier once.' "

The palaver between Wilhelm II and Beyers was also conveyed by other sources. German agents in South Africa were busy spreading the rumor that the Emperor had made a tremendous impression on the Union's commander in chief. The German noose was tightening around the braggart's neck.

General Smuts, who had come to Johannesburg with Botha, ostensibly to visit the headquarters of the semi-military committee in charge of the Witwatersrand administration, was fully informed about the real mood of his commandos and their commander in chief. But he was coolness personified. A journalist asked him about the conditions of the men and horses he had conjured up from the *veld*. *"Eerste klas; spekvet!"* (First-class; sleek and fat), he answered with perfect unconcern. But instantly he ordered the officer commanding the Rand Light Infantry to exercise the greatest severity. "Don't hesitate to shoot on provocation!" Simultaneously General de la Rey, about whose allegiance to the government of his close friends Botha and Smuts there was no doubt, trained his guns on the Trades Hall. He sent an ultimatum. Staring into the muzzles of the howitzers, the strike leaders surrendered.

All nine of them—among whom there was not a single South African-born—were immediately sent to jail. They were only kept in their cells for a few hours. At midnight they were transported to Durban, and immediately dispatched aboard the S. S. *Umgeni*, to be deported to England. On the next day the case of the nine strike leaders came to the Supreme Court. But Judge Wessels could only utter a subdued protest from the bench. The nine culprits had been spirited away by General Smuts. They were already on the high seas, and the S. S. *Umgeni* was under orders not to interrupt her voyage before reaching the port of London.

The kidnapping of the strike leaders was undoubtedly a high-handed and unconstitutional act. Smuts had to defend it during three weeks of debate in Parliament. Accusations were poured on him from all sides. Mr. Creswell and his Labor Party were now definitely through with him. Hertzog used his first speech as leader of the Nationalist opposition to express his tender concern for the Imperial government that would be embarrassed by having to take over the strike leaders. Smuts defended himself in three masterful speeches. His main argument was that the strike leaders had, by all manner and means, committed high treason in their effort to choke the economic life of the country in time of grave international crisis. But the law, dating back to the Middle Ages, recognized as high treason only crimes against the army. Crimes against the national economy, he insisted, were just as treasonable and dangerous. Since there was no paragraph to deal with them in a manner that would guarantee the safety of the country, he had, at least, to purge the country of the pest.

Parliament agreed. By a majority of 95 to 11 votes the House expressed its full confidence in Smuts. But the country disagreed. Innumerable agitators, nationalists, socialists, the dissatisfied from every camp, called him "the inventor of *platskiet politiek*"—the policy of shooting down people ruthlessly. At the provincial elections in the Transvaal Labor, for the first time, gained an absolute majority in the Provincial Council. Fickle Johannesburg had unanimously voted Labor, perhaps because the solid citizens wanted to insure themselves against the red flag waving everywhere, and against the mass choirs singing the *Internationale*. But that even conservative, traditionalist Pretoria had voted red was a terrific blow to Smuts. He knew that he had gravely impaired, perhaps ruined for good, his political career. But he was no longer a politician. His only program was enshrined in a word that gradually became unfashionable and began to sound archaic; duty. He would again do his duty by the country, he insisted.

He was as good as his word. A few weeks after the House had adjourned, war was declared. In South Africa they at first called it: the European War. General Smuts said: World War.

AN EPIDEMIC OF GERMAN MEASLES SWEPT SOUTH AFRICA AS THE Great War broke out. It was a grave affliction. Soon it became the German plague. The country was swamped with German agents. Hundreds of them congregated in Pretoria. "In Cape Town the personnel and activities of the German Consulate General are out of proportion to those of other German Consulates, or to Germany's actual interest in the Union," Lord Buxton, the Governor-General during the war, reported to London. "There can be little doubt now that the Germans had, before the war, been carrying on an assiduous anti-British propaganda in the Union; and had been engaged in acquiring political and military information."

Smuts spoke in the same vein. "All this German talk, all this rumor of German sympathies, has been spread by German commercial agents and German dealers," he said. "I hope the people will realize that these Germans are placing a dagger into the heart of South Africa which they are eager to press home."

His hope betrayed him. The openly pro-German elements among the Boers probably did not form a majority, but they were certainly the most vocal part of the nation, which, as a whole, was not keen to support England, France, or Russia. In vain Smuts pointed out the fact that German South West Africa was being used as a base for intrigue against "this part of the Empire." In vain he stressed how dangerous it was to have next door a neighbor such as the German Empire. The constant accumulation of military power in the German African territories was essentially unwelcome to most of the Boers. But their overwhelming desire was to keep out of the war. German money was inundating the *platteland*. It was received gratefully like fertilizing rain. The farmers, accustomed to making money with politics, smiled, which was rare with them. The untamable soil of the *veld*, ageless and immutable, sad, gray,

and barren, not, like the jungle, the natural enemy of man, but
not his slave either, rather a quiet spectator of human effort—
this soil of South Africa needed one thing above all: irrigation.
Now the German irrigation flowed in a golden stream, whis-
pering that the *verdomde*—damned—British had obtained complete control of the government. They were going to tax the
land, or to take the farms away.

Hertzog fanned the smoldering embers into flames. Now it
proved that his dismissal from the government two years before
had in fact turned him into a revolutionary. His political downfall had ruined him financially as well. He possessed no money
of his own. After losing his comfortable salary as Minister of
the Crown—2,500 pounds a year—he was broke. He became an
undisguised rabble-rouser. His anti-British attitude was no
longer hidden behind equivocal phrases. He dropped his mask.

The very moment the news of the German invasion of Belgium reached Botha, he sent a message to London assuring
that the Union recognized her Imperial obligation, and, in the
event of an attack, was prepared to defend her territory by her
own strength. The seven thousand British soldiers guarding the
South African border could be released for the European theater of war. Six thousand departed instantly from Potchelstroom
via Cape Town to England.

The British Government, accepting Botha's offer, asked him
to take a further step. He would render a great and urgent
service to the Empire by occupying the two ports of Luederitz Bay and Swakopmund in German South West Africa,
and the wireless station at Windhoek, which was in constant
communication with Berlin, and imperilled the movements of
the British fleet.

Botha replied by pointing out the critical situation in his
country. His people were unwilling to commit an act of aggression. "The wireless station at Windhoek is a menace that must
be exterminated," London answered.

Three weeks had passed with these negotiations behind
closed doors. All the other Dominions and Colonial Dependen-
cies had already sent their messages of allegiance and their

promises fully to participate in the war effort. Everywhere in the Empire domestic quarrels had stopped. South Africa alone was torn asunder. The Union Government, it appeared, had lost its voice.

The Nationalist Party met in Bloemfontein, and adopted a violent anti-war resolution. Only one of Hertzog's closest followers dissented. He was all out for war, but for a war against Great Britain. Now was the Boers' golden opportunity. Everyone understood that the leader had spoken, as was his habit in critical moments, through a mouthpiece.

Johannesburg, still shaken by its social upheaval, was panic-stricken. The De Beers, Premier and other mines closed down. The Labor Party, since the last provincial elections the ruling power, was split from top to bottom. Its great majority now consisted of fanatically anti-British young Boers. But Mr. Creswell, still the leader, declared stubbornly that he, for one, would support the war effort to the hilt. He signed up immediately, and subsequently won distinction in both African campaigns, from which he returned a Colonel, but still as a radical Leftist and a violent foe of Smuts. Foreign "syndicalists" did their best to incite the masses of the townspeople. The Imperial Military Stores at Roberts Heights, insufficiently guarded after the hurried departure of the British troops, as well as the magazines of Smuts' Defence Force at Potchefstroom, were stormed by Dutch crowds, and burned down.

Pretoria, the capital, remained the center of events. The press, mostly English, did not conceal its dissatisfaction with the hardly comprehensible hesitation of the Union government. The solid citizens were aroused at the aspect of the German agents, who, although well known, were neither arrested nor even deported, but could still, grinning, go about their business. They mingled with the bearded Boer farmers now filling the town. A coffeehouse in Church Street was soon known as the headquarters of the German conspiracy. Beyers, commander in chief, who a short time before had returned from a trip to Germany, was a habitual visitor to this coffeehouse. Middle-sized, rather on the paunchy side, his short, trimmed beard scented with perfume, swaggering in military fashion, his right hand gripping a dagger of honor, a present from Wilhelm II, he stood his boon companions innumerable rounds of coffee and liquor. He disposed of a million Mark with which the German treasury had entrusted him to manufacture the revolution. Besides, a premium of fifty thousand pounds was waiting for him in the sealed vaults of the now abandoned German Consulate General in Cape Town. He had simply to conquer the town.

Yet, during the critical days, General Beyers still went carefully about his business. He inspected the Civil Militia in Johannesburg. During the general strike the men had been equipped by the government with brand-new rifles. Under the pretext that the Defense Force wanted them, Beyers collected all rifles in the possession of English citizens. The burghers were permitted to retain theirs. The confiscated rifles were subsequently added to the large stores of German Mausers and machine-guns already distributed throughout the *platteland*. From Johannesburg Beyers returned to Pretoria. There he gave a bibulous farewell party for Lieutenant-Colonel Maritz, Smuts' lieutenant during the guerrilla raid in the Cape, later an officer on the Defence Force of Beyers' making. Maritz, a compound of enormous strength, inordinately vain, and entirely uneducated, was adorned with a gigantic—*Es ist erreicht*—it is achieved —mustache after the pattern of the Kaiser's trademark. When he was drunk, he freely admitted that he was going to start a revolution for what he could get out of it. One could, after all, not live on an officer's meager pay if one had a beloved wife and two children to support, and was, at that, a frequent visitor in the shebeens. Already in 1913 he had received 100,000 Mark —some £20,000—from an unknown admirer. Now he was about to march to the border of South West Africa with a Defence Force of six hundred men—and to cross it under the white flag, to join the Germans.

The Loyalist population of Pretoria was aroused by the shameless behavior of the traitors. They staged a huge mass meeting on Church Square. Their speakers, Mayor Andrew Johnston and Dean Gordon of the Anglican High Church, voiced their feelings in determined words. The meeting went off without the slightest disturbance. The traitors hid in their rat holes. But as the days passed, and the government still kept silent—although Smuts and Botha were feverishly active behind the scenes—an uneasy feeling overcame the Loyalists. Again the German agents and their Boer associates raised their heads. Commandant F. G. A. Wolmarans of the district of Lichtenburg, west of Pretoria, galloped from farm to farm, preaching sedition to the burghers: "You will soon hoist the *Vierkleur*— the old Transvaal Republican Flag—and march to the German border to get ammunition!"

General de la Rey was the great old man of the Lichtenburg district. He had been the last successful Boer general in the war, and yet had sided at Vereeniging, after some grave inner conflict, with the peace party under Botha and Smuts. Smuts, who is sparing with his personal feelings, loved him like a father. De la Rey was one of the three or four men in his life of whom Smuts spoke with veneration and emotion. After the peace, General de la Rey held office continuously. At the outbreak of the Great War he was probably the most highly respected member of the Senate. But he could never reconcile himself with the loss of the Boer War. Deeply imbued with religion, he sought comfort in anti-Semitism, mysticism and superstition. His father confessor was a man named Nicholaas Van Rensburg, a soothsayer, worshiped in every Boer house. As General de la Rey's adviser in the Boer War, he had won fame by his visions. He had dreamed exactly where small or scattered groups of British soldiers could be surprised and annihilated. In fact, he had organized an excellent Kafir spy organization.

"Oom Niklaas' " dreams made South African history. His hold over the credulous burghers, including their generals, was tremendously enhanced when he dreamed the exact date of the end of the Boer War and of the peace. He had added to his Kafir spy system a no less remarkable white intelligence service. In 1914 he was already an aging gentleman, suffering from cerebral disturbances which, however, sharpened his faculty of seeing visions. In the spring of this year he published a book containing hundreds of his dreams. Since the Boers were not great book buyers, the tome went almost unnoticed. But on the second day after Great Britain had declared war on Germany, Van Rensburg's volume of prophetic dreams was in everybody's hands.

So far Oom Niklaas' most popular dream had been the vision of a furious fight between seven bulls. The red, blue, black, gray, brown, white and orange-colored bulls represented the different European nations. The gray animal stood for Germany, the red for Britain, the blue for France. After terrific goring first the black bull, then the red, and finally all save the gray bull went down. The interpretation was obvious: Germany was to conquer Britain, France, and the whole world.

Now the visionary dreamed as if on the assembly line. He fitted two dreams to his patron De la Rey's personal measure. He dreamed that the Union government was finished. The English were leaving the Transvaal, and trekking to Natal. When they had gone far away, a vulture left them, and returned to the Transvaal. The vulture stood for Botha. Smuts, an ugly sparrow, would fly all the way to England, and never return to South Africa. In his place, a man "representing the Godhead"— a God-fearing man—would appear as a leader. He would not shed blood, but arrange all peacefully and bring everything into good order. The prophecy would come to pass when the Transvaal would see the "sifting" of British on one side and Dutch on the other. The dream ended in an apotheosis: General de la Rey pulling down the Union Jack and hoisting the *Vierkleur*, General de la Rey as God's instrument, delivering the people from the British, Botha and Smuts.

The outbreak of the war had already crazed the God-fearing general. His son-in-law ceased to regard him as accountable for his acts in those disturbed days, and considered it necessary to have him watched day and night. The young man could, however, not protect him against Van Rensburg. The prophet had another dream. He saw the number *15* on a dark cloud

from which blood dripped. In the second version of the dream
De la Rey returned—from nowhere—with his hat. He was followed by a carriage, covered with flowers. Van Rensburg himself could not interpret his reverie. He could only conclude that
something very splendid for De la Rey was written in the stars.

All the farmers of the Lichtenburg and Rustenburg districts
knew instantly that this number 15 stood for the fifteenth of August. Those who were too ignorant to draw their own conclusions were enlightened by the numerous German agents in the
Western Transvaal, stirring up the burghers with fabulous
promises and flagrant lies. De la Rey observed all the commotion with a benign, senile smile.

A Sunday meeting was arranged in Lichtenburg for August
15. The burghers were instructed to *upsaddle* with rifles, blankets, all the ammunition they possessed, and food for at least a
fortnight. They were told that after the meeting they would
move to Johannesburg, where resistance was expected. But De
la Rey would lead them, and *allsal reg kom*—all would be
right. Others would proceed directly to Potchefstroom, the central camp of the Imperial troops of South Africa, now held only
by the remaining one thousand men. The commandos of that
district would join the men from the Western Transvaal. The
last British soldiers would be killed. The Republic would be
proclaimed.

Botha and Smuts got wind of the conspiracy. No secret could
be kept in the country riddled with spies, and counter-spies.
They sent an urgent message to De la Rey to meet them in
Pretoria. Smuts was too gravely shocked to speak. He must
have realized that his beloved paternal friend had lost his
senses. Botha attacked his old follower where he was most vulnerable: Did the Lord's word teach falsehood and treason? he
asked. It was a God-sent opportunity, De la Rey replied. But
he had no longer the strength to withstand Botha's persuasion.
Faint-hearted and dejected, he left the *indaba*. The day was
the fourteenth of August. On the next morning, the morning of
the appointed day, De la Rey appeared at the meeting. He was

accompanied by Sammie Marks, of all people, the richest and toughest Jewish speculator in South Africa. Eight hundred burghers were gathered to heed the General's call to action. Instead, De la Rey admonished them to go home and be good. If the government wanted them in connection with the war in Europe, they would be called out in the regular way. The burghers listened in stony silence. Impassively they voted for De la Rey's resolution of confidence in the government. Slowly they trotted home. Some lashed their horses unmercifully. Others got drunk. All cursed. They had been fooled. The revolution was off.

On the same day the government issued the first official statement about the war. It was vague and inconclusive. Yet its meaning was somewhat clarified by a simultaneous call for volunteers to join the Defense Force for active service inside South Africa. Parliament was convoked. The government assured the country that all measures would be taken to insure, as far as possible, normal conditions within the Union for the duration. Subsequently the Second (Pretoria) Regiment was mobilized, whereas the regiments from Johannesburg and the Witwatersrand entered the huge new camp at Booysens. In the cities the "town units" were called out to get infantry training. The burgher commandos, now grouped into regiments, made a splendid cavalry.

The country awoke. The English section, to one man, relished the prospect of having a go at the Germans in South West Africa. A large portion of the Boers fell in line. They were aroused by three incidents. The Kaiser had sent a replica of his Kruger telegram, promising his recognition of the Boer Republics if the revolution would start immediately. The Germans had crossed the Union border at Nakob, and had entrenched themselves on South African territory. Furthermore at the Schuit Drift on the Orange River, they had attacked a party of Boer farmers, and forced them to seek refuge on one of the tiny, unnamed islands in the river.

After this affront even the hotbeds of Boer nationalism, like

Bloemfontein and Potchefstroom, pretended loyalty and waved the Union Jack. Yet, secretly, most of their people strongly disapproved of the forthcoming attack on the "peaceful" German neighbor. Johannesburg, despite its cosmopolitan character, proved to be an intensely English town. The mines could reopen, and resume production. Nevertheless, gang rule, one of the most distinct features on the Rand, continued practically unchecked.

Pretoria was the hottest spot. The English inhabitants were jubilant. But again streets and coffeehouses were jammed by bearded men from the *veld,* who predicted openly that they would refuse to serve if an attack should be made upon the Germans beyond the frontier. Indeed, many *backvelders* mutinied when they were called up. They rode off into the *veld,* where they strayed without the slightest notion what to do next.

They got their clue from Hertzog. He chose the days of gravest unrest to hold a Nationalist congress right in embattled Pretoria. Significantly, on the door to Town Hall, where the congress met, a daub was painted representing the burning of a Boer farmhouse by British soldiers. The police arrested the painter, and charged him with incitement to disaffection. He got away with a small fine. Smuts did not want to create martyrs.

Hertzog blamed Botha and Smuts for the division in the country. The chairman, a Senator by the name of Wolmarans, declared: "We will not take part in any invasion for robbery." General De la Rey, who had come as an onlooker, pleaded for unity in time of crisis.

A Pretoria English paper attacked the congress for spreading seditious rumors and talking a lot of pestilential nonsense. "The Dutchmen are not as a whole responding to the call to join the colors," the paper stated. "There is in this town an unpleasant feeling of hostility against the British cause, and an open delight expressed at anything that savors of a check or reverse sustained by British arms. The place is seething with sedition." The government censor took the newspaper to account.

He did not contest the truth of its statements, but he described the article as "unpolitic." Botha and Smuts still held their protecting hands over their lost brethren.

In the meantime, the Defence Office under Smuts worked indefatigably at getting the burgher force into military shape. Even General Beyers felt the necessity to prove his loyalty. On August 29, he appeared at Camp Booysens, which he had thus far demonstratively shunned, and addressed the troops: "Whenever our country is threatened, Boer and British will stand together, and fight to the last man. Every man, I am convinced, will do his utmost, perhaps under very trying circumstances. But let him all the more be patient, loyal and persevering to the very end. Three cheers for His Majesty, the King!"

Smuts was astonished. He deeply distrusted his commander in chief. He went himself to Booysens, but Beyers had already left. Now Smuts spoke: "There are many people in this country who do not appreciate the tremendous gravity of the crisis in which South Africa, together with the whole Empire, is placed today. Although apparently we stand outside, and at some distance from the actual scene of conflict, yet at any moment we may be drawn into the vortex."

The soldiers cheered themselves hoarse. But the politicians were unimpressed. Feelings were running high. Private and social life was disrupted. Many families were torn apart. Under such conditions Parliament met on September 4 in a special session to consider the war situation.

Hertzog leapt up to speak in defense of Germany. It was simply not true that the Reich had committed an act of aggression. Moreover, it was quite wrong to provoke a nation as powerful as Germany. If the Emperor lost, South West Africa would anyway become a part of the Union. If Germany should win the war, and the Union was in it, South Africa was doomed.

In his reply Smuts called Hertzog a "German advocate." He insisted that South Africa was threatened by a military autocracy in the worst form. He counseled the Germans not to bank too heavily on rumors that South Africa was unarmed. The House understood the allusion. Smuts had, indeed, not distrib-

uted nearly as many rifles as the burghers in the border districts
of the Cape and the Free State had clamored for. He kept them
for his own troops. Subsequently, his foresight was entirely vindicated. Those border districts became the very center of the
revolution.

The parliamentary debate had continued for three days when
rumors sprang up that the Twelfth Regiment had left the
Booysens camp for an unknown destination. A new storm broke
loose. The poor boys were being sent to the slaughterhouse, the
Nationalists shouted. As a matter of fact, the boys, English and
Afrikaans alike, marched merrily along, and were eager for a
scrap with the Germans. But even the government's own South
African Party was appalled at the presence of war. Botha and
Smuts assembled their party in caucus. They had to exercise all
their persuasion, and even to threaten resignation, to induce
their own members to support Botha's resolution expressing the
wholehearted determination of the House to co-operate with
His Majesty's Imperial government in order to maintain the
security and integrity of the Empire. After a week of discussion
the resolution was adopted by an almost unanimous House.
Only Hertzog's followers dissented.

In the meantime Maritz was already in Upington, some
thirty miles from the border of German South West Africa. He
sent an old friend, a man by the name of P. J. Joubert, a Boer
who was a large estate owner in the South West, back to Pretoria to inform Commander in Chief Beyers that the negotiations with the Germans were proceeding excellently. Governor
Seitz of German South West Africa was expecting Beyers on
September 15.

On this very day a strong contingent of the Union's Defence
Force was leaving for Luederitz Bay, as the Imperial Government had requested. Beyers was not with them. Two days earlier he had published an open letter announcing his resignation,
and protesting against the decision to attack South West Africa
"without provocation." The letter contained an atrocious attack
against the British Empire, which had, in view of the "barbari-
ties" committed during the Boer War, no right to protest

against alleged German atrocities. At the same time Beyers sent a letter of encouragement, and of comradely greetings, to the traitor Maritz.

Smuts, in his capacity as Minister of Defence, replied by rebuking the insolent vilification of Great Britain, and concluded: "It may be that our peculiar internal circumstances and our backward condition will place a limit on what we can do; but nevertheless I am convinced that the people will support the government, and fulfill their destiny to South Africa and to the Empire, and maintain their dearly won honor unblemished for the future. . . . Your resignation is hereby accepted."

Smuts himself became the Commander in Chief of the Defence Force. He moved to headquarters, put on a uniform, and did not take it off for the next five years.

Governor Seitz of German South West Africa waited in vain for the visit of Beyers. Instead of keeping the appointment, the renegade went to Pretoria, to win over General de la Rey to the cause of the revolution. The two had an all-day palaver, the contents of which remained a secret. It appears that old De la Rey was vacillating; certainly he was no longer capable of a balanced judgment. In the evening he consented to accompany Beyers to Johannesburg. Beyers' car raced along the roads. Every corner was heavily policed. The Foster gang was at large, one of the worst bands that had ever ravaged Johannesburg. On the morning of this very fifteenth of September three gangsters had shot a detective, and escaped in a car. The police were under orders to inspect every car, particularly those with three passengers, on the main roads to and from Johannesburg. But Beyers had ordered his chauffeur to disregard signals. He was in a hurry. At four o'clock in the morning he was expected in a training camp near Johannesburg, where, at his and De la Rey's appearance, a large group of recruits would rise in rebellion. They were to march to Pretoria, proclaim the Republic, and elect, by acclamation, Beyers President and De la Rey Commander-in-Chief. Whether De la Rey was in on this plan, or whether Beyers wanted to confront him with a *fait accompli* was never established. At any rate, conscious or not, the saintly, aged General was on a treasonable mission, while his country was at war—when it happened.

A constable jumped into the middle of the road, when he saw Beyers' huge motorcar approach. The car was similar to the one the Foster gang had stolen. Three men sat inside: the two generals and Beyers' driver. Moreover, the car did not stop. At full speed it raced right to the place where the constable stood. Beyers, not eager to be investigated by the police at that particular moment, ordered his driver not to stop, and De la Rey, in his senile sullenness, nodded consent.

The constable leaped aside, aimed at the tire, fired, missed, hit the road. The bullet ricocheted and entered De la Rey's head. He was killed instantly.

De la Rey's funeral at Lichtenburg led to a tremendous demonstration. Botha, Smuts, and Beyers stood together at the grave. It was another proof of that overwhelming feeling of racial oneness that unites the Boers, even the arch-foes among them. But the masses jeered at their ministers. Everyone was persuaded that Smuts and Botha had had De la Rey murdered. They did not heed any pathetic protestation to the contrary. They only understood that Van Rensburg, the seer, had been right. After all, the tragic day was the fifteenth. Behind De la Rey, who was returning from nowhere, a large carriage laden with flowers rolled along. Many onlookers even saw red blood dripping from the dark clouds.

Beyers stole the show. He swore on the dead man's memory that he himself was not a traitor. On the same evening he met his fellow conspirators.

Smuts returned to headquarters. He sat at his desk, as if glued to it. Immediate action was imperative. He fully understood the significance of what had happened.

ON THE THIRTIETH OF SEPTEMBER SMUTS ORDERED MARITZ BY wire to come to Pretoria. Insolently, Maritz in his answer referred to a speech he had delivered a few days before, pouring abuse and contempt on his minister. Smuts, for his part, feigned astonishment. He made inquiries "whether there was any reason to fear an act of treason in connection with Maritz' movements." It was a ruse to gain time. Colonel Brits had already been appointed to the command of the Union forces around Upington, where Maritz lay in wait. The Colonel was under instructions to arrest the rebel if he refused to resign and submit peacefully.

Maritz learned from his Kafir spies that a big Union force was moving in his direction. Immediately he broke up his camp in Upington to proceed to an undisclosed destination. One of his officers smelled a rat. Major Enslin inquired where the whole force with all its ammunition was supposed to be going. "I am carrying out secret instructions!" he was told. Thereupon the Major excused himself, and disappeared. He had no desire to accompany Maritz into open rebellion.

After a two days' march Maritz' troops, six hundred youngsters, most of them in their teens, arrived at Van Rooisvlei, near the German border. After another two days a mysterious motorcar appeared, and drove Maritz into German territory. When he returned to his troops on October 7, the secret was solved. Not the Germans, but the English were the enemy.

Only a few of the men had advance knowledge of the planned coup. To most of the soldiers it came as a surprise. Maritz assembled them at a full parade which was so shrewdly arranged that the gun section, whose loyalty was notorious, was completely surrounded. At a prearranged signal the plotters attacked the gunners. Maritz himself helped by stabbing a few of his victims in the back. The Loyalists were made prisoners of war.

Now the traitor, standing on a soapbox, delivered a grandiloquent harangue. Botha and Smuts were in the service of capitalistic oppressors. The country was ruled by Englishmen. Now was the time for the Boers to regain South Africa. It was quite unnecessary to be killed in German South West Africa, England had already lost the war. The German wireless reported it every day. This was the moment to hoist the old republican flag on Table Mountain. Those who disagreed should step forward.

Lieutenant Bossouw and fifty men stepped out. They were disarmed, and marched into a German camp in South West Africa. Finally a sergeant by the name of Engelbrecht, a German-born Boer, moved the election of Maritz as commander. The traitor was elected in the best old commando fashion.

But Colonel Brits was already hard on his heels. Instructed by Smuts to use persuasion rather than force, he sent Major Bower with the flag of truce to Maritz' camp. Clad in a pompous German general's uniform, the traitor received the major, showed him German howitzers, and a number of German soldiers who had joined him. He boasted his abundance of German arms, ammunition and money. He even displayed a treaty he had concluded with the German Imperial Government, and demanded finally safe conduct for Hertzog, De Wet, Beyers and "General" Kemp, to come to him to discuss the situation. Otherwise, he threatened, he would instantly attack.

Smuts, hearing of this ultimatum, issued a brief statement, accusing Lieutenant-Colonel Solomon Gerhardus Maritz of having shamefully and traitorously gone over to the enemy, and declaring: "In view of this state of affairs the government is taking the most vigorous steps to stamp out the rebellion and inflict just punishment on all rebels and traitors."

Colonel Brits advanced. Twice, at Keimoes and at Schuit Drift, he beat Maritz' soldiery, and took a number of prisoners, among them German officers. The inglorious rebel retired into South West African territory. He used a light wound on the knee, received at Keimoes, as a pretext to drop out of action.

Elsewhere, in the Free State and in the Western Transvaal, action was just beginning. Nationalistic intellectuals, lawyers and a great number of *predikants*, were preaching open sedition. The country was perturbed. Even the Synod of the Dutch Reformed Church, an arch-reactionary body which had no love for Smuts, addressed an open letter to its divines warning them against an attempt to cause a bloody civil war. At the same time the Synod adopted a resolution, expressing its profound indignation at the treacherous conduct of Maritz. It called upon all the members of the Church to support the government in every way possible to maintain law and order.

A few reverend gentlemen were deaf in both ears. On October 13 the Reverend Mr. Ferreira opened the dining room of his parsonage at Keppers to a secret meeting. A group of his fellow clergymen, under the leadership of the Reverend Van Broekhuisen, De Wet with a delegation of Free Staters, the Boer General Liebenberg, Piet Grobler, Kruger's kinsman, and Pienaar, both lieutenants of Hertzog, were present.

After the host had invoked God's blessing, General De Wet started the row. He exploded in one of his violent fits that had, even among friends, earned him the nickname *Bobiaan* (baboon). He had a terrible story to tell. He had been fined five shillings by a tyrannical magistrate, one of those "pestilential English," for having assaulted a native servant. (In fact this tyrannical magistrate was a brother-in-law of ex-President Steyn, and had received his seat on the bench when Hertzog was Attorney-General in the Free State.) This insult, De Wet insisted, was enough to justify immediate revolution. There was not a moment to be lost. Maritz had already started. He had plenty of money and arms. "We start here," De Wet concluded, "and join him later."

Opposition came from the most unexpected quarter. General Liebenberg, who had led the campaign of protest against a march into German South West Africa, was firmly set against revolution. Hertzog was not with the conspirators, he pointed out.

"The general is a lawyer!" purple-faced De Wet cried. "I saw

221

him yesterday. He is a man you can trust in the dark. He fights for us in the political sphere. There he is in his proper place. Don't ask where he is. He told me he would not attend our meeting, since he has already been made the scapegoat. However, he is to be found when he is wanted."

Stubbornly, General Liebenberg insisted: "Where is Beyers?"

Pienaar, the Hertzog man, found an excuse for Beyers' absence. While his car was parked in front of the Opera House the tires had been slashed. He could not drive to the meeting.

The fact was true. But General Liebenberg found it an unsatisfactory explanation for the commander in chief's absence. He declined to go into rebellion, and proposed to send a delegation to the government.

De Wet and Kemp, the fire-eaters, shouted against this proposal. It was, however, accepted as the only way of dealing with Liebenberg. On the same afternoon a deputation, including De Wet, left for Pretoria. The delegates met at the Reverend Van Broekhuisen's house, who promised them to bring them in touch with Beyers the next day. On the following day, however, he had to admit pusillanimously that he could not keep his word. Beyers was in hiding. Nor could the reverend gentleman himself accompany the deputies to Botha.

Beyers hiding? It boded ill. The deputation lost heart. But De Wet drove them on. They called upon the Prime Minister, and were immediately received. Botha welcomed the rebels with his accustomed affability. They talked for four hours and a quarter. In fact, the delegates were playing for time to convince General Liebenberg that they had done their best. They spoke so evasively that Botha, after their departure, asked: "What do these people really want?"

De Wet had left the conference while his colleagues were still hoodwinking Botha with their pretended grievances. He returned to the Reverend Van Broekhuisen's house, where he met Beyers. The two chief conspirators made their plans.

On the next day Botha's question was answered. De Wet wired him from his home in the Free State: "Resign immediately."

Smuts entrenched himself at headquarters. Nothing in his face, no loud word, no nervous movement betrayed his high tension. He was not only calm and collected, but he displayed indefatigable patience. His manner had greatly changed since the days of his struggle for power. Harshness and stern austerity had faded. Instead he showed solicitude for each of his innumerable callers, and that wonderful unembarrassing courtesy that was to mark him for the rest of his time. Some visitors observed a repeated gesture: "As if he were washing his hands with invisible soap in imperceptible water." But that was the only way of working off his emotions that he permitted himself.

He was in the throes of a tragic dilemma. He was about to take stern action against his own brothers in arms. Perhaps he would have to impose the death penalty upon the same Maritz, who, some years before, had lain with him under the same blanket to share what little bodily warmth was left in the exhausted guerrillas. (Incidentally, throughout the decade following the Boer War, self-styled old comrades called upon Smuts by the hundreds and thousands, reminding him that he had shared their blanket in those happy days, and asking for a job for a son-in-law. Smuts could never believe that the entire South African textile industry could have produced as many blankets as that.) The tragic death of De la Rey must have weighed still more heavily on his mind. Mrs. Smuts was just expecting another baby. The boy would be christened De la Rey. It was a girl. Nevertheless, she was baptized De la Rey.

Undoubtedly, Smuts himself had once been a rebel against the British. What difference, he was asked, was there between his revolt during the Boer War, and De Wet's or Beyers' insurrection today? A world of difference, he explained. The English had attacked the Boers. (At least he saw it this way.) But after the war the English had acted more magnanimously than any victor in history. They had returned to the Boers their complete independence; indeed, the nation enjoyed in many ways more liberty than ever before. Moreover, the English were trusting the Boers. Trust was a sacred word to Smuts.

His hardest task was to wrestle with himself. Smuts is one of those rare human beings in whom intellect and instinct are happily harnessed. Yet the day comes inevitably, in every life, on which the impulses at the roots of a man clash with his convictions. This moment had come. On an October day in 1914 Smuts received in his house the journalist Nathan Levi, a friend of old standing. Mr. Levi reported: "Modern tendencies and latter-day beliefs were discussed. Smuts admitted that, having drunk at the source of transcendentalist wisdom, he could not stand precisely where generations of his ancestors had stood. Yet, he added that deep, deep down in the recesses of his nature, which he himself could not plumb, the religious conceptions and feelings learned at his mother's knee in that little corner of Riebeek West remained unpolluted. As she had inherited them from her forefathers and passed them on, so his apperception (he used the Kantian term) showed them to be there still, at his core. He remained a child of his race and of his Church, though a new garment might cover him."

He decided, however, to follow the call of the "new garment." In the Transvaal he called up five rifle regiments, four mounted, one unmounted. Volunteers flocked in in droves. Thirty-five thousand men registered. Most had come to help. But every one could well be a potential traitor. Yet Smuts decided that the matter was an affair between Boer and Boer. As far as possible he sidetracked English volunteers. Finally, ten thousand English South Africans served shoulder to shoulder with twice and a half their number of Boers. But General Smuts was unable to find Boers well enough qualified to serve as his personal liaison men. After a few unavailing tryouts with young Afrikanders, he appointed Mr. Ernest F. C. Lane—later to become a captain in the South West African campaign, and finally to join the Heavy Artillery in Flanders—his private secretary, and Mr. H. R. M. Bourne, later the permanent head of the South African Defence Department, his aide-de-camp.

On the night of Sunday, October 25, Smuts proclaimed: "The government has to announce with deep regret that at the instigation of certain prominent individuals a number of burghers

in the Northern District of the Transvaal have been misguided
enough to defy the authority of the Union government, and to
make preparations for armed resistance and rebellion. The government learns that in the northern Orange Free State burghers
are being commandeered and military supplies requisitioned
under the authority of General Christiaan De Wet, and in the
Western Transvaal by General Beyers. An armed rebel commando is already in existence. The town of Heilbron has been
seized, and the officers of the government in this town taken
prisoner. A train has been stopped at Reitz. Armed citizens and
members of the Defence Force have been taken from the train
and disarmed." Simultaneously Maritz was declared an outlaw,
and "all Magisterial Districts in the Union of South Africa, until further notice, placed under Martial Law."

Nothing happened, at least not on the government's side.
Smuts and Botha advised the rebels that no measures would be
taken against them, if they went home quietly. Twelve days
later the same invitation was addressed to the rebel leaders.
Defiantly the Generals De Wet and Beyers replied that their
only object was "the honor of God and the welfare of people
and country." Furthermore they were bound by the Treaty
with the Kaiser in Berlin, which Beyers had concluded.

The government reacted by twice extending the deadline
within which the rebels should go home without being called
to account. But almost twelve thousand Boers were already
honoring God and taking care of the welfare of people and
country.

They were primarily occupied with looting their own land.
True, they were under orders. Many Boer wives, exercising the
real power, had allowed their husbands to join the commando
only on condition that he would loot something pretty and
practical for her. Accordingly, ladies' stockings were the first
booty of war. But since the husband was already in the *winkel*
—village store—he requisitioned everything not clinched and
riveted. There was an excellent opportunity for the sale of saddles and provisions, even for the overcoats shabby civilians
were wearing, for carts and cattle, harness, wagons, and horses.

Payment was not on a strictly cash basis. The commandos compensated the storekeepers for their purchases with bills, redeemable by the nonexistent South African Republic, and frequently written by the customer while he watched his goods being loaded upon the cart.

Smuts waited until he saw Pretoria threatened on three sides by rebel commandos. Only then the innermost conflict between his roots and his garment was definitely decided. The Minister for Defence ordered the second battalion of the Transvaal Scottish and Irish Regiment from Johannesburg to Pretoria. Strong patrols occupied the encircling hills and guarded the approaches to the capital. Inside Pretoria, the town police, carrying rifles and full bandoleers of cartridges, paraded the streets. At night the whole police force was on the alert, assisted by a thoroughly efficient citizen civilian guard.

Still the regular troops were under orders to avoid, if possible, bloodshed. They were told only to hustle the commandos, and to take prisoners. Colonel van De Venter, who was later to become Smuts' chief of staff in the South West campaign, captured Captain Joubert, Beyers' go-between. Two days later Colonel-Commander Celliers took prisoner the disloyal Major Ben Cotzee, a general staff officer of the Defence Force. The rebel prisoners were disheartened. They cursed Van Rensburg, the fake seer, who was guilty of all the trouble. Some prisoners did not even know for whom or against whom they had been fighting. Their commandant had just said: *"Upsaddle!"* and with cattlelike docility they had obeyed.

Not before the beginning of November did the fight start in earnest. Colonel Alberts, operating in the Lichtenburg district, where the whole affair had begun, arrived in Treurfontein. He surprised, and beat, a strong party of rebels under the self-styled General Kemp. Loyalist Commander de Villiers met a strong rebel force under Commander Classens, a German Boer. The rebels immediately hoisted white flags on their rifles. Expecting their surrender, de Villiers approached them, whereupon the rebels attacked and captured de Villiers with one hundred ten men. The triumph of treachery, however, was short-lived. On the next day Colonel Alberts picked up the whole rebel group, and liberated de Villiers and his men.

Beyers fled to the Free State, where he hoped for sanctuary. Colonel Lemmer was hot after him. His Lieutenant De la Rey Swartz attacked the traitor from the rear as he passed near Bloemhof. Beyers did not stop to fight. He escaped across the Vaal River.

In the meantime Japie Fourie, the sinister hero of the revolution, was making trouble. Fourie was a friend of Beyers, and of the same mind. Personally he used to be a very pleasant man. But since a bullet in the Boer War had wounded him in the knee and hampered him by a limp, he had had to give up his famous athletic activities, and became diseased by Britain-hatred. Beyers had procured him a commission as Major in the Defence Force. Fourie followed his friend and leader into the revolution. Beyers was already on his ignominious escape when Jopie Fourie collected the broken and scattered remnants of the rebel forces in the Rustenburg district. Many of them were weary of their hopeless enterprise. But the Reverend Van Broekhuisen lifted the cross, and thundered that deserters went straight to hell. Japie Fourie supported him. The rebels returned to the thick of the fight. They blew up railway lines to hamper the movement of the government forces, and fought to the end with the cruelty of cornered beasts.

Only one leader of the revolution got away: Kemp. He had inherited De la Rey's mantle—he had been the general's lieutenant in the Boer War—and with the mantle the prophet Van Rensburg. Thus protected by Providence, he gathered anew eight hundred recruits, among them many *predikants*. On November 3 he occupied the small town of Schweizer Reneke, hoisted the *Vierkleur,* soiled the Union Jack in an unspeakable manner, and commandeered forage and supplies from the storekeepers, government-owned wagons and mules, all the horses of the civilians. He summoned the inhabitants in front of the courthouse, informed them that the two republics had been

proclaimed, and that he intended to form flying columns of men
with good horses. "When I get Jannie Smuts," he concluded, "I
will make mincemeat of him!"

After this oration he went to the pub, invited all the young
men in the town to have a round of beer on him, paid with
good money, not with requisition scraps, and let the cat out of
the bag: strictly confidentially he announced to all and sundry
that forty thousand German soldiers with three hundred guns
would arrive in the Transvaal within three weeks.

The drunken crowd haggled, in the best Boer fashion,
whether Oom Jannie should be put in front of the muzzle of
a Krupp gun, or executed with the help of an old-fashioned
sjambok. A free-for-all ensued over this difference of opinion.
The next morning, before most of them had slept themselves
sober, eleven hundred excellently mounted men, some with
two or three spare horses, cleared out of the town. Day and
night they rode, six hundred of the best horsemen forming the
main advance body, men so much one with their beasts that
they never fell from their saddles although they were constantly drunk. They left a bloody trail behind them. They pillaged every farm and store they passed, plundering horses,
food, and forage.

At Kheis Drift the Natal Light Horse under Colonel Royston
as well as a loyal commando were waiting to intercept them.
At 2:30 P.M. the Colonel, expecting reinforcements, saw a large
body carrying white flags and white armbands, the emblem of
the Defence Force, approaching him. Colonel Royston was
overjoyed. His men trotted to the appointed meeting. When
they arrived within safe firing distance, Kemp's disguised advance guard dismounted, and fired a murderous barrage into
the trapped ranks of the Natal Light Horse. He tried to rush
their camp. But here he was beaten back. Sniping continued
all night. Kemp, however, was already galloping to the German
South West African border.

God was with him, he afterwards boasted. The Kalahari
Desert he had to cross was miraculously drenched by torrential rains, which happened only once or so in a century. He

gulped down the rain. It tasted even better than the best beer. His horses did not starve either. The tropical vegetation of the desert provided ample forage. The Loyalists traced him in the sands. They found along the way remnants of his meals, quantities of half-emptied bottles of beer, evidently placed there earlier by his German accomplices, methodical people who did not trust in God alone. At the Sand Dune the troops caught up with him. Kemp made a last stand. He had seventy drunken followers left. He threw them against the troops. He himself turned his horse, fled, and slipped across the German border.

The trouble in the Transvaal was subdued. Beyers was on the run, Kemp in safety with his German friends. But the Free Staters were now on the point of rising. In order to avoid further bloodshed Botha and Smuts asked Hertzog to use his formidable influence with his fellow citizens. Hertzog did not reply. Maritz and the other rebel leaders asked for safe conduct to receive instructions from Hertzog. Permission was denied. Hertzog remained mute. Now everyone, friend and foe, believed that he was privy to the revolt.

Above all, De Wet believed it. One night, crazed by his superstitious obsession and blinded by his red-hot Britain-hatred, De Wet called his entire family from their beds. They gathered outside Memel, De Wet's farmhouse. The bearded old man in a disreputable nightshirt pointed to the dark sky. "See our Lord Jesus Christ!" he exclaimed. "Hear him calling us to save his people! Now is the time!"

The next day gang rule broke out in the district. Volunteers were attacked, trains seized, Loyalist meetings broken up. Mr. J. A. Joubert, the aged State Attorney, and Mr. Steenkamp betook themselves to the farm Memel. They pleaded for an end of the uproar. The irate old martinet challenged them to go outside and to repeat their counsel of moderation to the burghers. Both refused. They had come solely to talk to De Wet. Yet they were dragged on to the *stoep*, where they meekly faced an infuriated crowd, and uttered a few words of advice. Everyone looked at De Wet. He burst out: "Hold them as prisoners, and treat them as spies. If they try to escape, shoot them dead!"

Joubert and Steenkamp wrote letters in English to their wives. They were using the language of the hellhounds! De Wet barked. By way of punishment the two aged men were forced to accompany his commando on its first sallies, and to perform Kafir service. He also took them along to a secret meeting with Hertzog, where he learned that Smuts and Botha had appealed for the lawyer's intervention. De Wet laughed uproariously. "A strong government does not deal with traitors!" he exclaimed. Evidently Botha's and Smuts' was a weak government.

The news came that De Wet's youngest son had been killed in an encounter. The insane old man went into another paroxysm of laughter. "The apple of my eye!" he repeated time and again. Then he set up headquarters in the town of Reitz, which remained for six weeks in his possession—six weeks of organized thieving and terrorism. The same martyrdom was imposed on Kroonstad, Bethlehem, Heilbron and a dozen other purely Dutch towns in the Free State.

Finally, De Wet with one hundred fifty mounted men entered Vrede. A post-office clerk, watching on the outskirts of the town to estimate the strength of the onrushing commando, bicycled to the post office, and managed to shout through the open window: "One hundred fifty. . . . One hundred armed. . . ." By a hairbreadth Postmaster Evans could wire the message to the government in Pretoria. Then the commando caught up with him. He was knocked senseless. The post office was devastated. All precision instruments—which the rebels could not handle—were smashed. One group galloped through the streets, ordering every passer-by to come to the monument in front of the Dutch Reformed Church, unless he wanted to be driven there by *sjambok*.

De Wet, leaning majestically against the monument, called for the Magistrate. With true English sang-froid Mr. Colin Fraser refused to shake grinning De Wet's outstretched hand. He was not going to attend a rebel meeting. Six bodyguards assailed the Magistrate, and dragged and kicked him in front of their boss. Bruised, wounded, and bleeding, Mr. Fraser still defiantly faced the mad baboon.

De Wet poured out a collection of obscenities which *Taal* alone among all languages expresses. He delivered a crazed speech. "Magistrate, get a shorthand writer to take down every word I am going to say because whatever I may do in the future, I can never commit a greater act of rebellion than I have already committed." Then he babbled incoherent words about the *Vierkleur* and German arms and his misfortune in front of the British Magistrate who had fined him five shillings. Obviously the King of England had demanded this sinister act of oppression and so the peace of Vereeniging was void. Botha and Smuts were serving the "dead dog" England, and he would choke them with his bare hands. God willed it. Suddenly he switched into logic and precise language: "I am now going through the town to take the following six articles: horses, saddles, bridles, halters, arms and ammunition. If anyone should refuse to hand over these articles, I'll personally give him a thrashing with the *sjambok*. I herewith order the storekeepers to open their shops, and I will select men to go round and to take whatever I require, apart from the articles I mentioned. I will open closed shops in my own way. I have got my eight sons and sons-in-law here," he ended, with the strongest affirmation of Boer pride.

Vrede was pillaged. Then the pretty little town of Parys was systematically looted by the rebels now deteriorating to the level of common thieves. In Kroonstad, the Town Guard held out for fourteen anxious days behind a fortification line of sandbags, until Colonel Manie Botha came to relieve them. The *bywoners*—the poor whites living rent-free on farms—joined with the rebels. But the rest of the Free State was *takharen*—ashamed of themselves. They even rebuked Botha—who had let Beyers get away at their first encounter at Rustenberg in order to avoid spilling blood—for his exaggerated tolerance. Beyers was quick to spread the rumor that the government was secretly directing the Defence Force to inflict no harm upon the rebels. In view of Botha's and Smuts' evident disgust of the fratricidal strife, this rumor found wide credence. Smuts, indeed, sent an agent by the name of Cecil Meintjes to negotiate with Beyers, who pretended that he was ready to call off the revolt if the government agreed to carry out the action against South West Africa only with volunteers. But Mr. Meintjes was prevented from delivering this message in time. He was arrested, and kept under guard, until Beyers with the rest of his commando was at a safe distance. Instantly Beyers attacked, and sabotaged, the Northern Transvaal railroad line.

Appeasement was entirely discredited with the Loyalists. They chafed under the inactivity of the government. No one understood Smuts' deepest, almost enigmatic trait: his complete indifference toward hostility. Once more he tried to reconcile the traitor. He dispatched the Magistrate of Wolmaransstad, unescorted and unarmed, to follow up Beyers. The aged gentleman took his life in his hands, trailed Beyers, whose route was easily discernible by a line of burned farmhouses, blown-up railroad lines, and broken telegraph poles. One night, in a small town in the Free State, he caught up with the man he was after. Beyers drew his gun, but the old English Magistrate disarmed him with a smile. "You were too, how shall I say, too impatient, I believe, to wait for the Minister of Defence's answer to the message you most kindly sent him by Mr. Meintjes. Well, here I am with General Smuts' reply." The reply reaffirmed all previous promises on behalf of the government, and added two new enticements: a safe conduct for Beyers to meet De Wet, and a promise of amnesty for all crimes committed during the rebellion. Beyers demanded time to communicate with De Wet before he would give a definite answer.

De Wet, however, was dead set against compromising. He dodged President Steyn and his son, who wanted to meet him as mediators. He insisted that Hertzog was the only authority he would deal with. In the House of Assembly Hertzog spoke for the revolutionary cause. He mourned "the poor, downtrodden burghers who had been murdered, robbed, and wronged!" But he stubbornly refused to exercise his influence with De Wet in order to bring him to the conference table. This double dealing caused General Tobias Smuts, a distant relative of the Minister, to make the observation: "Hertzog always keeps silent when he ought to speak, and speaks when he ought to keep silent."

De Wet finally announced that he did not wish to see ex-President Steyn or any other go-between. He had every inten-tion of going to Maritz across the German border, and return-ing with him and his German allies to Pretoria, where "if God, in whom we all trust, so wills" independence would be pro-claimed. Simultaneously, his gang continued looting, burning and pillaging with a vengeance.

On November 11, on the last day before the promise of am-nesty was to expire, Botha placed himself at the head of a large force in the Free State, attacked De Wet's gang, which by then had been increased to 3,500 men, routed them, and drove them toward Koraanberg, where General Lukin was to trap them. But due to what was later explained as "faulty transmission"—probably an act of insidious sabotage—General Lukin got his orders a few hours too late. Once more De Wet slipped away. He fled toward the German border.

But his losses were irretrievable. His whole *laager* was gone, he had lost two hundred fifty prisoners, the casualties among his followers were heavy. This was against Botha's intention. He owed his victory primarily to two machine-guns, new weap-ons against which the rebels, only familiar with old-fashioned rifles, were entirely helpless. When Botha observed the enemy's heavy losses, he immediately silenced his machine-guns. His was a humanitarian warfare, no mass slaughter. Only a stray casualty here and there was permitted. Indeed, on Botha's or-der, the commanding officers had given the machine-gunners misleading ranges. But the gunners, not to be fooled, aimed correctly. After victory, which was chiefly due to them, they were severely taken to task by Botha.

A second encounter, the famous battle at Mushroom Valley, completely annihilated De Wet's gang. He had only twenty-five exhausted followers and dead-tired horses left when he attempted to cross the Vaal River. Nineteen of his men were beaten back at this attempt. De Wet with six others managed to negotiate the river late at night.

A new enemy arose: the motorcar. Commandant S. P. Du Toit with his motor patrol swept the country near the point where De Wet supposedly had crossed the river. At Karreeboskuiel he received the information that seven horsemen in full gallop had been seen racing westward. He soon came upon the group. But the cars could not follow the horsemen into the dense pathless jungle. Du Toit's patrol fired a volley at the fleeing men. They killed two horses. One horseman, De Wet's son-in-law, was taken prisoner. The other, H. Oost, until a short time before the editor of Hertzog's weekly in Pretoria, escaped.

Six men were left out of three thousand five hundred: De Wet, Brand Wessels, Koos van Coller, Wessels Potgieter, Gert Muller, and H. Oost. They hid in the woods. De Wet sent Brand Wessels to Bloemfontein to ex-President Steyn. Now he was prepared to confer with him about chances of peace.

Steyn urged Smuts strongly to accept. But when Smuts, after long and painful hesitation, makes up his mind, he sticks to his decision. In a letter dated Pretoria, November 17, he accused Steyn and Hertzog of allowing De Wet to claim them as allies. "We feel," he continued, "that the position has entirely changed since General Botha's first appeal to you to use your influence with De Wet and Beyers to avert bloodshed. Now the military situation is different. Even now we do not know whether this is not again an attempt to gain time." The letter ended demanding the unconditional surrender of the rebels.

Smuts had his "eyes and ears," his informers, throughout the length and breadth of the country. He knew every move of the fugitives. He was well aware that De Wet had got across to the Schweizer Reneke district in the Free State, where the last flames of the rebellion were still smouldering. In fact, De Wet had collected a few hundred more Free Staters. He took them westward, with the object of escaping across the desert to German South West Africa. He had made many forced marches in his adventurous life, but never one against such heavy odds. He trekked through a waterless, sandy country, ever changing his direction, hard pressed to escape his pursuers, and harder still to find a water hole now and then.

Colonel Brits pursued him with a fleet of motorcars. The cars, mostly American-made, proceeded in the desert sand with great difficulty. But Colonel Brits kept tracing the *spoor* of De Wet's horsemen. Besides, the few water holes in the desert were patrolled by Loyalists. At Marokwen Colonel Brits halted. From here, General Smuts had instructed him that there was not a single water hole until the farm of Waterbury, right at the German frontier. De Wet would have to stop either in Marokwen, or at the farm.

On Sunday the sentries at Marokwen saw a cavalcade of horsemen slowly passing at a distance. They offered a wretched sight. Men and horses looked like skeletons. Some decrepit horses were carrying two men. De Wet and his men had killed a few of their horses to quench their unbearable thirst by drinking the animals' blood. It would have been easy to annihilate the forlorn handful of men in a single attack. But that was exactly what Smuts would never have forgiven. He wanted Colonel Brits to bring De Wet home alive.

The cavalcade crept on. Colonel Brits guessed that they would take all Sunday as well as the following day to reach the farm Waterbury. So the night between Monday and Tuesday would bring the kill. On Monday Colonel Jordaan arrived to reinforce Brits. Acting as their own scouts, the two colonels approached the farm. The house was teeming with newcomers. De Wet, haggard, terribly aged, his beard snow white, grinned happily. He could not tear himself away from the fountain. He drank and drank.

On Monday night Colonel Jordaan picked out seventy men. He spoke to each of them separately, explaining exactly what each was to do. Before dawn the men crept through the bush, encircled the farmhouse, attacked De Wet's stable guards. The bandits were not able to utter a word before they felt the cold steel of the rifles at their temples. Then Colonel Jordaan called in ringing tones: "Surrender!"

De Wet and the faithful Oost were the first to come out of the house. They attempted a run for the stables, but they found themselves encircled. There was a moment of deadly silence. Then De Wet threw up his arms. "The race is run!" he grinned.

He and his men were disarmed, brought to Vryburg by motorcar, and then by train to Johannesburg. Throughout the whole journey De Wet tried to maintain his poise. But his looks betrayed him. His clothes were rags, his broad-brimmed felt hat was riddled with bullet holes, his face was deeply lined and crumpled. Nevertheless, his eyes had kept their shrewd glance, and the broad gold chain across the shrunken belly recalled that he had once been a prosperous burgher. He was still bragging. "I will hang higher than any of you!" he told his fellow prisoners. To the military police he said: "Your motorcars beat me. I never believed they would get through the sand."

Beyers, too, was a beaten man. He had lost his old equanimity. His moves were marked by a complete lack of resolution. Here and there he made minor raids with his commando, shrunk to twenty-five men. On his last day he was seen near the farm Greyling's Request on the Transvaal side of the Vaal. A little boy who had waded through the river brought this news to the farmer Jacobs, who, in turn, informed the Loyalists. Troops moved up from all sides. Beyers was cornered. But he told his field-cornet, the Reverend Boshoff: "As long as there is life in me, I will make a fight for it." These were his last coherent words.

He removed his garters, spurs, revolver, and threw off his mackintosh. He mounted a stolen horse—his own had been killed—and plunged into the river. His guide, a man by the name of Jan Pietersee, also mounted, pushed ahead of them into the swiftly running, swollen stream.

In the meantime the Loyalist forces had occupied both banks of the river. Captain Uys' men, on the Transvaal side, opened fire at about fifty or sixty yards. Beyers' horse, frightened, swung around, and struggled in the water. It refused to go into the hail of bullets.

Beyers could no longer even manage a horse. He slipped out of the saddle, and started to swim back to the Free State side, which was much nearer. Whether his mind was still able to grasp that he was swimming straight toward capture and the firing squad, was no longer discernible. Pietersee made good progress. Spurred by the fanatic loyalty of a typical Boer follower, however, he turned back to assist Beyers when he saw his leader in difficulties. A bullet struck the faithful man. The water around him was red with blood. Still Pietersee struggled desperately toward Beyers. Suddenly he disappeared.

Beyers, swimming on his back, was heard shouting: *"Ek kaunie meer nie!"* (I can't do any more!) The soldiers on the Transvaal side thrust a big branch from a tree in his direction. Beyers could not grasp it. One of Captain Uys' men nearest to him shouted to ask whether he was wounded. Beyers cried back: *"Ik kan nie swem nie; die jas is tussen my bene!"* (I cannot swim, the coat got between my legs!) Suddenly he threw up his hands, and dropped like a stone beneath the muddy waters. It was panic-suicide by drowning.

When Captain Uys saw Beyers going down, he asked for a volunteer to jump after him into the swollen river. Private Reneke obliged. But while he was undressing, Beyers' last men, who had, entirely unmoved, watched their leader's death struggle, opened fire. Reneke was forced to seek cover. The handful of remaining rebels, under the Reverend Boshoff, were captured and disarmed.

For an hour and a half the troops tarried along both banks. The flood receded some eight or ten feet. Many dead fish were left on the banks. The body of Beyers was only recovered after three days of torrential rains. He was coatless. He had stripped off his coat before leaping into the water. It appeared that his shoelaces had become entangled, and thus his feet had been tied together. At his last outcry he had mistaken his shoelaces for his jacket.

Smuts was deeply shocked when the story of Beyers' death was reported to him. "I must write to his widow," he said. "She must hear it from a friend." He sat down at his desk, his head leaning on his left arm, his open left hand supporting his forehead and protecting his face from onlookers. He wrote with flying speed.

Japie Fourie was the last man to surrender. In Smuts' words, his band "was the only one to remain contumacious." Defying all rules of warfare, the treacherous Defence Force Officer discarded his rebel uniform and fought on in mufti. He let his wild, black beard grow so that his cheeks, his chin, and his mouth were almost hidden behind his whiskers. Yet everyone recognized him by the piercing look in his eyes, by his long, irregular brows, and by the enormous flower he wore in his buttonhole, as was his custom. He assailed and ambushed straggling officers and soldiers, and killed them with calculated cruelty. However, he remained faithful to the hallowed Boer tradition. On Dingaan's Day—South Africa's Fourth of July—he refused to fight.

It was on this very Dingaan's Day that Colonel Pretorius, the grandson of the founder of the Transvaal, and Fourie's own cousin, trapped the outlaw at Nooitgedacht. He asked Fourie to surrender. Instead, the bandit and his men opened fire at a range of twelve yards. Twelve of Colonel Pretorius' men were killed before Fourie was captured. He was immediately brought to Pretoria. A court-martial was arranged, strictly according to military law. One of its members asked General Smuts to be excused from the jury, since he was an old friend of Fourie's. So much the more he should sit on the bench, Smuts replied.

The trial took place on Saturday. Japie Fourie made a defiant speech. He asked for mercy to be shown to his brother, who had only followed his own lead. He did not try to conceal his crimes. He boasted of them. He concluded with a curse against England. The verdict, condemning him to death, was unanimous.

Friends of Fourie tried to interfere on his behalf with Botha. They could not reach the Prime Minister, who spent the critical week end in strict seclusion at his son-in-law's farm.

On Sunday morning a volley in the Pretoria prison yard put Japie Fourie to death. The echo of the shots resounded for many years throughout South Africa. The irreconcilable Boers had their martyr.

In Parliament, Smuts defended the decision of the court, pointing out that the case was not a question of "Khaki versus Boer," but "the pith of a nation against a marauding band."

Even Hertzog declaimed in the House of Assembly: "The government has done its duty in suppressing disorder and violence in the country. I have never accused the government of having done anything wrong in so doing." This miserable opportunist and fence-sitter wisely passed over in silence the potent fact that a single word of his at the right moment would have prevented the whole revolution.

A commission of inquiry was appointed, and a Bluebook on the rebellion laid on the table of the House. The nationalists attacked both the commission and the Bluebook, edited by an outstanding university professor, in unmeasured terms. Hertzog was again back where he belonged. He led the choir of vituperation. He asserted that Maritz had used his name without his authority. "Why did Hertzog not repudiate him?" a heckler asked. "I would have lost all my influence over the people!" came the frank reply. "If I would have spoken openly, I would have been placed where others were already—in jail. If I had reproached the rebels, I would have prostituted myself. I was never much a man of hollow protests, nor was I inclined to go to jail to please the Minister of Defence."

The Honorable J. W. Quinn, Unionist member from the Rand, expressed the unanimous feeling of the majority: "I would have shot the honorable member from Smithfield. But his is not the kind that gets shot. He is safe. He walks in the dark, and you can't shoot men in the dark."

The surviving traitors were dealt with extremely leniently. Although De Wet was captured as he was about to go over to the Germans, Smuts testified on his behalf that there was not the slightest evidence of his having had any connection with the enemy. The martinet was condemned to a term of six years, but released after less than a year and a half.

General Kemp and his prophet Van Rensburg, who had escaped to South West Africa, surrendered as Botha invaded the German colony, while Maritz fled to Germany. They were permitted to return. No punishment was inflicted upon them. General Kemp is still today a Member of the House of Assembly, and one of the most ferocious opponents of Smuts.

The five shilling revolution ended ignominiously. None of its objects was achieved. Only military operations in German South West Africa were delayed for three months, greatly to the advantage of the not-quite-prepared South African Defence Force.

When Smuts was duly indemnified in Parliament, he joined Botha, who was already at the front, in driving the Germans out of the South West.

Chapter 20   TWO-FRONT WAR

IN THE MIDDLE OF APRIL, 1915, GENERAL SMUTS SAILED TO GERman South West Africa, to take command of the southern forces, while General Botha was operating in the North. There was little doubt about the outcome. Forty-four thousand men of the Defence Force were pitted against nine thousand Germans. It was, however, the baptism of fire for the South Africans, the first military action in the short history of the Union, whereas the Germans were seasoned colonial veterans. Moreover, the equipment of the Defence Force was rather sketchy, its organization was still in its infancy, and there was no trained general staff.

While Botha operated from Swakopmund, Smuts' force pushed in from Luederitz Bay, which an English formation had taken months before, and went on, struggling against sandstorms, torrid heat, and venomous insects. The Germans had abandoned the flats along the coast. But before retreating they had littered the soil with land mines, and poisoned every water hole. The Union soldiers had to rely on distilled sea water, hauled over the desert sands for hundreds of miles. Not before they reached Garub did they find fresh natural water. Garub lies on the edge of the desert, only a few miles before the highlands begin. Here the Germans had entrenched themselves in strong positions. The only pass leading through the pathless hills was the neck of Aus, which was fortified with trenches cut in the solid rock.

Smuts applied the lessons the Boer War had taught him. The commandos had rarely ventured upon frontal attacks. They preferred to swing around the flanks, and by-pass the enemy. True to his old pattern, as guerrilla raider, Smuts outflanked the obstacle. The Germans were threatened in the rear. They fled. The dreaded neck of Aus passed into the hands of the Union forces.

Throughout the time this operation took, Smuts had secretly dispersed four powerful columns. The first column executed a brilliant march across the Kalahari Desert, trekking a distance of over seven hundred miles of desolate country with practically no grazing for the horses, and very little water for the men. A few canisters were transported by motorcar. The horses could chew the thorn bushes. Most of the animals had to be left behind, but the column made a beeline for the German railway center at Keetmanshoop. At the same time the three other columns pushed on from the southeast and the south. Finding themselves menaced on all sides, the Germans precipitately retreated to Windhoek, the capital, and the seat of the wireless station which was the first and most important goal of the campaign. Botha anticipated the enemy's move, and hurried in forced marches to arrive before the Germans. At this stage Herr Seitz, the German Governor General, made his first suggestion for an armistice. He pointed out that, despite the retreat in his own territory, the Germans were winning everywhere in Europe, and that this factor would decide the war. South Africa would have incurred the wrath of a world-dominating German Empire. Why not avoid this fate? Why not call it a campaign? Each side should remain in the possession of the territory held at this particular moment. Fighting should stop.

After consultation with Smuts, Botha insisted on the surrender of all South West Africa. Seitz refused, left the conference, but reappeared on the next day to announce his unconditional surrender.

Some of his followers carried on their struggle for a short time. But when they felt the first bombs from British airplanes, they ran. However, they did not forget to strew mines behind them. Six thousand were removed by the South African engineers, for a loss of only six lives. Now the last German commander resisting, Colonel Franck, approached Botha with the insolent words: "I come to give up, Mr. . . . hm, Mr. . . . Shall I call you Mr. Botha, or how else? Of course I cannot recognize you as a general. Generals are made in Germany."

Botha replied that his rank did not matter, as long as his terms were accepted: unconditional surrender. The German bully threw up his hands.

Peace was concluded a few days later. The Union of South Africa had conquered a territory larger than France. But Smuts insisted immediately that the vanquished should get a fair deal. He issued an order of the day: "All ranks of the Union forces are reminded that self-restraint, courtesy, and consideration of the feelings of others on the part of the troops, whose good fortune it is to be the victors, are essential."

The conquest of South West Africa, executed with clockwork precision, was the first Allied success in the First World War. Due to Smuts' constitutional leniency, the Germans in the territory, however, never learned that they were beaten. Mono-

cled, horsewhip in hand, their disarmed officers strutted along
the streets of Windhoek. Every night German national songs
were chanted. German South West Africa, although later at
Versailles made a mandate of the Union of South Africa, remained the hotbed of Pangermanism, and became the stronghold of incipient Nazism in Africa.

Flag-waving, and covered with garlands, Pretoria received
the victors, Botha and Smuts, toward the middle of July. But
this demonstration of loyalty was deceptive. The capital was
flooded by witnesses to the inquiry into the five-shilling revolution. Although the nationalists boycotted the inquiry, without
being punished for their defiance of the law, the tension was,
once again, almost unbearable. It was increased by the aftermath of the *Lusitania* demonstrations. After the Germans had
committed the crime of sinking the *Lusitania*—a crime that
materially affected feelings in the then still neutral United
States, and undoubtedly contributed to America's entry into
the war—the Loyalists in most important towns in the Union
lost their patience with the government's complacency toward
the Germans in South Africa. It was particularly Smuts who
had warned the people against "persecuting" the Germans in
the country. "Myself," he had stated in Parliament, amidst peals
of laughter, "I am frequently taken for a German." When the
news of the *Lusitania* came through, however, Johannesburg
patriots got out of hand. They had already held a number of
protest meetings against the lenient way in which the Defence
Department dealt with the internment of Germans, and against
continued trading with the enemy—meetings against which
Smuts had protested in a telegram to the mayor. Now aroused
masses occupied the premises of firms which continued business as usual with Germany via the Portuguese colonies. Offices,
shops, warehouses and even private residences of subversive
elements were wrecked. Similar scenes were repeated at Kru-
gersdorp and elsewhere in the mining area. They also occurred,
though on a smaller scale, in Pretoria and Natal.

The government was compelled to step up the internment

of Germans. In a way this measure backfired. It kindled the
flames of hatred among the rapidly increasing number of nationalist Boers. Suddenly half of them claimed their own German descent. The victorious campaign in South West Africa
was not popular with them. Smuts tried to minimize the new
wave of agitation. Dismissing the recruits from South West
Africa, he warned them ironically that they would hear terrible
atrocity stories about their conduct during the campaign, as
soon as they returned to their farms and *dorps*. In fact, such
stories mushroomed. On the other hand, complaints about alleged cruelties were intermingled with derision of Botha and
Smuts for not having taken more prisoners. Hertzog, who stood
behind the new upheaval, carefully, as ever, in shadow, played
both ends against the middle.

Johannesburg repeated the triumphant welcome Pretoria
had given Botha and Smuts. In the hope of bringing the English population and the sensible and decent part of the Boer
people together, the government decided to hold general elections. The House was five years old. It no longer represented
the opinion of the nation.

Smuts and Botha found the going worse than rough. Even
Johannesburg was in a miserable state. The Rand industry was
faced with almost insurmountable obstacles. Yet it had to carry
on. Its output of gold was of vital importance for the Empire
at war. Other difficulties were due to war conditions. Military
priorities as well as the dangers of the U-boat made impossible
replacements from England of obsolete machines, whereas
South Africa, at that time, had no steel industry of its own. The
labor situation was even more of a menace. All able-bodied
Englishmen, to the last man, had joined the forces, both the
Defence Force and the Imperial troops overseas. Among them
was Mr. Creswell, the Labor leader. His place in the Labor
Party was taken by power-drunk, illiterate Boer union bosses
who instigated a rule of terror. The miners, now mostly Dutch
peasant boys, exacted conditions which all but ruined the industry. They extorted unlimited and exorbitant concessions in
wages, working hours, paid holidays. Discipline was entirely

gone. Directors, managers, and even foremen lived in constant fear for their lives. In the end, working costs per ton far exceeded the value of the gold won at standard prices. These absurd circumstances prevailed throughout the war.

The Nationalists under Hertzog, although arch-reactionaries, encouraged "syndicalism," as the forerunner of Communism was called, in the mines, in order to cause trouble to the government and to impede the war effort. Hertzog declared at Edenburg: "South Africa has done enough for the Empire. Personally, I object to any more money being expended on the cause of the Empire."

Smuts retorted that South Africa was fighting for her own cause. It was impossible to tolerate Germany as a neighbor. Besides, the whole expenditure of the South West African campaign had been less than fifteen millions, an amount worth the conquest of a country almost as big as the Union itself, and opening the gates to further expansion.

This very argument incensed the Nationalists still more. They hated Smuts' budding conception of Pan-Africa. They did not want to be mixed up with countries settled by non-Boers. They feared the idea of losing their scant majority among the white people.

Smuts carried on the fight for his vision of the future, African brotherhood, which was later to develop into the ideal of human brotherhood. "Our northern boundaries will not be where they are now, and we shall leave to our children a huge country, in which to develop a type for themselves, and to form a people which will be a true civilizing agent in this dark continent. That is the large view!"

The large view? "Rhodes reborn!" shouted the Nationalist press. "Civilizing agents!" To hell with this nauseating civilization! The children should become God-fearing Calvinistic plantation owners, as their forefathers were. Among the three sects of the Dutch Church, only one, the United, gave the government a modicum of support. The other two, the *Hervormde* and the *Gereformeerde*, sent their somber *predikants* right into the fray, to attack and curse the government.

The paper that had called Smuts "Rhodes reborn," was a newcomer to the South African press. Its first issue appeared in Cape Town the very day Botha returned from the South-Western campaign. Its editor was Dr. Daniel François Malan, Hertzog's henchman. The unfrocked clergyman was entering the newspaper world, he insisted, to raise the level of political debate, and to reinstate the old dignity of controversy. *Die Burger* was soon involved in more slander, libel, and blackmail cases than the rest of the whole South African press together. Today it still leads the choir of the pro-Nazis. Keerom Street, where *Die Burger's* premises stand, sounds as Cliveden sounded once in England.

At the same time another debutant bowed his way into the public. *Herr* Oswald Pirow, then the Hertzogite candidate on the Rand, declared ominously: "The ill-advised policy of our opponents will ruin South Africa, and thereby, for all practical purposes, rob the British Empire of the fairest of its colonies." His Dutch audience had difficulty in understanding the words the round-cheeked, pale-faced young man with the piercing, small, black eyes behind rimless spectacles, was sputtering. Herr Pirow had difficulties with the Dutch language, which he has not yet quite overcome.

De Wet was released from prison, where he had been treated like a patient in a sanitarium. He pledged himself not to get involved in politics. Immediately, however, he stumped the country, predicting "great changes in the constitutional position of South Africa" and confiding to his adherents that he still regarded himself as the George Washington below the equator.

Perturbed by the competition, Hertzog summoned his men to a congress of the Nationalists in Pretoria. Advocate Tielman Roos, the chairman of the Transvaal branch of the party, and Hertzog's right-hand man, opened the attack by calling Botha and Smuts "no better than hysterical old Kafir hags." The joke was received with uproarious laughter. Ever witty Advocate Roos' future in the Nationalist movement was assured. A delegate by the name of Roux told the Congress that he had been walking some time "with dynamite in his pocket for Botha and Smuts."

Hertzog remained conspicuously silent. The frail little man, much too carefully attired for his surrounding, simply nodded when the congress rose to cheer him at the end of the session.

Smuts was the principal speaker on the other side, both on behalf of the government and for the cause of the war effort. He conducted his campaign on the pattern of a khaki election. He expressed his pride in the success of the first campaign which should not be the last. In the face of furious resentment he continued to call for volunteers, even for the Imperial forces on the European battlefields. Vigorously he defended Botha against the Nationalist slander that the Prime Minister had "become an Englishman." He appealed to the English voters for support, asking them the very English question: "Have we not played the game?"

"You have!" roared the Boers in reply. The hatred of the irreconcilables became pathological. In all his meetings Smuts was confronted with pictures of the dead men, De la Rey, Beyers, and Japie Fourie. The latter's widow complained that the corpse of her late husband had been desecrated. When Smuts refuted this crazy insinuation, she insisted on seeing the body. But the government had buried Japie Fourie in an undisclosed place, lest his grave should become the scene of rioting and demonstration. After the elections it would be, and indeed it was, opened to Mrs. Fourie, and she was satisfied that her husband was resting in peace.

Mrs. De la Rey published an open letter laying the responsibility for her husband's death squarely at Smuts' door. The letter kindled the flames of the Boer racialists into white heat. There was general talk of a new revolution. The talk did not even stop when the fact was revealed that the infuriating letter had been written while Mrs. De la Rey was staying as Mrs. Smuts' guest at *Doornkloof*, and that it was a fake.

Like the furies the nationalist Boer women plunged into the

upheaval. Thousands of families were torn asunder. The father's hand was raised against his son; neighbors became deadly enemies.

On September 23, the pandemonium climaxed in the infamous outrage at Newlands, the Dutch suburb of Johannesburg. Smuts was warned against speaking in this center of hooliganism. He braved the danger. A terrific din arose as soon as he entered the hall. His "dynamic" friend Roux, whom Smuts later described as an "unkempt, desperate-looking man," was among the audience, as was Mary Fitzgerald, in spite of her English name one of the fiercest Boer furies. She had taken an innocent tot along which, she pretended, was the orphan of one of the "murdered" revolutionists of 1914, a man by the name of Labuschagne. Jostled by the mob, the child cried, and thus beyond doubt established its identity.

The rowdy meeting that ensued was well organized. First rotten eggs were thrown at the speaker, then brickbats, and beer bottles. When Smuts tried to speak, the crowd howled him down with the words *"Zuid Afrika Eerste"* (South Africa First!), the battle cry of the racialists.

Smuts remained immovable. His friends urged and beseeched him to leave. He did not listen. The first heavy stones were thrown. Then only he decided that it was time to close the meeting. Some innocent by-standers would be killed, he feared. Personally fearless as ever, he battled his way right through the densest crowd, who belabored his followers with sticks, pick handles and *sjamboks*. Some even hit the Minister. He returned blow for blow.

In front of the hall Smuts' faithful chauffeur, Hodgson, was twice pulled out of the driver's seat before he could start. When the car left, a few shots were exchanged. One was fired by a detective, into the air, to frighten the hoodlums. A few shots were undoubtedly aimed at Smuts, who did not bat an eyelash. He was always sure that his was a charmed life.

A social gathering should have followed the political meeting. Smuts' only comment was: "Verily, a social!" But a few days later he acknowledged: "I am the best hated man in South

Africa." Yet he refused a worried friend's well-meant advice to
relax or better to resign, in order to save his life. He was no
quitter. Fate had burdened him with a great task. He rejoiced
in carrying his load.

The elections left the South African Party—the governmental
party—with fifty-four seats, as the strongest in the House. But
the absolute majority was gone. The Unionists, the English,
under Sir Thomas Smarrt won thirty-nine seats. Hertzog's following leaped from five to twenty-seven. The Labor Party returned in the old strength of four men. There were six independents.

A complete volte-face had taken place in the Free State. The
South African Party, which had carried all but one seat in 1910,
lost every constituency. In turn Hertzog, who had won his own
constituency in Smithfield with the overwhelming majority of
1,315 against 272, gained all the seats in the Free State but one
in Bloemfontein which went to the Unionists. More than 30
per cent of the voters were revealed as Nationalists, among
them a majority of the rural electorate.

In the first session of the new Parliament the government
passed important consolidating measures, attempting seriously
to deal with the industrial and social troubles. Parliament col-
laborated loyally. But restiveness was ever increasing on the
platteland. Incessantly Hertzog reiterated his battle cry: South
Africa First! When the government introduced a most modest
bill to curtail trade with the enemy and, in order to stave off
more radical demands by the Unionists, declared that South
Africa proposed to follow the United Kingdom's policy on that
matter, but not to go a step further, Hertzog jumped up from
his seat. "The government says that South Africa's interests
need not be considered, but that only the Imperial interests
count. The Ministry is intimating that what is good enough for
the United Kingdom is good enough for the Union. I warn the
government. That is a fatal policy."

Throughout the First World War South Africa remained an
unhappy and torn-asunder country. Anti-British feelings were

widespread. Even the Dutch press supporting Botha and Smuts could not refrain from gloating over English reverses, and from mildly advocating the new creed of Hertzogism. Yet the position of the government was assured. The Unionists, His Majesty's loyal opposition, lent their political foes all their strength. Colonel Creswell, the Labor leader, declared: "The Nationalist speeches betray a wish that we may lose the war." He swung his party into an all-out effort to see the war through. Hertzog remained the leader of defeatism. Both on African soil and on the blood-soaked European battlefields the South African soldiers, Dutch and English alike, put up an excellent show. Once more they proved that South African troops, affectionately called Springboks, in the right hands, are great and gallant fighters.

On the fifth of January, 1916, Smuts, at Potchefstroom, reviewed a body of volunteers for East Africa. He emphasized the hardships they must expect. German East Africa was the haunt of the tsetse fly, the deadly enemy of man and beast. His "beloved sons" would not find the sandy flats of South West Africa. They would have to march through a country covered with thick, in some parts almost impenetrable, bush. He regretted that for compelling reasons—the foremost of which, it went without saying, was Hertzog—he could not accompany them. But they would have a gallant leader: the British General Smith-Dorrien, the hero of Mons. Moreover, General Crewe of the Defence Force, an English officer during the Boer War, would look after the Springboks.

General Smith-Dorrien arrived at Cape Town. Immediately he fell gravely ill. His illness, however, could not delay the departure of the South African contingent. The rainy season was drawing dangerously close, and the move had to be made instantly.

London sounded out Smuts whether he would accept the command. Smuts seized the opportunity with both hands. It was an escape into the most advanced, most perilous fighting

line. But it was an escape from a hated fratricidal strife at home
into a good fight against a real enemy in a hostile land.

On the tenth of February he was officially appointed Lieutenant-General in the Imperial Army, and Commander in Chief
of the campaign in the German South East. Both the London
newspapers and the South African English-language press
showered him with praise. *Die Burger*, Dr. Malan's venomous
sheet, congratulated him, too—now he would draw double pay.
It was a miserable lie. Smuts served the British Empire without
pay. He only drew his salary as a South African Minister.

On Friday, the eleventh of February, in the late evening, he
left Pretoria, where he had spent the last hours with routine
desk work. His family and a few friends gathered at the railroad station. One of them asked why he was leaving the country at such a critical period to venture into the land of the
anopheles, malaria, the tsetse fly, and the jigger flea. With a
quiet glance of his steel-blue eyes Smuts answered: "Do you
know that there are seventeen thousand of our men there?"

He kissed his grandchild, little Klein-Jannie, good-bye. The
train thundered away. A handkerchief waved from the window
of the reserved car. A few minutes after midnight, on February
12, the General had joined up again.

He was now an Imperial general, not only a Boer commander. Yet he remained Springbok number one. He shared
the almost unbearable hardships of his men. Once he saw a
soldier in the ranks collapsing with an attack of malaria. The
Commander in Chief jumped from his horse, lifted the poor
devil on to his own saddle, led the horse, walking at the bridle,
and talking to the delirious patient, to impart to him something
of his own strength and confidence.

In due course Smuts himself was stricken with malaria. He
refused to yield to the disease. He lived on quinine pills, and
carried on. His very appearance was a tonic to the troops. His
big Vauxhall, in which, according to François Brett-Young,
then an officer in the campaign, "Smuts daily risked his life"
was cheered wherever it was seen.

251

There was nothing of the showman in him. On the contrary. Once more he seemed inaccessible, not in his private conduct, but in his conduct of the expedition. Probably he had already learned that there was somewhere an invisible, but unbridgeable gap between him and lesser human beings. Even his most intimate collaborators, ranking among whom were General van der Venter, his faithful companion during the Cape raid, and the Boer General Joubert, were only let into his plans as far as they were immediately concerned.

The men in the ranks knew nothing of this self-seclusion. They chanted to the tune of *John Peel*:

> D'ye ken Jan Smuts when he's after the Hun?
> D'ye ken Jan Smuts when he's got them on the run?
> D'ye ken Jan Smuts when he's out with his gun?
> And his horse, and his men in the morning?
>
> Yes, I ken Jan Smuts, and Jourdain too,
> Van der Venter and the sportsman Selous,
> Springbok, and Sikh, for they're all true-blue
> When they're strafing the Hun in the morning.

Unfortunately it was not as easy as that to strafe the Hun in the morning. Germany had entrusted her most brilliant World War number one general, von Lettow-Vorbeck, with the defense of South East Africa. He was under Wilhelm II's special order to hold the "gem of the German Colonial Empire" at all costs.

When Smuts arrived, a reconnaissance force, on its first march to M'buyuni, where the railway ended, had scouted the enemy entrenched in great strength upon the eastern slopes of the very difficult Kili terrain. The German "pom-poms" and mountain guns were admirably placed, and difficult to locate. Smuts reconnoitered the situation for himself. Again he permitted himself one of his rare smiles. T'Chaka, the Lion of the Zulus, had known a method of handling exactly this strategic position. The great black swordsman had based his idea on the horns of a bull, enveloping the enemy by an outflanking movement. On this principle Smuts sent his mounted brigade, based on the

Kili, to sweep along the western foothills. His Springboks, born on horseback, were just the right men to do that. The main force was concentrated for a thrust at Moshi, the terminus of the Tanganyika-Kili railway. Stubbornly contesting every foot of the ground, the Germans fell back. Emperor Wilhelm's Askaris, shining black sons of the bush, grinned at the white troops assailing them on this difficult territory that only a native could really negotiate. To show them how wrong they were the South Africans went at them in a most workmanlike and effective manner, with butt and bayonet.

The second position of the Germans was protected by seven miles of dense bush, behind the River Lumi. In an arduous night march the South Africans passed the Lumi. Their mounted men occupied Chala Hill and other slopes. On March 11 Smuts' infantry brigades attacked precipitously the bush-clad hills of Reater and Latema. They worked their way through thick, thorny scrub, which, however, offered little protection against the guns of the sunken German cruiser *Koenigsberg,* now defending the hills. It was a slow and costly advance. Its main objective was a green *kopje,* surmounted by a fort, that alternately flaunted the German and, in honor of the Askari garrison, the prophet's green flag. The Springboks rushed the first and second lines of the trenches. By night, from the third line of defense, the Askaris made a counterattack. They fought like demons. The explanation of their reckless ferocity was revealed in the morning. Water bottles filled with raw spirits were found on the bodies of their dead. At dawn the Germans were driven out. For the first time they practiced what from then on was to become their habit: to leave behind their wounded, sick and dead, for their foes to care for.

Smuts' own troops were plagued with diseases. He understood that only colored troops were really able to withstand, both constitutionally and morally, the conditions prevailing in East Africa. He reported to London that it was impossible to keep white troops for any length of time in this particular battle area, that produced not only bodily unfitness, but mental depression. Moreover, native troops were immune to the scourge of malaria. Raw recruits from Nigeria and the Congo were dispatched to him, and he trained them, while he had already made up his mind to send home most of his South African boys. But as long as they were on duty, he tolerated no fatigue. "Fear? Hunger? Thirst?" he asked, when his generals warned him against overstraining his men. "No time for that!" He himself took no time out "for that." He looked pale, thin, emaciated. But he drove the Germans from what General von Lettow-Vorbeck believed to be a practically impregnable position around Kilimanjaro. Smuts captured this highest peak in Africa, though at a cost in human lives that surpassed all the losses of the South West Africa campaign together. Now he was in the undisputed possession of the richest part of East Africa, the Moschi-Aruscha region.

After the seizure of Moschi, the railroad of the Tanganyika line, and with van der Venter threatening the central line from Dar-es-Salaam to Tanganyika, Smuts' men made steady progress through dense bushes, under a blazing sun and torrential rains, encircling elaborately prepared positions, fighting fiercely and winning an endless series of minor engagements. The first task was to clear the railway. Smuts proceeded methodically. With three mobile columns he swept the country from the frontier to Pagani. It was an adventurous enterprise. For the first time human beings in concerted action worked their way through the virgin bush along the foothills of the Pare Mountains. The tire tracks of armored cars mingled with the *spoor* of the ostrich. Airplanes, protecting the advancing columns, frightened away the startled game by the thousands. Man appeared in the jungle.

On June 13 Smuts' troops occupied the important center of Wilhelmstal. In the meantime van der Venter, assaulting Kondoa-Irangi, attracted as many soldiers as Lettow-Vorbeck could spare. For four days this German stronghold was besieged by starving South Africans. But when the news spread that Smuts in person was coming, the mounted Springboks with empty bellies charged, drove out the German defenders, and chased Lettow-Vorbeck's dwindling forces in the direction of Handeni.

There Smuts himself went after them, but found the nest empty. Again the native spies had warned the Germans. Colonel Byron, with some British platoons, followed them through the thick bush, correctly in the prescribed English battle formation. He engaged the more numerous enemy, and, after three hours of bitter fighting, when dusk fell was forced to retreat. German machine-guns fired into their rear. This was too much provocation. Colonel Byron commanded: turn about! The German machine-guns revealed themselves by their spurts of flame. In a night-long fight, Englishman against machine-gun, the machine-gun lost. They were silenced. Once more the Germans fled.

On June 23 Smuts issued secret orders for a night march with "unwheeled" transport. The guns had to be carried on mule back. Late in the afternoon long lines of infantry in "Indian file" vanished in the dark recesses of the jungle. No light was shown. Smoking was strictly forbidden. On the next day the enemy was located as he waited behind the heavily fortified Lukigwra River. General Sheppard advanced to make a frontal attack. His raw men raised a terrific din. The Germans immediately fell into the trap. They attacked while Sheppard's men retreated in perfect order, but rather in a hurry. General Hosken made a wide encircling movement. At noon his British Fusiliers and Kashmiris took the hills protecting the flank, but Sheppard, reinforced and this time in earnest, repulsed the German attempt to break out of a trap by crossing the river.

Simultaneously Brigadier-General Crewe, the "co-operating officer from the artillery," sent a mounted platoon forward, as a reconnoitering patrol. Returning, the horseman could suggest the distance and the direction of the targets, imparting a knowledge particularly useful for "indirect" fire from guns firing from a covered position at an unseen target. British artillery was thus converted to an offensive weapon. Its accurate, deadly fire exterminated the German contingent. Smuts showed himself rather pleased. He had not made a frontal attack, which he hated for its cost in human lives, but again one of his precious flank attacks, so heavy with memories of the Boer War.

Naval landing parties arrived. With their co-operation Smuts could, at his leisure, occupy smaller ports. Now supplies streamed in by sea. Smuts redoubled the energy of his drive. On September 6 he entered Dar-es-Salaam, ironically called Haven of Peace. The Union Jack was hoisted over the colonial capital. The German administration fled to the native *kraal* of Moro-Moro. But there they were driven out by Belgians from the Congo after ten days of desperate fighting. Smuts controlled practically all of South East Africa.

But the indomitable General von Lettow-Vorbeck now played Smuts' own guerrilla game in reverse. Although his last men had no more military importance, but only a certain nuisance value, they were still roaming East Africa on the day the peace of Versailles was signed.

Soon after his departure from East Africa, Smuts received a letter containing the perfect indictment of the German colonial power which he had smashed. This letter, incidentally, was, on October 24, 1918, presented to the American Senate by Mr. Lodge, and embodied in the Senate Document of the Sixty-Fifth Congress as Document 296.

The letter is dated Magila Mission, Mukeza, Tanganyika, November 7, 1917, addressed to Lieutenant-General Jan Christian Smuts, "relative to German rule in East Africa," and written by Frank Weston, D.D., Bishop of Zanzibar, Head of the Universities' Mission in the Eastern Districts of German East Africa, who had served as a porter, commanding African carriers in the coastal column of the East African Force. It reads:

Many thousands of porters and carriers who served the forces of Great Britain would be executed by the authorities if the German administration should return. If we let the Kaiser have East Africa again, we would be guilty of a monstrous betrayal of thousands who gladly trusted us and followed us into the war.

I have won my own personal experience in my twenty years of residence in East Africa. I have many friends among Mohammedans and heathen Africans. Swahili became "my language." So I can say that the Germans rule entirely by fear. Their failure is due to their inbred cruelty which they encourage their African underlings to copy. Cruel punishments are their means of spreading terror throughout the land.

Flogging is the German's pleasure. Twenty-five lashes are given as commonly as in London on a big day the police cry "Move on!" Fifty lashes are very frequently given in two installments. Now there are floggings and floggings. The African does not easily cry out. But those who have had to pass government buildings at flogging times will bear me out that it was no ordinary flogging that produced the shrieks to which we had to listen. The German *sjambok*, or rhinoceros or hippopotamus hide, is cut to damage, not merely to hurt. The colored soldiers who lay it on are past masters in the art, and the German himself presides at the ceremony to see that no mercy is given. To make it still more cruel there is a notorious law of floggings. It is this: the condemned man is not tied up as he ought to be. He lies on the earth, his face in the dust or on a hard floor. After the first two or three strokes, he usually has to be seized, and forced to keep still. If he continues to wriggle and scream, he is liable to receive the same number of strokes again, there and then. Again, when the punishment is over, if in his pain and excitement he forgets to come to attention and salute the German, he receives the whole punishment for the third time. Cruelty is a mild term to describe it.

Torture is another recognized method of dealing with the black man. The Germans always accept the word of their African underlings against a native. Torture is employed to produce confession or evidence. I will give two cases of my own knowledge, both of them concerning friends of mine: My first friend was sent by his German officer into the woods. Policemen accompanied him, and beat him with *sjamboks* for a whole week, until his body was a mass of wounds and sores. My second friend was put into the "iron hat." A band of iron was passed around his head, and tightened by means of a vicelike screw, so as to press more especially his temples. The agony is unspeakable. Another dodge is to tie a string to the middle finger, pass it back under and round the forearm, and tighten it steadily, till the man confesses whatever the German wants to hear. With a system such as this the police can supply a criminal to meet any exigency, and can also wipe out all private grudges they may have against their fellow subjects. In fact, the colored underlings are as bad as their German masters, and no one dares complain. Revenge is, in my experience, always taken on those who venture to appeal to the German.

Again, the punishment of the chain gang is a most serious cruelty. Eight men, or thereabouts, are chained by the neck to one very

257

heavy chain. They are not unchained at all, till their sentence is finished. Day and night, at all times and under all circumstances, the eight men live and move as one, while they are entirely at the mercy of the jailers, who freely use on them *sjambok*, heavy-nailed boots, or the butt ends of their rifles. I have seen women in chains. . . .

Many of my friends have been through this; some have died under it. My teachers, who were caught during the war and locked up, only because they taught an Englishman, have also told me their experience of chains. A flogging, they say, is preferable. They should know, because they have had a taste of both.

Deaths in jail are a common event. Of the brutality and ill treatment causing them, there can be no question; there are too many who have suffered it. The Germans encourage their colored police in cruelty. Even in court, before his conviction, the native is knocked about by the police. The German quite approves. If the accused, or a witness, does not stand strictly at attention, if he moves his hands while making his statement, if he calls the German *bwana*—master—instead of *bwana unkubwa*—great master—if he shows hesitation in answering, or if he does not understand the German's broken Swahili, or if, as it so often happened, he blunders in the effort to express his own vernacular in Swahili, the policeman boxes his ears, or hits him with his fists. This is the custom. This exalts German dignity.

The colored schoolteachers, appointed by the Germans, were brought up in the same way. They were themselves so often flogged, that they turned into great floggers. They find a *sjambok*, freely used, necessary to educate small boys between seven and thirteen. It is a disease, this flogging. It makes the German feared everywhere. But it poisons the German's mind as well as the mind of his African underling.

The vicarious punishment the German loves to mete out makes parents and wives suffer for their sons and husbands. Another peculiarly German habit is the persecution of native chiefs. Metaka, one of the highest Yao chiefs, a sultan to his own people, died in German chains. His offense was that he had written a letter to his brother in Portuguese Nyasaland, warning him lest he move into German territory. German spies intercepted that letter.

As a final example of German terrorism let me add that Germans on inspection tours require to be supplied with a young girl at each sleeping place. These are but a few typical examples of how the German colonial system works. It is cruel, relentless, inhuman. And the reason for all is that it is German.

| *Chapter 21* | ON THE ROOF OF THE WORLD |

ON MARCH 17, 1917, SMUTS ARRIVED IN LONDON. HE HAD COME
to take Botha's place at the meeting of the Imperial War Cabinet. The Prime Minister could not leave South Africa. The
country was in the throes of the gravest crisis since the Boer
War. Unrest was worse even than in the summer of 1914, when
some ten thousand rebels had taken up arms. This time there
was no bloodshed. But more than half the Boer people clamored furiously for republican independence.

Hertzog was carrying his crusade one step further. Thus far
he had only demanded the Boers' supremacy in a South Africa
loosely connected with the Empire. Now, while Great Britain
was entirely absorbed in her tremendous war effort, Hertzog
found the moment propitious to demand complete severance of
even the formal ties between the motherland and the Dominion. He published a "manifesto"—he issued such highfalutin
manifestoes throughout his ensuing career—stating the three
points of Hertzogism: (1) All people have a right to choose for
themselves the sovereignty under which they wish to live. (2)
The small states have the same right to their sovereignty and
territorial integrity as the big states. (3) The world has a right
to be free from any disturbance of its peace that has its origin
in aggression and disregard of peoples and nations.

It sounded very well. It almost tallied with a diplomatic note
that the British Government was then addressing to the neutrals: "No peace is possible until reparations have been made
for violated rights and liberties, nor until the principles of
nationalities, and the independent existence of small states is
recognized."

The difference was only that London was pleading for the
invaded, devastated, and white-bled countries of Belgium, Serbia and others, whereas the Union of South Africa was, of its

own free will, an independent, self-governing partner in the Empire.

Hertzog and his gang, however, distorted the British note as a complete justification of their own policy. Always a jump ahead, Tielman Roos, the lion of the Transvaal, proclaimed, on his own authority, the restoration of the Republics of the Transvaal and the Orange Free State. He sent this declaration to Lord Buxton, the Governor General, for transmission to the British Government, and received a formal acknowledgment. After long months of silence, he got in answer to his question the reply from London: "Your earlier communication was entitled: 'A statement as to the attitude of the Nationalist Party' toward a certain question. His Majesty's Government naturally assumed that they were not being asked for, and were not expected to offer, an expression of opinion in regard to a statement issued by a particular political party in a self-governing Dominion."

This cool correctness on the part of the English, who at that time had more weighty matters on their mind than the moods of Messieurs Hertzog and Roos, only intensified the repeal agitation which, under Hertzog's incessant urging, now swept the *platteland* like *veld* fire. To an accusation by his own government that he was going back on his pledge and signature at Vereeniging, he answered with his typical ambiguity: "Personally I have always been true to Vereeniging, and always will be. But, nevertheless, a republican system would be better for South Africa. Every nation has received its liberty in due course. And, whether it lasts a hundred or a thousand years, South Africa, too, will win back her freedom."

The lion of the Transvaal had no intention of waiting for the millennium. "Now, right now, we must be a republic in practice as well as in theory. The idea of a sister state, as set forth by General Smuts, is ridiculous!"

Minister D. F. Malan accused Hertzog of dishonesty, once more pointing out the latter's endorsement of Vereeniging. The crafty advocate found another ruse. "Vereeniging," he insisted, "has merely stated that the burghers recognized Edward VII as their lawful king—it did not make them agree to become a part of the Empire."

When rumors of an impending new revolution became so thick that one could cut the air with a knife, Botha decided on a showdown. He moved a resolution in Parliament, to pray that the Almighty might grant complete victory to the armies of Great Britain and her allies. The House adopted the resolution by sixty-three to twenty-one votes. Mr. Henwood, M.P. for Durban, cheered: "The King!" The Cabinet, the members, the public galleries, rose and sang: *God Save the King!* Hertzog and his followers remained seated.

It was against this background that Smuts came to represent South Africa in the Imperial War Cabinet, which held its first session on March 20. Lloyd George, the new Prime Minister, opened the meeting with a declaration of British war aims. The Central Powers must be punished and pay reparations, he said. It was a bold demand, considering the almost desperate situation. Russia was clearly on her way out of the war. America was not yet in, and no one could foretell her ultimate decision. Moreover, the "unlimited" U-boat war had just been unloosed by Germany.

Within a few days Smuts had made his mark, not only on the Imperial Conference, but on the members of the British Cabinet. It proved no handicap that he was a Boer. He did not disguise it, either. Proudly he stressed his being "just a Boer from the *veld*" while his people were in a state of open uproar. The very fact that he was a Boer, and yet, as everyone could see, a passionate adherent to the Empire's cause, gave him a lofty standing. In one of his first speeches in England, he eulogized the Empire. "It is not founded on might or force," he said, "but on moral principles—on freedom, equality and equity. Our opponent, the German Empire, still believes that might is right, that a military machine is sufficient to govern the world. She has not yet realized that ultimately all victories are moral. . . ."

Barely two weeks after the first meeting of the Imperial War Conference, Smuts, almost a stranger, speaking with a distinctly foreign accent, was entrusted with a mission to the King of Belgium and to Paul Painlevé, the President of France. Painlevé insisted that it was time for the Allies to prepare their minimum demands in case Germany should make peace overtures. What, then, was the situation in Africa? Smuts left no doubt that the Union would not consent to handing back the German colonies, which he himself had conquered. Moreover, a German-African Empire would endanger British sea power, and her communications with both South America and India.

Albert, King of Belgium, was despondent. He had nothing on his mind but his own country. President Wilson's first peace feelers, he grumbled, had not been readily enough taken up by the Allied statesmen. He even declared Alsace-Lorraine a matter of secondary concern. All that counted was the restitution of Belgium.

Disappointed, Smuts returned to London. He felt that France was too strongly influencing the development in Europe, and he continued to think so for many years. Nor did heroic little Belgium seem the hub of the world to him. Smuts' world has no hub. Smuts' world is universal, with perhaps a slight priority for South Africa.

He translated his universalism into global strategy. He agreed with Lloyd George that all fronts were one battlefield. He argued for the opening of many fronts. Perhaps one should first attack the Turks, the weakest link in the chain of the Central Powers. Churchill's Gallipoli expedition had been excellently planned, Smuts insisted. It had been wrecked only through inept direction from London.

In his survey of the general war situation, written toward the end of April, Smuts expressed his regret that the British forces had become entirely absorbed by the Western Front. The British and French, the two most important Allied armies, were stalemated in a theater of war of the enemy's choosing. It was a war of attrition, gradually wearing down the enemy, but immensely trying for the Allies themselves. "In that kind of warfare victory is the costliest possible." He hated bloodshed.

Relentlessly his mind centered on the question of how to make victory cheaper in expenditure of human lives.

Again his thoughts reverted to Turkey. One could attack them from Palestine, knock out the already tottering Ottoman Empire, and push forward to the "soft underbelly" of the Central Powers from the East.

Lloyd George was quickly persuaded. He offered Smuts the Palestine command. But the War Office was against the idea. Lord Robertson, chief of the Imperial staff, as he had been in the Boer War, opened his heart to his newly won friend. The Allied strategists did not think much of the "Eastern conception." Smuts listened, and kept silent. He did not agree with Lord Roberts. But, always a realist, and mostly prepared to compromise on matters of tactics, he feared the influence the strategists and the War Office would have on Lloyd George. He himself would be far away, and perhaps stuck with an unfinishable business—unfinishable for lack of support in the center—until the end of the war. So he declined Lloyd George's offer. A year later Lord Allenby carried out what Smuts had planned, and won a historic triumph.

Lloyd George understood the reasons for Smuts' hesitation. He gave Smuts, in exchange for the Palestine command, a seat in the British War Cabinet. Now the "Boer from the *veld*" was indeed in the center of things. The British War Cabinet, as distinct from the larger council, the Imperial War Cabinet, in fact conducted the war. It was a body of six colleagues, Smuts, co-opted as number seven, being the only "colonial" among them. In the best English tradition his position in this supreme council was never clearly defined. Sometimes he was called "Minister without Portfolio." But he never alluded to this ministerial rank. He was Defence Minister of the Union of South Africa. That was enough. Finally he joined the Cabinet Committee, the innermost chapter, where he sat next to the Prime Minister, Viscount Curzon, and Viscount Milner, the man whom in his youth he had, so bitterly pursued. Sir Maurice (later Lord) Hankey acted as secretary. The committee was to supervise the entire political, military, and naval situation. Smuts sat on the roof of the world. He called himself the Empire's handy man.

By the end of May, ten weeks after his arrival, Smuts was recognized as unparalleled among Dominion leaders, and unsurpassed even by English statesmen. In the House of Lords a banquet was held in his honor, which all the British leaders attended. Smuts, eulogized by Lord French, whose troops had harassed him throughout the Cape Colony, delivered a speech that entered history. It was on this occasion that he coined the phrase: "The British Commonwealth of Nations."

"Do not forget in these times the British Commonwealth of Nations," he exclaimed. "Do not forget that larger world that is made up of all the nations that belong to the British Empire. Bear in mind that, after all, Europe is not so large, and will not always continue to loom so largely as at present. . . . Your Empire is spread all over the world. This great commonwealth to which we belong is peculiarly situated. It is not a compact territory; it is dependent for its very existence on its worldwide communications which must be maintained, or this Empire goes to pieces. . . . The British Empire is much more than a state. I think the very expression 'Empire' is misleading. We are a system of nations, a community of states and of nations, far greater than any Empire that has ever existed. . . . We are not one nation, or state, or empire, but we are a whole world by ourselves, consisting of many nations and states, and all sorts of communications under one flag. We are a system of states—not only a static system, but a dynamic system, growing, evolving, all the time toward new destinies. . . ."

By the autumn of 1917 all the Allies were weary of war, France most of all. America, it is true, had come in, but the United States was not yet in a position to render decisive aid. Great Britain alone had to carry the brunt of the burden. But England was imperiled by the U-boat war. Robertson and Haig as the army leaders, and Jellicoe for the navy, evolved their plan for a great offensive to free the coast of Belgium, deprive Germany of her most menacing U-boat bases, and finally to annihilate the German fleet. Lloyd George was cautious. The measure of French assistance obtainable, he was well aware, was doubtful. The French had already lost two million men. Milner and Bonar-Law sided with the Premier. But the knock-out blow at Caporetto, under which Italy crumbled, proved that there was only the choice between strong counteraction or collapse. This was Smuts' opinion, and, according to Lloyd George, it determined the decision. And so to Passchendaele. . . .

The British gained a few miles, and lost four hundred thousand men. But Smuts never regretted that he had assumed the responsibility for a disastrous loss. Passchendaele, he still insists, staved off the German attack at the moment of gravest crisis, gained time, and in its consequences led to victory.

Apart from his strategic activities, Smuts was concerned with innumerable problems of a military, diplomatic, social, and economic nature. He was again the man who once had held four cabinet posts simultaneously. He was a member of the Middle East Committee that helped and supervised Allenby's glorious campaign. At the same time he was a member of the Northern Neutral Committee, and third, of an unnamed, secret committee to watch over the Netherlands, which could at any moment be invaded by Germany. All this did not consume his restless urge for activity. With his restlessness he combined, then as always, a strong desire for tidiness. He made it his business to tidy up the difficult and involved relations, the internal struggles and rivalries, between the service departments. He devised a War Priorities Committee, and was elected its chairman. Once more he excelled as a mediator. Peace was declared between the Admiralty, the War Department, the Ministry of National Service, and the Secretary of State for War. Even England's fightingest man joined in the general appeasement. The Minister for Munitions co-operated without the slightest friction. His name was Winston Churchill.

Among Churchill's predominant interests was aviation, then

a comparatively new arm. The rapid development of British aircraft during the first three years of the war had been primarily due to his insistence. But the enemy, too, had made progress in mighty strides. London was no longer threatened by helpless and slightly ridiculous cigar-shaped Zeppelins alone. Scattered full-scale raids gave the first taste of things to come.

Smuts could not neglect a problem of such great importance. Already he had demanded "an increase of aircraft not only for the sake of defense, but to assist in an offensive bombing policy against the industrial and munitions centers of Germany." Seen from today's point of vantage, he certainly shared Winston's visionary belief in air power.

Smuts organized a committee to deal with the air defenses of London. Then it fell to him to unify the entire air service, which had thus far been divided between the two service departments. He urged the establishment of an Air Ministry, and demanded that, until such a Ministry could function, an Air Organization Committee should discharge its duties. He presided over this committee, which came into being in August. In October all regulations in their minutest details had been worked out. The R.A.F. was born. Undoubtedly Winston Churchill was the father. But Smuts played a not unimportant part at this birth. He was the midwife. Instantly the R.A.F. proved its mettle. The air raids over London ceased.

After an unbroken chain of speeches which had moved and shaken England, after having been showered with honors and distinctions, after having validly and efficiently helped to tide Great Britain over the perilous crisis, Smuts sensed the approach of peace, while the Allied staffs were still preparing a great offensive for 1919.

Immediately the war lord turned pacifist. His last oration in England, delivered on May 18, 1918, asked for clemency for the Germans. "I am persuaded," he said, "that this war will end in decisive victory, and not merely in a stalemate. But when you talk about victory—victory is a vague term—you must know what you mean. There are people who mean by an Allied victory that we must completely smash Germany, that we must march to Berlin, occupy the capital of the enemy, and dictate terms there. I am not of this opinion.

"I do not think out-and-out victory is possible any more for any group of nations, because it will mean an interminable war. It will mean that decimated nations will be called upon to wage war for many years to come, and what would the result be?

"The result may be that the civilization we are out to save may be jeopardized itself. It may then be that in the end you will have the universal bankruptcy of government, and you will let loose the forces of revolution which may engulf what we have so far built up. Civilization is not an indestructible entity. As it has been built up, so it can be broken down, and you revert to barbarism."

Chapter 22	GENERAL SMUTS' DILEMMA

SMUTS' PROPHECY PROVED ONLY HALF ACCURATE. THE FORCES OF revolution were subsequently unloosed, but the greater part of mankind did not revert to barbarism. On the contrary. In their fight against barbarism many people in many countries outgrew themselves. They rose to a stature unprecedented in their history. Great Britain, in particular, to whose commonwealth Smuts had addressed his warning, turned the years of her gravest peril into her "finest hour." Toward the end of the first war Mr. Smuts, the "simple Boer from the *veld*," yet twice British, by birth as well as by choice, had, in pleading for Germany, out-Englished the English. The match was nearly over. The captains of the opposing teams were supposed to shake hands. Or so it appeared.

General Smuts' dilemma, which beset him as the war drew
to a close and plagued him for many years to come, was rooted
in his innermost nature. An irrepressible urge in his otherwise
so well controlled system had burst forth when President Wilson, in January, 1918, published his first conception of a League
of Nations. Smuts was already a confirmed Wilson man, although the two had thus far never met. However, the great
President's defense of the Hay-Paunceforte Treaty, which
opened the gates of the Panama Canal to the world, although
most Americans wanted the canal exclusively for themselves,
had deeply impressed Smuts. His sympathy had always gone
out to men who stuck to a great cause, in the teeth of a whole
nation's opposition. He was himself of this ilk. Woodrow Wilson was another. Moreover, the American President thought in
world-embracing terms, as did the prophet of "Holism."

Smuts had valiantly participated in the British war-leadership until the last hour. But for many months, already, his
thoughts had been rotating around Wilson's great project.
While the last bullets whistled, he took time off to blueprint his
own League of Nations plan. On December 15, about a month
after the surrender of the Central Powers, when Smuts' job in
England was done, he resigned from the War Cabinet, and, on
the same day, came out with his League of Nations plan. It
was, by coincidence, the day Botha arrived in London.

Much of Smuts' blueprint was subsequently incorporated in
the Covenant of the League of Nations. Its central idea was
this: Three Empires were dismembered, the Austro-Hungarian
Monarchy, Tsarist Russia, and the Caliphate. New states were
arising, some of them, Smuts admitted, "deficient in the quality of statehood." Their supervision and guidance should fall to
the League, not to the white-bled and embittered conquerors.
As he saw it, Europe was completely broken. Of all the little
leagues which had made up the former empires, only the British Commonwealth remained, "the embryo league of nations,"
based on the true principles of national freedom and decentralized political federation. As to the continent, he found "the
map of Europe dotted with small nations, embryo states, dere-

lict territories, reduced to its original atoms." "Europe," Smuts said in his most pregnant phrase, "is being liquidated, and the League of Nations must be heir to this great estate."

This phrase enthused Wilson in turn, who for his part had kindled Smuts' ice-cold flames. The American President, Secretary of State Lansing reported, repeated Smuts' words again and again.

Was Smuts right? His phrase, "the liquidation of Europe," and the League's obligation to administer a forlorn heirloom, was, history has borne out, simply a catch phrase. Europe remained the heart of the world. A fantastic development, originating in the geographic center of Europe, in Germany, appealing to the frustrated, the unbalanced, the misfits everywhere, set the world for the second time aflame. But as this is written, a new Europe is about to emerge from the purgatory, a Europe to which no lesser man than Winston Churchill proudly announced his allegiance.

General Smuts was rather hasty in writing off Europe. And he was wrong, entirely and definitely wrong, in taking Germany to his heart. He believed in that fallacious difference between Prussian militarism and the German people that for twenty years confused the minds of world democracy, and he was foremost in creating that perverted guilt-complex, prevailing, above all, among English-speaking peoples, that made the victors of Versailles throw away their bitterly won supremacy, and allowed a charlatan to plunge the world into the gravest catastrophe of all time. If Versailles erred, it erred on the side of leniency. If Versailles blundered, it blundered in not partitioning Germany, in Balkanizing, instead of federating, Austria-Hungary, and thus removing what might have become a powerful stumbling block against German expansionism and ravenous "hunger for living space."

This development Smuts did not foresee. Can one blame him? *Interdum dormitat Homerus.* Smuts' visionary foresight is mingled with a good deal of hindsight. A builder of a new world, he remains the Boer from the *veld*. He is proud of it, and his roots in the *veld*, are the very element from which he draws his indomitable strength. At Versailles he recalled Vereeniging. Then he had been a loser himself. Since that time sympathy with the underdog was in his blood. Vereeniging was a gentlemen's agreement that had worked miracles. Why should one not conclude a similar agreement with the German gentlemen? The German gentlemen. . . . The vital difference between his own little nation and the Germans did not occur to him. The Boers, barely more than a million people, struggled, frequently with an animal's ferocity, for their privileged place in the sun, where they best liked to do nothing at all. The Germans lusted for world domination. They wielded the tremendous, dark power of robots, technically streamlined and mentally schizophrenic, equipped with every device of modern science, applying them mainly to perennial preparation for war, sixty-five millions in serried ranks, clamoring for the liberation of another thirty-five millions of alleged brethren (who, for themselves, wanted nothing of the Germans but to be left severely alone) and expressing their innermost desire in the anthem: *"Und willst du nicht mein Bruder sein, so schlag ich dir den Schaedel ein!"* (If you don't want to be my brother, I'll crush your skull).

Essentially, these Germans did not fit into Smuts' "holistic" conception. But the whole conception depended on not admitting this fact, not even to oneself. To concede the element of human, national, or racial inequality—which does not deny that we are all God's children, but which allows for the fact that God, like most of his images, has children of all sorts and kinds—would shatter the whole building of Smuts' lofty thoughts. He allowed that sometimes the Germans were prodigal sons, and he was the first to help punish them when they erred. But to Smuts, in whose visions the millennium loomed, the passing events of a day, or of a mere century, did not matter. Even if the Germans were sometimes wrong, one could not wrong them perennially.

Other personal experience, all acquired in his own South Africa, increased his tendency to acquit the Germans. First came his own complete indifference to hostility. He did not take it amiss that "General" Kemp had sworn he would make mincemeat of Smuts. He bore no grudge against Hertzog, whose every breath expressed insane hatred against him. More than once Smuts insisted that, under the skin, Hertzog loved him. His own hide had grown thick. The change from the shy, easily hurt youngster was complete. He had learned to take it, for otherwise he could not dish out his heart to human brotherhood.

Finally, he deprecated both France and Russia. During the war he had repeatedly declared that France's influence was out of proportion to her actual achievement. The real reason for his distrust of France, however, lay deeper, and further back. It was the color question, South Africa's fatal question. France was giving a bad example on the dark continent. France accepted the natives as equals. Theoretically England did so, too. Nevertheless, England relied essentially on her own strength to maintain her power in Africa. France, on the other hand, trained hundreds of thousands of black troops. The Senegalese and the Moors from Morocco were the French elite troops. What would happen if and when all the natives of Africa would demand arms? The Boers had had their experience with the great Zulu fighters. Smuts did not hate the natives. He had grown up among them. His children played with their children, and natives accompanied him and served him on all his campaigns. During his raid in the Cape Colony he had watched with pain while one of his two faithful colored men was killed and the other had both legs shot away. He was permeated with the humanitarian English attitude. He regarded the natives as his wards. Yet he was a Boer. And the Boers in South Africa were outnumbered one to eight by the blacks. A tremendous emergency would have to materialize before he would arm them. The French had done so in the most tranquil days of peace.

As for Russia, it was now Bolshevist. Smuts was a realistic statesman. He was among the first to understand that the West had to come to terms, or at least in contact, with Lenin. But had the Bolshevists not caused all the trouble on the Rand?

Had their agents not poisoned Labor, particularly his own Boer young men from the *platteland,* who now, by the thousands, were streaming into the mines, into the towns, singing the *Internationale,* and becoming easy prey for the arch-reactionary Hertzogites, with whom a hatred in common against the existing order united them?

Germany was the natural counterpoise to France and Russia. Smuts, and, in a more subdued way, Botha, were among the very few delegates at Versailles who sympathized with the Germans.

Smuts, inaccessible as ever, kept his personal problems, predilections, and aversions to himself. But his strong, forthright, wise, and yet somehow innocent personality made its mark upon Versailles. He was immediately recognized as an intellectual and moral leader in a great Empire. His influence far exceeded even the importance of his exalted rank. He was elected a member of the Commission of the League of Nations, the body under the chairmanship of President Wilson himself, that finally formulated the Covenant. The Commission included Lord Robert Cecil, the other delegate from the British Empire, Léon Bourgeois for France, Roman Dmowski for Poland, and the sharp-witted and blade-tongued Patriarch Venizelos for Greece. Its work, done in daily sessions in the Hotel Crillon, certainly achieved more fruitful results than the labor of any other instrument of the Peace Conference.

Before he went to Europe, President Wilson had prepared a draft for the Covenant. Smuts, for his part, produced a paper out of his breast pocket which he termed "some practical suggestions." It was a draft he had worked out in London—ironically with the help of the Round Table Group, the brilliant young men who had emerged from Milner's Kindergarten. Smuts' "practical suggestions" impressed President Wilson so deeply that he prepared, and had printed at Paris, a new paper of his own, embodying many of Smuts' ideas. (This paper was subsequently published at the hearings before the Senate Committee on Foreign Relations.) No other delegation had prepared any sort of a proposal.

On January 19 the question came up how to reach an agreement between the British and the American ideas. Toward the end of the month the delegates of the two English-speaking countries decided to get together in a separate meeting. President Wilson was accompanied by Colonel House. Smuts left most of the talking to Lord Robert Cecil. Both men, incidentally, were strikingly similar. Cecil, too, possessed that austere simplicity combined with the most charming manners. His arguments were supported by his almost unbelievable frankness and shining sincerity. Like Smuts, Robert Cecil was a combination of the conservative, the realistic, and the idealistic. With Wilson's and Smuts' ardor, he espoused the cause of a League of Nations, and became its leading protagonist in Great Britain. Several important decisions emerged from the separate meeting, among them the plan for a Permanent Court of International Justice.

During the period between February 3 and February 13, the Commission held three-hour meetings every day. Orlando of Italy, the Czech leader Dr. Kramarsch, and M. Hymans from Belgium, were loquacious. The Chinese Minister Wellington Koo spoke rarely. The Japanese delegate was almost entirely silent. But Smuts out-silenced even the Jap. He left to Lord Robert Cecil the task of explaining the proposal dealing with the thorny problem of the protection of minorities, which was an important part of Smuts' paper, published in London on December 15. The American delegation agreed with the proposal. Smuts' brain child was incorporated with the Covenant as Article 22.

There was a single difference of opinion between President Wilson and General Smuts. Strangely, on this occasion Smuts found himself on the side of those who wanted to burden Germany with another retribution. President Wilson had most vigorously declared that reparations should be limited to what might actually be called material damage. Upon his strong insistence the other chiefs of states withdrew their further-reaching claims, and agreed to the great principle.

Only Smuts begged to disagree. "What was spent by the

273

Allied governments on their soldiers, or on mechanical instruments of war, might perhaps not be recoverable from the German Government under the reservation that these expenses do
not in a plain and direct sense result from damages to the
civilian population. But what was spent, or is being spent, on
the citizen before he becomes a soldier, or after he has ceased
to be a soldier, or on his family at any time, does represent
compensation for damage done to civilians, and must be made
good by the German Government."

Wilson was convinced. When the lawyers attached to the
American delegation advised him that all logic was against the
resolution, the President exclaimed: "Logic! Logic! I don't give
a damn for logic! I am going to include the pensions!"

Smuts' innate Boer thriftiness had scored a double triumph:
over his warm clemency for the Germans, and over the cold
rules of logic. And a warm shower of pensions would compen-
sate the Springboks for hardships, gallantly borne.

Originally Smuts had dealt with the Germans according to
advice the unforgettable Oom Paul had given him in his youth:
"Smack him hard on one cheek, and rub him gently on the
other!" But now, as everyone was smacking him hard on one
cheek, and the German stubbornly refused to offer the other,
Smuts' pity came to his help. The weakness of a strong man is a
formidable weapon, particularly when this strong man is recognized as the highest moral authority. Again the patriotic
Boer, Smuts declared the return of the German colonies impossible, but in almost every other matter he protested against
those who wanted to punish the guilty Reich. By March he had
already earned the reputation of being not only a moralist but
a gadfly into the bargain. His best friends shook their heads.
The delegates from the many countries which *furor teutonicus*
had devastated agreed that the man from comfortably located
South Africa did not know what war really was. Even Lloyd
George became nervous. Could one not find an adequate job
for the incurable peacemakers? A job on the side lines?

Indeed, one could. The line led straight to Vienna and Buda-

pest. Vienna was to be only the halfway house. Budapest was
the terminus. A sort of comic-opera government, though of the
most sanguinary red color, was set up in Hungary. Bela Kun,
a Jewish trustee of Lenin, was the midget dictator. He was
famishing for world-wide recognition of his awkward, but entirely unrepressed, terror system. Here was an excellent job for
an appeaser, made to measure for General Smuts.

Smuts decided to go and see. On April 1 at seven-fifteen in
the evening, he left the Gâre de l'Est, accompanied by Allen
Leeper, Colonel Heywood of the Military Institute, Cyril Butler of the Food Control Commission, Colonel Lane, Smuts' personal aide-de-camp, an Italian and a French officer, a small
clerical staff, some orderlies, and last but not least Harold
Nicolson, whom Smuts described as "a brilliant chap," and
whom he had personally invited to come along. Mr. Nicolson
afterwards gave a delightful account of the tragicomedy of this
journey.

The ostensible purpose of the mission was to delineate a line
of demarkation behind which Hungarian and Rumanian troops,
locked in their unending struggle, should retire. In fact, Smuts
wanted to find out whether Bela Kun was the man whom he
could use as a go-between for getting in touch with Moscow.
With his habitual reserve he let no one into what he believed
was his secret. During the journey he primed Allen Leeper
thoroughly. Austere and super-correct General Smuts could not
well soil his hands with a Bela Kun. The young British diplomat should assume the responsibility for possible negotiations.
Mr. Leeper obliged, and serenely played the fool to the chief
of the mission.

The mission arrived in Vienna on the next forenoon. For the
first time the gentlemen got an inkling of how life looked on
the wrong side of the blockade. The appalling misery of starving and grippe-ridden Vienna, immediately after defeat impressed the visitors. Mr. Nicolson was polite enough to un-
derstate the terrible aspect as, "a town with an unkempt
appearance." It is doubtful whether General Smuts relished the
word "unkempt": it was the trade-mark of his Boers.

The Viennese had never had their hearts in the fight for Germany's greater glory. Toward the end of the First World War they were completely subjugated and as miserably under the Prussian jackboot as Germany's "allies" are in this war. The first sight of Allied uniforms, of those blessed uniforms that had, while ruining them, yet freed them from the unbearable field-gray rags, came as a tonic to the Viennese people. A respectful crowd, eager to demonstrate their sympathy, but too badly beaten to venture to open their lips, gazed at the resplendent regimentals. That inexplicable sympathy that he always evoked sparkled around Smuts in khaki, walking the streets of Vienna, silent, dignified, visibly reserved. The men about town in Vienna, who, too, had gathered to have a first happy look at the harbingers of peace, admired with unspoken envy Messieurs Heywood, Lane, and Nicolson in their spotless civilian attire. The Viennese gentlemen were wearing their four-year-old Sunday best for this occasion. One could not hear them sighing. But it was a long way to Savile Row.

At the British Embassy Sir Thomas Cunningham, head of the inter-Allied military mission, and Mr. Philpotts of the British Consular Service met Smuts and his entourage. From the first moment, Mr. Nicolson observed, Smuts preferred the unassuming Philpotts to Sir Thomas. The party went off to *Sacher's*, the legendary restaurant, again followed by a respectfully staring crowd. The luncheon vindicated *Sacher's* fame as one of the best eating places in a world gone down. The bill was 1,200 *Kronen*. It would be paid, Smuts was told upon inquiry, with reparation funds. His eyes froze as he looked at Sir Thomas. "This was a gross error in taste!" he said in front of everyone. "From now on the mission will live entirely on our army rations. We will not take the least bit from a starving country." Slowly he calmed down, while he listened to an explanation of frontiers and armistice lines. He took dinner in a patrician Jewish house, whose owner acted as right-hand man to the Inter-Allied Food Commission. During all his months in Paris, incidentally, Smuts had never accepted invitations to private houses. At ten o'clock in the evening the mission traveled on to Budapest.

Bela Kun awaited the train at the station: a fat, little man in his thirties, with an unhealthy, bloated face, an almost bald head on which only a few short red hairs remained, he had the restlessly shifting eyes of a professional killer who incessantly fears the police on his tracks. Immediately he explained that, personally, he wanted to make peace. But his government had come in on a wave of nationalism. His Red Guard was under the command of officers of the Royal Hungarian regime. They didn't give a damn, Bela Kun admitted cynically, whether his system was Communistic as long as the fight was for Hungary. He was afraid of these mad dogs. He dared not let them down. Yet he would proceed to a conference of the quarreling succession states either in Prague or in Vienna, if His Excellency could guarantee him safe conduct. And now, he asked His Excellency to luncheon. The Hotel Hungaria was reserved for the mission. Budapest's leading hotel had hoisted the Union Jack and the Tricolor to give the population the impression that an Allied delegation had arrived to beg dictator Kun for peace.

Smuts refused to leave the train. None of his entourage was allowed to get out. The mission lunched off beans and cheese: the army ration. At three o'clock Bela Kun returned from a "Cabinet meeting." He had, in fact, telephoned to Moscow to get his orders. Reluctantly, he entered Smuts' wagon-lit, looking carefully around, as though he lived in eternal claustrophobia.

Smuts asked for the release of the British prisoners of war in Hungary. Personally, Kun was inclined to release them. But he could give no assurance without the consent of his "cabinet colleagues." He seemed relieved when he escaped from the sleeping car, unkidnapped and alive. Again he telephoned to Moscow. He returned in the evening, and was ready to sign the release of all British prisoners of war. Smuts treated the rat, Nicolson observed, "as if he was talking to the Duke of Abercorn: friendly, courteous, but without a trace of surrendering his own tremendous dignity."

Neutral visitors called upon Smuts in his rolling residence. Everyone, including the Swiss and the Spanish Consuls, was agreed that Bela Kun was a bloodthirsty jailbird. His Red Guard looted the streets, the prisons were crowded, there was general fear of a night of long-knives. Smuts had satisfied his curiosity, when Bela Kun returned on the fifth of April. Smuts handed him the draft of an agreement providing for the occupation of a neutral zone between Hungary and Rumania by Allied troops. If the Prime Minister agreed, the blockade would instantly be lifted.

The Prime Minister scratched himself behind his ear, his tongue licking his swollen, pale lips. His breath came quickly, but heavily, from his drooping belly. He was visibly excited. The document in his hands meant nothing less than international recognition of his gangster rule. But the dictator of Hungary was still a puppet, dancing on the Moscow wire. He would convey his decision the day-after-tomorrow. "On the seventh of April," which was the day after the next, "we are to leave at seven fifteen," said Smuts.

Precisely a quarter of an hour before this deadline Bela Kun reappeared with three equally uncouth accomplices, Ministers of the Hungarian Government, this time escorted by a company of honor of the Red Guard. He was clearly staging a grand affair of state. Yet, in the dining car of Smuts' special train, the lights dimmed, the whole scene set for departure, he was again the harassed, suspicious, uneasy fugitive. He gave Smuts a note. Smuts read it twice, and handed it to Mr. Nicolson. "No, gentlemen," he addressed the gangster government. "I cannot accept any reservations." The note had agreed to Smuts' demands, but added that the Rumanian troops must withdraw behind the Maros River. In his final word Smuts emphasized that the conference he was representing would not go a single step further than his proposal had indicated. It was in the Hungarian Government's own interests to accept.

The gangsters looked at one another. Fear was written in the faces of gunmen who suddenly found themselves without orders. What if they accepted and Moscow refused? What? One of the gangsters, a brute by the name of Kunfi, made a significant gesture toward his comrades. He lifted his hand toward his neck, describing a semi-circle. It meant hanging—liquidation, in Lenin's Russian language.

Only Kun did not lose his poise. He had been in much tougher spots. As the danger increased that he would miss the bus—recognition of his rule—and certainly be taken to task in Moscow for his failure, he straightened his misshapen body, tried to grin, and proposed what Smuts would have called a Kafir bargain. "One could perhaps find a third line of compromise . . ." he suggested.

Smuts looked at his wristwatch. It was seven fifteen. He rose. "Well, gentlemen, I must bid you good-bye." Staggered, the gentlemen retreated, step by step, much too polite to show their backs to His Excellency, tumbling over one another's flat feet.

With exquisite courtesy Smuts accompanied them to the platform. He shook hands with every member of the Hungarian Government. He nodded to his aide-de-camp, while standing already on the step of his car. The train moved off. Four gangsters, baffled, looked after the engine. Then, in the same breath, they muttered something in Hungarian which means, translated in its mildest form: "Double-crossed!" It was a new experience: they were on the receiving end.

Smuts went to Prague, where he met Masaryk. For hours the two men remained closeted in the President's study. It was never disclosed what they had spoken of.

Back to Vienna. The people, no longer frightened, gave Smuts a jubilant welcome. If nothing else came of his visit, his presence meant at least that he would protect them from the Bolshevism ravaging the land across the border, less than an hour by railway. Perhaps his visit meant also food. Small groups followed him respectfully. But as Smuts and his group entered a cheap restaurant—the military rations had given out—no one wished to disturb him. Even the few guests in the place left, the ladies curtseying, the men bowing. The headwaiter took the liberty of explaining *"Die Herrschaften* (the gentry) certainly wish to be alone among themselves." Then he served, with great ceremony, heaps of *épinards*, 1918-Viennese for boiled grass. There was, however, still a pre-war bottle of sweet and golden 1911 *Tokay*.

As the train rolled back to Paris, Smuts spoke of those really indescribable nights on the *veld*. Mentally, he made three notes: relief for Austria instantly necessary. The destruction of the Austro-Hungarian State must be repaired, best by a union of the succession states. Austria-Hungary is as much an indivisible entity as the Union of South Africa. Thirdly, Bela Kun is not a desirable negotiator with Moscow. The newspapers called it "fiasco of a mission." To Smuts it was not a fiasco. He is insatiably curious, and always satisfied when he has learned what he wanted to find out.

Upon his return to Paris, he plunged again into his fight against the Treaty, and for what he called a fair deal for Germany. The line he stubbornly followed was to draw a sinister picture of the terrible retaliation Germany would take at some future date, visualizing most of the horrors that actually came to pass. But he explained, nay he excused, this horror by the unjust treatment the Germans were receiving at Versailles. Subsequently even the advent of Hitler to power, and his first crimes in power did not change Smuts' opinion about the causes that had produced Nazism. To him it was the wrongs the victors of 1919 had inflicted upon Germany.

Incessantly, he harped on the evils of the peace treaty which was gradually taking final shape. In the middle of May he wrote identical letters to Wilson and Lloyd George, asking for "drastic revisions at the eleventh hour." He demanded the revision of the occupation, reparation, and punishment-for-the-war-guilt clauses. He rejected changes along the German Eastern frontier, the occupation of the Saar Valley, military and air clauses preventing German rearmament. All these minimum insurances against Germany's taking to arms immediately and unloosing the next war within a couple of years were "pin

pricks" to Smuts, "such as I had to suffer at Vereeniging."
(Where he had emerged top dog.)

Wilson answered: "I feel the terrible responsibility of the
whole business, but inevitably my thought goes back to the
very great offense against civilization which the German State
committed and to the necessity for making it evident once
and for all that such things can lead only to the most severe
punishment."

Smuts beseeched the British Empire delegation to use their
influence for modification of the border regulations at the
German-Polish frontier ("Poland is a historic failure, and will
always be a failure"), for limiting the German reparations to a
fair sum, possibly five billion *Reichsmark* (in fact Germany
paid ten billion and borrowed thirty, so that American and
English creditors had the privilege of paying for much of the
German rearmament), and for Germany's immediate inclusion
into the League of Nations.

In another letter to Lloyd George Smuts stated bluntly: "As
far as I am concerned I wish to make it quite clear that I cannot agree to anything less than to the recasting of the Peace
Treaty and to its transformation. . . . I very much fear that we
are endeavoring to make a peace of the twentieth century
which might have had its place in the seventeenth or eighteenth."

Lloyd George became irritated. He replied with a few questions: "Am I to understand that it is your proposal to depart
from the principle of nationality, and leave great numbers of
downtrodden Poles under Prussian rule? Are you prepared to
forego your own claims for pensions? Are you prepared to allow German West Africa and South East Africa to return to
Germany?"

Lloyd George hit where it hurt. Of course Smuts could not
return to his people with empty hands. No delegate could.

But he still stuck to his dismantled guns, again prophesying
the right thing, but offering the very worst solution: leniency,
which the Germans had always interpreted as weakness. "This

Treaty breathes a poisonous spirit of revenge" (which it did not, by any means) "that may yet scorch the fair face—not of a corner of Europe, but of Europe" (which happened).

On June 23 old General Foch threatened to reopen war and cross the Rhine—although the British Empire delegates had unanimously refused to authorize the British Army and Navy to renew hostilities in order to enforce acceptance of the terms of peace—if the Germans resisted further the laboriously patched-up peace treaty compromise. Foch was the only man who knew how to deal with the Germans. They surrendered. On June 28, 1919, on the fifth anniversary of Sarajevo, the peace treaty was signed.

The last struggle was no longer between the conquerors and the vanquished, but between General Smuts and his friends. Botha made it perfectly clear that, for his part, he must sign, since this was the first international document which the Dominions were adhering to under their own responsibility. Without the signature of the Prime Minister of South Africa the Union would clearly not demonstrate its independence within the framework of the Empire.

The question was discussed whether Botha should sign and Smuts protest. Resigned, Botha agreed with the proposal. There was no more fight in him. He was a dying man, stricken with a liver disease, hereditary in his family, and plainly doomed. He hated to part company with Smuts, at least on the surface, now that their lifelong teamwork, the very symbol of the Union of South Africa, was coming to its crowning fulfillment.

For once Smuts was forlorn. Lloyd George found the solution. Why not, he suggested, sign under protest? General Smuts could publish his protest at the very moment he put his signature to the Treaty.

Smuts did so. His signature, one among a great many, went all but unnoticed. His ringing protest, however, resounded around the globe. Indeed, his very blunder catapulted him to world fame. The great moralist, the purest of the pure was for the Germans! For years his hard-hitting phrases of condemnation of Versailles were quoted by the Germans, whose chief witness he was to remain for many years. For years the appeasers and the defeatists claimed Smuts as their man, although he was, despite his one grave error, the very opposite of the yellow crowd. For years the sentimental as well as the mercurial-minded friends of the new Germany silenced their opponents with the single syllable: "Smuts!"

Throughout the ensuing ups and downs of his political fortunes, Smuts' moral authority grew. His shadow loomed large over the globe, which his vision embraced as a whole. The testimony of such a man was worth more to Germany than the secretly built Luftwaffe.

Paris had broken Smuts' heart. He repeated it over and over again. He had seen through the hollowness, the emptiness of human civilization. When he returned home, after four years in uniform, he was but forty-nine. Yet his hair was white. Oom Jannie was the *Oubaas*—the Old Master. He developed more and more into a character of Greek tragedy. At Versailles he had burdened himself with his innocent, his tragic guilt.

IN DECIDING TO RETURN TO SOUTH AFRICA, SMUTS WAS WELL
aware that he was sacrificing world fame for personal misery.
England wanted to keep him. It was suggested that he should
stand for a constituency, and, as a duly elected member of the
House, join the Cabinet. He was offered the Vice-Royalty of
India, and also the Governorship of Palestine. The budding
League of Nations needed his supervision, his support, his inspiration. World opinion held him in high esteem. His aberra-
tion on the treatment of Germany did not impair his prestige.
His critics bowed to the patent sincerity in his pigheadedness.
His following increased by leaps and bounds. His arguments
persuaded millions. English-speaking people are not endowed
with the capacity for hatred. They are not revengeful. Moreover, the inevitable reaction to the war rapidly materialized.
The United States of America was disgusted with the whole
business, and retired into its shell. Europe was exhausted. A
wave of cynicism and indifference engulfed the world. Smuts
stood out, in bold relief, the great impartial, the umpire, the
man with the clean hands, the reconciliator. Everyone loved
him. There was only one country in which he was loathed with
an insane hatred: South Africa.

Smuts did not waver. Botha was dying, and the leader's mantle would fall on him. His family could only live in South
Africa. His children must grow up as South Africans, there was

no doubt about that. After years of absence, he hardly knew how family life felt. But he knew where his duty lay. Before leaving for England in 1917, when he had been attacked as an Imperialist for attending the Imperial Conference, he had given his solemn pledge that, as long as there was breath in him, wherever he worked, whether on the battlefields or in the Imperial Councils, he was working for South Africa. Now was the moment to redeem his word. He shouldered his cross.

He did not come with empty hands. In South Africa the war boom did not end as abruptly as in most parts of the world. England was still buying the most important products of the country, particularly wool, at those exaggerated prices on which the Dutch farmers had insisted during the war. The depreciation of the British currency in America, in July, 1919, came as a relief to the already tottering gold industry. Now Johannesburg sold gold for good dollars and translated them into devaluated pounds. The margins thus obtained enabled the industry to carry on without the losses of the war years. It was, however, only a transitory amelioration. The currency value of gold reached its peak in February, 1920, but already the costs of mining had caught up with it. By then wages were inflated. Union leaders made not only the reduction of wages, but even the slightest relaxation of their cramping regulations impossible. By the middle of 1920 half the industry was again working without profit, and some mines actually at a loss. The Nationalists did not care whether the mines went to pieces. Mostly farmers, they did care for the wool prices, but they would have never acknowledged that the boom in wool, as well as the expansion of the country's trade and industry, was due to the war. The gain of German South West Africa did not impress the Boers. It was a large, neglected country full of agrarian possibilities. They wanted it. But not from Botha and Smuts.

Botha's heart was broken. By innermost desire he needed the same sympathy he offered. He received it from many adherents. But the majority of Boers slandered and cursed him. Gravely affected by his physical disease, he died in the early morning of August 27, 1919, the time he had, a year before, predicted his death, and three weeks after Smuts' return to South Africa.

Smuts and Mrs. Smuts were in Heidelberg when they heard the news. They hurried to the house of mourning. There Louis lay, his body shrunken, his eyes closed. It appeared to an eyewitness that Smuts envied his dead friend.

The passing of Louis Botha was more than a terrible bereavement to Smuts. With him fell the last bridge between the old-fashioned Boers and the government. Many Afrikanders who had felt affection for Botha's ways and manners could not understand the new Prime Minister. Even his friends agreed that there had never been a South African like Smuts. In this they were right. Smuts had to muster all his strength to explain to the country, seething with contempt for his personal success abroad, that he, in fact, had advanced the cause of South Africa's independence, and he had won full international recognition for the country. For the first time the Union had signed an international treaty as a full-fledged free nation in her own right. He challenged the believers in what he called "the eternal yesteryear" to remember the conference at the Hague, at a time when the Transvaal was an independent republic. Then the nations of the world would have nothing of the Boers. A motion to invite the South African Republic to join the Conference had been defeated. How, on the other hand, had all the delegates, the British, the Americans, even the French, this time, at Versailles, clamored for the signature of South Africa's second delegate! What a change in the Union's position!

Smuts' explanation was in vain. Hertzog heckled the new Prime Minister. He wanted to know whether South Africa had the right to secede from the Empire; whether the Dominion could renounce the king or whether it could petition the king to renounce South Africa. Three times Smuts answered: Decisively, no.

The elections were fought exclusively over secession. For the first time Hertzog emerged as the leader of the strongest party. He received over one hundred thousand votes, his party got forty-four seats. Smuts was second victor. He trailed the Nationalists by ten thousand votes and three seats. Colonel Creswell, with twenty-one Labor members, staged a triumphal come back. The Unionists—English—Party received twenty-five seats. Three were Independents, sympathizers with Smuts.

To the outside world the elections in South Africa, where a mere handful of votes decided things, was a storm in a teacup. To Smuts South Africa was the microcosm.

After the inconclusive outcome of the polls, certain peacemakers talked of a coalition between the two main parties. Smuts immediately took up the suggestion. But Hertzog stubbornly refused. He was biding his time. Smuts had to fall back on the help of the English Party; it was his only means of getting a parliamentary majority. But open coalition with the Unionists would have meant open revolt in the *platteland*. Hertzog was just waiting for this chance.

This was one more of the many occasions on which detached observers could not understand why Smuts, the statesman of world stature, the helpmate whom Great Britain repeatedly claimed, the friend who was the solace of Woodrow Wilson in his sudden political isolation, the thinker who belonged to humanity—why this damned fool Smuts did not give South Africa a kick that would resound around the equator, and return to the center of men and things.

Duty, said Smuts. His stubbornness disheartened his best friends, his greatest admirers.

Smuts demanded from others the same sense of duty, the same self-sacrifice, he imposed upon himself. He summoned the leader of the Dominion Party, the official opposition, to an *indaba*. In the most critical hour he found the savior, a man who, in his tough, yet casual manner, would have laughed uproariously had someone called him "the savior," a man whom history has all but forgotten. His name was Sir Thomas Smarrt. He was twenty-odd years Smuts' senior, a fighting Irishman by birth and disposition, a medical man by profession, and had come in Smuts' birthyear to the Cape Colony as District Medical Officer at Britztown. In many ways he was Smuts' perfect counterpart. Sir Thomas, too, had the secret of eternal youth. He, too, had gone through an anti-British period. He, too, was helplessly in love with the *veld*. Like Smuts, he became a model farmer, like Smuts, he served his political apprenticeship in the Afrikander Bond, and finally, like Smuts, he was a discovery of Cecil Rhodes.

He was attracted to the Dutch cause, he confessed, not only by his Irish blood, but above all by the doggerel:

> We want no British government
> No cumbrous code of laws,
> No grand, expensive officers
> With plunder-seeking jaws.

As a follower of Cecil Rhodes he entered the Cape Legislative Assembly, where his pungent Irish wit immediately attracted attention, and caused much hilarity. Like many of his ilk, he had the time of his life in the old Cape era, which came to an end with the raid of his friend Dr. Jameson.

Thomas Smarrt belonged to the few Bondsmen who followed Rhodes and Jameson into the political wilderness. His sympathy with the Dutch had always been more fun than conviction. He really did not know what sort of convictions he had, he admitted. He was only sure that he always had a tremendous thirst. The Boer War taught him conviction. The fighting Irishman jumped headlong into the English camp. He fought well, and returned to the Cape Assembly, a convinced Imperialist. He was inseparable from Jameson during the latter's Premiership. After Union, the crowning conclusion of "Dr. Jim's" adventurous political life, Smarrt succeeded him in the leadership of the English Party. He changed the name of the party from Progressives to Unionists. For his merit in helping to bring about Union he was knighted in 1911, at a time when London showered titles and distinctions upon their new partners in South Africa. He had reached the pinnacle, but somehow the man of the gay Seventies in the good, old Cape felt, in spite of his insatiable zest for living, that he was surviving himself. He became the darling of the Union Parliament, his jokes still amused the House, but he was also smiled at when he spoke in gravity and pretended earnest.

It was this old war horse, still going strong, to whom Smuts appealed in the emergency. He told Sir Thomas that he needed the Unionists' voices, but that he could not enter into an open coalition with them. All he demanded of his good friend was complete self-effacement. The founder of the Unionists should dissolve his own party, and merge with the South-African Party, Smuts' Dutch group.

Sir Thomas thought that Oom Jannie was in one of his rare jocular moods. He chuckled: "Shall we dissolve and merge tomorrow?"

There was a Unionist meeting on that very evening. It was decided to give up the identity of the English Party, in order to reinforce Smuts' battalions. This supreme self-sacrifice was made to stave off the threat of Hertzogism. For three years this policy succeeded, until, in 1924, Hertzog's landslide swept away the English. In spite of forming almost 45 per cent of the white population, they have, since then, played no political role of any great importance. But they do not complain as long as Smuts watches.

"Smuts' party is swallowed by the Rand capitalists and by the jingoes!" yelled Hertzog. "He can never more be regarded a true Afrikander!" This time he overreached himself. The conservative Dutch were ready to swallow a lot of nonsense, but that Oom Jannie, whatever his faults, should not be an Afrikander would not go into their stubborn heads. The *platteland* remained quiet, although the embers of dissatisfaction smoldered on.

But there was never a dull moment in South Africa. On the Rand, labor that since the prewar strikes had not settled down once more became rebellious. Thousands of poor whites, once *bywoners* on the farms, streamed into the big town. These men, who had never worked, were entirely unfit for any sort of productive occupation. Moreover, unabashed, they transgressed the South African taboo, the color bar. They taught the natives,

who were by nature not eager to work either, how to make a
living by trouble-making. The Kafirs formed their own illegal
unions. They struck in all the factories and mines as soon as
they had their organizations, mostly under white bosses. First
minor disturbances flared up. Soon over seventy thousand natives were on strike. Bloodshed ensued.

The government remained passive. Had Smuts taken protective measures for the mines, the cry that he had sold out to the
jingoes and the capitalists would have been vindicated—on the
surface. Chaos prevailed. The Nationalists rubbed their hands.
"General Smuts has brought South Africa to the verge of ruin,"
Hertzog said. His lieutenant Tielman Roos expressed himself
more distinctly: "Smuts must break his own neck before he has
the chance to break ours."

"I am like St. Paul," Smuts confessed. "I die daily." This sigh
of resignation was his signal to attack. Early in 1921 he called
the people to a new election. His ear to the ground, he heard
the tide of fanaticism receding. From Russia came atrocity
stories about the Bolshevist regime that frightened many Hertzogites away from their leader's unnatural coddling of the
Reds. The threatening words the trade-union bosses used
brought about a healthy reaction, indeed resistance, among the
politically indifferent masses. The nearer Hertzog's threat of
secession seemed to come, the more the calculating Dutchmen
realized that they would cut off their noses to spite their faces.
They would lose their best customer, which, after all, was England. Besides, secession from the Empire could not be accomplished without revolution, and revolution would entirely wreck
both business and the country.

Smuts conducted a whirlwind campaign, to whose speed
Hertzog, a man of slow brains, was not equal. Instinctively,
however, Hertzog felt that the call for secession would not sufficiently appeal to the country. He made another volte-face.
"Secession," he declared, "is not an issue at this point. It will
come in time. But the time is not yet here!" Instead, he invented a nonexistent Great Empire Banking Trust, whose mysterious henchmen squeezed South Africa's economy. He as-

serted that the British shipping companies were robbing the South African trade. Why, he asked, did Smuts promise our whole production to England? Why does he exclude the free world market? The reason was that England, for political reasons, paid higher prices for some South African products. But Hertzog only saw, and cried out in the market place, that England was getting the better of South Africa, and that Smuts was aiding and abetting the Imperialists in enriching themselves.

Not to be outdone, his henchman Dr. Malan had discovered a plan according to which England and Japan would force the participation of South Africa in a war against the United States. Tielman Roos wisecracked: "I do not speak of deporting Smuts to Europe, but a free ticket to Europe will be at his disposal as soon as we come to power!"

There was much excited talk about deportation. Prices were skyrocketing. Both wings of the opposition, Nationalists as well as Labor, demanded that the government should deport the hoarders and profiteers.

Smuts could not speak in a meeting without being interrupted by shouts: "Hang the profiteers! . . . Why don't you deport them, at least? Once you knew how to do that!"

"I am no longer as ruthless as I once was," Smuts admitted with a faint smile. "We all mellow."

Behind him were the English, who owned all the big newspapers in the country. Incessantly the press reminded Hertzog of his old secession babble. The dangers of a Hertzog victory were painted in dark colors. A "Conference of International Socialists and Communists" came, most involuntarily, to Smuts' aid. This conference resolved to vote for the Nationalists, since a Hertzog victory was more likely to plunge the country into turmoil and civil war than any other event.

In March, 1921, the country voted. Smuts' South African Party won seventy-nine seats, Hertzog forty-five. Labor lost more than half its representation. Its members were reduced from twenty-one to nine. Even Colonel Creswell went down. Smuts had a safe majority of twenty-four members in the House of Assembly.

After victory he no longer had to conceal his English allies. He reconstructed his ministry, and took in three Unionists. Sir Thomas Smarrt, the lover of the *veld,* made an excellent Minister of Agriculture. Mr. J. W. Jagger, nicknamed the "merchant prince," applied sound business methods to the railways, and cleaned up their permanent deficit. He is still remembered as the best Minister of Railways—a job otherwise noted as a graveyard of political reputations—the Union ever had. Patrick Duncan, once Milner's principal private secretary, became Minister of the Interior. He was later knighted and is now Governor General of the Union.

All decent people sighed with relief. For the next five years at least, for the normal duration of the new House, one could lock the skeleton of a new civil war in the closet.

Chapter 24   DOWNFALL

"IF WE LOOK TO WORLD PEACE, WE MUST DO NOTHING TO ALIENate Japan. . . . I am anxious that we should avoid this, because Japan is the danger of the future: there is no doubt about that." The Imperial Conference, gathered in London in June of 1921, listened attentively. Here in two sentences was their friend Smuts in a nutshell: prophet and appeaser. He said a few more visionary things: "The only path of safety for the British Empire is a path which she can walk together with America. In a certain number of years we shall be in a great crisis in Europe, and not all the time in a position of independence, but involved with France and all the odium which her policy may bring

upon us, and not really strong and independent to act according to our own interests. That is why I am looking more and
more in the other direction—that is, to America."

But for his permanent inclination to burden France with
most of the evils for which Germany was responsible, the future, "in a certain number of years" bore out his prediction.
Once again he was in top form. Smuts belongs to the few people who like the London climate, and with the great many who
are happy in the London atmosphere. He likes English sur-
soundings best, his friends assert. His heart? His heart, of
course, he leaves behind in South Africa.

Back in South Africa things were deceivingly quiet. For
once, the Union was not the noisiest spot in the world. The
noisiest spot was Ireland. Inevitably, Smuts had to rush off to
the Emerald Isle.

These were the days of the Black and Tans. King George V
was about to go in person to Belfast, to open the Ulster Parliament. The rebels in the South regarded this as a provocation.
It all depended on what sort of address from the Throne His
Majesty would deliver. Smuts was received in audience. He
remained overnight at Windsor and drafted a speech which,
after some minor alterations, the King delivered on the next
day at Belfast. It was an appeal to appeasement.

Now de Valera sent a secret emissary to Smuts. The rebel
leader was in hiding, somewhere near Dublin. Perhaps Smuts
would kindly visit him to talk things over. Lloyd George, to
whom Smuts faithfully reported the overture of the conspirators, was perfectly willing to let his friend go. Smuts was the
right choice for peace negotiations. Lloyd George, and with
him England, wished for nothing better than to arrive at a
peaceful settlement with the Irish rebels. Smuts sent word to
Dublin that he would come. A few days later Mr. Smith betook
himself to the appointment.

The Irish rebels did not expect an unassuming Mr. Smith.
They were looking for a gold-braided general. There was a
slight comedy of errors. Finally Mr. Smith—Smuts' *nom de paix*
when he is on peace missions—and de Valera met. They met

for the first time, but to Smuts, de Valera's every word sounded familiar. He was Hertzog all over again. Hertzog spoke of "severing the British connection," de Valera called it "cutting the painter." That was the only difference.

Once more Smuts had to repeat the exhortation with which for years, desperately and entirely without success, he had tried to convince the Hertzogites. A republic, he said, does not necessarily mean freedom. South Africa, for instance, had much more freedom as a self-governing member of the British Government than the Transvaal ever had had as an independent republic. He knew what he was talking about. He had been a leading administrator of, and had given his blood for, this republic. A midget republic had no position, no dignity in the world. It was, due to its very narrowness, torn by parochial strife and dissension. A Dominion within the Commonwealth is happy. There are only happy Dominions. Why shouldn't Ireland ask for self-government, which, Smuts was sure, would be granted, and become a Dominion? Because of Ulster? For the time being, he advised, leave Ulster in peace. Natural development will bring both parts of John Bull's other island together. Members of the same Commonwealth . . . islands growing together . . . natural fusion . . . Smuts was in his element.

De Valera was evasive. He never used the upright pronoun. He always said: "They . . ." to indicate that he was only the servant of his people, and that "they" would have to be persuaded.

Yet he accepted an invitation from Lloyd George, which Smuts had suggested upon his return to London. Smuts was already long back in South Africa when that painful truce between Great Britain and Ireland was negotiated, which, during long years, was again and again amended to Eire's greater advantage. Undoubtedly, Smuts had negotiated the first steps. He was quite pleased. He remained a friend of the Irish. In the present war, he points out, two of the fightingest regiments of Springboks are the Irish Transvaal and the Cape Colony Irish. One hundred and fifty thousand Irishmen are volunteering in the British Army. About Mr. Eamon de Valera, whose hospitality has made Dublin the world center of wartime Nazi espionage, there is not a single word by Smuts on the record. He does not speak about unspeakables. He sticks to this habit.

On his return to Cape Town, aboard the S. S. *Saxon,* Smuts was accompanied by Sir Thomas Smarrt, his cabinet colleague, and Sir Lionel Phillipps, the mining king, patron of art, and philanthropist, who, by this time, had become the elder statesman of the English Party in South Africa. Both men used the long voyage to discuss cold facts with their premier. "You must save the government from plunging over the economic precipice for which you are blindly headed," Sir Lionel put it. Smuts, his head still full of the Irish trouble, admitted candidly that he was really little familiar with the state of affairs. "State of affairs? . . . The imminence of catastrophe!" Sir Lionel corrected him.

The S. S. *Saxon* arrived belatedly in port. A fire had broken out aboard the ship. It took more than a day to bring it under control. Perhaps it was a foreboding.

Soon after his homecoming Smuts, with a staff of technical advisers, went up to the Rand. Although not an expert in financial questions, he surprised the shrewdest members of the Chamber of Mines with his rapid understanding of the situation. He gauged the damages. He saw which of the shut-down mines could not be reopened. He understood that millions of tons of gold could no longer be recovered. But the shutdown of half the mines still functioning (under almost unbearable conditions), could be averted if the right, and, alas, unpopular, measures were taken.

Smuts was fully aware of the consequences of a complete shutdown of the mines; wholesale unemployment, general depression, a crippled treasury, finally the collapse of his own government. He began to share Sir Lionel's anxiety. He got in touch with Colonel Creswell, the Labor leader, and wrested from him his consent to the employment of more natives, and to a modification of the union conditions hampering efficiency. Unfortunately, Colonel Creswell, although still leader in name, and again spokesman of the parliamentary Labor group, no longer represented the real feelings of the unions under the new boss system. To them striking was a game, played without rules. Every minor disciplinary measure provoked a new strike wave. Such scattered strikes mostly backfired. The strikers had to return to work, after losing a good deal in wages, without gaining anything. Even public opinion, usually not sympathetic to big business, was angered over the irresponsible strikes.

Smuts tackled the situation determinedly. Due to the paralyzing crisis on the Rand, the Union's revenues showed a deficiency of £6,435,000, an appalling amount for a large, but little developed country, as South Africa was at that time. The situation of the railroads, next to the gold mines the country's only big industry, was precarious. Mr. Jagger saved them by a slight increase in the fares, and by cutting down inflated wages. The society of Railroad Employees threatened to strike. But they had not yet quite forgotten their own sad experience with Smuts, and so they chose for a while the better part of valor: caution. Taxation was increased, causing an uproar in a country that had thus far only paid infinitesimally small direct taxes, and those grudgingly or not at all. Heavy retrenchment was imposed upon the civil service. Smuts himself set the example by cutting his own salary in half. He also cut the allowances of officials and employees, from the cabinet minister to the local postman.

The Boers could not take it. Since time immemorial they were used to living on nepotism and patronage. Now every man in the street had to pull in his belt. Retrenchment and economy saved the nation, but hit everyone.

Hertzogism was in clover. On the *platteland* the leader still attacked Smuts as a "lackey" of England, and presented himself as the god-sent, one-hundred-per-cent, dyed-in-the-wool Afrikander. But in the towns his anti-Imperialism yielded to a poisonous exploitation of social and economic grumblings. In this way he killed two birds with one stone. He hurt Smuts, and gradually approached the Labor Party which, under Creswell, had always resented his anti-Imperialism. Hertzog brooded over captivating Labor. Some day this small group in the House might tip the scales. Tielman Roos and Dr. Malan encouraged him. Dr. Malan recalled that the Dutch Reformed Church had dismissed him for his "social" inclinations. Tielman Roos peeled off his coat, and stumped the *veld* in his shirt sleeves. His popularity mounted by leaps and bounds.

Smuts felt painfully that his own popularity was waning. His triumphs in Europe had only aroused the suspicions of the Boers at home. Tielman Roos scored in accusing the Prime Minister of having brought the "khaki pest" into the country. The peasants, whose cattle were already cursed with Rinderpest, were frightened. By-election after by-election went against the government.

Beneath the surface, economic grievances, racial hatred, and the dislocation following the war were merging. Returning soldiers found their jobs already taken. They were unemployed. And if they did get their jobs back, their displaced substitutes sank another step lower on the social ladder: they augmented the hundreds of thousands of poor whites. During the years of regimentation, both at the front and on the home-front, people had forgotten how to decide for themselves. Now they could neither think nor act on their own. They formed groups, mobs, masses. The worst were the bands of young *backvelders*, who had serenely sat out the war and occupied the posts of the fighting Englishmen. Both great industrial enterprises in the Union, mines as well as railways, were teeming with a new Boer youth: constitutionally lazy, inbred rebels, swaggerers, and blackguards. Most of them followed Hertzog's slogan that the Afrikander should be *baas* everywhere. This they claimed as their reason for keeping out the English. Some of the new unions accepted no English members. While the South African Trade-Unions had been traditionally affiliated with the Labor Party, they were now an annex of the Nationalists. The Labor Party, in turn, had to outbid the Hertzogites, to recover some of the lost ground. In both camps radicalism flourished tropically. It was strengthened by the repercussions of the general social unrest in the world, above all by the exciting tales flowing in from Bolshevist Russia. Illiterate young Boers sang the *Red Banner* and the *Internationale*.

Yet each of these Boer Communists had a master-complex. In a country in which practically all heavy manual labor was done by Kafirs, there was a premium on white skins. Most of the English disregarded it. But the lower the Boer, uprooted from the *veld*, forlorn in the towns, and forming the first white proletariat in South Africa, the stronger his claim to be *baas*. Racialism and Communism blended. Hitler was still an unknown beer-cellar agitator in the suburbs of Munich when the National Socialist combination burst forth on the Rand. The ensuing trouble was not as much directed against the government, as against the genuine working class in South Africa: the Kafirs.

The similarity between the Rand rebels of 1921 and 1922 and budding Nazism is striking. A "Committee of Action" replaced the Council of the Trade-Unions. It formed commandos everywhere. Boer commandos, some Irish commandos, and even women commandos, who subsequently behaved like the furies themselves. The men drilled and got practice with the rifle. Calisthenics and athletics, their leaders called it. Imported Bolshevist agitators worked hand in glove with Hertzogite estate owners, who promised the rebels food from their farms, if and when. . . .

The embodiment of this unholy union between arch-reaction and undiluted Communism was Advocate Tielman Roos. Witty as ever, but already gravely ill, and thus spurred on to direct action—for he had not much time to lose—he summoned a conference of Nationalist and Labor leaders in Pretoria. This "Roos's Parliament," as it later came to be called, issued a resolution, passed by six thousand crazed followers: "The time has arrived when the domination of the Chamber of Mines and other financiers should cease. To that end we ask the Members of Parliament assembled in Pretoria to proclaim a South African Republic and to form a provisional government for this country." Since the rabble leaders, however, could not agree who should lead this provisional government (differences as to whether Lenin or Hertzog should be asked to decide could not be solved), the South African Republic, latest edition, came to nothing.

The white miners, dominating the unions, were the only well-organized class in a country, four-fifths black, with only a very thin upper crust and with farmers and burghers still living in yesteryear's seclusion. The miners terrorized the Rand, and the whole country. "The miners" were the bugaboo, particularly for the poor shopgirls, cobblers, or little storekeepers, whom they could, at will, "pull out" of their places of employment when strikes were proclaimed, and reinstate, if they pleased, when the strike was called off. They were the holy terror to the natives. If General De Wet had lashed his Kafirs with the *sjambok*, the Boer miners had worked out an elaborate system of pin pricks, anything from a kick in the pants to a slight case of manslaughter, to make work difficult for their black mates, who were guilty of the crime of sweating for a tenth of the white man's wages.

When the depreciation of sterling was fully compensated by inflation, the mines had one problem: cut down expenses or shut down. The reduction of expenses affected inflated wages first. A Boer miner, mostly raw and always undisciplined, could earn over twenty pounds a week. An unskilled coal miner, it is true, earned only thirty shillings a week.

On January 1, 1922, the anniversary of the outbreak of the great strike eight years before, the workers in several Transvaal coal mines walked out. They refused a reduction in wages to twenty-five shillings. The owners of the coal mines, already working at a loss, insisted on their demands. The whole country was scared. For three uneasy weeks the haggling went on. Then the employers dismissed the miners. Smuts' heart did not beat on the left. Himself a farmer and a farmer's son, at home on the *veld*, and a lover of the *platteland*, although it rejected him spitefully, he compared the miners' lot, even the worst paid of them, with the farmers'. There was not a farmer who made twenty-five shillings a week all year round.

But he did not interfere. He stayed his hand. Dictatorial inclinations, if, indeed, he had felt them in his youth, were gone with the years. He understood that in a democracy public opinion was the supreme judge, and in spite of his terrible experiences with South Africa's public opinion he was, now aging, a confirmed democrat. He did not yet know how painfully and slowly democracy works in a miners' strike. He confined himself to pleading with the gold miners: they should not follow the bad example in the coal mines. Never strike before all possibility of negotiation was exhausted, he advised them. In their low economic condition the gold mines would not survive a strike. Half of them would close for good, and the miners themselves would no longer be strikers, but unemployed.

Uproarious hilarity on the Rand answered Oom Jannie's pleading. Man by man, shoulder to shoulder, singing obscene songs, beating up the foremen and officials, killing a few Kafir bystanders, the gold miners of the Rand walked out. For the first time all mines were closed.

The strikers were in high spirits. The Hertzogites would come to their aid. They had the promise, not from the leader himself, but from scores of his underlings.

They fought the employers, the public, the natives, but the real target of their hatred was Smuts. They only rarely used his name. Everyone knew who was meant when "the agent of the Chamber of Mines" was cursed.

Smuts divided his time between Pretoria, the seat of the executive, and Cape Town, the seat of the legislature, receiving deputations, appealing to the strikers, dealing with the employers, trying to calm the country, and yet to make it aware of its peril. All his attempts failed. Milner's shadow loomed over him, black and menacing. "Everyone who has a bad hand at bridge damns Milner!"

In the middle of February the Council of Action urged the strikers to hold out. Many, particularly among the oldsters, were disgusted. They did not relish the outrages of their young mates. They wanted their work and pay. But woe to him who whispered it! The *sjambok* dealt with the "scab." The *sjambok* was not the only weapon. Provocatively, the commandos of strikers paraded the streets with rifles and guns; once they produced a machine-gun. The commandants were mostly Hertzogites. None of the new Union bosses had ever worked in a mine.

In the House of Assembly, Smuts put the onus where it belonged: at the door of the Hertzogites. They were inciting labor with their infamous slander of the government. Personally, he did not care. But the country should care. The government, he insisted with a stubbornness that was unanimously criticized, would keep out of the struggle. "We shall draw a ring round the disputants, and allow them to fight it out," were his words. They were long remembered throughout South Africa, and never forgiven. Public opinion refused to think and act for itself. As late as on March 1, Smuts insisted: "I think we shall allow things to develop." "I think I shall not get married today," was not nearly as often quoted.

The Chamber of Mines, in its despair, grew stubborn, too. They refused a conference with the strike leaders. They were fed up with eating humble pie. Upon their refusal a general strike throughout the country was proclaimed. And now, as the popular saying in Johannesburg had it, "the balloon went up."

The general staff of the strikers, who were open revolutionaries, established headquarters in Fordsburg, one of the mining towns around Johannesburg. The sixty miles of the Rand were under their terror. Strangely, they left a few business streets and the railroad station alone. One of their strongest citadels was in a school building on, paradoxically, Jan Smuts Avenue.

Smuts called up the burgher commandos. A few days before the Hertzogites had tried to do the same. But in a grave emergency the solid burghers hearkened to the call of the law. In their own right they established martial law in and around Johannesburg. Smuts was still saying in Parliament that this was not a government order. He still wished to avoid bloodshed.

On March 10 the burgher commandos sailed forth in a frontal attack. Now the Prime Minister sanctioned their attack by legalizing martial law. Fighting was going on almost all over the Rand. Where and as long as the revolutionaries were still top dog, they stormed private houses, assaulted the people, insulted the wives, terrified the children. Another terror spread over the Rand. The Kafirs were in an uproar. Some of the revolutionaries killed them on sight. But they could not kill 260,000, the entire black population of the town. The natives staged a fantastic uprising, half blood-crazed, and half desperate. Smuts had addressed them when the trouble began. He had asked his colored people to stay in their houses, and to be confident that the government would give them protection.

Protection? . . . Government? . . . Where were they?

They were on their way. Smuts had left Parliament without disclosing his whereabouts. He took the train to Johannesburg. Only the Revolutionary Committee of Action knew that he was coming. And only Smuts knew that the committee knew. Eighty miles before reaching Johannesburg he transferred from the train to an automobile. Some twenty miles nearer the embattled town the train was held up, while Smuts, in his motorcar, drove through a hail of bullets. One of the tires was blown out. But nothing happened to him. Again a charmed life.

He arrived in Johannesburg on March 12, before dark. He directed the end of the fight. He watched his airplanes dropping not bombs but pamphlets which urged all loyal citizens to leave the town. They went. A great many of them were disloyal —fugitives from their own revolution. Perhaps Smuts had had this aim in mind. He did not care to have people shot, when all was over. Only four of the revolutionaries were subsequently sentenced to death. They had been caught as snipers.

Toward noon the white flag was hoisted over the revolutionary headquarters in Fordsburg. Almost three hundred policemen and burghers, one hundred and sixty revolutionaries, some one hundred bystanders, and an undisclosed number of natives were killed or wounded.

In Parliament an acrimonious debate ensued. Tielman Roos asked the House for mercy for the revolutionaries. The word mercy from the bloated lips of the most vitriolic speaker in South Africa sounded strange. There was no reply. Hertzog criticized the government's attitude in the strike for which he himself was largely responsible, but in which, as usual, he had taken no active part. The reactionary of reactionaries accused Smuts of an attempt to crush organized labor by force.

A judicial commission inquired into the "chief causes of the revolutionary movement," and found three explanations: "First, the belief held by a large part of the strikers that they would receive armed assistance from the Nationalists in the Orange Free State and in the Western Transvaal. The strikers expected that the burghers would accept the suggestions of Tielman Roos and decline the government's call for assistance. Secondly, the actions of certain members of the Nationalist Party in endeavoring to make political capital out of the industrial upheaval. Thirdly, the desire of the Nationalist element among the strikers to take advantage of the industrial dispute to obtain a republican form of government for South Africa."

Each one of these carefully chosen words lashed Hertzog. The House rejected his motion of non-confidence in the government. Smuts' majority was fourteen. He was fully vindicated.

He was doomed. He knew it.

His coalition government had started with a majority of twenty-four. After the Rand revolution fourteen were left. Patriarch Merriman, Smuts' political godfather from the Cape and now his most important supporter, was bedridden. For all practical purposes he had to be counted out. That left thirteen. A few other veterans were similarly, if not quite as completely, incapacitated. The South African Party was definitely over-aged. Smuts had a habit of recompensing old friendship with seats in the House. It was his only form of nepotism, or rather avunculism. Not all his veteran comrades were still going strong in their advancing fifties. Like the little nigger boys, soon there were seven, six, five. . . . The fate of important divisions in the House sometimes depended on three or four votes, and on an equal number of attacks of gout, influenza, and gastric calamities which kept legislative patriarchs at home. Smuts himself persistently refused to acknowledge his recurrent afflictions of malaria, acquired in German East Africa. When they came, he looked tired and pale. But he never missed a single session, except when he went abroad.

He visited Rhodesia at the time when Cecil Rhodes' contract with the British Government, handing over the colony to the Chartered Company, had run its course, and when the Rhodesians were free to choose their own future destiny. Smuts had come, he asserted amid general hilarity, only as a simple tourist. But he could not refrain from talking of Pan-Africa, the Dominion of the Federated States of Africa, self-governing under the Union Jack. A merger of Rhodesia and the Union would be a decisive first step on this long way.

The cartoonists at home depicted Smuts *vrying* in the best old Boer manner, a candle in one hand, and a moneybag in the other. He appeared as a senile curmudgeon, whereas "Miss Rhodesia" was prim and demure. The Boers wanted no increase in the British element. Least of all did they want to be burdened by the colony's permanent deficit.

The white population of Rhodesia, all English, was strongly attracted by Smuts. Even in his decline his enigmatic personal magic was as strong as ever. But the Rhodesians wanted nothing of the Afrikander *baas,* no strikes as in Johannesburg, no Kafir-baiting. They felt safer, and very much more cozy, under British protection. A plebiscite rejected union with the Union. Smuts fully understood. The Union of brothers, his daydream, was not established even in South Africa. He was ahead of his time.

In 1923 he attended again the Imperial Conference in London. The French had just marched into the Ruhr basin to enforce the delivery of coal which Germany offered to transfer by way of reparations. But the Ruhr mining magnates withheld the coal under flimsy pretences. Yet Smuts thundered against the Ruhr "invasion." He impressed England strongly, and finally succeeded in driving the first wedge between the English and the French. In Berlin, Dr. Stresemann listened. He had always been a long-distance admirer of Smuts. Both men dreamed the same dream of international co-operation and brotherhood. Both were, each in his own country, apostles of the League of Nations. And both were equally hated by their own people. Stresemann died of a kidney disease, which was, as in Botha's case, in truth a broken heart.

When Smuts returned home, Hertzog and Colonel Creswell were engaged in a series of hands-across-the-table talks in the *koffeehuis* of the House of Assembly. Their meetings were so plainly in the open that even Smuts scented no evil. Hertzog, it appeared, wanted to display his beautiful English. Creswell wanted to cure his conversation partner of his anti-British obsession. Both men wanted to oust Smuts.

Personally, Hertzog was prepared to continue preaching his gospel of Britain-baiting until he had converted a majority, and could establish an independent government, to sever the British connection. But there was no majority obtainable against the English voters plus Smuts' followers, the progressive Boers. Most of Hertzog's followers were becoming weary of wandering in the political wilderness. True Afrikanders, they famished for the fruits of office. Tielman Roos, ever a good mixer, had brought Hertzog and Creswell together.

Both forgot their previous vicious attacks on one another. The last campaign lay three years back, an eternity for South African politicians. Hertzog could no longer resist his henchmen's hunger for pork and patronage. He was the leader; he had to follow. Creswell, for his part, saw his influence on the Rand vanishing. The beaten mob wanted action. On April 23, 1923, Smuts was stabbed in the back. The unnatural coalition of Nationalists and Labor united in voting against the government.

Immediately Smuts dissolved Parliament, and appealed to the electorate. On June 17, 1924, after a bitter campaign, he went down in defeat. Hertzog had won sixty-three seats against

Smuts' fifty-three, and Labor, now Hertzog's vassal, had gained eighteen seats into the bargain.

Oom Jannie resigned before the new House met. Hertzog was sent for. He swore his oath of allegiance to the Crown. After twelve years of political exile he was back in office, this time at the helm of the state.

Smuts had been in office throughout all his mature life, except during the time of Milner's proconsulate. He remained unruffled. Gladly he relinquished his official residence in the Groote Schuur, which had always been a bit too grand for his tastes. He would farm again, and read a little more. Worries? Certainly, the family would have to retrench. Smuts' law practice was long gone. He had never been in business. The Smuts tribe would have to subsist on the meager salary of an M. P. All of them, father, mother, and the children, looked most hopefully into the bleak future. Smuts did not worry that his bank account was overdrawn. He did not even know it.

| *Chapter 25* | **THE LEAN YEARS** |

THE FUNDAMENTAL CAUSE OF SMUTS' POLITICAL DOWNFALL LAY deeper than the accumulated social, economic, and racial troubles which, on the surface, brought about his undoing. In spite of its turbulence, South Africa was bogged down in bread-and-butter politics. Smuts' vision became broader, wider, cosmic, as the years went on. His feet still firmly planted on the *veld*, he had grown too big for his narrow frame.

It was entirely characteristic of him that he did not seek revenge for his defeat. Although he played his part as the leader of the opposition, he gave little thought to politics. He spent most of his time on his farm, brooding over the central problem of his intellectual life, and writing his chef-d'oeuvre, *Holism*. As a mere achievement of industry and energy it was a remarkable piece of workmanship. The bulky volume, exploring and analyzing the most subtle philosophical and psychological problems, surveying the thought of all the great philosophers and founders of religion, of artists and scientists, was written within six months, without assistance, without even, it was said, the help of a secretary. The book makes difficult reading, although it contains some almost poetic passages, yet it is unforgettable as a perfect blend of cool science, deeply felt religion, and a philosophy, deriving from Aristotle, developed by Spinoza and Leibnitz, and siding rather with St. Thomas Aquinas than with Darwin, to whose theory of material selection Smuts opposes his own law of the human personality, rising from its physiological origins to a fusion of body and mind, and becoming a part of the whole—*holos* in Greek—which is greater than all its parts.

A book of this kind could never become popular, but Smuts' endeavor "to attain a Holistic universe"—in which there would, of course, be no war—won him recognition throughout the scientific world. The highest tribute paid to him was an invitation to preside over the Centenary Meeting of the British Association for the Advancement of Science, which was to meet in London, in the autumn of 1931. He accepted the invitation with hardly concealed emotion. "I can only tell you that nothing in my chequered life has made me prouder," he answered. It appeared that Smuts had done with politics, and was about to devote himself to the vast realm of the spirit. At home things were going from bad to worse. In the elections of 1929 he had taken another bad beating.

The ruling government of reaction and revolution, of fire and water, was a combination of amateurs. Hertzog himself, who took the Ministry of Native Affairs in addition to the Premiership in order to carry out his long advocated native policy, was the only member who had previously held office. His colleagues were mostly job-hunters. Labor had to confine itself to two members in the Cabinet. Colonel Creswell took the posts of Labor and Defence, his comrade Boydell got the portfolios of Post and Telegraph, as well as Public Works. The stalwarts of the Nationalists reaped a rich harvest. Advocate Tielman Roos became Minister of Justice, Dr. Malan grabbed three offices at once—Education, Public Health, and the Interior—Charlie Malan and Willie Beyers, both furious rabble rousers, shared between them the Railways and the Mines. Two rebels of the 1914 uprising came into power. General Kemp, of "Smuts into mincemeat" fame, became Minister for Agriculture, and Piet Grobler, Oom Paul's kinsman, received the Lands, the juiciest post, since he could not allot farms to meritorious party members.

This combination of intriguers and know-nothings was favored by incredible luck. Hertzog had barely come into office when the shadows of world depression began to recede. Torrential rains, such as the country had not experienced for fifty years, made for a record corn harvest that brought the farmers six million pounds from overseas. This superstitious lot was now convinced that the Lord approved of Hertzogism. When platinum was found on many farms, the last doubts about Hertzog's divine mission were dispelled. Smuts had reorganized the mining industry. His successors thrived on the outcome of the measures they had so violently opposed. With industry again profitable, the government had large revenues to spend. "Klaasie" Havenga, Hertzog's man Friday, and Minister of Finance—the only member of the government, incidentally, who had lasting success—spent the money wisely. More white labor could be employed, the wages of the railway workers rose, the poor whites, Hertzogites to the last man, were settled on the land, and tax-exempt. Yet Klaasie Havenga could show a modest surplus in the Treasury from year to year.

The biggest boom was the arrival of the Prince of Wales. The Prince had been expected a year earlier. But when Smuts dissolved Parliament, the state visit was postponed. Now His

Royal Highness came, saw, and scored. Trade boomed. The
Boer belles, most of them venomous Britain-baiters, bought silk
stockings and white gloves, ostrich-trimmed hats, silver shoes,
and even lipsticks. They hoped for a dance with the Prince, or
at least to help to prepare tea for him. The Rough Riders from
the Boer War joined with the English ex-soldiers at mounted
parades in honor of *"Ons Prins."* Hertzog, the weathercock,
crowed in Parliament: "I say positively that I have not the
slightest intention of recommending secession from the Empire.
I say here again that I am strongly in favor of the British connection being maintained."

But as soon as the Prince had left and retail trade was again
reduced to normal proportions, the old racial quarrel was reopened. Hertzog proceeded step by step, and, as usual, under
cover of front-men. To the general astonishment of the House
of Assembly, the Laborite Arthur Barlow, himself an Englishman, proposed an address to the King, praying that he "hereafter may be graciously pleased to refrain from conferring any
titles upon your subjects domiciled or living in the Union of
South Africa or the mandated territories of South West Africa."
Thus the visit of the Prince of Wales was not followed by the
shower of titles which the leaders of society, predominantly
English, would otherwise have had conferred upon them.
Hertzog himself came into the open. He attacked titles as a
danger to democratic ideals, and called them "a pestiferous
institution that even Europe would like to be free from if it
could." Moreover, titles were conferred upon those who pleased
the British Government. Hertzog was no longer prepared to
tolerate such tampering with South Africa's independence.
"Don't let us be the lackeys of anybody!" he concluded. He
had dug out one of his oldest stock-in-trade phrases.

Preferential tariffs for British goods were abolished. Large
government orders for railways were, for the first time, placed
in Germany. A ferociously conducted battle of flags ensued
which tore the country for two whole years. Hertzog wanted
a "purified" flag, without the Union Jack. The British section
insisted on the Union Jack, but conceded that the two flags of

the defunct republics could be included. Both Houses of Parliament, all political parties, even the courts were involved. In the end the Earl of Athlone, the Governor General, brought about a compromise settlement.

The time had come for Hertzog to attend an Imperial Conference in London. Before leaving he shouted that he intended to ask for a clear definition of the free and independent state of the Union. It was not sufficient, he said with his shyster lawyer's insistence, that Great Britain and the Dominions were agreed on the matter. The world should be notified of the existing full equality within the Commonwealth.

This was one of the rare occasions that brought Smuts to his feet. At a mass meeting in Johannesburg he said: "A declaration such as General Hertzog has proposed would mean the breakup of the British Empire."

Hertzog, however, succeeded in London in obtaining one more statement on the problem of equality, which no one had contested. It was, essentially, a reassertion of the existing status. But for home consumption Hertzog turned it into a personal triumph: "The Old British Empire exists no longer," he told his listeners at the *Paarl:* "As a result of what the Imperial Conference has done, nothing remains of the old Empire." In Parliament he claimed that, after the decision of London, every Dominion had the right to neutrality if Great Britain were to be involved in war! Smuts rose, and said quietly: "I doubt whether such an interpretation would be finally and definitely acceptable." It was only a short exchange of thrusts. But years later these two sentences were to make history.

The first five years of Hertzogism-in-office were characterized by a muddle of thinly veiled anti-British legislation. Every South African Trade Commissioner abroad was elevated to the rank of Minister Plenipotentiary. A Press Act endangered the personal security of opposition journalists. All political articles had to carry the full name and address of the writer. Hertzog's hooligans were waiting around the corner. Afrikaans was made the second official language. A new trade agreement with Germany, Hertzog boasted, "breached the Imperial Preference System." Finally a Department of External Affairs was set up. Hertzog himself took it over. Almost all the budding South African diplomats were Afrikanders.

This sort of selection embittered the English part of the population. Their protests were unavailing. But a good many Boers joined them in attacking the shameless favoritism now practiced. More than one minister—as the old saying goes—while providing for his relatives, did not forget his in-laws, either. These "jobs for pals" became a bone of contention even within the ranks of the Hertzogites. The government declared that it would favor the appointment of those men who were most eager to apply its ideas.

At the same time the coalition began to crack. The first split occurred within the Labor Party, the English wing of the anti-English government, a queer mixture of gentlemen and rabble rousers. There were now two Labor parties: the Creswellites and the National Councilites. The leader of this leftish wing, Mr. Madeley, had to be co-opted into the government, in exchange for a right-wing Labor man who was kicked out. Mr. Madeley became Minister for Post and Telegraph. Immediately, he trebled the wages of the Kafir employees. This was too much for his Nationalist partners. Hertzog asked Madeley to resign. The latter, copying Hertzog's stubbornness in 1912, refused. Hertzog aped Botha, resigning on behalf of the whole Cabinet. He was sent for again, and built a new government, excluding Madeley. The whole maneuver took him three hours, while Botha had taken six days. Hertzog boasted that he was a better man than his dead, but still hated, antagonist.

The little incident of the Kafir pay was the snowball that became the avalanche. The general elections of 1929 were approaching. Hertzog decided to make the native question the chief issue. Smuts, although not very active in politics, was still the principal enemy. He must get at Smuts.

It so happened that Smuts delivered a speech at Ermelo, dealing with his favorite topic. In his best Cecil Rhodes manner he pointed out the rapid development of the vast British territory in Central and South East Africa, and suggested the Union's co-operation to form a great African Dominion extending all over the continent.

This was the cue for which Hertzog had been waiting. Together with his henchmen Dr. Malan and Tielman Roos, he issued a violent manifesto, unsurpassed in its falsifications and slander. Smuts was called "a man who puts himself forward as the apostle of a black Kafir State, of which South Africa is to form so subordinate a constituent part that she will know her own name no more. Smuts preaches political equality for all— Kafir and white man, everywhere on an equal footing. This means the downfall of the white man and his civilization in South Africa. Shall the people of this country stand passively by and watch how South Africa is being wiped off the map, as General Smuts desires, in order to be dissolved into an English-Kafir State?"

It was the most vituperative attack, even for the rowdy politics of South Africa. But it hit the people on their sore point. It pointed out the approach of the menace under which the Boers had lived ever since they had conquered the land by slaughtering the blacks. Throughout *dorp* and *veld* the manifesto was distributed. "Smuts for votes to the Kafir!" was incessantly repeated, and the question was asked: "Do you want to save your children from the blacks? Vote Nationalist!" Finally, the condensed form of racial appeal emerged, and swept the land: "Dutch vote Dutch! Dutch means Hertzog!"

The townspeople kept their heads. But the *platteland* was swept by a nationalistic landslide when the elections came. Hertzog got seventy-eight seats, Smuts sixty-one. The Cabinet was reorganized. Tielman Roos retired, and left for Germany, allegedly to consult a doctor. The Ministry of Justice went to Oswald Pirow whom Smuts had beaten in his constituency, Standerton, but who succeeded in getting himself elected elsewhere. The first avowed pro-German joined the government, in fact, the first pro-Nazi.

Smuts accepted an invitation to deliver the Rhodes Memorial lecture at Oxford, where he breathed the fresh air of England for two months. Then he carried out an old plan. The League of Nations' tenth anniversary was about to be celebrated in New York. Simultaneously he received, after many similar invitations, an offer from a lecture agency, which had managed ex-President Taft and Prince William of Sweden, for fifty lectures throughout the United States and Canada. It was a great opportunity. It was not the lecture fees that lured him, although they too may have exercised a certain spell, but the chance of impressing America with his world-embracing ideas.

He crossed the ocean at the end of 1929. He was showered with civic honors and university degrees. The entire press offered him bouquets. Many editorials called him the greatest living statesman. Only the Irish extremists attacked him ferociously. He might, they feared, end the British-Irish impasse in such a way that Eire would not realize her republican aspirations. The *Christian Science Monitor* presented the most accurate view: "He has always served high ideals in a way that has ever inspired a strange confidence. He was not closing his eyes to mistakes, one felt, where mistakes were made. His devotion was inspired by a much larger conception of things than that involved in the generally accepted meaning of the word patriotism."

American visitors were startled by his intimate familiarity with Irving, Poe, and Emerson. No one knew that he had written an unpublished book on Walt Whitman. Yet he disguised his bookishness with that shyness that is an important part of his make-up. "I am 80 per cent a farmer, and, at that, a Boer," he said, adding smilingly: "Most people think a Boer must be a barbarian." He showed little interest in seeing skyscrapers, but he was intent on visiting the farm belt in the Middle West. "You people have made farming a science. I wish that South Africa could emulate you. We have farms in a vast area. But we have not yet attained an adequate development."

In America he made his famous declaration on behalf of a Jewish home in Palestine. He would serve their cause, he promised, not because it was Jewish, but because it was a great human cause. He soon had an opportunity to prove that he stood by his word, even at his own political peril. On the ship returning to South Africa, he received the news that Parliament in Cape Town had voted a bill that would practically exclude "Eastern Europeans" from immigration. Most terrifying was the fact that not the Hertzogites alone, but almost all his own party, had voted the so-called "Quota Bill." He arrived in the nick of time to take part in the third reading. He found no support. Again he went down in defeat.

The lower his fortunes sank in South Africa, the higher surged his fame in England. Now was the time for the Centenary Meeting whose Presidency he had so gladly accepted. He had some of his happiest days in England. He needed them. Five thousand scientists from all over the world were congregated. Respectfully, this most distinguished group listened to Smuts dwelling on *The Scientific World Picture of Today*. He was in his element. He presided over illustrious meetings, took part in the work of no less than thirteen commissions, spoke in public halls and exhibition grounds packed to overflowing with plain people. He was given the freedom of York, and had, several times a day, to acknowledge distinctions and honors. Everyone sought his company: fellow botanists, fellow agriculturalists, fellow philosophers, fellow historians, fellow—what not. He had long and elaborate talks with leading economists, thoughtfully discussing what would happen to the world now that England had gone off gold. Suddenly the lights went out. Only very few days of undisturbed happiness at one time are allotted to General Smuts. South Africa refused to go off the gold standard. It was insanity. If she did not want to become the most expensive country in the world, to paralyze her trade and business, she must immediately follow England, Smuts urged in repeated cables.

The Hertzogite Cabinet received his urgent messages and explanation with riotous chuckles. Did Oom Jannie not know that he was already surviving himself? Did he indeed fancy that South Africa would still follow England slavishly as in the bygone days of his power? Did he want to stage a come back? They refused his pressing advice hilariously, but with grave suspicion. What was the old devil scheming? He could not be as stupid as that to propose that the country producing half the world's gold should go off the gold standard!

The Chamber of Mines, and a few experts, understood perfectly well. Moreover, they would not be adversely affected by an increase in the price of the gold they were producing. This simple fact everyone understood, even the bearded Boers on the *platteland,* and now it was clear beyond doubt that Smuts, in England, was again plotting with industry and the Jews.

In November he returned to South Africa. His country was choked with its own gold. Prices were far above world market levels. Exports had stopped. The farmers did not know where to sell their crops. Every other country that had gone off gold, including all the other Dominions, undersold them. Australia had even gone further than England. One could get Australian cattle, wool, corn for half the South African price. But General Hertzog, in Parliament, lifted his finger accusingly against Smuts and said that Smuts' off-gold propaganda was ruining the credit of the Union.

It happened rarely that Smuts defended himself against insults. It was his habit to gaze into the air, while a torrent of abuse poured down upon him. Sometimes he explained: "The dogs bark, but the caravan marches on." That was as long as he was in power. Now he was out. Now he said contemptuously: "This is no government. This is terror." He piled figure upon figure to prove his simple facts. He was still derided—until bankruptcies followed one another rapidly, shops closed down, mass suicides occurred, and the farmers, the real power in the state, began to lose their patience. They had been plagued by another drought, already in its fourth year. Persistent bad weather always brings government changes in the Union. The impossibility of selling their expensive crops, their own inability to buy fodder, forage and tools at excessive prices, in addition to the drought, bode ill for Hertzogism. One by-election after another went to Smuts' followers.

It was at this moment that Tielman Roos came in. After his return from Germany, he had no longer played a role in politics. His health was too badly shattered. He had received a seat on the Bench of the Supreme Court in Bloemfontein. But he could not stand the dignified tranquillity of a supreme justice. The toothless Lion of the Transvaal roared again. At Christmas 1932, after having resigned his seat, he had a new message for the country. It was exactly Smuts' message: "Off gold!"

Now things were different. Now people listened. Tielman Roos, everyone's pal, the most popular jolly good fellow in the Transvaal—had he forgiven his lifelong arch-foe? Indeed, he came as a peacemaker. He suggested the adoption of Smuts' proposal with Hertzog's consent. Both men should join a "best-men" (coalition) government. And since one could not expect either of them to submit to the other, he, again plain Advocate Tielman Roos, would bring the supreme sacrifice of acting as Prime Minister.

The time was January, 1933. It was just before Hitler came to power in Germany. But South Africa had only one problem: gold. Hertzog yielded. The Union followed the devaluation of sterling. A riotous off-gold rush ensued, unprecedented even in the annals of Johannesburg. The country was flooded with money. Smuts' prophecy was vindicated a hundredfold. But Tielman Roos had stolen the show. His tremendous popularity had forced the government to give in, while Smuts had been the crier in the desert.

Roos made a formal offer to Smuts to accept his leadership. For his part, he would win over the majority of the Hertzog-ites, if necessary, against the will of the leader. Who were his followers? Smuts asked. Roos could not yet disclose them. Smuts declined. Tielman Roos was not a newly won friend. He was a successful turncoat. Smuts did not sacrifice his principles for a share in the power.

Once more Smuts had proved his infallible instinct. The tide that had carried Roos sky-high ebbed as rapidly as it had surged. People lost interest in politics. It was disclosed that

Roos had no political followers of any importance. He had no financial backers. He was reduced to his natural proportions. Now Smuts could deal with him. He offered him a minority in a cabinet which he himself would lead. Roos insisted on all or nothing. He got nothing. Heartbroken, he returned to Bloemfontein. He was now fifty-five, diseased, penniless. He had to start life all over again. It proved impossible. He still hung about for a little while, ever joking, ever the good companion. Then his light went out. Smuts eulogized him at the unveiling of his memorial. He has the habit of praising his enemies.

He resumed his lonesome walks in the *veld*. The country, he reflected, needed peace after all this excitement. The people were sick of political haggling. A dark cloud was appearing on the horizon over Germany. A very distant cloud, not yet bigger than a man's hand, it was true. Smuts was not so far too badly concerned about this fellow Adolf Hitler. The decision of his own lifetime was at stake. Hertzog's government was shaken. The recurrence of this eternal racial conflict could perhaps be prevented. Should he try to return to the government? Upset Hertzog, if possible, and establish the rule of his own tottering party against another party of about equal strength, and against the shadow of Roos, that still loomed behind the scene? Would that be union? Fusion? Brotherhood?

It was at this moment, when both Smuts and Hertzog stood at the crossroads, that the kingmaker of South Africa interfered. "Old Bailey"—Sir Abe Bailey—had almost twenty years before dropped out of active politics, although he might have become the dominant power. Yet he had refused to stand again when the first Union Parliament expired, excusing himself in his inimitable way with the words: "As I was always at cross fire in politics, I had the wonderful achievement of keeping myself out of office. I wish to keep my record straight." In fact, no other man's record was as chequered as his. He had inherited Cecil Rhodes' Midas touch, as well as the colossus' contempt for money not serving a higher purpose. He was the man to carry on Rhodes' self-imposed mission. Like his spiritual predecessor, "Old Bailey" was one of the greatest latter-day

Imperialists, perhaps the last one of the honorable line, and again, like Rhodes, he wanted to make the Dutch in South Africa a pillar of the Empire.

His methods were shrewder and more direct than Rhodes'. He had, after all, not made his millions in diamonds and gold, but in odd adventures: as a prize fighter and a stock broker, a "farmer," as he modestly called himself (he became the world's largest estate owner), a land speculator. "I always tried to keep up appearances by keeping up the payment of my debts, especially the small ones that squeak the loudest," he once confessed.

But he was not particular about his "friends"—including everyone in South Africa—paying their debts. Practically all Dutch leaders knew where to borrow funds, either for themselves or for their causes. Botha had built his house in Pretoria with a loan from "Old Bailey" which was punctiliously repaid. Hertzog sought capital for his multiple newspaper enterprises. He never touched a penny for himself. But for the good of his mission he frequently visited *Rust en Vrede*—rest in peace—Sir Abe's manor in Muizenberg, the fashionable beach near Cape Town. Old Bailey lavished money on enterprises to advance whatever Afrikaans culture there was. He founded, and richly endowed, a *Voortrekker's* scholarship for research into the history of "our pioneer ancestors," although he was the son of a Yorkshireman from the West Riding. This scholarship was entrusted to the University of Stellenbosch, which had once been Victoria College, Smuts' *alma mater*. The university was, and remains to this day, the Mecca of the British-baiting Afrikanders. The Union Club in Johannesburg, at the corner of Bree and Joubert Streets, which Old Bailey founded and supported, was the only club in the country where British and Dutch gentlemen met on an equal footing. Time and again he used his great influence, and spent some of his wealth, to foster in London the cause of the Union of South Africa.

This was the man, with one foot in the English, the other in the Dutch camp, his heart beating for the Empire, who wielded perhaps the greatest influence in the decisive hour. He spoke to his friend Hertzog and then to his friend Smuts. He urged them to sink their differences and to work together. "You must both recognize that the cause is infinitely greater than the quarrel."

Hertzog, his position shaken, had to listen. Smuts was impressed. Old Bailey had spoken with his own voice. But it fell to his young friend, Mr. J. H. Hofmeyr, at present Smuts' right-hand man in the Union's war cabinet, to help him make up his mind. Mr. Hofmeyr was informed that the Nationalists were finally convinced that they could no longer run the country alone. Hertzog was ready to share his power, but he was reserving the Premiership for himself. Smuts had no objection to playing second fiddle. He had felt very comfortable as number two man in the team with Botha. Of course, Hertzog was not Botha. Smuts would have to swallow much of his pride, to sacrifice whatever hope of return to full power he might have. He would not be able to devote himself to writing, thinking, preaching Holism. He made a last attempt to escape. He would send his party into a coalition government, but himself remain outside.

It proved impossible. The designated party ministers would not go without their leader. Smuts agreed to a conference with Hertzog. They decided that Smuts was to become Deputy Prime Minister. But it was he who had to suggest reconciliation in Parliament. It was not difficult. Had he not preached reconciliation throughout his life? He stood up in the House. . . .

In May, 1933, the new Coalition Party swept the country. Smuts had done his duty by his idea. It was sublime self-sacrifice. He took it in his stride.

IT TOOK THE OUTBREAK OF THE SECOND WORLD WAR TO REVEAL Hertzog's true nature, perhaps even to himself. During the first thirty-odd years of his running feud with Smuts both men's aims differed only in degree. The father of Holism always wanted South Africa first. This was Hertzog's own slogan. But in Hertzog's mouth it was an understatement. He wanted South Africa to stand alone.

Now they were steering the ship of state together, a strangely met pair. Smuts stood in the shadow, his favorite place, provided he does not happen to be in England. In England he is a different man, although even there he maintains a certain air of detachment. As member of the War Cabinet he was not of the government. He never joined the Liberal Party; he was satisfied to be a fellow traveler. He examines British questions as an outsider, but he understands their ways of moving forward better than most Britons do themselves. He is steeped in the idea of the British Empire, but he is not dogmatic about it. He does not wish a closer organization, or any sort of assimilation between its members. He stands for a more varied way of life inside the Commonwealth. He loves it above all because it is Holistic, in his own words "the only League of Nations that really existed." His attitude is most characteristically expressed by his use of English. He has, some of his listeners believe, little feeling for the flow and rhythm of the language. But he phrases things in a new way, and he has mastered the art of reducing complicated phraseology to its simplest terms.

His repeated triumphs as an orator in England are largely the triumphs of his personality. He knows that he is among friends. Before speaking, he looks about him with an expression of serenity, even curiosity, that immediately bridges the distance between the speaker and his audience.

He has always been much celebrated in England (whereas

Botha was lionized). During the First War Mr. Garvin, one of the most influential journalists, suggested retaining Smuts as Foreign Secretary. Sir Philip Gibbs even looked upon him as the obvious successor of Lloyd George. Similarly, many Englishmen wanted to keep him in the country, when he visited London during the present war. Smuts never seriously considered such suggestions. But he likes to come to the tight little island as a friend. It is the only place on earth where he does not shun the limelight.

In his own country even his friends say that aloofness is his predominant quality. He finds his chief solace in philosophy, and in his model marriage. (About Mrs. Smuts, South Africa's much beloved *"Ouma,"* the story made the rounds that she runs her house with a grandchild at one hand and the Greek grammar in the other.) Everyone knows Smuts as a superlatively clever, singularly subtle, extremely cautious, but, by the same token, unusually daring statesman, and as a glutton for work.

But only a very narrow, limited circle knows the real Smuts. Some have suggested that he should occupy a chair for metaphysics at an ancient seat of learning. Others call him a country gentleman, interested in herds and crops and in the wide open spaces. Even those who see him predominantly as an out-of-doors man, understand, however, that it is not only his passion for mountain-climbing and his inbred horsemanship that make him a part of the South African landscape. The grass of the *veld* has a particular meaning to him; Smuts is one of the world's outstanding botanists, specializing in grasses. Country life also gives him an opportunity for mental repose, communion with himself, for reflection on the eternal verities. He has made most of his great decisions after a solitary walk. Before he at once signed and protested the Treaty of Versailles, the most spectacular incident in his career, he marched, since no *veld* was at hand, up and down the Champs Élysées.

Most of his admirers wonder about, some even regret, his complete indifference to jealousy, rivalry, ambitions, disappointments, and to the bitterness of public life that no contemporary statesman has experienced to anything like the same degree. No one who has ever watched him from the gallery of the House of Assembly can forget the faraway, transcendent look with which he, immovably, without response, without any reaction, tolerates the outpouring of abuse that has been heaped upon him as upon no other living man. His enemies loathe him because they know that he towers sky-high above them. He appears detached even among his followers in the House. One can see him striding along the corridors, lost in reflections, but always with his ear to the ground, lest he miss a single word of the debate behind the door.

In social contact he is candid and courteous, but intimate with no one. Even his relations with Botha, it is said, were confined to their work and vision in common, to that telepathy that united them, but this did not extend much beyond their common interest in their cause. Botha took time off for his famous bridge games, for golf and tennis, whereas Smuts crammed every moment with a double order of work and study. It is doubtful whether his knowledge of card games goes beyond a little old-fashioned whist. He relaxes now and then with his family, his horses, his wanderings, his books. His life is austere. He drinks only coffee, the mother's milk of the Boer, and although he likes his *biltong*—dried venison—he eats modestly. He has succeeded in keeping his weight steady for many decades.

His handwriting is noted for its illegibility. His manner of speech is forceful, convincing, persuasive. Sometimes he speaks with vigor, more and more rarely with emotion. In great moments he has the rapid, passionate speech of the seer and prophet. In private conversation he is frank and cordial, but he does not allow familiarity. Whatever he says and however he presents it, his words ring on.

South Africa calls him "slim": crafty, cunning, sly. But everyone is aware that only pure and enlightened motives direct his political game of chess. For reasons which must lie in invisible depths, all South Africa also calls him "Oom Jannie." Even Botha, eight years his senior, used to call him so. No one ever called Botha, the man with the magic touch, radiating sympathy, "Oom Louis." Perhaps a comparison with Cecil Rhodes, who was, already at the age of thirty, "the old man" to everyone, is permissible. He used to refer to himself in these words.

Smuts has but two passions: his romantic patriotism, which makes him call the story of South Africa "the only romantic adventure story in modern history," and his passion for bigness, an obsession he certainly shares with Rhodes. He has also frequently been compared with Alexander Hamilton, particularly for his work as the chief architect of the Union. He has, indeed, Hamilton's world sense.

The word for Hertzog, his antagonist, later his chief, is: petty. His very narrowness made him the idol of the *kraal-walled* Boers. Physically, he was undersized; mentally he was slow. He owed his success to his limitations. His brand of nationalism was exclusive and jealous. He fitted well into a time in which the envious, the dissatisfied nations—big ones like the Germans and the Japanese, small ones like the Irish and the Boers—were everywhere in the ascendant.

When he was at Victoria College (at the same time as Smuts), he was not a bookish youth like his younger colleague, but rather a bookworm. Painfully, he wormed his way through bulky tomes of the Old Roman-Dutch law, while Smuts, until his mind became oversaturated at Cambridge, was known for his capacity of learning a book by heart after one reading. Hertzog, descendant of a family of German immigrants, refused to study at an English university. Hence he was not admitted to the bar in the then British colonies. He had to confine himself to practicing in Bloemfontein, the capital of the furiously anti-British Free State. After the Boer War, in which he only played an insignificant part, he entered politics, of which he knew nothing. But the Free Staters saw in the foreigner their own flesh and blood. He became the champion of all those who could not understand why they had been defeated by the tools of the "Jews and the capitalists." Hertzog devoted himself to the task of rebuilding a downhearted and broken nation. His program was merely the airing of grievances, his outlook entirely racial. He hated the world, and sympathized only with other "downtrodden" peoples: the Indians, the Egyptians, the Irish. All were members of the British Empire. He came to loathe the Empire with an abiding hatred. He hated progress and civilization. To play down the fact that he was an outlandish newcomer—as it must have appeared to the proud descendants of the *Voortrekkers*—he appealed to their deepest and basest racial instincts.

The First War not only intensified his hatred for Britain, it made him set all his hopes upon Germany. Whereas to Smuts the Germans were prodigal sons of the great human family, who should be welcomed back after the good spanking they had received—but, by all means, kept out of Africa, where they were liable to build up and train enormous black armies—to Hertzog the Germans were the redeemers of the future. At the Imperial Conference in London he told the members of the British Government frankly that he disapproved of their apparent distrust of Germany. Why, German blood was flowing in his own veins, and did he not, despite his wild words, prove a perfectly amiable business partner? After the First War a picture of Frederick the Great hung over Hertzog's desk, opposite the picture of his own German grandfather.

His predilection for national isolation in a thinly populated and faraway country made him the natural enemy of Smuts' Pan-African conception. Smuts' Holism was treason to Hertzog. Smuts' eloquence was a challenge to his own manner of losing himself in cumbersome, never-ending sentences, which, incidentally, many Boers liked, since they need not listen quite so attentively and could have a good nap during the three hours Hertzog took to speak. Yet his persistence, his dogged repetitions, the fact that his creed, Hertzogism, consisted of four or five ever-recurring platitudes, made his appeal popular. There was this smoldering flame in him that kindled the *platteland*. He was obscure, often unintelligible, habitually cautious, until he burst out in a rage.

His was a double life. As if to offset the wild man from the *veld*, his conduct in private life was gentle and ingratiating.

325

He had many English acquaintances, provided they were good
South Africans, not *jingoes*. He spoke their language without
the slightest foreign accent. Megalomaniac in politics, he was
simplicity incarnate in his off-stage bearing. In society he felt
insecure, but he was sure of his hold on his old friends and
liked their company. He cared little for money, and not at all
for amusements. He was entirely deficient in humor. He was
single-minded, and an introvert. Some day the little man would
no longer be satisfied with play acting the big boss. Some day
his repressed passions, the true ones, would burst out.

Smuts strove hard and honestly to make the coalition work.
Hertzog remained stubborn and evasive, although he, too,
wanted to give the new combination a working chance. For
the time being it was the only instrument that would keep him
in power.

Dr. Daniel François Malan had different aims. He attributed
Tielman Roos' downfall to providential dispensation. He had
loathed his chief competitor with that Old Testament hatred
that only the Dutch Gereformeede Church can teach. When he
heard of Tielman Roos' punishment by the Lord—that the ail-
ing, prematurely aged man could scarcely eke out a living, and
that his family suffered direst need—he spent all day in church
praying, he said, that the Lord may have mercy on a sinner.
When he left the church, Alderley Street, Cape Town's Fifth
Avenue, saw a show that no one had ever seen: Dr. Malan
strolled leisurely down the promenade, and, good Lord, Dr.
Malan laughed.

He was now the undisputed chief lieutenant of, and heir
presumptive to, Hertzog. But at the age of sixty it was no
longer enough to be a lieutenant, or an heir to the throne. Dr.
Malan, a faultfinder throughout his life, saw through Hertzog's
emptiness. Hertzog was a relic. What the nation needed was a
reformer. Had he himself not borne the burden of reforms during the coalition government with Labor? Had he, Dr. Malan,
as Minister of the Interior, not made *Afrikaans* the official language? Curtailed the power of the old-fashioned, pro-Smuts

Senate? Appointed reliable Britain-baiters to all offices of income under the Crown? Destroyed Smuts' educational system, so that the Boers should remain on the soil, and become farmers as their fathers and grandfathers had been? Who else, if not he, had borne the burden of the struggle in the flag quarrel? Should all his reforms be marred by a compromise with Smuts? This was a good time for reformers. Germany had this man Hitler, another Bismarck, another Frederick the Great. He, Dr. Daniel François Malan would be damned—forgive, Lord, forgive!—he would be most unhappy if he did not become the Luther of the Boers.

Although he had saved his mandate in a faraway Cape district only due to the help of Smuts, who had come to campaign for his perennial vilifier, Dr. Malan now refused to join the new Cabinet. Instead, he organized a head committee of the irreconcilables in order to outbid Hertzog's now necessarily somewhat subdued racialism and to steal his leader's thunder.

As duly elected chairman of the head committee, Dr. Malan asked Prime Minister Hertzog whether he agreed "that the British Crown, in so far as the Union is concerned, is divisible, that we possess the right of neutrality, and that we have the right of separation."

Hertzog was trapped. He could either agree to renew the anti-British campaign at this moment, which would endanger the coalition, or lose his aureole as Britain-baiter number one. This seemed the graver menace. He answered Dr. Malan: "With regard to the question of sovereign independence and the removal of court anomalies it gives me pleasure to be able to state that the intention is as presumed by your head committee." The British Crown, to which Hertzog had four times sworn fealty, was now "court anomalies" to him.

The head committee went one step further. It demanded a status bill to bring the Prime Minister's declaration into legal form.

Hertzog agreed. He would move the bill.

To Smuts this decision came as a terrible blow. The Cabinet to which he belonged was about to deceive England. Perhaps the merits of the act did not matter so much. Smuts felt confident that he could stave off the worst. But the breach of confidence involved, the fact that South Africa adopted an attitude which must appear as if the Union was going back on *Vereeniging*, and on the Statute of Westminster, on both the great declarations of freedom which he himself had materially helped to bring about—the double-dealing, the foulness of his coalition partners, aroused his wrath. Should he break out of the *kraal?* It would mean a renewal of fratricidal strife. It was impossible. He had to fall in line.

For the whole duration of the coalition government such conflicts recurred, on a smaller or larger scale, conflicts not important because of a thinly veiled split inside the Cabinet, but terrible because the split was inside Smuts. It was the conflict between the South African and the philosopher. The Old Master surpassed himself in exercising his strongest power: self-control. He preserved South Africa for the great test that was approaching.

He turned to Hertzog. Smuts implored him to watch his step. With all his persuasiveness he wrestled for what he called Hertzog's soul. The weathercock yielded a few inches. He gave Smuts a written promise that those points on which they had disagreed in the past would not be touched by the new act; he and Smuts would merely continue to disagree about them.

In Parliament Smuts fought valiantly to keep the new act within the frame of the Statute of Westminster. On this occasion he delivered one of his historic speeches, celebrating the Statute of Westminster as the *magna charta* of freedom. To the people of South Africa he gave the promise that they would not be asked to do anything they should not be asked to do. He pleaded with London not to be unduly disturbed.

But the Dominion Party, the small group of independent South African English under Colonel Stallard, was distrustful.

The new Status Act was passed with a great majority. Both Hertzog's and Smuts' followers voted for it. The Dominion Party was opposed and, strangely, the Malanites as well. Although Dr. Malan's head committee had declared: "When the

present Status Bill is passed by Parliament South Africa will be
more free than Paul Kruger's Transvaal was in 1884!" the act,
suddenly, did not go far enough for their appetites. Having
tasted his first victory, Dr. Malan wanted more elbow room.
With a handful of followers he seceded from the United Party.

The Boers had won the Boer War in 1934. It was the common opinion in South Africa. The English in the country knew
it best. Smuts saw their confidence waning. They had but a
couple of seats in Parliament. They were no longer a political
factor of any importance. But their distrust hurt Smuts deeply.
He addressed a few heart-rending words to them: "If I cannot
be trusted after what I have done for a lifetime, then who
can be trusted in this country? . . . If I cannot be trusted,
who can be trusted in this world?"

On the same day Dr. Malan founded his party of "Purified
Nationalists." Its constitution was drafted on the pattern of the
National Socialistic Labor Party in Germany.

Nazism grew tropically on South Africa's hot soil. Its tenets
confirmed what most of the Boers had always suspected. Already during the Boer War they had unanimously assured Winston Churchill, their prisoner of Pretoria, that "the Jews and
the capitalists" were responsible for the war. While Adolf Hitler
was still a schoolboy in Linz, Upper-Austria, Boonzaier, South
Africa's foremost cartoonist, discovered that one could make a
good living on *Hoggenheimer* alone! on the caricature of a fat,
apelike, bejeweled Jew, standing for the Rand capitalist. Hoggenheimer held an enormous cigar in his left hand; his right
hand pulled the strings on which a shrimp with Smuts' likeness
danced.

Against a flood of rabid anti-Semitism, Smuts stood out to
protect the Jews, almost alone. A little assistance came from an
unexpected quarter. In 1933, Tielman Roos, shortly before his
death, lifted his fading voice against anti-Semitism. But by then
the Nazi locusts were already swamping the land.

Smuts did not yet know Hitler's secret weapon: the hypo-
dermic. Methodically, Nazism poisoned South Africa's blood

stream. Nazi propaganda mushroomed on the hot soil. Nowhere else were conditions for spreading the gospel of racialism as favorable as among the race-crazed Boers. Moreover, in no other civilized country was there so much destitution. South Africa fell prey more easily to Nazism than Germany itself.

Twenty-two per cent of the white population were poor whites: men of European descent who could not make a living on civilized standards and who did not keep clear of the color bar. Crushed between the haughtiness of skilled white labor, from whose ranks they were barred, and cheap native labor, with which they could not compete, three hundred thousand poor whites, many of them *bywoners* on the farms, others slum dwellers in the towns, lived in a state of physical and mental decay that made them ripe for every revolution. According to a report of a Carnegie Commission of Inquiry, another 34 per cent of South Africa's white population were unable to feed and clothe themselves, to be decently housed or to send their children to school without government assistance. There were neither English nor Jews among them. They were Boers to the last man.

The bigoted Calvinists who loathed the English with Old Testament hatred, as well as the irreconcilable Republicans, who dreamed of the return of Oom Paul's golden days, set all their hopes on Hitler. Moreover, the "national awakening" in Germany appealed irresistibly to that third of the Boers who claimed German descent. Most of them had long forgotten their ancestors, mercenaries, who had come as soldiers of fortune in the pay of the Dutch or of the East India Company. But now, as Hitler thundered at the gates of the world, it became a promising proposition to recall a German great-grandfather.

Hitler's urge for living space was essentially the Boers' own craving. They could not see the smoke of their neighbor's chimney. It was proverbial. And if the Hitler-Germans claimed to be the master race—why should not the Boer himself be the *baas* in South Africa?

Throughout the year 1934 Nazism in South Africa spread

like the plague. Smuts was disturbed. But he was not yet prepared to antagonize Germany. The German measles would be cured as soon as the world gave the Third Reich a square deal. Delivering his rectorial address at St. Andrews, Scotland, however, he made Human Freedom his topic.

He returned to South Africa by airplane. Bodyguards received him at the airport. They followed, and screened him, everywhere. Smuts protested. Would they not, at least, let him alone when he was mountaineering? They would not. They were under orders. Nazism was rampant.

Chapter 27	PRELUDE TO WAR

SOUTH AFRICA SEEMED A PRIZE CATCH TO HITLER. HERE WAS THE nucleus for the vast German colonial empire of which Wilhelm II had once dreamed. He who holds South Africa holds the whole continent below the equator. He also commands the confluence between the Atlantic and the Indian oceans. He has the key to the world. Furthermore, he has the earth's richest gold output.

The Nazi penetration of South Africa was entrusted to Ernst Wilhelm Bohle, boss of the "League of Germans Abroad," who also founded the *bunds* in this country. But Bohle's heart was never in the United States of America. It was always in Cape Town. Son of a professor of electrical engineering at the Cape Town University, he had grown up under the shadow of Table Mountain, but he remained an undiluted boche whose every thought was treason to the land of his birth. His right-hand man was his venerable father, then living in Berlin in "retirement," in fact as chief of the African Division of Dr. Haushofer's "Geopolitical Institute," Hitler's brain trust.

The Bohles, father and son, sent masses of German immigrants to South Africa, particularly to the mandated territory of the former German South West. Four thousand alleged German "miners" who wanted to disembark at Windhoek, were refused admission, and had to return on their ship. But this was the only case on record in which the Hertzog government protected the country against Nazi infiltration. Even the Prime Minister did not wish to hand South West Africa back to Germany. Hertzog declared that the return of the Reich as a great colonial power in Africa was both inevitable and desirable, but he tried to persuade the Germans to help themselves to the Belgian and Portuguese colonies. He disposed as magnanimously of other people's countries as his model, Hitler, himself.

He did nothing to stop the influx of German agents into South Africa proper. Eighteen thousand Germans, less than 1 per cent of the total white population, were German settlers. They had no influence in politics, but their little hamlets were scattered all over the map.

Bohle's agents, arriving in droves, took care that the Nazis obtained majorities in the committees for German schools and in the councils of elders for German churches. All Germans, including Jewish refugees, were registered by Nazi functionaries. If they did not want to contribute to the German Winter Hilfe —winter relief—their relatives in the old country would be herded into concentration camps. The funds, allegedly for charity, were used by the Nazi press fund, headed by Manfred Zapp, who later shifted to New York. German businessmen in South Africa were forced to hire Nazi employees, if they did not want to lose their trade with Germany. German residents had to see movies from Bablesberg, the German Hollywood. German steamers in South African ports arranged "socials" for the Germans in town. The friendly invitations carried the words: "Attendance obligatory." Hitler was shown in the newsreels, and the bored crews in the audience had, time and again, to feign enthusiasm. By way of relaxation, they staged propaganda marches through the streets of Cape Town.

An army of agents and spies was unloosed over South Africa.

Botany professors, pretending to draw samples of the rare South African flora, sketched bridges, harbors, the site of munition dumps. Ethnographers came to study the vanishing bushman. They brought literature with them. Between covers with scientific titles were folded reprints of articles from the *Stuermer,* the notorious anti-Semitic sheet. German exchange students and professors proved so charming, although admitting their undying devotion to Hitler, that the Nazis could not be so bad, after all. Missionaries from Germany preached neo-paganism.

Occasionally, more important visitors came. Miss Rutkowsky, a fanatic Nazi schoolmistress, toured the country with a camera, and showed in hotels and schools films of the Nazi movement. Her preferred shots were pictures displaying the neo-pagan rites of the believers in Wotan. This disgusted even the pro-Nazi Dutch Reformed Church, and she was asked to leave the country. Another case of attempted religious infiltration occurred in the Trappist monastery at Marianhill, in Natal. The brothers extended their hospitality to a group of German missionaries who talked incessantly of the unholy combination of Judah and Rome. Trappists, for their part, do not talk at all. They are bound by an oath of silence. Silently, they went at their German brethren, who, within a few minutes, collected their bones outside the monastery.

A Nazi with the suspiciously Jewish-sounding name of Hirschfelder represented the heavy industry in the Ruhr. He penetrated South African big business, and offered, not unsuccessfully, such barter agreements as Dr. Schacht had introduced to get imports free of cost. At present Hirschfelder enjoys the hospitality of a South African detention camp.

The most sinister uninvited guest was Gestapo chief Diverge, assistant editor of the *Schwarzes Korps,* mouthpiece of Hitler's elite guard. He visited Johannesburg, Pretoria, Cape Town, and Durban, and reported on every single German in the four biggest towns of the Union. His accounts were detailed: did the man drive a German car, or did the traitor use a car of American make? Did he employ a German chauffeur or a Ne-

gro? His wife and secretary took down his interviews in shorthand, and sent them to Berlin. Diverge was also commissioned
to investigate the German Legation and the Consulates in the
Union. He was not satisfied with Dr. Leitner, the Minister, and
relegated him to third rank in the Nazi hierarchy, subordinated
to boss Jasper, who had had a hand in the rape of Austria, and
to the second in command, a gunman by the name of Lierau,
who later became notorious in fomenting trouble in the Sudetenland. To prove his reliability as a Nazi, Dr. Leitner protested to the Prime Minister when the City Councillors of Cape
Town had refused a German offer for harbor installations, although cheaper than the British tender. After profuse excuses,
Hertzog sent his Under Secretary for External Affairs, Dr.
Bodenstein, himself a German by descent, to the Town Fathers
of Cape Town. Dr. Bodenstein was told that Hertzog might
betake himself to the opposite place to Heaven. He had no
right to interfere in matters of local jurisdiction.

Hertzog, a bad loser, compensated the Reich by giving large
orders for railway construction to the German industry. Moreover, he sold to Germany South African wool to the tune of
three million pounds sterling for clothing the Reichswehr, and
manganese for the German steel industry, working full speed
at rearmament.

Smuts, smarting under his exclusion from real power, toured
the country, and addressed the crowds. He spoke about irrigation, the fight against locusts, the introduction of new improve-
ments in agriculture, and ended regularly with an appeal to
keep faith with the British Commonwealth. Only once he hit
out against Nazism, but even on this occasion he carefully
spoke only by implication. A German hairdresser in Cape Town
by the name of Weichardt had founded the Greyshirts, an organization which trained Boer and German youth in throwing
stones, some day to be replaced by hand grenades. "The Greyshirts are subsidized from abroad," Smuts warned. Nothing
happened. The Nazis took heart. The Blackshirts sprang up.
Soon they outnumbered the Greyshirts.

After more than two years of superhuman patience, Smuts, in the end, had one success. When Italy grabbed Abyssinia, everyone understood that the Union itself was menaced. All Mussolini's balderdash about the great Italian Empire he was creating certainly did not refer to Ethiopia alone. The Duce meant Kenya, Uganda, the Congo, and Tanganyika. The majority of the Boers did not care about British and Belgian colonies. Yet even Hertzog understood that Italy on both sides of the Transvaal would mean the end of South Africa, and thus of his own regime. Under Smuts' influence, he consented to the strongest representations in Geneva on behalf of sanctions against Italy. But the democratic powers shied away from imposing oil sanctions, the only ones that could have broken Mussolini. The stock of world democracy sank lower and lower among the Boers.

Early in 1938 their resentment found violent expression at the Centenary Celebration to commemorate the mass slaughter of their pioneers, the *Voortrekkers,* by the Kafirs. *Voortrekker Day* is the day when Afrikanders think with their blood. In 1938, when another war was looming, another mass slaughter in which the majority of the Boers wanted no part, all previous celebrations were surpassed. From all parts of the Union ox wagons, the ark of the *veld,* in which the *Voortrekkers* had traveled, and lived, and made their homes, rolled slowly to Pretoria. Groups of Boer youths, in relays, marched from Cape Town to Pretoria, carrying the torch of liberty. Tens of thousands of men and women in *Voortrekker* costumes congregated; the women in long frocks and bonnets, the men in breeches and colorful waistcoats. All the men, including hundreds of Nazi agents, had for many months carefully grown luxuriant beards. The Centenary Celebration ended in a gigantic demonstration for the Republic.

The Boers were where Hitler wanted them. Innumerable offers from would-be spies flooded the German Consulate in Portuguese Lourenço Marques, where the Nazis still maintain their African espionage headquarters. One of the most significant of these letters was revealed in Parliament by Mr. Harry Law-rence, Union Minister for the Interior. It read: "My sentiments are with Germany. I feel that my knowledge of South Africa, its people, its political parties, its armaments and defense in-stallations may be of great use to you in Germany. I have first-hand information about the Jewish question, and about the possibilities of trade with Germany. Knowing all sections of the community so intimately, speaking their language fluently, and having access to influential political, military, and financial quarters, I feel I could provide information of use to Germany. I know Mr. Bruckner de Villiers, who controls *Die Burger*, and on whose behest Dr. Malan adopted the policy of open anti-Semitism. I know Mr. Pirow. I could even easily invite myself to General Smuts' farm at Irene, and obtain definite informa-tion on his opinions. I could without difficulty arrange to see the airports at Robert Heights, or find out more about the great harbor works at Cape Town and their fortifications."

The writer of this letter was a man by the name of J. W. Gadow, the secretary of the Greenside Branch of the Purified Nationalist Party in Johannesburg. The letter was intercepted by the Union Intelligence Service. The ensuing investigation disclosed that it had been the third of his offers, that Gadow, indeed, had been in Germany, where he had been treated as a guest of honor, and equipped with money. Mr. Bruckner de Villiers, though gravely compromised, remained silent. He was not only the backer of the leading Nationalist paper, but also one of the most influential members of the mysterious *broeder-bund* which wields the real power behind the scenes of politi-cal Afrikanderdom. Entrenched in this strong position, he felt certain that the law would not dare to lay hands on him. He guessed right.

During the days of Munich, secession seemed near. Smuts had neither protested Hitler's rape of Austria, nor did he find the Fuehrer's claim to the Sudetenland improper. Why, it was the first step to Holism: the fusion inside the individual nation preparatory to the fusion of all nations. The facts that Austrians and Germans were entirely different nations, and that the people of the Sudeten had never been, nor did they wish to be, incorporated with the German Reich were too trifling to arrest his world-embracing attention. Yet Hertzog was suspicious that his deputy might, in the case of a showdown between England and Germany, want to drag the Union alongside Great Britain into a war that appeared menacingly near.

In his neat longhand Hertzog wrote the memoranda on his official stationery. The first, written on September 1, 1938, was headed: "A statement of the standpoint to be taken by the Union of South Africa in the case of war in Europe with England as one of the belligerent parties: South Africa will remain neutral, but stick to the contracted obligation in connection with the naval base at Simon's Town." He signed formally: James Barry Munik Hertzog.

Four weeks later he penned another memorandum: "In case war should break out in Europe as a result of the quarrel between Germany and Czechoslovakia, and England should be involved in it, the attitude of the Union would be as is explained in greater detail in the accompanying documents A and B, signed by myself." These documents had been communicated by Hertzog to Smuts in the early days of September, during the Sudeten crisis. They stated that South Africa would not be involved in a war to safeguard the Sudetenland for Czechoslovakia. Smuts had accepted them as referring simply to the situation in these days, but not as a declaration of a general policy of neutrality in the future.

Neither Hertzog nor Smuts, it appeared, saw the warning beacon of the agreement of Munich. However, Munich taught South Africa a lesson. Hitler's technique of creating dissatisfaction among German minorities as a pretext for interfering on behalf of the "oppressed" might well be applied in South Africa, too. The general nervousness increased, when the Fuehrer announced that his next demand would be the claim for the return of colonies.

With the half-hearted consent of Hertzog, the Union authorities began to take an active interest in the German spies and agents who thus far had operated quite unmolested. Missionaries, exchange students, lecturing professors, and traveling salesmen from Germany were put under control. But no measures to stop or deport them were applied.

The English part of the population as well as many Dutch followers of Smuts expressed their anxiety over the miserable state of the defences in no uncertain terms. On October 24, 1938, a sensational newspaper article laid the responsibility for this state of affairs at the door of Oswald Pirow, the Minister for Defence. Mr. Pirow, the paper said, was responsible for the grave neglect of Simon's Town, the British Naval Base in South Africa, the maintenance of which was entrusted to the Union. The guns of Simon's Town were obsolete. They were incapable of keeping out of range any modern cruiser armed with six-inch guns. The material for the repair of these deficiencies had been available for many months, but it had not been installed.

Pirow answered with the subterfuge that he wanted to wait until more powerful modern guns could be shipped from England, even if this should take another two or three years. Moreover, he would soon travel to England to discuss the defense plans with the British War Office, and to supervise the purchase of arms and equipment.

On the very day of this acrimonious debate, a "German South-West African League" was founded in Windhoek. Dr. G. E. Conradie, the administrator, asked his government's permission to forbid the league. Hertzog only allowed the administrator to forbid civil servants to join any sort of political organization.

The Germans in South West Africa profited from the apparent weakness of the Union government. They formed about a third of the white population of the territory (8,500 against almost 20,000 Boer post-war immigrants and 2,500 English settlers), but they found help among the Boers. "Manie" Maritz, the traitor of 1914, had returned from Germany. He came as a Hitler agent, distributing his pamphlet *My Lewe and Strewe—My Life and my Strife*—which contained such vulgar anti-

Semitic passages that the author had been fined seventy-five pounds. This mild punishment encouraged the Germans and their Boer fellow travelers. Dr. Hirsekorn, Hitler's appointed *gauleiter* of the South West, called up all Germans to enroll in a "German Fighting League."

The trouble in the South West caused immediate repercussions in the Union. A Nationalist paper in Pretoria demanded measures against the refugees who were endangering the Union's friendly relations with Germany. Dr. Malan, at a congress of his "Purified Nationalist Party," adopted anti-Semitism as an official point of the program, and passed a resolution congratulating the Sudeten Germans upon their return to Germany.

In the midst of the general turmoil, Pirow, the stormy petrel, slipped out. He did not go to London, as he had announced. Instead he toured the Fascist countries. His first step was Lisbon, where Dr. Salazar, the dictator of Portugal, received him to the tune of *Die Stem of Zuid Afrika,* the Boer republican hymn. Pirow was a minister under the British Crown. But *God Save the King* was not played. Sir Eric Phipps, the British ambassador in Lisbon, who was present, froze.

While the Spanish republican government at Burgos was still officially recognized, Pirow called upon General Franco, committing, as it was generally put, a "blazing indiscretion." He duly eulogized Franco, and hurried on to the real aim of his journey: Berlin. Hitler received him with high honors. The Fuehrer and his presumptive *gauleiter* of South Africa drove through the Berlin streets, where a million people were lined up to cheer. Photographs, immortalizing the handshake between the two "kinsmen" were displayed in all German shop windows.

Pirow ordered his daughter to follow him. The half-grown girl took an English ship. Innocently, she told interviewers at Southampton: "I am really a German girl. All my four grandparents are German. My father spent his youth in Germany. German is our household language. I once visited England. But

I felt every moment that I did not belong. I belong to Germany." Upon her arrival she immediately joined the *Deutschen Mädchenbund*—the League of German Girls. She still lives in Germany. Unfortunately, her father returned to his adopted country. He presented the bill for his traveling expenses. The South African taxpayers had to refund him £1,329.

The new session of Parliament opened on February 2, 1939. Shrewdly, Hertzog calmed the storm that was awaiting him. He published an exchange of letters between himself and his son. Advocate Albert Hertzog had demanded that his father should assume leadership of a movement to be called *Afrikander Unity* with the aim of excluding the English-speaking South Africans from all political rights. With great dignity Hertzog *père* stated that he had immediately refused this demand. The English-speaking section should henceforth be "considered" as before.

The first measure of consideration was a bill, presented by Dr. Bodenstein, Under Secretary for External Affairs, with the aim of forbidding the English-language press to criticize Hitler and Mussolini. At the same time Pirow, as Minister of Defence, moved his "emergency bill" to suppress hostile demonstrations and propaganda in the case of a European war. "Hostile" referred to any demonstrations and propaganda in favor of England. A number of anti-Semitic bills were introduced by Nationalist members.

On March 15 Hitler invaded Prague. The whole world realized that sooner or later this meant war. The rumblings that followed were loudest in South West Africa. On the very evening the occupation of Prague became known, the streets of Windhoek were crowded with German insurgents. Dr. von Oelhaven, the former German Consul in Windhoek, returned surprisingly and told a meeting of Nazi athletes: "If you trust the Fuehrer and rely on him, he will keep his pledge and liberate us in South West Africa."

Now Smuts acted. Appeasement was dead. Smuts fell in line. On Monday, April 17, three hundred policemen with armored cars, machine-guns and Bren guns, grenades and rifles embarked from Cape Town and Pretoria for South West Africa. Legally, Union police had no right to interfere with the mandated territory. But this was one of the repeated moments in Smuts' life in which he was the law. He had acted in time. Papers were seized in Windhoek disclosing that the Nazis had planned a *putsch* for April 20, Hitler's birthday. They wanted to seize Walfisch Bay with its radio station, and broadcast the signal calling for a general upheaval. They had planned to give short shrift to the two hundred twenty-four local policemen scattered over a territory almost three times the size of the British Isles. Instead, twenty trucks with Union police and machine-guns drove through the streets of Windhoek on Hitler's birthday, and the Exhibition Grounds were transformed into an armed camp. The jubilation of the Boers in the South West, the great majority of whom had no intention of returning their farms to the old German owners, forced Hertzog to smile bittersweetly on his deputy's resolute action.

Behind Hertzog's bittersweet smile and Smuts' stony mask the struggle for power had broken out openly. The majority of the Boers were easy prey for uninhibited racialism. The United Party, torn from top to bottom by the thinly veiled strife between the two leaders, but on the surface still intact, lost, on the day after the police action in the South West, a most significant by-election at the *Paarl* to the "Purified" followers of Malan. The Hertzogites became nervous. On the next day Smuts moved a bill in the House of Assembly to put the mandated territory under the permanent control of the Union Police. Dr. Leitner, the German Minister, rushed to Hertzog to protest on grounds of international law. The Hertzogite majority within the United Party heeded the protest, and defeated their Deputy-Premier's bill.

But Smuts was again in his stride. He acted on his own responsibility. He established a burgher force in the South West, which was well able to take care of the Germans. He called out volunteers for National Service. Not only the English people—

among whom not a single appeaser was left after Munich—but also a great part of the Boers responded. Youngsters left school to join up. Even German immigrants who had served during the First War in the Imperial Army, volunteered. The cleavage between the Boers became apparent. A determined minority, the aggregate of the best elements, followed Smuts. The majority, however, became day by day more infuriated against the English. Three English teams, a tennis, a soccer, and a rowing team were just visiting South Africa, and, except for a single football match in the Southern Transvaal, the "bloody foreigners" took all the honors.

On the evening of April 24, the Naziphiles, as usual, tuned to Zeesen, the German shortwave station, were amazed to hear a voice addressing them in Afrikaans. They felt honored, but disappointed. They were accustomed to Naughty Naughty, the Lord Haw-Haw for South Africa. With his spicy reports on boxing matches, with his subtly understated translations of Hitler speeches, with his ever-recurring assertions that he could not forget England, although he had not really been treated well under the government of war mongers, with his Nazi poison sugar-coated with perfect English gentleness, Naughty Naughty had attracted even a wide circle of English listeners in the Union. In a quiet, unobtrusive manner he used to address fans who had written him to Berlin, and he promised every South African that he would speak via Zeesen to his beloved ones at home, if he came to visit Germany.

Unfortunately, on the twenty-fourth of April the charmer Naughty Naughty was replaced by Eric Holm, a dyed-in-the-wool Afrikander. His speeches were unconcealed hymns of hate. He addressed the republicans, the racial fanatics, the poor whites. He started to speak to Dr. Malan himself. Referring to Smuts as "Jan Smutskowitz," he excelled in Jew-baiting, unhampered by the fact that the Government Information Service soon disclosed that Eric Holm's father was an Elder of the Synagogue Council in Cape Town. Kate Voss, the self-styled nightingale of South Africa, now in Berlin, and generally recognized as the only friend Ribbentrop and Goebbels shared in common, was another great attraction. Radio Zeesen scored. Today still the German broadcast in Afrikaans is the strongest medium of Nazi propaganda in South Africa.

On July 1 Hertzog celebrated his fifteenth year as Premier. Smuts eulogized him duly, and most of South Africa jubilated: "Another fifteen!" Hertzog promised he would remain in office as long as his mental and physical strength would hold out. His main objective was to keep South Africa out of war if Europe should go up in flames.

Two months of almost unbearable tension ensued. Greyshirts and Blackshirts demonstrated freely. The Afrikander students of the University of Pretoria organized a "peace strike." Smuts toured the country, appealing for racial co-operation.

On August 25 Hitler told Sir Nevile Henderson, British ambassador in Berlin, that he could no longer tolerate the persecution of the German minority in Poland. When Zeesen broadcast the news, Pirow rushed to Hertzog's farm. Pirow had just received Lord Francis Scott, the leader of the English settlers in Kenya, who was perturbed about the colony's complete lack of defenses, and had assured Lord Francis in the most folksy and engaging manner: "If you people in Kenya will allow us, we should like to look on your northern border as our own frontier, and if you should get into trouble there, we should be prepared to send you at once three hundred airplanes."

It was a different Pirow who now put pressure on the wretched, aged Prime Minister. Pirow's receding hair stood up like a brush in Prussian fashion. His small, dark eyes under the broad, bushy brows, his tight lips, even his bat ears, trembled. He was playing the game of his life. Although he knew that Hertzog would not like it, he appeared in his hurry informally, in a sloppy, rumpled black suit, and with a gray, loudly striped tie around a German stand-up collar. That is how his bodyguard, appointed by a watchful Government Information Service of Smuts' creation, described the Minister of Defence, as he buttonholed the Premier. Now was the moment to declare neutrality and to break away from England. He was in league with the Blackshirts, he disclosed; they would march upon Johannesburg if the great leader would give the signal.

Hertzog was not good at giving signals. He preferred to be dragged along by events. Yet Pirow must have made a deep impression upon him. Throughout the ensuing fatal days he kept the dangerous adviser at his side.

Dr. Malan was the next visitor to Hertzog's farm. In stark contrast to the unbalanced German Pirow, the ex-*predikant* and frustrated professor of theology, did not lose his dignity for an instant. His square, heavy-set face, clean-shaven and rosy, was expressionless. His high thinker's forehead, looking twice as high due to his baldness, remained unlined as he spoke in an unctuous voice. Even his ample double chin did not lose its natural poise. He had come with an offering. He offered Hertzog reunion. The full support of the Purified Nationalists—"more dangerous a competition than we care to be"—would be his for the mere asking. The Prime Minister should declare South Africa's unwavering neutrality. The Purified members of the House had often proved the power of their vocal cords. They would again shout down Smuts, and Parliament would be stampeded into submission.

No bodyguard accompanied Dr. Malan. No one was within hearing distance during the interview. Smuts had no report of the meeting beyond the mere fact that it was mentioned in the papers. Yet, in a parliamentary spech he delivered a few days later, he reconstructed the negotiations between Hertzog and his two visitors with translucent accuracy—indeed, with the visionary insight of a man who knows human fallacy.

Saturday morning, the second of September, Smuts stalked into the Prime Minister's Chambers. Pirow and Havenga shadowed Hertzog. Simultaneously all three assailed Smuts with their policy of neutrality. "Impossible!" said Smuts. He fell into silence. But silence, his habitual protection, was not permitted when the fate of the world was at stake, and, what counted more, the fate of South Africa. With unending patience he tried

—in his own words—"to show them why neutrality was an impossible policy." The argument lasted the whole forenoon. Hertzog remained intransigent. Smuts demanded a full Cabinet meeting to lay the matter before their colleagues.

After luncheon, while all the police squads of Cape Town were mobilized, the whole Cabinet gathered. The discussion lasted throughout the afternoon, the evening, the night, until dawn. All the time Hertzog had Dr. Malan's written offer of support in his pocket, but he did not mention it.

After the first inconclusive day, the Cabinet met again on Sunday afternoon. In the meantime Hertzog had received another promise of support from the "Purified," which he also concealed.

Smuts and his six followers in the government advised Hertzog to summon a party caucus. Again Hertzog refused abruptly. With the letter, his secret weapon, in his breast pocket, he felt sure of obtaining a majority in the House.

The negotiations led nowhere. Smuts expected Hertzog to dismiss him and his followers, reform his cabinet, and appeal to the electorate. Instead the Prime Minister appealed to the House. When Smuts bowed his way out of the Cabinet council, Hertzog whispered, grinning: "I have my majority, Oom Jannie. I do have it . . . in the pocket."

Parliament met on Monday, September 4. Hertzog dropped his mask. The outburst, long overdue, revealed the little man as an undiluted Nazi. "I understand the Germans perfectly," he said. "I sympathize with Hitler. I know how he feels. I, too, have been downtrodden. We, too, the Boers, are a downtrodden people. We have no quarrel with the Germans. This is not South Africa's war. If Hitler were out for world domination, no one would oppose the Germans more fervently than I," he continued. "There is, however, no proof that this is Hitler's object. . . . I have gone through Hitler's struggle myself, and I know what it is to be trampled underfoot so long that eventually one prefers destruction to further humiliation."

Replying, Smuts was again complete master of his feelings. His voice never wavered. Only his fist struck the desk occasionally to emphasize his arguments. Once or twice he showed anger when the Nationalist benches made foolish "humorous" noises. Until then the House had listened in deadly silence to Smuts, who said: "We are up against the most vital issue for the future of this country. The position we take is that it would be fatal for this country not to sever relations with Germany at this stage. In September, 1938, the country had been prepared to recognize that Hitler had a strong case when he claimed the return of the Sudetenland. Since then we have seen an entirely un-Germanic people, the Czechs, absorbed by the Germans. These developments have shown the real objectives and motives of the German Chancellor. The next demand, after Danzig has been wiped off the slate, will be the return of the German colonies. What will our position be when we are treated as Austria and Czechoslovakia have been, and Poland is now being treated, when we have to surrender what we consider vital to the Union at the point of the bayonet? We are not dealing with a faraway problem, but with an issue which may touch us here. If we dissociate ourselves deliberately from the line of action taken by the other members of the Commonwealth, we are going to get what we deserve." He concluded with a motion to sever relations with Germany, to continue cooperation with the associates in the British Commonwealth, to defend South Africa's interests and territory, but not to send forces overseas as in the last war.

While the debate continued all day, Zeesen had already broadcast: "Union of South Africa remains neutral." The division took place shortly before nine o'clock in the evening. The Speaker put Hertzog's neutrality motion to the House. A roar of "Ayes" was out-thundered by a hurricane of "Noes!" The division bells rang. Across the gangway the whole opposition came to Hertzog to reinforce his thirty-odd supporters in the United Party. On the other side the balance of the United Party, Labor, the Dominion Party, and the three representatives of the Natives gathered. The tellers swiftly ticked off the names. There were sixty-seven Ayes against eighty Noes. Smuts emerged with a majority of thirteen.

On the fifth of September Hertzog resigned. Smuts was sent for. He formed his cabinet within an hour. He himself took the Ministry of Defence, his own creation, in addition to the Premiership. On the same day, the Prime Minister of the Union of South Africa severed relations with Germany. On the next day he declared war.

Hitler, it was said, laughed at this declaration.

Chapter 28   *ELL—GAMELAYO—WAAH*

ON THE DAY AFTER THE DECLARATION OF WAR GUNNERS MANNED battle stations at Simon's Town, which, for more than a century, has been the South African base of the British Navy. "It is the cornerstone on which our freedom was built," Smuts said on this occasion. "The Dutch-speaking South Africans hold the might and power of the British Navy in high regard. For centuries she has ruled and policed the seas, and never once during those centuries has that power been abused. Picture for yourself what would be the position if Germany ruled the seas today. No nation would have the right to trade or ply the oceans freely. It is not guns and power of weapons which in the end will make victory certain. It is the great tradition on which the British Navy is founded, the morale of its seamen, men who could well be excused if in the heat of action they left their swimming foes to drown, but who at their own risk stick to the great tradition of their service that, friend or foe, human lives must always be saved wherever possible."

Smuts' first statement in the war was humanitarian. His first action was to crush the enemy within. The Union government issued Emergency Regulations which gave them the power to

347

deal effectively with Nazis and their fellow travelers. It proved
that Smuts had not been idle while the moles were undermin-
ing the country. His office possessed authentic lists of each
Nazi organization in the principal towns of the Union, as well
as a register of Nazi agents working in the rural districts. Pho-
tostatic copies of documents disclosed the contacts between
these and the Blackshirt leaders. The documents revealed a
Nazi plan for using the mob of the Blackshirts for a march to
Johannesburg and Pretoria. Smuts had known this conspiracy
all the time. He had been informed of every step of the chief
organizer. This man was Counsellor Stiller of the German Legation. Hertzog would never have permitted any action against
a German diplomat. Smuts' world record in patience had remained unbroken. But now he hit out with both fists. In concerted action, all over the Union, the police swooped down on
the Nazi agents and Blackshirt leaders. Those who did not
cross the Portuguese border in time were arrested and sent to
camps of detention. Thus Smuts prevented a repetition of the
1914 revolution. To general surprise there was no uprising and,
at the beginning of the war, only very little sabotage. However,
Hertzog was still a formidable foe. Many Boers, by no means
all Nazi sympathizers, expressed their traditional devotion to
their "personal leader." A crowd of twenty thousand people,
mostly women, celebrated Hertzog in Pretoria. Within a week
after the beginning of the war, the fallen man had captured
the United Party machine in the Transvaal, thus far Smuts'
stronghold. The *platteland,* however, remained quiet. Many
more farmers than had been expected supported Oom Jannie.

Smuts understood perfectly well that he had to bring his
house in order before he could approach the other problem of
the war effort. The miners on the Rand used the outbreak of
the war to make exorbitant demands for wage increases. Smuts
spoke to their bosses. The old English Trade-Union leaders,
who, in recent years, had played a rather shadowy role, re-
asserted their authority. The miners received a slight rise in
wages, which were stabilized for the duration at a reasonable
level. A National Supplies Control Board was created. Prices

were fixed. Stringent measures to prevent hoarding and profit-
eering were introduced. All volunteers received the promise
that their jobs would be safeguarded for them. The social problems, in peace times South Africa's headache number one, were
solved within a fortnight after the beginning of the war. On
the social and economic front there has been no unrest up to
this day.

Now Smuts could throw all his strength into the task closest
to his heart: to transform the world's most pacifist country into
a fighting unit. He passed the War Measures Bill in the House,
which empowered the government to suspend Acts of Parliament by proclamation but did not allow any interference with
already existing legislation. The bill reaffirmed the provisions
of the Defence Act that no one could be compelled to serve
with the colors beyond Africa south of the equator. Military
service would be compulsory only for the suppression of civil
strife or for defending the borders of the Union.

Recruiting started instantly. Smuts himself took the lead. His
usually repressed romanticism blossomed. He appealed to local
and provincial traditions, to the tribal pride both of his own
Boers and of the Scottish, the Irish, the North Country English,
and the stubborn Welsh who formed the British part of the
population. Had the Cape Colony Artillery not proved its mettle a hundred years earlier? Were the great traditions of the
commandos in the Boer War forgotten? He was well aware
that he was addressing romantic realists. The South Africans
would be the best fed, the best paid, the best looked-after soldiers in the world. They would draw at least their peacetime
wages. Their employers would make up the difference, and
where small employers could not do so, a pool, richly endowed
by the mining industry, helped out. In time, Smuts promised,
the whole South African force would be mechanized. Every
man would learn a trade that would greatly help him in the
technocratic world of tomorrow. They would get the best medical care available. Above all, it would be a democratic army.
Each man carries the marshal's baton in his knapsack. All men
applying for commissions must first enlist in the ranks. If they

are worth their salt they will soon prove that they are able to lead men. The most amazing part was that all these high-flown promises were carried out, word for word.

The largest part of South Africa's youth knew that Oom Jannie would be as good as his word. All able-bodied English males enlisted. Among the first units organized were the Cape Town Highlanders and the Irish Brigade. The Boer youth was in commotion. The Nationalist section had no desire to die for Poland, a country full of hook-nosed Jews, as some were known on the *platteland*. But the majority of the Boer youth heeded the call to the great adventure.

"Old Bailey" emerged out of his retirement. Again he issued one of his manifestoes: "You are up against Hitler, a clever man, but one whose veracity requires confirmation, and it should warn all but those who wish to be deceived. Fortunately we have a great Afrikaner, General Smuts. He is holding us together, and with great dignity devoting his individual talent to South Africa's future. It will win him perpetual renown that he brought order and common sense into a dangerous position. When I see some of the papers attacking General Smuts, and I look back at their birth, I might easily be called their illegitimate father. The Dutch and the English prefer living together to dying together. So let us discard racialism and unite as one people throughout our country. Nothing will stop our collective march." At this time "Old Bailey" was already more of a legend than a man. The South African youth knew little about the tremendous sum of his life's achievement. But his fame as a prize fighter, as a huntsman, a soldier in a dozen encounters lived on. His manifesto was a tonic to the recruiting campaign.

In a way the rush to the colors was even embarrassing. There were no uniforms, and many of those in existence had no buttons. There were plenty of suspenders, but no trousers to attach to them. There were neither guns nor airplanes. When Smuts took over his old department, he found the Defence Force in a state of chaos. Pirow, who had held the office for almost ten years, had sabotaged the country's defenses because he feared the force would protect important industrial and urban areas against Nazi sabotage. Mr. Pocock, M.P., leveled this charge against the traitor in open Parliament. Colonel Stallard, the leader of the Unionists, concurred. He had himself been asked by Pirow—when the turncoat was still Minister under the Crown, and before he had dropped his mask—to form a Voluntary Citizen Force. But he had been so badly hampered by the Minister that he could not carry out his task.

In fact, after ten years of Pirow's regime the Union was defenseless. Smuts found an actual shortage of 548 trench mortars, 780 anti-tank guns, and 833 Bren guns, a shortage of almost the whole artillery the Union had—on paper. But for 500 Lewis guns which Great Britain had sent in the midst of her own feverish rearmament after Munich, South Africa would have had no guns at all. Pirow had also falsified the figures of men in the air force. He boasted of having 2,000 skilled mechanics at Roberts Heights. He never disclosed that many of them, after having been trained, had gone into "the industry" for higher wages. When Smuts took over, he found only 1,350 mechanics at Roberts Heights, 500 of them unskilled apprentices. Officers of the Ministry of Defence had investigated the ammunition supply. They found only stocks enough for one day under battle conditions, and bombs for three air squadrons for three days. They reported these conditions to Pirow. But the Minister never informed his Cabinet colleagues of this report.

The coastal defense was entirely neglected. Port Elizabeth and East London, two of South Africa's four principal ports, had not a single gun.

Early in 1939 Parliament had passed three million pounds for extraordinary Defense Services. "How much of this sum was spent when Mr. Pirow resigned on September 4?" Mr. Pocock asked.

Pirow lowered his head.

"Nothing!" interjected Mr. Hofmeyr, the new Minister of Finance.

"The House has adopted one of your schemes calling for 137,000 men, including three divisions totaling 67,000 for the Union's normal defenses," Pocock continued. "Could you, Mr.

Pirow, have only put two equipped divisions into the field?"
Other questions followed like hammer blows: "Only one? . . .
Was even a single brigade fully equipped? . . . You once told
the House that the Union had trained and prepared 150,000
riflemen able to take to the field. How many rifles had we at
the outbreak of the war? . . . How many of them were fit for
service? . . . You have assured us that the Union could place
28,000 men in the field on very short notice. Were there last
September 28,000 sets of equipment in this country to arm
these men? . . . There was nothing but an Emergency Plan issued by you last March," Mr. Pocock concluded his accusations.
He quoted contemptuously: "No one in the forces should en-
gender or aggravate feelings of hostility towards a state or a
country with which the Union was at peace. It is forbidden
to listen to overseas broadcasts, such as the British Broadcast,
for example. . . ."

Pirow jerked. "Why does the Prime Minister not say these
things?"

Smuts did not yet "say these things," because he did not talk
at all. Once more he spent day and night at his desk, building
up his model army from scratch. The coastal defenses came
first. He got a last consignment of guns from England, already
shipped in the face of the U-boat menace, while the pocket
battleship *Graf Spee* was plying the waters off South Africa.
Now Table Bay, the harbor of Cape Town, was protected by
nine-inch guns at Robben Island, and other coastal guns were
placed in strategic positions. The two so far undefended ports
were armed with six-inch guns, powerful enough to keep off
enemy cruisers. Smuts, who had always warned South Africa
against building a "tin-can fleet" of her own, now created the
Seaward Defence Force to clear the sea of mines and hunt
down U-boats. It was an entirely new beginning. When he had
come back to office, the Union's whole navy consisted of an
obsolete, engineless, immovable, discarded English sloop, rechristened *General Botha,* and converted to a training ship.

It was, however, impossible to protect 2,500 miles of coast-
line with a handful of converted trawlers and whalers. Smuts

founded the Coastal Command of the Air Force, the forerunner of the R.S.A.A.F., which covered itself with laurels as the war proceeded. It was again a very modest beginning. The South African Airways, the company in charge of civil aviation, had some twenty German Junkers with American engines. Some of them had already served to punish rebellious native chiefs and to drop food parcels to flooded areas. Now they went to war. The Junkers were fitted with bomb racks. Some of them did very well within a short time. Other machines were so old and obsolete that they came to pieces during the test flights.

At the same time the Volunteer Defence Force was called up to guard the land approaches to the ports, power houses, ammunition stores, bridges and other key positions. The air was thick with rumors of sabotage. Pirow stumped the land and talked unabashed of organizing storm troops on the German pattern. He chose his men among the Nationalist slackers who were determined to sit out the war. Among a white population of two million, most of them *spekfet*—strong and healthy—to use Smuts' word, some three hundred thousand were able-bodied men, fit for military service. Two hundred thousand listened to Smuts' call for *eer en plig*—honor and duty—and volunteered. A great majority joyfully accepted the orange flash, indicating first that they were ready to serve anywhere in Africa, not only south of the equator, and later that they would fight anywhere in the world. Finally, only volunteers for a global war were taken. Some twenty thousand men were essential war-workers or holders of industrial key positions, carrying a badge that identified them, but wearing it with an uncomfortable smile, almost apologetically. Farmers and farm hands were not exempt. The racialist youth listened to Pirow, the foreign adventurer, until a more seducing little Fuehrer appeared.

Smuts built his army while watching one man. Mussolini was his personal enemy. Smuts never doubted that the Duce would decay until he became a mere slave of Hitler, and, in Germany's iron grip, plunge the dagger into the back of the French.

But Smuts was more concerned about Africa. It was clear to him that Mussolini would thrust southward. He observed Mussolini's preparations. Under the poor subterfuge of having to "pacify" restive native tribes, the Italians built a large highway south from Addis Ababa. Gasoline and oil, tanks, guns, and men streamed into Eritrea and Somaliland. The ports of Massawa and Mogadiscio were crammed with Italian submarines, torpedo boats, and all sorts of small craft. In Addis Ababa enormous assembly shops for bombers and fighters were built. All this indicated that as soon as France faltered an attack would be made on Kenya, Uganda, and finally South Africa.

Smuts confirmed in earnest Pirow's traitorous promise of protection to the British colonies. He took instant measures to strengthen their border defenses. He surrounded himself with a staff of ranking officers, some of whom had fought on the other side in the Boer War, others who were veterans from the First World War. He made Colonel C. H. Blaine Assistant Secretary of Defence, and General J. J. Collyer, the famous strategic theoretician, his private military secretary. Both officers had been his enemies in the Boer War, but his close assistants in the South West and East African campaigns. Sir Pierre van Ryneveld, a hero of the First World War and one of the first ace pilots in the budding R.A.F., was appointed Chief of the General Staff. Brigadier-General Dan Pienaar received the Command of the First Division.

The men were ready. The army was built. Voortrekkerhogte, the Aldershot of the Union, produced a gallant new officers' corps, mostly with instructors who had been officers in the last war, and had taken a short refresher course. Medical services, map-printing units, scouts, engineers, anti-aircraft units, and an ever-increasing corps of women auxiliaries made Oom Jannie's Force a perfect, self-contained, small model army. Racial differences were entirely discarded. The brothers in arms were the grandsons of the men who had fought one another in the Boer War.

A true miracle was the shift to war production on the home front. Before the war, South Africa had only two industries of importance: mining and railways. A small factory, a department of the Royal Mint in Pretoria, had produced some .303 ammunition. The total number of shells available would have barely sufficed for one day of active combat. Every other item of equipment had to be imported from Great Britain. Now England herself was hard pressed to manufacture enough arms for her own needs. South Africa must help herself in order to contribute effectively to the war effort of the British Commonwealth. Fortunately, the "Iscor," the Iron and Steel Corporation in Pretoria, was prepared for the job. Dr. van der Bijl, the manager general, became the czar of the entire South African industry, which sprang up almost overnight.

He developed South Africa's steel production to such an extent that subsequently half a million spare parts a year could be shipped to the African battle fronts. The "Iscor" is now producing small arms as well as howitzers, and armored cars with American engines and chassis. Not only satisfying almost all her own military needs, the Union became famous as the repair shop for the Allied armies in the Middle East. No less great is her contribution to the Allied naval war effort. Within the two-year period ending in March 1943, 6,428 Allied ships—among them American ships in increasing numbers—were repaired and refitted in South African ports.

Smuts and his men were ready when Mussolini struck. In fact, Italy had already muscled into the war before the Duce's balcony speech of June 10, 1940. Some two weeks previously a lighthouse keeper at Agulhas, the most southerly point in South Africa, had detected floating mines. They were duly removed by South African mine sweepers. Zeesen bragged that the furthermost reaches of the seas were no longer inaccessible to German U-boats. But the mines were identified as being of Italian make. An investigation disclosed that some Italian craft, sailing under the Portuguese flag, had sown them in the Allied shipping lanes.

On June 9 the Commissioner in the Italian border fortress Moyale dined and wined his colleague from the other side of the track, the British Assistant Superintendent of Police, P. L. Carter. In the dawn of the following morning Mr. Carter, together with a sergeant of the sappers—engineers—and a Somali police sergeant, was kidnapped by a party under the hospitable Italian Commissioner's leadership.

Some hours later Mussolini thundered from the balcony of Palazzo Venezia. Smuts replied in a broadcast from Pretoria. All South Africa was agog. Now they would have to defend their own skins.

A squadron of South African Air Force took to the air and blasted Moyale almost out of existence. For the first time the war cry of the Springboks resounded:

ELL—GAMELAYO—WAAH.

| *Chapter 29* | TWO-FRONT WAR AGAIN |

WHILE THE ARMY EXPANDED IN MIGHTY STRIDES, AND THE COUNtry's war industry, as it were, was born, the home front was torn by dissension. The first serious crack was revealed when the *Sunday Times* of Johannesburg disclosed Nazism inside the South African Broadcasting Corporation. A Committee of Inquiry was set up. After weeks of painstaking investigation the committee admitted that a section of the staff was "animated by anti-government spirit."

Already before the war the Nazis had tried, not altogether unsuccessfully, to penetrate the South African radio. Insidiously, they had parked a few fifth columnists in the offices. There were a number of incidents on the prewar record. Reuter's correspondent in Berlin had reported the lack of essential foodstuffs for the German Christmas holidays. The Afrikaans

speaker refused to transmit this news; it would be an affront
to Germany. Although regulations prescribed that English and
Afrikaans broadcasts must be identical, the stubborn Afrikander received permission to omit the passage to which he
objected. On another occasion, Dr. Leitner, German Minister
in Pretoria, complained to Hertzog that one Dr. Trimmler, a
broadcaster imported from Berlin, had not enough liberty of
expression; his political diatribes had been trimmed.

After the outbreak of war, every member of the staff was
asked to sign a declaration of loyalty to the new government.
A number of Afrikander members refused their signatures;
they even refused to join the Company's Employees Association on account of its partly English membership. Some refused
to join the Civilian Wireless Reserve. They wanted no part in
the war effort. When *Sapa,* the official South African Press Association, distributed news from Germany which rubbed the
Afrikaans speakers the wrong way, they would not transmit
"sensational and possibly misleading" stuff. A few Afrikaans
staff members were declared Nazis. They left, before being
weeded out. On the others rested the Committee of Inquiry's
blame of "neither giving loyal support, nor co-operating in
carrying out the policy of the board."

The government made every effort to play down such incidents. Smuts was hounded by the specter of a renewed civil
war. He confined himself to the most necessary measures for
safeguarding the law. For the rest he trusted to his old proverb:
"The dogs bark, while the caravan marches on."

Hertzog led the opposition choir. He was still respectfully
listened to, but his unprincipled vacillations confused even his
most gullible adherents. Within a single week he was able to
produce the following statements: On Monday he shocked the
whole Parliament with a spiteful attack on Smuts. On Tuesday
he addressed the caucus of his shrunken group, the Afrikander
Party, pleading for unity, and fulminating against racialism.
On Friday he spoke under the Kruger Statue in Pretoria: "I
am convinced that General Smuts has acted sincerely and with
conviction. We others must fight for neutrality by constitutional

means." Yet he stood while speaking between Dr. Malan and Pirow. Next he warned his listeners in Bloemfontein that no division should be permitted between Afrikaans and English-speaking South Africans. Rather than have to watch such a division, he would prefer to retire from the political scene. On the following day he appeared, arm in arm with Dr. Malan, at a meeting at the Voortrekker Monument in Pretoria, and shouted: "The union of the Afrikanders is reborn. The war in Europe is no concern of ours. We must by all means struggle for neutrality." He nodded, when Dr. Malan added: "A republic should be the ideal of all of us."

Smuts replied to this muddle: "General Hertzog has rendered great service to this country. It grieves me to see that in his old age he is busy destroying the great work which he did in the past six years, and I deeply regret that he has become a tool in the hands of Dr. Malan. I do not accuse him. He was misled by collaborators around him, and especially by one who pretends to be a 100 per cent Afrikander. But upon this man the people of South Africa look with deepest suspicion. This counsellor of General Hertzog was the cause of his downfall. Today this man is busy seeking favor with Dr. Malan. Now the nation must be brought into confusion, and must be torn in two, because General Hertzog has lost the day. We shall hear a good deal more of the personalities to which I have referred in the days to come."

Hertzog replied by moving a peace motion in the House. "Germany," he said, "is being encircled and crushed while fighting to regain living space. Hitler's persecution of the Jews may be ugly, but it is only a passing phase of the struggle. Reports about alleged German barbarism in occupied Czechoslovakia and Poland are nothing but atrocity stories. I sympathize with Hitler's leader-principle. My own party is very much run on the same line. Hitler has always encouraged loyalty to the leaders rather than to dirty politics."

Even the Afrikaner members of the House shook their heads. Was the great, little, old man mentally disturbed? At second glance it did not seem so. He was still as alert as ever. He could simply not reconcile himself with his personal disappointment. He exhibited the stubbornness which had always been his most formidable weapon, now that his set opinions and prejudices clashed with the country's interest.

Pirow answered Smuts' criticism in his own inimitable way. He announced that he had already organized storm troops, and that he would build up "cells of action" inside the Nationalist Party.

Rarely in his long career had Smuts bothered to attack a personal opponent. But Pirow's challenge could not go unpunished. Smuts took off the gloves. In the session of Parliament on March 15 his slashing blows hammered the foreign adventurer.

Smuts started with a dangerous smile, pointing out that Pirow had, during five years in office, omitted to carry out his defense plan announced in 1934. "I have no objection to the plan itself," he said jovially. "I will fulfill it just as I have fulfilled other promises made and broken by Mr. Pirow. Mr. Pirow's work," and now Smuts' smile faded, "was more a danger to the country than a protection. His plans were all right, but they were just grandiose plans and talk. It was all something on paper. Mr. Pirow has nothing to boast of." A long list of Pirow's sins of omission followed. Mr. Pirow left only two bombers and a few unusable old fighters behind, while he had planned three squadrons of aircraft consisting of twenty-six bombers and twenty-six fighters each. The artillery, ten guns instead of the promised ten batteries, had not enough ammunition for a single day's fighting. The whole tank force consisted of two obsolete tanks. And so on and so forth. . . . "Mr. Pirow dreamed for five years, publicly and before all the country," Smuts concluded. "Now we are working day and night, not to make a plan, but to make an army. That was Mr. Pirow's duty in those five years. But he left it completely to us. We have to do it today."

Pirow took his punishment silently. His head was sunk between his high-lifted shoulders. Nervously, he licked his lips. When the chastisement was over, his shifty eyes looked to the Nationalist benches in search of aid and comfort. The Nationalists, for their part, looked the other way. They had not forgiven the turncoat his "sins" in the coalition government. Pirow's seat-neighbor heard him cursing: *"Verdammt!"* Then he got up and walked into the wilderness.

Even his brother disassociated himself from the Nazi disciple. Dr. Hans Pirow, President of the South African Boy Scout Association, declared pointedly: "The religious persecutions taking place in the world, and even fostered by irresponsible trouble-makers in South Africa, and the use of racial hatred to serve political interests make it evident that the time has come to fight that type of mental disease."

Brother Oswald was incurably contaminated. He got mixed up in every political mischief that occurred in war-time South Africa. He tried his hand as a mixer, negotiator, go-between for the rival racialists. Sometimes he was used, more often abused. He became the lone wolf.

The first Allied reverses filled the racialists with joyful expectation. The complete breakdown of the British Empire seemed near, at least from the perspective of the African bush. The German invasion of Norway was hailed by both Hertzog and Dr. Malan. Hertzog appropriated the lie that Hitler had been forced to act in order to remove the English-sown sea mines that menaced peaceful German shipping and trade. Dr. Malan insisted that the Germans had anticipated an Allied invasion.

But since only few of the bearded denizens of the *platteland* knew that Norway was a country, and almost none where this strange land might be located, the opposition returned to harping on domestic issues. Smuts was attacked for locking up Nazis and fellow travelers in internment camps. He replied by disclosing new putsch plans which the Information Service had unearthed. Every man on the new lists was immediately arrested. He could appeal to the courts, and was sure of obtaining a legal hearing if he felt injured. Moreover, Sir Theodore Truter, the chief control officer of the internment camps, had been vice-chairman of the Transvaal United Party when General Kemp, one of the most noisy rabble rousers, had been chairman, and was, as chairman of the Transport Board, an appointee of Pirow, during the latter's term as Minister for Railways. A man with this record was certainly above suspicion of undue harshness against Nationalists.

Hertzog, Havenga, his man Friday, and Pirow interrupted Smuts persistently whenever he spoke. The choir of Nationalists raised a racket so loud that no one could hear his own words. Rowdyism had broken out in the venerable House of Assembly, and it had come to stay.

In April, however, the noise was silenced by one of Smuts' master strokes. He had negotiated a wool bargain with Great Britain that saved the wool farmers from being choked by their unsellable crop. Before the war the average price of South African wool was 8s 3d. This season's price was raised a third. Moreover, England pledged to share with the growers any profit that might accrue from reselling part of the wool abroad. The wool farmers in the Free State were Hertzog's staunchest followers. But they grabbed with both hands the profits Smuts had procured them from much maligned England. The Free State Branch of the National Association of Wool Growers resolved that the agreement should continue after the war. They had now a personal stake in England's survival. Britain also bought the entire export of South African butter, cheese, and eggs, thus saving the agricultural market from an inevitable crash, since no other outlet was open to them.

Smuts had secretly negotiated the agreement since December, 1939. His position in the country was markedly strengthened. A "Union Truth Legion" sprang up. More than 650,000 signatures, far the most numerous petition ever signed in South Africa, urged General Smuts to carry on to peace through victory. At a tremendous meeting in Cape Town scores of white-clad girls handed over to Oom Jannie seventy volumes containing the signatures. Brigadier-General H. N. W. Botha, M.P., assumed the chairmanship.

Strokes of luck, good or bad, never come singly. A bombshell exploded in the House when Mr. Wallach, member for Pretoria-

West, read a letter which, he said cautiously, had been addressed to one of the most distinguished families in the Free State. The writer was Dr. Leyds, once the arch-enemy of Great Britain, who had left South Africa during the Boer War to intrigue in Germany, and who had spent the next forty years in seclusion in Holland, writing books in which the Boer War was fought over and over again. His letter read: "We are sitting here, waiting what Hitler will do, and in this uncertain atmosphere one never knows what will happen the next day. History can take queer turns. I with my feelings of abhorrence and contempt for the old Joe Chamberlain would gladly stand shoulder to shoulder now with his son in his fight against the Germans who, in my eyes, are a curse to the world. This nation, particularly the youth, is receiving an education which is reducing them to something worse than barbarians. Fortunately, I have no business in Germany, because my wife and I would undoubtedly and expeditiously be consigned either to a concentration camp or to death."

Dr. Leyds, the man who, by egging on Kruger, was more than any other individual responsible for the bloodshed of the Boer War, had now reached his eighty-first year. He was still going strong. The giant with the white lion's mane had, more than a year previously, been celebrated at a banquet in Cape Town, at which all surviving officials of the two Republics had been present. Smuts had eulogized him as the greatest figure, after Kruger, in Transvaal history.

This man's conversion made a strong impression on the country. But it was utterly lost on Hertzog and his followers. Hitler invaded the Lowlands on May 10. The abortive resistance of Holland and Belgium was unavailing. Two days after the rape of Holland Dr. Leyds died. He had retired into a hospital when the Germans came, but he could not bear the incessant tramping of the Nazi jack boots. His son had already been for some time in London. He had obtained British citizenship, and, although himself advanced in years, joined the English Home Guard.

A fluctuating majority of the Boers, comprising the progressive part as well as most of the fence sitters, received the news of the fall of the Netherlands, their mother country, with a deep shock. Only the racialists appeared completely unperturbed. They had never felt any sympathy for the older, richer, and more civilized country from which their ancestors had once been kicked out. Furthermore, they hated the arrogant Hollanders in their own midst.

Hertzog, who, fifty years before, leaving the University of Utrecht, had written the well-meant verse: "Adieu, thou land of freedom sprung, By freedom's bracing power sustained . . ." shunned the special session of the House, convoked for a sympathy demonstration toward Holland. He retired to his farm, leaving behind the message to his people: "Let us not become partisans toward one or the other nation or country." In Parliament, Dr. Malan, substituting for the leader, declared that he felt sympathy for Belgium or Holland, but that the nature of modern warfare explained Hitler's lightning invasions sufficiently, and that the Fuehrer's desire to seize the important naval bases of Flanders was perfectly legitimate. Neither Holland, nor Belgium, nor the Hollanders living in South Africa could expect him, Dr. Malan, to erase his neutrality motto on their behalf.

Smuts cabled to Queen Wilhelmina in London: "All South Africa would consider it the greatest honor to offer sanctuary to the Netherlands Royal Family." The officers of the Secret Service sighed with relief when this friendly offer was most graciously declined. The Hertzogite Press was so viciously sputtering at refugees, royal or Jewish, that the task of protecting the Queen's life would have been immensely difficult.

Smuts broadcast an impassionate speech about German aggression. "Now you see," he addressed his own people, "that neutrality does not mean protection. Germany stops at nothing. Unless we resist, our day will come as it has come to other nations. But Dr. Malan still sticks to neutrality. He is getting deeper and deeper into the mud. I leave him there."

Even in Stellenbosch demonstrations of sympathy with Holland occurred. Professor Keet of the Theological Seminary, the stronghold of Calvinistic reaction, confessed: "We should no longer be civilized people if we did not condemn this crime. In our hearts there can never be neutrality toward this act of barbarism." Yet the great majority of Stellenbosch professors displayed their Nazism ever more shamelessly, and the university, already the Mecca of the fighting Afrikaners, was soon to become the parade ground of a new revolutionary movement.

On the whole, Hitler's rape of Holland strengthened Smuts' position in the country. Parliament passed a special credit of eight million pounds—four times the amount of the normal military budget—for the Defence Force. The bill was voted without debate. The Nationalists did not appear in the House. Evidently they feared to provoke the prevailing sentiment too outrageously. But on the next day Dr. Malan resumed his vituperations. Germany had invaded the Netherlands for the Dutch people's own good, he said. Zeesen had broadcast the same phrase a few hours before.

Thousands of new recruits flocked to the colors. Cape Town was in a patriotic ecstasy. Table Bay was crammed with British sea giants. A merchant fleet of almost 300,000 tons, among them the *Queen Mary,* the *Aquitania,* and the *Mauretania,* protected by some 200,000 tons of naval vessels, had brought the greatest convoy of troops that thus far had crossed the seas, to proceed through South Africa to the Middle East. Smuts and Wavell had laid out the plan a month before, when Wavell had been in Cape Town on a flying visit. Shoulder to shoulder with the Aussies and the New Zealanders, whom the ships had brought, the first contingent of the Springboks left for the front. They were in high spirits, lusting for a go at the "Eyties." The railway coaches were chalked with inscriptions: "Attention, Musso! . . . Next stop Rome! . . ."

In his old general's coat, which he had worn on the Western front, but now with the orange flash on the shoulder, Smuts was among his men. He bade them farewell: "More no man can do than offer his life for his friends. That offer, the highest and most solemn offer a man can make, you are now making.

You are going to face hardships, danger, and sacrifice, perhaps death itself in all its fiercest forms. But through it all you will gather the experience of life and enrichment of character which is more valuable than gold or precious stones. You will become better and stronger men. You will not return the same as you went. You will bring back memories which you and yours will treasure for life. You will not be mere items of the population. You will come back as builders of your own nation. Your children will be proud of you. A nation is never proud of its 'hands-uppers,' its fence sitters, its players for safety."

Oom Jannie was now truly his soldiers' father. In the teeth of an incessant campaign of hatred and slander, such as no other man in public life is exposed to, living in a world of thoughts, hard realism and dreams of the millennium mingled, he felt and acted, above all, as the guardian of his happy warriors. Each of his "beloved sons," as the otherwise reserved old man repeatedly called them, was his personal ward. He appointed a committee, composed of Cabinet members and medical men, to investigate conditions in the Defence Force. There were initial difficulties, inevitable in view of the rapid growth of this fine volunteer army, to be overcome. There was too much red tape. Professional officers were in some cases not sufficiently versed in handling problems of administration and organization. Inter-departmental rivalries blossomed as in every new and great establishment. In the purely military sphere, however—in regard to training, discipline, mechanization—the job was supremely well done.

Smuts appointed Dr. A. J. Orenstein, an American, Director of the Union's Military Medical Service. Dr. Orenstein had for seven years served as a member of the Panama Canal Medical Service, and had won fame for his mosquito control. Then he was called to become chief medical adviser to the Corner House group, the largest mining combine in Johannesburg. Now he worked miracles in protecting the Springboks against the poisonous flies and insects, the principal enemy in the African theater of war. Smuts himself saw to it that his beloved sons should get the right diet: no longer the *stormjaegers* and the *maagbomme* on which their grandfathers in the Boer War had thrived, but vitamins and calories. The Springboks were the first combat troops to get concentrated orange juice with their rations. They were treated according to General Smuts' own prescription: give them plenty of good, wholesome food, combined with hard training and ample opportunity for recreation.

On the tenth of August they took Kornidil, south east of Moyale. The drive against the Italian Colonial Empire was on, with the Springboks in the vanguard. At the same time the South African Air Force went out daily to intercept the air pirates of the *Regia Aeronautica.*

While watching and supervising the progress his troops were making, Smuts set himself another task. He was going to make "the South African coast no place for hostile battleships." Colonel Craig, Deputy Director of Fortifications, who had just finished the work on the great new harbor of Cape Town, perfected the fortifications on Robben Island and on the mountainside above Llandudno, where General Smuts' 9.2-inch howitzers now occupied the sites of Pirow's blue-funk 15-inch guns.

A few days after South African forces had entered active combat, the doom of France was sealed. Smuts was not surprised. He had always believed that France was gravely overrated. But this darkest hour of the war, the moment of the gravest shock, spurred him to a renewed confession of faith: "The Dominions are unhesitatingly ranging themselves alongside Great Britain in her resolve to continue the war, even if she has to stand alone. Of all the Dominions South Africa is in the gravest danger, and her interest in taking this stand is therefore the greatest of all. Germany has her historic ambitions in Africa, and South Africa with her gold and mineral resources and her strategic position in this world is the prize most worth having on our continent. If Germany wins this war nothing will save this country. We can therefore but choose to stand with Great Britain to the end in this mortal struggle. . . . Don't be downhearted! By next year Germany's war effort will be crippled, and the tide of war will begin to turn. Germany's ambitions and her thrust toward world hegemony will have raised a world war in which the alignment of powers will be very different from what it is today. The end might come with the same suddenness of collapse as that which ended her victorious career in the last war. This war, which began as Hitler's war, will end as God's war!"

Only Winston Churchill, and no third man in the world, could speak with the same great vision and determined confidence. Churchill, indeed, replied: "The great General Smuts of South Africa, that wonderful man with his immense and profound mind, his eyes watching from the distance the whole panorama of European affairs, does well deserve our gratitude."

Hertzog, on the other hand, thought differently about Smuts' merits. The fallen leader was already surviving himself. Mentally unbalanced, he had retired into the seclusion of his Sabine farm at Waterval. There he wrote a letter to Smuts: "In view of the disastrous course of the war and the collapse of the Allied forces, our further participation in hostilities against Germany and Italy threatens the existence of the country and the people. You will forgive me if I say now that as far as South Africa is concerned the time has come to put an end to this game of self-deceit, and of deception of the people. I demand immediate steps to withdraw from the war."

Smuts firmly rejected Hertzog's "dishonorable proposal," pointing out that it had already been rejected by Parliament on September 4, 1939, and would undoubtedly meet the same fate again. "The government," he concluded, "will carry out the policy on the mandate of Parliament, and will not allow the execution of that policy to be nullified by propaganda or threats of violence." He did not comment on the fact that Hertzog's letter, in violation of all rules of decency, had been published by *Die Vaderland,* Hertzog's mouthpiece in Johannesburg, before it had reached its recipient.

The open letter kindled the ire of all the Nationalists in Johannesburg, a particularly spiteful lot, living as a small minority, submerged by an overwhelmingly English population. Two hours after *Die Vaderland* was sold on the streets, three

Hertzogite hooligans, disguised as policemen, called upon Mr.
F. M. B. Ferreira, a member of the East Rand Board School
and a local leader of the "Truth Legion." They kidnapped him,
drove him to a lonesome spot, stripped him of his clothes, and
tarred and feathered him.

On the home front the rule of terror began.

While the war went from bad to worse for the British Commonwealth, now alone defending the ramparts of human freedom, the seditious movement in South Africa increased by
leaps and bounds. Hertzog lent it whatever strength he had
left, although he was already more a shadowy figure than a
protagonist. Dr. Malan had achieved the aim of his hypocritical
life. He had dethroned his leader, and was now boss himself.
He founded the *Herenigde* (re-united) *Nasionale* Party. Most
of the Nationalistic rabble congregated around him. Only a
handful of faithful followers remained true to their "personal
leader." They offset in noise what they lacked in numbers.

Dr. Malan coined a new slogan: "Smutskowitz's"—he used
the name Eric Holm, the traitor of Zeesen had coined—"*dwang-
maatreels* (measures of enforcement) must be stopped by all
means, and the *broeder-oorlog* (fratricidal strife) between
Boers and Germans must come to an end." He was little concerned about the fact that he himself was inciting to *broeder-
oorlog* in his own nation.

His underlings outcried and outbid one another. Following
Hitler's advice to make one man the single scapegoat for all
evils, their barrage of lies and calumny was concentrated on
Smuts. General Kemp, the traitor of 1914, later minister in the
coalition government, invaded Smuts' own camp. In Malmesbury, Cape Colony, whence Smuts hailed, he addressed a
meeting crowding the town hall: "England has become the de-
fender of the small nations only to plunder and rob them of
their possessions. Never again will I hold out the hand of
friendship to General Smuts."

Pirow, the foreign adventurer, went more slyly to work. In
Pretoria he said calmly: "The occasion might well arise that

South Africa would voluntarily side with Great Britain in a war, for instance if Japan were the enemy. But never, never against Germany."

The first rumblings about the *Ossewa Brandwag*—the sentinels of the oxcart—were heard. Smuts insinuated, ever in his cautious legalistic language, "that this new movement had negotiated with the Nazis with a view to its being used as an instrument for acts of an illegal nature." It was a deliberate understatement. Smuts knew perfectly well the name of the Nazi official involved, a former counsellor of the German legation in Pretoria, as well as the identity of the *Brandwagters* who had met him in Portuguese Lourenço Marques. But Mr. Sauer, the chief whip of the Herenigde Party, shouted: "The *Ossewa Brandwag* is a purely cultural movement! If Smuts looks for treason, he shall look before his own door."

Messieurs Bruckner de Villiers, Nationalistic Senator and chairman of *Die Burger*, and Senator Oosthuisen, another sponsor of Dr. Malan, themselves two of the fattest moneybags in South Africa, called Smuts "the slave of capitalism."

In Parliament Dr. Malan and his followers lavished praises on Adolf Hitler, and bolstered up the demand for neutrality with fulminations against General Smuts, "himself the most ruthless dictator."

Herr Pirow, and General Kemp, not satisfied even with these excesses of the Herenigde Party, founded splinter groups of their own. Pirow's program was: proclamation of a Republic, immediate peace, cancellation of the Simon's Town agreement, recognition of *Die Stem* as the sole national anthem, stricter censorship to stop "imperialistic propaganda." When he left the University of Pretoria, where he had made this declaration, deliberately in an old-fashioned horse and buggy, the enthused students *outspanned* the horses and themselves dragged the car to the railroad station.

His followers closed the ranks around the Old Master. Hofmeyr, Steyn and Reitz—the latter two sons of republican leaders in the Boer War—fought valiantly for their chief. Once more "Old Bailey" came to help. Although both his legs had been amputated within the last year, he was still possessed with his old zest for life. He could not pass away without a last joke, full of a deeper meaning. His swan song read: "I have always joyed in Africa. Here I am, maybe the largest landowner and farmer in the world. I grow horses, cattle, sheep, tobacco, and over five thousand tons of fruit a year. As the Yankees say: 'We eat what we can, and can what we can't!' I have had a colorful life, unique, perhaps, in the history of the world. Now I am old, and a little deaf. So I cannot hear anyone speaking about me behind my back. With all my increasing infirmities I shall soon be taking a non-stop into the next world. I shall certainly not live long enough to see my legs grow again. But I do not wish to hear some people talking of how they hate living in this period. Personally, I should think they would be proud of the experience, and do what they can to win the war."

To Smuts, his own fate, the fate of one individual mattered little in this time of storm and stress. He was satisfied with the rapid growth of the Union Army, and with their proud progress. In Groote Schuur he gave the prescribed annual garden party for four thousand members of the United Party. Each of the guests was astonished at how well the Old Master knew all his visitors' names and families, and how he even remembered where their farms were located.

On July 27, street rioting flared up in Cape Town. Nazi pamphlets in large bundles had been left in the tram cars. The population was sick of the constant provocation. Nazi fellow travelers had a bad time. Smuts spoke over the radio, beseeching his people not to follow the example of lawlessness. His voice sounded harsh. Was he heartbroken? Smuts heartbroken? It was simply that he had a heavy cold. Since he believed the situation to be firmly in hand, he heeded his doctor's advice, and retired for a few days to the *lowveld*. There he botanized with a vengeance, and returned, his cold worse than ever.

Chapter 30
BLITZ OVER ENGLAND—THUNDER IN SOUTH AFRICA

"THE MAN WHO CAPTURED CHURCHILL!" YELLED THE SCREAMER headlines of the Nationalist press.

So Hitler had done it. He was in London. The swastika was waving over Buckingham Palace and Westminster Abbey. Now was the moment to unfurl and to hoist all the hidden *Vierkleurs,* from Table Mountain to the Limpopo. Now was the chance to bring Smuts to account.

Unfortunately, the man who captured Churchill had done so almost forty years earlier. Now, at the blessed age of seventy-nine, Mr. Richard Alexander Knipe, of Zoekmakaar, headmaster of the *Christelike Nasionale Onderwys Skool*—one of those private schools under the supervision of the Dutch Gereformeerde Church in which the children learned the A B C from Nazi pamphlets—had peacefully passed away. The Nationalist press told the story of his life and death in that sensational manner that passed in Keerom Street for "Americanism."

The much-mourned headmaster had also been a popular author, a regular contributor to *Die Kerkbode* (The Church Messenger) and *Die Huisgenoot* (The Home Companion), except for the Old Testament the only reading matter on the *platteland.* For almost forty years he had repeated the same story, and ever again it kindled the imagination of the nation with the longest memory. Mr. Knipe, his story went, had captured Winston Churchill during the Boer War. Somewhere near the Germiston station, he pretended, he had seen a horse that could not possibly have belonged to a Boer. The mare looked suspicious, and so did the small house with the shuttered windows in front of which she stood. Far from venturing upon a dangerous frontal attack, such as kicking open the door, Mr. Knipe boasted of having "besieged" the hut, until a hatless, beardless man came out. He threw up his hands. "My name is Winston Churchill," he introduced himself.

In itself the story was of no importance. South Africa is still seething with old-timers who have singlehanded taken prisoner the British warlord. But the headlines caused by the death of a small fry from the *backveld*, characterized the state of mind of many Boers. While their sons sweated their way through Italian Somaliland, the fathers and grandfathers fought the Boer War all over again.

So did the mothers. On Sunday, June 23, 1940, more than seven thousand well-organized Boer mothers, their gray hair still severely brushed back, clad in cheap imitations of the costume the *Voortrekker vrouwe* used to wear, duly primed and assured of the Lord's blessing by the Reverend P. J. de Klerk, staged a peace-at-any-price demonstration in Pretoria. Smuts refused to receive their delegation. Until Monday night no respectable citizen of the capital ventured on to the streets, for fear of being attacked by the parasol-armed, peace-minded furies.

The Afrikander universities were rebellious. In Johannesburg, on July 1, Smuts addressed a meeting of the National Union of South African Students. He tried hard to explain the problem of the war. "If the enemy attack succeeds finally, this noble order into which we were born will be destroyed, freedom and justice, mercy and humanity will be blotted out, and another dark age will settle over this fair world. The State will be totalitarian, omnipotent, and will be the new deity. The human individual will become an automaton, without freedom or rights, without a soul to call his own. Instead of the upward reach to the stars, we shall follow the downward and backward road to the beehive or the antheap. The lights of the mind and the soul will be dimmed or extinguished in the new blackout of the human spirit."

Whereupon Constable Gert Hendrik Theunissen, of the Cleveland Police Commissariat, Johannesburg, on duty at the door of the hall, remarked to Constable Verwey: "I wish I had a revolver. Then I could shoot the —— dead, when he comes out!"

The subsequent investigation disclosed that Theunissen had been transferred from the alien registration branch of the police special staff, where he had easy and pleasant duties, to the fatiguing job of tramping his beat, because he had failed to take the oath. Of course, that —— Smuts was guilty for his transfer. Theunissen declared unabashed that he wanted to go to Pretoria to help the students in their contemplated revolt, because "the police were treated just like slaves." He admitted frankly that he was a champion of the Nazi cause and in the habit of giving the Hitler salute.

Innocently, Constable S. R. Excell, a witness, testified: "It is fashionable at Cleveland barracks to discuss politics openly, defying the government. Theunissen is by no means the only one at Cleveland to hold anti-Smuts views. Many comrades have said to those who did take the oath of allegiance to the government that they were now on Hitler's blacklist, and if he wins, they will be in for it. Theunissen would not take the oath since he had no intention of fighting for a dog like Smuts. And if it were in his power, he said, others would not fight either. At least not on the English side. A large section of the Johannesburg police celebrated the fall of Paris, and other Nazi successes."

On Smuts' personal intervention, Theunissen was only accused on a charge of using improper language in a public place, or, alternatively, with conduct incompatible with the proper conduct of a member of the police force.

A few days after Smuts' address to the students in Johannesburg the first open disturbances broke out. Characteristically, they occurred in the internment camp at Baviaanspoort, where 1,200 Germans were detained. The internees were leading most comfortable lives, under conditions far excelling the regulations prescribed by the Geneva Convention. Their food was good and ample, beer and tobacco were among their privileges; they were allowed radio sets, newspapers, and visitors. Thousands of racialists obtained, under the most flimsy pretenses, visitors' passes. They assured the poor Nazis that the whole country was in sympathy with them.

Incited by such assurances, the entire body of internees revolted. The unarmed wardens, among them a good number of Nazi sympathizers, were either too weak or unwilling to restore order. Police had to be called in. Only using their batons, they broke up the upheaval. A hundred internees suffered slight injuries and bruises, two ringleaders were moved to the Johannesburg prison. German arrogance had suffered a defeat.

But what would Hitler think of the beating up of his faithful followers? The collapse of France was still a fresh memory, and an invasion of England seemed not unlikely. Certainly the Allied cause was done for, and the internees from Baviaanspoort would be South Africa's *gauleiters* and district-leaders of tomorrow. Senator Brebner, otherwise a comparatively moderate Nationalist, declared: "General Smuts is in the position of the former French Prime Minister Reynaud, who could not conclude an honorable peace because of his previous invectives against Germany. This is the danger General Smuts represents. His words are worse and more scandalous than Reynaud's. General Smuts will continue to speak about the 'beast of Berlin' and will continue to bring South Africa more and more into danger. The time will come when another government will have to be set up to do the things General Smuts will not be able to do!"

Instead of answering the calumny, Smuts broadcast to the people of Great Britain and America. "Although the Germans can show an uninterrupted series of most spectacular successes, England will prove an impregnable fortress if Hitler attacks her. If Hitler does not attack, he is equally lost. He will in the end be unable to hold down the vast populations whom he is dominating, starving, and seeking to enslave. To the specter of a Nazi-dominated Europe we oppose the vision of a truly free Europe. Freedom still remains our sovereign remedy for the ills from which human society is suffering. But we have also learned that discipline and organization must go hand in hand with freedom. We therefore aim at a society of nations which will possess a central organization equipped with the necessary authority and power to supervise the common concerns of mankind. In such an international society there will be no place for self-appointed leaders and fuehrers. He who will be master, shall be servant. Our aim and motto will be a nation of free men and women, an international society of free nations."

It certainly took courage to prophesy a new world during the very hours the blitz struck London with bestial fury. England was no less courageous than General Smuts. While the battle of Britain was at its peak, a large number of heavy Martin bombers, originally destined for France, were diverted to South African pilots, enabling them to wreak havoc on Mussolini's African positions. "The South African Air Force plays a vital and brilliant role," Sir Archibald Sinclair attested.

·At the same time the various groups of Boer Nationalists and racialists, defeatists and pro-Nazis struggled for position on the home front, each outbidding the other for Hitler's grace. Secret societies mushroomed, others came out into the open, all were the objects of violent rivalries between the republican leaders and underlings. Colonel J. C. Laas startled South Africa with his sudden demand for supreme authority for his *Ossewa Brandwag*, since only a "military group" could maintain order. The O. B., a prewar growth, started in the beginning of 1939, had thus far deceitfully claimed to be nothing more than a cultural and social society, devoted to the "awakening and development of the Afrikander's national pride." Smuts had known for a long time that a great number of O. B. leaders and members had been using their "cultural" organization for sinister ends. He knew that supporters of his government had been eliminated, and that the O. B. was developing along military lines. Yet he did nothing to root out this weed. Watchfulness, he trusted, would be enough.

Perhaps the old tactician also relied on the ferocious competition going on within the Afrikander camp. Pirow tried to best the O. B. in adding a *Handhawersbond*—league of artisans

—to his storm troopers, assigning to his new foundation the functions of a South African Gestapo. But when the *Handhawersbond* was making headway, the same dark forces that really dominated political Afrikanderdom, and to whom the German turncoat was never more than a contemptible instrument, kicked him out of his own foundation. A *Reddingsdaad Bond,* an economic league to promote Afrikander small business at the expense of English and Jewish, and an *F. A. K.* (Union for Afrikaans Culture) added to the number of subversive groups. Keerom Street, Dr. Malan's headquarters, wrangled violently with the last Hertzogites, now practically led by Mr. Havenga, for domination of these societies. Malan's personal enemies attempted to set up a *Boerevolk* organization to unite the gray-bearded survivors of the Boer War and their descendants in an Afrikander elite, which would exclude the instruments of Keerom Street. They succeeded in driving Dr. Malan from Cape Town, where he had spent most of his life. Under the pretext that the center of South African politics had shifted to the Transvaal, the old man with his wife moved to Pretoria. The change of air did him no good. The capital smiled at dour Dr. Malan who could so ill conceal his nostalgia for the bustle of Adderley Street, the Table Mountain mists, the oak-lined avenues, and the *koffiehuise* of the mother city. He tried to work off his personal ill-feeling in redoubled radicalism. His Purified Nationalists, *Die Suiderstem,* Smuts' mouthpiece, disclosed, had worked out a plan for a Christian-Nationalist Republic on the Nazi pattern. Mass meetings in the four provinces should culminate in a National Convention at Bloemfontein: "the one great meeting before we are free."

Smuts called in all the rifles in the hands of the civil population. His object, he explained, was not to disarm the people, but simply to get the small arms which were so necessary for the defense of South Africa. Rifles, he insisted, were the scarcest war-requirement in today's world. But he added: "The government cannot be accused of having abused its powers. If there is any charge against the government with a semblance of substance, it is the charge that the government is being far too lenient. There is not a single government anywhere in the world which would have allowed what the Union government has allowed. The government has done so because it realizes the peculiar position in South Africa. It appreciates the political differences between the people, and knows that it has to make allowance for exaggerations in speech. We shall continue to be patient with the people of South Africa," he concluded, "but if there are minority influences doing subversive work, I wish to tell the country that the full powers of the War Measures Bill will be used."

To test his determination, the racialists invented a particularly insolent provocation. Cape Town observed a two-minute pause at noon. When the bugles sounded, all traffic, walking, speaking on the streets stopped. In reverent silence the population paid homage to the heroes and the victims of the war. Eric Louw, a Nationalist youth leader, suggested to the students of Stellenbosch that they should band together and parade Adderley Street in Cape Town during the noon pause, to disturb the sacred and solemn moment which most passers-by used for a short prayer. On July 29, a group of Stellenbosch academic hoodlums, indeed, appeared in the center of Cape Town. The very moment the bugles had sounded the pause, the hooligans crossed Adderley Street, laughing and shouting raucously. For two minutes the noise-makers remained undisturbed. Then literally all Adderley Street turned on them, and they received an unforgettable thrashing.

At the same time other university hoodlums, back in Stellenbosch, attacked and beat up the colored news vendors, children between six and twelve, who sold English-language papers. Some grown-up natives tried to defend the newsboys. The local police interfered. They pushed back the natives, and protected the academic rabble.

The score in the South African Civil War was 1 to 1—Cape Town pro-war, Stellenbosch anti-war—when, on August 1, 1940, the Springboks entered active combat. Ten days later they occupied Kornidel, south east of Moyale. It was a glorious baptism of fire.

Within a fortnight the R.S.A.A.F. had established its superiority in the skies above Italian East Africa. Overnight the budding air aces became national heroes, better known by their nicknames such as "Sultan" or "Sheik." The most hilarious among the many stories about them was the account of "Sultan," who was sitting in a tree, clad only in drawers, when an air-raid warning announced the enemy's approach. "Sultan" rushed through the bush to his plane in a minute, and was climbing skyward. It took him another five minutes to shoot down a *Caproni*. The Italian mechanic was killed. But the pilot, although burned and sorely wounded, still looking smart in his snow-white uniform, glanced at his victorious foe and remarked acidly: "To think that I, an ace of three wars, should have been shot down by a naked ape!"

The Air Force was the pride of South Africa. The artillery and the tankmen ran a close second. The Union was proud of its new tanks and howitzers, the first to be manufactured in the country, and already coming rapidly off the assembly lines. The old Imperial barracks at Potchefstroom were converted into a huge training camp for the South African Artillery. Potchefstroom is also the site of University College. The attitude of the hopeful youth was explained by the chairman of the Students' Representative Council, a youngster by the name of Coetzee: "We stand aloof from the soldiers. We walk out of the movies while *God Save the King* is being played. We should all be interned for republican sympathy. We refuse to fight against Germany."

But they did not refuse to attack solitary soldiers who had come from the camp for an evening stroll through the town. A sergeant by the name of Poth was pushed off the sidewalk and kicked into the gutter. "Soldiers are not allowed with decent people on the sidewalk," his assailants said. A few minutes later a number of other students dragged a soldier from his motorcycle. He had a bad fall. "Serves him right for wearing khaki!" commented a belle. "It's a pity he was not killed outright," nodded another. Both girls wore Normal College blazers. Corporal Oats was attacked by five young men, mercilessly beaten, and had to be taken to a hospital. It became the general custom among the blazer-wearers to give the Nazi salute when they saw a soldier approaching. A gunner's wife was spat at by three women. "We don't want General Smuts!" was the explanation. Even Colonel Noel Poulton, commander at Potchefstroom, was waylaid by students on a narrow street corner, where he was turning his car, spat at, insulted in the most obscene manner, and followed by a jeering crowd as he drove off.

For a few days rowdyism went unchecked. But on the evening of August 7 five hundred artillerymen, who had lost their patience, gathered in front of University College, and gave every student that fell into their hands a severe beating. The young rowdies retreated into the building. Armed with nothing more than sticks and make-shift weapons, the artillerymen followed them into the premises. The students retreated to the upper floor. A few soldiers pursued them. The first to place his hand on a stair-rail received a violent shock, and was thrown back. The ingenious students had charged the stair-rails with electricity. After suffering three or four casualties, the soldiers understood the device, and applied their hands where they rightly belonged. For weeks scores of students went about with black eyes. The King's uniform was no longer insulted in Potchefstroom.

But the students were by no means disheartened. They received support of the Church. The Reverend J. D. Vorster addressed the *Afrikaanse Nasionale Studentenbound:* "Hitler's *Mein Kampf* points the way to greatness. Afrikanders must be fired by the same holy fanaticism that inspires the Nazis. . . . The foundation of the republic shall be that the Afrikander shall no longer co-operate with the Englishman. He will lay down the conditions, and the Englishman will be compelled to subscribe. The Englishman must also surrender his language. We want to hear nothing more about this liberal-democratic swindle!"

The Reverend Jacobus Daniel Vorster, Minister of the Nuwe Kerk, Bree Street, Cape Town, was a "general" in the *Ossewa*

Brandwag, like many of his brethren, and a very zealous one into the bargain. He induced Corporal Broegart of the Coastal Command in Simon's Town to betray defense secrets, the numbers of batteries, caliber of guns, the strength of the garrison, which immediately found their way to the German espionage center in Lourenço Marques. Broegart suffered pangs of conscience, and went to the police to confess. "General" the Reverend Vorster was arrested and tried. During his trial Mr. Hartoges, the magistrate, received a threatening letter, signed *"Trou En Trots, Die Memse wat Verraaiers doodskiet"* (Faithful and proud, the people who shoot traitors dead). Also the Crown witnesses were threatened with murder. Nevertheless, Vorster was sentenced to a long term.

His Church did not dare to side openly with the traitor. However, the Synod of the Dutch Reformed Church in the Free State sent a message to Smuts: "The Church cannot be convinced that the German people are out to destroy Christianity and its principles. As to Hitler's alleged plan of world domination, the Church does not know what goes on in Hitler's heart. He who sheds blood and tears merely on suppositions goes too far. The Afrikanders did indeed choose to stay out of the war, but in Parliament they were outvoted by the representatives of the other section which in origin, tradition, vocation and interest are opposed to the Afrikaans-speaking people. Now these people are not only being governed by an alien majority who are themselves afraid of going and fighting a bloody war, but they are also being dragged, life and property, into this war. The people, therefore, do not recognize a government ruling at its own discretion. The people must always and in everything be more obedient to their God than to their government. The Church urges the government to make immediate peace, and bases its request on the Word of God. In the name of the Synod: P. H. van Huyssteen."

Exactly one week after this message was published, one of its authors, by the name of Christiaan Rudolph Kotzé, a Minister of the Chief Dutch Reformed Church in Bloemfontein, was indicted by the Circuit Court for common assault.

The *Ossewa Brandwag* was encouraged. It organized political demonstration in the Churches. The Wolseley congregation, which had been united for two years after having been split for longer than a century over a previous dispute, was again torn asunder. The *Kerkraad* (Church Council) asked the minister to cancel a service to which men and women of the local O. B. marched in serried ranks. The minister declined, whereupon the greater part of the congregation left. Old women wept: "There is no longer room for us in our church!" Having won the day, the O. B. group roared, in front of the crucifix, the hymn *Afrikanders, Landgenote,* which is sung to the tune of *"Deutschland über Alles. . . ."*

Strangely, the strongest resistance against Nazification of the Church came from a German minister. The Reverend Wilhelm Luckhoff, Minister of the German Lutheran Church at Bloemfontein, declared that Nazism and Christianity were in an irreconcilable conflict. The members of his church council censored him. During the first week of the conflict he received three threatening letters, one of which read: "Pastor, you are a marked man. I must earnestly request you to leave the country at the earliest possible moment for your own safety. They know everything about you: all the information you have given about your countrymen, your trips up here, your contacts with the heads of departments, etc., etc. Your life is in danger. Friend." The strangest thing about this letter was its envelope. It bore the imprint of the Office of Patents, Designs, Trade Marks and Copyrights, and was posted at Johannesburg.

When members of the congregation asked the Reverend Luckhoff to pray for Hitler, the Niemöller of South Africa replied: "To ask God's blessing on Hitler's person would be a mockery of prayer." He was instantly dismissed. His farewell sermon was based on the text: "He that is not with me is against me, and he that gathered not with me, scattereth abroad."

Pirow covered the country, speaking darkly of the coming social and economic revolution, a new system of government,

military education for the nation, and a new relation between
state and citizen. "We require nothing less than an economic
and socialistic revolution," he asserted. "The state will have to
look after the citizens in a manner which today would be regarded as Utopian. The citizen should have to submit himself
to a control which today would be regarded as militaristic. The
domination by capitalism and by the capital-controlled press
must stop." Even Keerom Street was afraid of this undiluted
Nazism. Pirow's speeches were tucked away in the Nationalist
press. Yet the difference was only one of degree: while Pirow
dreamed of a sub-Nazi dictatorship, he himself lording it over
South Africa, with a privileged class controlling the people by
a gestapo and storm troopers, *Die Burger* had no moral objections to such methods of achieving domination of South Africa
for one narrow section, but only feared the dangers involved.

Pirow's *Handhawersbond* grew into a sixth column. It regarded itself as the political police of South Africa. The moment for action would come with Hitler's invasion of England.
Then the *Handhawersbond*, all of whose members were calling
themselves "generals," would give Smuts forty-eight hours to
resign and hand over the government. A president "with the
powers of Hitler" would succeed him. "If things in Europe
should not go as we expect," the program cautiously added,
"and if we must remain within the British Commonwealth, we
demand that the reins of government shall be taken over by
the *Handhawersbond*, which stands for action. The trouble is
that we have too many timid Afrikanders. In the *Handhawersbond* we want only the bulls who are unafraid. We want to
play the role of policemen in politics, and in this way get control of the government." A number of prominent government
and railway employees accepted leading functions. They were
swayed by Pirow's promise: "Under the present system things
are measured in terms of gold; under the new system the yardstick will be the happiness of the people and their progress.
The disciplined labor power of the people will be our new
wealth. There will be a place for youth in the national administration." Eagerly the underpaid white collar men and the job

hunters listened. No one knew that Pirow was simply parroting Hitler's words. No one objected to his aping Nazi manners at his meetings. The speaker on the platform began: "We demand. . . ." Short pause. The crowd fell in: ". . . freedom." It was Nuremberg all over again.

But the *Handhawersbond*, for all its martial pretences, was only a mere shadow of the real thing: the *Ossewa Brandwag*. On September 13, 1940, Lieutenant-Colonel J. C. C. Laas, the founder of the "purely cultural" organization (who, incidentally, had received from the Hertzog-Smuts government the difficult task of organizing the Commandos in the Free State), declared that there was no longer any necessity for secrecy. The O. B. was strong enough to come into the open. Its aim was to obtain political leadership and supremacy in South Africa.

A few days afterward the Reverend J. S. du Toit, another of the innumerable self-styled "generals," described the O. B.'s military organization. At the top was the Commandant-General, under him the generals, then the commanders, each of whom had three field-cornets. This hierarchy formed the general staff, or, in the civil-war parlance which the O. B. preferred, the Vigilance Committee. Three assistant field-cornets were appointed to each cornet, three corporals to each assistant field-cornet, and every corporal lorded it over eight men. Thus the individual commando averaged two hundred fifty men, approximately the combat strength of a commando in the first months of the Boer War, before many of the mounted fighters had galloped home.

Already in May arrangements had been made to purchase twenty thousand yards of *veld*-green corduroy to equip at least the higher-ups with uniforms reminiscent of the Boer War days. But a government ban on private uniforms had put a premature end to this venture. Consequently, every O. B. officer was compelled to buy a fancy uniform of his own. He wore regalia at meetings, but arrived and left cautiously in mufti. The badge was worn openly. It was an exact replica of the German Nazi badge, the same, incidentally, the Youth Section of the *Bunds* in the United States of America used to display. The membership was as chequered as the first groups of Nazi hoodlums had been. Members of the civil service mingled with miners, lawyers, doctors, poor whites—everyone was welcome who proved his republican sentiment by undergoing a medieval blood oath.

The O. B.'s first "direct action," still carried out in secrecy, was the organization of a boycott of all those Boers who supported the government. Loyalists were socially ostracized and driven out of business, at least in the *dorps* in which the majority of the customers were Republican.

The prophet Van Rensburg, the same whose dreams had incited the revolt of 1914, emerged out of oblivion. Already a shrunken oldster, he rose to a new peak of fame by predicting the fall of Paris a few days before the tragedy actually occurred. During the battle of Britain he published a pamphlet which, at one and six, had a record sale on the *platteland*. Britain would shortly be blitzed to death, he prophesied, and a few weeks later the Smuts government would crumble. After two great battles five big German ships would come to South West and South East Africa, and to Cape Town. Parliament would be in session. It would rain heavily, and the grass would be green. Three blue letters would arrive. The third one would be read in Parliament. The members would scramble, and flee out of the Cape. "If they come here," the prophecy ended, "I see us sitting on horses and moving in the direction of Lichtenberg. There by a hill we meet, and there a man in a brown suit speaks to us."

The advent of Hitler in South Africa was predicted. Smuts had not another moment to lose.

Parliament was actually in session. Smuts appeared as dominating as ever. His tanned face beneath the white hair had lost none of its vigorous expression, although it seemed a little thinner than six months before. He still walked in his brisk fashion, a little impatient, as it were, with a nod for one member and a quip for another. He met Hertzog most courteously. His old foe had also visibly lost weight, but he, too, was still bronzed and fit. He made it clear that he still felt himself leader of the opposition, and that he did not mean to be driven out by the extremists under Dr. Malan, who themselves were shivering in their shoes for fear of the new competition: the O. B. Smuts and Hertzog had a brief and formal discussion about the co-operation of the opposition in operating the parliamentary machine. No agreement was reached. Hertzog reserved the right to spend hours in harping on his favorite theme: the poor, downtrodden Germans. But there were no precious hours to be lost. Smuts moved, and carried, his "guillotine" motion, which strangled any attempt at obstruction. Otherwise he treated the House with the full respect of a veteran parliamentarian democrat. Even the Hertzogite ex-President of the Senate C. E. van Niekerk thanked him for the friendly and tactful manner in which he was handling the business. "Yes, one must keep one's tongue under control," Smuts replied. "There are people who speak just a bit too harshly. Now, whenever I hear hard words it reminds me of the old days when I was young. President Kruger once said to me: 'Smuts, your whiplash cracks too harshly.' I think, as we grow older, so do our whiplashes cease to crack. Unfortunately, in some places there are still those who cannot keep their whiplash in leash."

Instead of his "whiplash" his police cracked down on the subversive elements. The offices and houses of the known leaders of the O. B. in Cape Town, Johannesburg, Pretoria, and Bloemfontein were raided. All lists of membership and a great number of secret documents were seized. In Pretoria the uniform of a woman general of the O. B. was found: khaki-colored casement cloth with epaulettes indicating the high rank of the wearer. In the Bloemfontein house of Colonel J. C. C. Laas, as well as in the houses of the Reverend D. G. van der Merwe and of Advocate Swart, the up-and-coming man of the racialists, explosives, arms, ammunition, anti-government pamphlets, heaps of Nazi literature in German, and precious membership lists were unearthed.

After the raid Mr. H. G. Lawrence, Minister of the Interior, could disclose a number of interesting details. In the O. B.

headquarters in Johannesburg, 403, Voortrekker Gebou, Hoek Street, a report about available arms and ammunition, supplied by Dr. Wertz, German Consul at Lourenço Marques, was found, also a circular to all generals and officers of the O. B. dealing with methods of organization, with special reference to the duties of various ranks. The "war council," the *storm-jaegers* (storm troops), and the women's section had each their functions assigned. "There is no room in the O. B. for anyone who is not prepared to serve in any capacity."

One hundred seventy thousand members, a terrifyingly high number, were prepared to serve. The type of service was specified in the papers of the organizing secretary Abraham Spies, who managed to escape to Portuguese territory. Some of the members had to obtain information about defense, railways, factories, troop movements. Others were to inform on dangerous persons "inside and outside" the O. B. A scout corps was formed for "immediate action." Attempts at infiltration by members of the O. B. into the police, railway services, and defense forces were made. Evidently some of these attempts had been successful. Among the confiscated documents were plans of Defence Camps with the number of men and their armament, and names of particularly "reliable" soldiers: Janse V. R. of Casseldale was specially qualified as an Air Force mechanic and machine-gunner, whereas W. J. Jacobs of Witport possessed expert knowledge of Bren and Vickers guns. The police found evidence that the O. B. had been behind the strike in the East Rand Proprietary Mines. The organization had promised the strikers its support, attacked the government, magnified the men's grievances and was responsible for a number of other wildcat strikes.

The worst crime of the O. B. was to unloose the sabotage wave, the true curse of South Africa. Bombing outrages occurred in widely separated areas. It was a new method of crime, imported after the outbreak of war. In spite of all perennial hooliganism on the Rand, the dynamiter had previously not been known. Now bombing was a daily event. The government introduced a bill setting the death penalty for dynamiters, and making it retroactive. For a time it helped. The raid had eliminated some of the worst elements in the O. B. Colonel J. C. C. Laas, the commander general, resigned. Hundreds of his underlings were sent to internment camps, where discipline was rigidly enforced. It was high time to take such measures. The camps at Leeuwkops, Baviaanspoort, and Andalusia were seething with insubordination. An epidemic of escapes had broken out. The Internment Guards had been permeated with Nazi sympathizers. Now they were replaced by troops. General L. Beyers, Commander of the Fifth Brigade, was appointed Camp Director with full powers. The First Battalion of the Sixth Infantry Regiment and the Sixth Battalion of the Infantry Reserve Brigade were at his disposal. Immediately all visits were canceled, broadcasts and newspapers were banned, the singing of the Nazi anthem was effectively stopped. At the same time the search for fugitives was vigorously conducted. Five Italians who had escaped into Swaziland were captured by the police after the greatest man hunt the jungle had ever seen, before the native chiefs, who had joined the hunt with a vengeance, could get at the heroes of Abyssinia and roast them on their spits.

Toward the middle of October Smuts organized a National Reserve of Volunteers in two sections: the military section took over internal security duties, whereas the Civilian Protective Services guarded the key positions. These measures, combined with news of the ignominious beating the Luftwaffe had taken in the skies over England, did much to restore order. With his infinite patience and unwavering determination at the critical moment, Smuts had staved off a revolution on an unprecedented scale.

Looking anxiously at her husband's tired face, Mrs. Smuts, who, a short time before had received the first evacuee children from bomb-torn Britain and was teaching those on her own farm, Irene, her old childhood games, *klip-klip* and *bok-bok,* decided that he needed a holiday. His Cabinet colleagues concurred in this opinion. They insisted that their beloved leader should take off at least a week.

Smuts yielded. "I might pay a visit to our boys up North!" he murmured. "But don't rush around too much!" Mrs. Smuts was reported to have warned. On an evening late in October the *Oubaas* got out some maps, and ran his fingers northward to Kenya, the Sudan, and Egypt. Pointing out Tanganyika he reminisced about the bush and wild life during the East African campaign. Peering through his spectacles, he remarked on the vastness and great possibilities of Africa.

Early on the next morning he put on his old general's uniform. A fast American-built bomber swooped over Pretoria. The General went north. After sunset he arrived at the Nairobi airport. It seemed almost as if his aircraft were falling from the deep-purple sky. The airport was illuminated by floodlights. Smuts inspected the South African guard of honor, and met large groups of senior officers. He attended a soirée at Government House that lasted late into the night. Yet he was the first —only accompanied by his aide-de-camp Lieutenant-General Barnard—to venture out before dawn. For hours he drove through rain, mist, mud and slush. At the first Springbok camp he met dozens of officers, who escorted him on motorcycles while the Old Master inspected the camp. He watched the signallers receiving their instructions. He observed maneuvers: machine-guns in action, a charge of soldiers with gas masks, a mortar attack through the bush. Back at the camp he looked at other units digging trenches in their mud-stained working clothes. He obviously did not feel in the mood for speeches. "The Union is behind you. I have no doubts for the future," was all he said. The soldiers were so impressed by his simplicity that they forgot to cheer. Only an old bald-headed man, with his helmet in his hand, replied quietly: "God bless you, Sir!"

A soldier among his men, the *Oubaas* strode along: in an old, worn gabardine uniform, with helmet and Sam Browne belt, swinging his cane. His mannerisms were familiar to all. While discussing, he fingered his Imperial reflectively; while simply chatting he stood hands on hip, drumming with his fingers.

He motored to the artillery park, called at the casualty clearing station, went through the operating theaters and wards, and smiled benignly when he came to "Jan Smuts Ward." At the air station he talked with all the members of the crews, pilots, navigators, gunners, wireless operators and mechanics alike.

Accompanied by Lieutenant-General Sir Pierre van Ryneveld, Chief of the General Staff, he toured the front with Lieutenant-General Alan Cunningham, then general officer commanding in East Africa, to whom Smuts introduced a great many of his Springboks in person. At a front-line outpost he was talking to a young man in battle dress who stood smartly to attention until the bomber arrived to take the General back. Only at that moment Second-Lieutenant Jan Smuts relaxed: "Good-bye and good luck, Pops!" he shouted.

Smuts' visit up North lasted eight days, within which he covered 7,500 miles by air, held a number of important conferences, attended social functions, delivered a few addresses, and had personally inspected the positions of the South African divisions as far as the most extreme outposts. In spite of this exertion he looked sprightly and refreshed when he returned to Pretoria on November 4. Only then his "holiday" was divulged. Until Casablanca it remained the best-guarded military secret of the war.

Chapter 31   *OSSEWA BRANDWAG*

"THE NAZI MENACE IS FELT TO BE WORLD-WIDE. SO MUCH IS THIS the case that I feel convinced that in the last resort America will not—as indeed she cannot afford to—stand out. Under the great and inspiring leadership of President Roosevelt she will once more freely and of her own choice dedicate herself to the greatest of human causes. In the spirit of Abraham Lincoln she will take her rightful place among the champions of a free world as against a slave world. Deeply as America desires to keep out of the war, they will find necessity laid on them, and in the last resort they will not let freedom perish from the face of the earth. Their stake is the great issue, transcending all other national or political considerations. Their way of life is menaced as truly as ours. None of the forces of democracy can be spared if a final and lasting victory shall be won. Of that I feel assured. America's intervention is just as necessary for the victory as for the peace which has to be shaped thereafter. The old order is passing away. A general plan for the world community of the future will have to be laid down in the new peace. Together that new peace must be won and planned. Together we must pass through the night in order to salute the new day for mankind. Let us all resolutely face our duty, and let us welcome the New Year with a cheer!"

Smuts spoke from his new home in Pretoria, into which he moved on New Year's Day, 1941. It was called *House Libertas*. A year of great achievement and remarkable expansion in military strength and economic activity lay behind his country. Thanks to the purchases of the British Government South Africa was able to sell its main agrarian exports at very favorable prices, and thanks to the Royal Navy the surplus could be transported to England. The gold-mining industry achieved new records. The armament production had expanded to formidable dimensions. Both the mining and the secondary industries benefited from a practically uninterrupted flow of machinery and raw materials from across the seas, to an important degree from the United States. The Union could have been the happiest among all belligerent nations.

But South Africa was the unhappiest nation of all. The fratricidal strife continued unabated; racialism gained ever more ground. Smuts had to divert most of his energy to controlling, and subduing, the smoldering flames of revolution. How this septuagenarian managed to combine the vigorous leadership of a tremendous war effort with the task of saving his country from a ruinous civil war—and that at the time in which the British Commonwealth stood alone against overwhelming odds —will remain one of the miracles of history.

Enemies outside and within worked in double harness. Toward the end of 1940 Pirow formally proclaimed the New Order for South Africa. He rejected democracy in form and spirit, and demanded the establishment of a South African Christian White National Socialist Republic under the guidance of God, separated from the British Empire, and founded on state authority and national discipline. Money as a yardstick was to be abolished. It was to be replaced by the "restoration of ethical values and moral considerations" in the relations between the people themselves and between the people and the state. These ethical values consisted of nationalization of the gold mines, capitalistic enterprises and banking, the expropriation of all big property holdings acquired for purposes of speculation (English-owned), state control of press, radio, theater, movies, all sources of propaganda and education, white trusteeship over all natives based on the principle of complete segregation and the National-Socialistic race theory; finally expulsion of all Jews and undesirable persons (of English descent), but encouragement of immigration having kinship with the people of this country—German immigration.

Fearing Pirow's competition, Dr. Malan, the veteran opportunist, threw himself into the arms of the *Ossewa Brandwag*. In a speech breathing defiance and fury he announced that he had concluded a pact with the O. B. His Re-United Party would take the O. B. under its wing. The two organizations had delineated their respective spheres of action. "I am ready to die a martyr's death for the O. B.," the unfrocked *predikant* shouted. "But I will not stop demanding that the British Empire must fall to pieces. It is already crumbling. The Union's participation in the war caused the most serious disturbance in race relations since the foundation of South Africa. The blame for all this rests with General Smuts. He is the greatest divider South Africa has ever had. General Smuts is a foreigner in this country. He does not know the Afrikander people. Ever since the time of the Boer War he has been the arch-enemy of the Afrikanders. Today he fights alongside the same English who, during the Boer War, had promised to the natives the farms of the Boers and *selfs hulle vrouens* (even their wives) if they would take arms against us. I repudiate Smuts root and branch."

On behalf of the O. B. the acting Commander General, a Boer by the name of Smith, endorsed the alliance with the *Herenigde* (Re-United) Party. The O. B., he promised, would see to it that no defections occurred. "Traitors will be driven back into our ranks with the *sjambok!*" he announced. To differentiate him from other bearers of his not infrequent name he was henceforth called *Sjambok-Smith*.

"South Africa will not change from democracy to a Fuehrer-system without blood and tears," Smuts replied. "The message for a new order came from Munich or Berlin. The O. B. has to be carefully watched. This is an organization of precisely the same character as the organization which brought Hitler into power in Germany. Its methods come straight from Germany, and its purpose is nothing else but to introduce into this country by underground means the system flourishing in Germany. Its organizers keep on saying that the O. B. is not a secret organization. Why, then, do they talk so much about traitors? The other day Mr. Swart, one of their leaders, said that traitors must be branded and treated as such. But if the movement has no secrets, how can it be betrayed?"

The Old Master's appeal to common sense was wasted. Presently, the same Mr. Swart, whom Smuts had singled out, won the by-election at Winburg, a 100 per cent Afrikaans constituency, by an overwhelming majority against the Prime Minister's old friend and supporter Theron.

In this dark hour Nazism seemed as invincible among the Boers as on the European battlefields. Both Dutch Churches condemned Bolshevism, but never Nazism. Many divines were profoundly influenced by the pamphlets the *Fichtebund* and the *Weltdienst* smuggled across the Portuguese border. The Afrikaans universities were hotbeds of Hitlerism. The students sang German songs, voted peace resolutions, and adopted *"Opsaal!"*—for Heil Hitler!—as a salute. The professors and instructors, particularly at Stellenbosch, taught philosophy, history, even gymnastics on the German pattern. The *Voortrekker-Youth*, the Afrikaans counterpart of the boy scouts, became "race-conscious," although its members were all of a tender age below fourteen. The boys in their advanced teens joined the *stormjaegers*—the youth-organization of the O. B.—or the Greyshirts. Many families were disrupted. Others were agreed on the blessings of Hitlerism. One Sunday a month they ate the one-dish-meal, as Hitler had ordered in Germany, to save some money for the O. B. English housewives on the Rand were terrorized into contributing to the collection.

At the beginning of 1941 two hundred thousand Boers, one-fifth of the whole nation, were committed to active Nazism. The drive to segregate the Afrikaner nation into a racial *kraal*, and to set up the dwarf-nation as Africa's *Herrenvolk*—master race—dominating in a narrow republic of Hitler's grace, insulated against foreign influences, wilfully blind to world collaboration, went on with ever-increasing vigor. It was the very opposite of Smuts' worldwide outlook. This was the principal issue in the fight for South Africa.

Strangely, the first casualty in this fight was the first avowed Nazi in the country: old man Hertzog. The man who spent the eve of his life aping Hitler and pitying the poor downtrodden Germans still remained a relic of the old days. Fanatically as he hated the Empire, he would not acquiesce in making the English-speaking South Africans politically rightless, provided they had abjured the devil of jingoism. He wanted a republic as passionately as anyone. But he wanted its proclamation by consent, not by a *coup d'état*. The new generation could not understand this reluctance. Hertzog's own son associated himself with the men of "direct action." Although his caution, inherited from his father, forbade him to take direct action himself, he defended a good many dynamiters, saboteurs, and traitors in court. As was said of his father, Dr. Albert Hertzog also became a lawyer, not a soldier.

Old man Hertzog's political career ended when the Transvaal Congress of the Re-United Party laughed, shouted, and voted him down, although he was again, after his conflict with Dr. Malan had been patched up, the nominal leader. The party decided to adopt the revolutionary course. Hertzog, who had preached sedition all his life, was devoured by the monster of his own creation. Even the constituency of Smithfield, which he had represented for forty years, rejected him. In the third week of December he resigned his parliamentary seat. One man alone followed his example: "Klaasie" Havenga. A few other veteran followers banded together in an "Afrikander Union" to promulgate the threadbare gospel of Hertzogism.

The only effective help came from Smuts. He passed a motion in the House, granting his fallen foe a pension of £2,000 a year. "General Hertzog has never thought of himself," he said, "although there was much temptation in a young country. He did not even make provisions for his old age. It is now our duty to make these provisions."

On the very day Hertzog retired from Parliament, another resignation occurred, an act that was to influence events in South Africa considerably more strongly. Dr. J. F. J. van Rensburg resigned from his post as Administrator of the Orange Free State. The country was electrified. "The old leader has gone. The new leader is coming." Then for two weeks nothing happened.

Business went on as usual. At night solitary unarmed soldiers, or preferably members of the air force, were attacked, kidnapped, taken to some lonely spot on the *veld*, stripped of their uniforms which the hold-up men needed for good, subversive reasons, and left naked, sometimes with profuse apologies. Afrikaans soldiers on furlough in their *dorps* were greeted by their neighbors as "loyal Dutch." English-speaking Springboks were assured that their "little England complex" would soon be shattered by a crushing German victory. Stories circulated, and even appeared in print, of casualties in the North so heavy that the blood-stained uniforms of the dead were ar-

riving at Voortrekkerhoogte in truckloads. The Boer-Nazis'
most tender concern went out to General Smuts. Poor Oom
Jannie had collapsed from a heart attack, scores of thousands
whispered on the appointed day. Smuts himself heard the rumor when he returned from his habitual ten-mile stroll around
his farm, Doornkloof. "How many doctors are attending me?"
he asked.

Occasionally the scare stories backfired. Gossip had it that
banknotes would soon be worth only paper. "Get silver and
hang on to it," friendly neighbors advised each other. The bank
was exposed to a rush for silver. The Pretoria Mint wished for
nothing better. It coined more silver at ample profit, and when
the panic had run its course, silver trickled back into circula-
tion. Then it was rumored that the government was going to
seize all investments. Not only the Boer-Nazis, but a great
many poor, misled people queued up at the Post Office Savings
Bank to cash their savings. Every penny was paid out, every
demand was punctiliously met. The money returned, and more
was put into bank accounts than had been taken out. Confidence in the South African currency was stronger than ever.

Jewish shops were blown up, railway lines were sabotaged,
telegraph poles were axed in the best Boer War manner. But
such incidents were no longer remarkable. No one paid much
attention until Dr. Malan announced: "Conditions in South
Africa amount to no less than the rule of jingo terror. Where is
General Smuts leading South Africa? Does he want civil war?
If he does, he is going in the right direction. I hope the day is
not far off when the *Brandwag* and the Afrikaner nation are
one and the same thing!"

This was the clue. Immediately after this speech, *Kleinbaas
Hans,* as the English-language press baptized him, took over.
On January 1, 1941, Dr. J. F. J. van Rensburg was appointed
"Chief Officer and Commander General" of the *Ossewa Brandwag.* Friend and foe alike recognized him as a man with whom
one would have to reckon. The van Rensburgs were the first
family of Afrikander society. Their ancestor had led the *Voortrekkers* some one hundred years before. He was a national

hero. His descendants were patricians in Stellenbosch. The youngest scion had served his apprenticeship as private secretary to Tielman Roos, the lion of the Transvaal. At the age of thirty *Kleinbaas Hans* was Under Secretary for Justice, a year later Secretary, and soon afterward Administrator of the Transvaal. Such rapid careers were rare in the Union. Dr. van Rensburg caused much attention. But no one was surprised when, shortly before the outbreak of the war, the remarkable young man visited Hitler in Berlin. The van Rensburgs had always been ultra-nationalists. None of the tribe, however, had ever looked the way *Kleinbaas Hans* looked upon his return from the Third Reich. Now he was the answer to every cartoonist's prayer: the "boche" incarnate. His slightly curled, carefully greased hair was parted on the left, while one wave drooped over his forehead. Furrows between his eyebrows, a pugnacious nose, tightened lips with deep lines running from the corners of his mouth to his receding chin gave his clean-shaven, fish-eyed face the perfect appearance of a Prussian lieutenant in mufti.

His first act after his resignation was to claim the handsome pensions which were due to him from the various civil service posts he had held. Then he delivered his maiden speech: "As long as our Supreme Council can maintain and improve discipline," he mingled promises with threats, "there will be no danger of disorder and violence among the two hundred fifty thousand men of the O. B. We do not want to cause disturbances in the country. We only want to see to it that Afrikanerdom shall not be crushed to death. This is the calling of the O. B. The Supreme Council appointed me, and if I cannot answer to this body, I will resign. The O. B. is mobilized Afrikanerdom—mobilized in economy and culture, and for mutual protection. Whatever Afrikanerdom may have in superfluity—droughts, pests, poverty and politics—discipline is not among these things. If we do not cultivate this discipline and mutual trust, no one need hope for new orders, worlds, republics. I have not joined the O. B. to start a rebellion or to spill blood. I am well aware that we would suffer defeat in such an attempt.

I have been an officer long enough to know how hopeless and reckless such an action would be. I give the government every assurance on that point. I wish to give General Smuts the assurance that the O. B. is at least as concerned as he is to maintain order and law in the country. As a philosopher General Smuts will realize that an idea always triumphs over violence, provided the idea is imbued by vitality. General Smuts knows that the Afrikaner, true to tradition, is peace-loving, unless he is too strongly provoked." It was polite blackmail.

No answer came from Smuts. The Old Master kept his ear to the hot African ground. He heard the first rumblings of the incipient revolt of native chieftains in Abyssinia. He was proud of his Springboks. On the last Dingaan's Day they had stormed El Wak in Italian Somaliland, capturing nine of fifteen guns and all the Italian transports. Brigadier Dan Pienaar, Smuts' personal favorite, had surprised and routed the enemy. He now received the D.S.O. for gallant leadership. At the same time the Union's Seaward Defence Force left their South African ports to assist the British fleet. For the first time South African warships co-operated with the Royal Navy outside their home waters. On October 22 Wavell announced the capture of Tobruk. The South Africans had been in the vanguard. Twenty thousand Italian prisoners were taken. Simultaneously, Springboks captured El Yiba and El Sardu, two Italian outposts on the Ethiopian border. This was too great a time for arguments with *Kleinbaas Hans*.

Not for the racialists, however. Pirow instantly espoused the cause of the O. B. under its new commander, who would take care, he hoped, that there should be more action and less *kultuur*. Van Rensburg, fully conscious of his importance as the new czar, tolerated Pirow for a while, but soon shook him off.

Was *Hänschen klein* really the new czar? To some stalwarts of nationalism he appeared merely an upstart. Professor A. C. Cilliers rose against him, a formidable foe, the kingmaker in political Afrikanerdom. Officially he was the spokesman of the Republican Nationalist majority of the body of Stellenbosch professors. In fact he had been Hertzog's brain-truster number one for many years, the champion of reunion of all Afrikanders long before the war, and, it was said, an influential figure in this mysterious *Broederbond* which never came out in the open, but wielded tremendous secret powers. Cilliers had his finger in every pie. He was endowed with a peculiar reputation as an "insider." He could allegedly outwit every man on earth but Smuts. This Professor Cilliers attacked the O. B. openly. He called it a curious organization that made the confusion in the confused opposition ranks only more confused. "It appears in front and behind, above and below and everywhere between the ranks of political leaders," he said. "The O. B. wants Afrikaners to subject themselves to a self-appointed group of anonymous leaders. It is a terrorist organization, to be disbanded as soon as possible."

The first bloody outrage, instigated by the O. B., occurred on January 31 in Johannesburg. The *Afrikaanse Taal en Kultuur Vereeniging*, the O. B.'s "cultural" section, met at a concert in the town hall of Johannesburg. A few sailors in uniform wished to buy tickets, but were refused admission. A brawl ensued, developing into a street fight. The police used tear-gas bombs against the sailors and a group of soldiers who came to the assistance of their comrades. Sticks, knuckle dusters and lead piping were used as weapons. All together some five hundred men were involved. But this was only the prelude.

On the next day, a Saturday, rioting assumed a much more serious character. Thousands of soldiers marched through the streets. They stormed and damaged the premises of the pro-Nazi newspaper *The Transvaaler* and of Hertzog's own mouthpiece *Die Vaderland*. On the other side thousands of Nationalists gathered in Simmond Street. They were protected by police, only a few of whom wore the orange tab of loyalty. "Where are your tabs?" the soldiers shouted. This was the signal for the police attack. The worthy descendants of the *Zarps*, the brutes from the *platteland* whom Kruger had pitted against the *uitlanders*, drove in trucks right into the crowds of soldiers, who were soon dispersed. One of the groups of soldiers, however, overturned a police van. Petrol streamed on to the ground. Someone lit a match. Flames roared sky high. Soon fire-engines raced through the streets. All the ambulances in the city were called out. The streets reeked with the fumes of tear-gas bombs.

The soldiers withdrew to the vicinity of the Soldiers' Club. There they were met by a group of police wearing the orange tab, accompanied by members of the Military Police. "Think of General Smuts!" the M.P.'s said. "The old General won't let you down! Don't make it hard for him!" These words had a magic effect. The soldiers returned to their camp.

The *Rand Daily Mail* wrote about the causes underlying the riot: "The soldiers' action was plainly stupid. But the riots did not arise without a strong cause, and the cause is evident. For months past isolated soldiers have been set upon by bearded men, knocked down, kicked when they were on the ground, and left unconscious. Rarely in such cases has anyone been brought to trial. In some of the country districts soldiers cannot walk alone. Their families are being boycotted and persecuted. In none of these instances did the government do anything really drastic. Is it not natural, is it not, indeed, inevitable, that the soldiers should eventually hit back?"

Smuts promised the House an impartial inquiry into the riots. The first findings were published within ten days. They proved that the police had indiscriminately hit, struck, and kicked soldiers. A few had been attacked who had been entirely unconnected with the riot, as they walked by, some with their wives. At the *Voortrekker-gebou*, the Brown House of Johannesburg, the police had even called O. B. men to "defend" the building against the soldiers.

The final findings of the Rand Riots Commission, published on April 8, were still more grave: "In order to restore public confidence in the Police Force it is necessary to enforce severe disciplinary measures against those members of the force who disobeyed orders or committed unnecessary acts of violence. At the outset there was no organized attempt on the part of the soldiers to create disturbances. The exercise of more tact and forbearance on the part of the police might have prevented the disturbances that followed. The baton charge by the police against the soldiers and civilians in the neighborhood of city hall was made without an order by a superior officer, and was unnecessary, violent, and brutal. Certain civilians, who had come armed to the concert and remained on the scene with the obvious intention of participating in any trouble that might occur, joined the police in the baton charge and further aroused the soldiers. Some of the South African police, in carrying out the charges, used unnecessary violence in striking on the head soldiers who were running away and soldiers who already had been felled and were lying on the ground. The police indiscriminately attacked persons, including women who were obviously spectators. The chief offenders were non-tabbed members of the force.

"Members of the O. B. incited crowds by their attitude outside the *Voortrekker-gebou,* and by carting missiles from the windows and roof of that building. Certain members of the O. B. joined the police in the baton charge. The vast disproportion between the numbers of wounded soldiers as against the numbers of policemen injured, as well as the severe nature of the injuries inflicted upon soldiers, is significant. Medical evidence shows that most wounded soldiers suffered head injuries of a serious nature which in a great majority of cases were received on the back of the head or in such a position that they could only have been inflicted from behind. The police indiscriminately clubbed soldiers and women, a body of police without badges went about beating soldiers and civilians.

"The O. B. contributed considerably to the feelings of division and friction which arose between soldiers, police, and certain sections of the public. This organization is distinctly sectional in character, with a racial bias. It is not only undemocratic and anti-government, but also un-Afrikaans. In the O. B. the Grand Council, not the three hundred fifty thousand members, choose the Commandant-General. Van Rensburg says, when speaking of democracy, that when you have worn out an old shoe you throw it away. The fifteen members of the Grand Council have the fate of three hundred fifty thousand people in the hollow of their hands, and can dictate a policy which their adherents willy-nilly must carry out. The Commander-General has openly stated that if his organization were at the head of affairs he would not under the same circumstances tolerate a body with a membership of three hundred fifty thousand opposing his policy and working actively against it. It seems to us that in the present circumstances the O. B. could have no just grounds for complaint if they received the same treatment as they admit they would, if in power, mete out to others."

The most terrifying statement in this document was the estimate of the commission that the O. B. numbered three hundred fifty thousand members. In the three months since van Rensburg had taken over, its ranks had almost doubled. In the middle of April, 1941, more than every third Afrikander (including women, children and even infants) was an organized Nazi of the South African brand.

Still Smuts was determined to ride out the storm. His government only took half-hearted measures. Civil servants were forbidden to join the O. B., or received two weeks' time to sever any existing relations. But a great many incidents proved that even this order was disregarded. The whole country was disturbed. Only the Old Master seemed in high spirits. Looking the image of radiant health, he flew to Nairobi on his second war-time visit to East Africa. His amazing vigor was evident when his plane flew at an altitude of twenty thousand feet over Mount Kilimanjaro. As a rule, pilots flying above fifteen thousand feet use oxygen. But Smuts refused it. He would not be disturbed. He was too deeply engaged in gazing at the snow-clad peak, towering thousands of feet above the clouds. When the aircraft landed in Nairobi, the pilot said: "The only passenger who seemed not the least bit affected by the altitude was—well, you know whom I mean."

From Nairobi Smuts went on to Cairo, where he conferred with Mr. Eden, Sir Archibald Wavell, and Sir John Dill. Asked by reporters whether he wished to make a statement about his conferences, General Smuts obliged most readily. He let the cat out of the bag: "The possibilities of the new situation called for careful consideration in our Cairo talks. A review of the whole Mediterranean position took place, which is certain to have an important bearing on future developments in that part of the world."

No one can call Smuts a chatterbox. Few have ever called him jovial. Yet it was a jovial Prime Minister who returned from the battlefields, just in time to attend the Victoria Fête at Greenpoint near Cape Town. He appeared in a lounge suit, and in his happiest mood since prewar days. As usual, his first tribute went to Mrs. Smuts, who, he proudly jested, was being called "Old Gifts and Comforts" in the Transvaal (on account of the Gifts and Comforts for Soldiers' Fund, over which South Africa's beloved *Ouma* presides). Then the *Oubaas* complimented the ladies "who have gate-crashed my army in the North. . . . They are better than the men," he said. "They are keener. They have even stopped titivating themselves. . . ." Finally he paid tribute to the colored transport drivers, although none of them happened to be a guest at the Victoria Fête. "They are partly responsible for our victories in the North!" General Smuts said earnestly.

Victoria Day was a day of many gatherings. In the best, almost Prussian fashion van Rensburg blared to his audience: ". . . and the O. B. has the right to decide whether it obeys the law, and upon whom it wishes to enforce it. . . ."

A thin, fading voice explained to a few faithful old followers who were spending the holiday at the Sabine Farm Waterval: "I have broken with General Smuts because. . . ."

Dr. Malan, the old man on the flying trapeze, tried desperately to have one foot in the O. B. camp and the other among the old Afrikanders. "But for Smutskowitz," he declared, "the Re-United Party embraces. . . ."

The Old Master made a bow to his guests at Greenpoint. His last words to the assembly are on record: "Thank God, this is not a country of bachelors. I dislike them. They are a sign of decadence."

Chapter 32	AS THE TIDE FLOWS

THE OLD MASTER WAS NOW CARRYING A BURDEN ALMOST BEYOND human endurance. In addition to running South Africa's war effort and keeping a restive, turbulent country on an even keel, his advice was sought by the Allied leaders before every strategic movement in the African theater of war.

The war, it appeared, proceeded on schedule. On April 5 the British forces, with the Springboks in the vanguard, marched into Addis Ababa. On the same day the Cape Town regiment returned from Cairo for a short leave, bringing with them 7,500 Italian prisoners. All went well. So Oom Jannie could take off an afternoon. In a khaki shirt open at the neck, the sleeves flapping loosely at his wrists, his feet in a stout pair of boots, he set off across the brown *veld* for a good twelve-mile tramp. A heavy stick in his hand, he swung along four to five miles an hour, striding in his eager, loose-limbed way, bent slightly forward. His companions—not to call them his bodyguards—were hard put to keep up with the Old Master.

Sometimes accompanied by his wife, he stumped the *platteland*, preaching confidence and good cheer, which he himself radiated. The wool farmers in the Free State received him with the anxious question whether England would renew her wool purchases. "If the German U-boats do not make shipping impossible. . . ." Oom Jannie replied cautiously. Many Free Staters had Hitler's picture hanging in their farms. But most of these disappeared rapidly after Smuts' simple remark.

A "War Train," rolling for six weeks through the length and breadth of the Union, did excellent propaganda. It carried an exhibition of the huge output of the six hundred new South African war factories. Thousands of *backvelders* came from the most distant hamlets. They could see for themselves the first howitzers made in South Africa. They thrilled at the boom of eighteen-pound guns and the rattling of machine-gun fire. The five-hundred-pound aerial bombs and the armor plates made of the toughest and finest steel, the shells, small arms, and ammunition in various stages of production, the mortars and mortar bombs, the steel helmets, bayonets and parachutes were most impressive. But the army boots on display made the biggest hit. The farmers were still accustomed to wear the wooden *veld-schoenen* of Oom Paul's good old days. Now they saw shiny brown leather boots, looking extremely comfortable. How did one get such a pair of boots? Nothing simpler. One must only volunteer. Every Springbok gets two pairs straight off, and six pairs during the year.

Freely, Oom Jannie mingled with his people. He chose the opening of an Easter Carnival at Benoni to expound his two favorite visions: America's entry into the war, and Hitler's downfall. "As time goes on, Germany's strength will be sapped," he foretold. "Her material resources will be exhausted, and her poisoned soul will shrivel. Germany's terrific initial successes were due to her long advance planning—but has she enough staying power? The people of Great Britain, notwithstanding the hardest blows in all their history struck against them, stand unmoved and rocklike in their attitude and spirit. The soul of this people is invincible, and growing only stronger under the hard blows and bludgeonings of fate. . . . Now wait until America comes more prominently forward and until she, too, will make her contribution, indeed a very great one, to the battle. When shipping was one of our greatest problems, we have seen that America sent her ships right around South Africa and through the Indian Ocean in order to supply our armies at Suez. America is coming in like the tide in flood. Still you may see many ups and downs, just as in the last war, when Germany won victory after victory on an enormous scale. But she will collapse from every moral and spiritual corruption at heart which her people has undergone, and from the hopeless cause for which she is fighting."

A few weeks later he reaffirmed in a broadcast: "With the United States of America and all her good will and vast resources behind us we may indeed look forward to the end in steadfast confidence. Hitler has mobilized America for us in a way we could never have done ourselves. Hitler has roused the American giant from his slumber. Hence the election of President Roosevelt, the Lend-Lease Act, the firm and unshakable alignment of all responsible American opinion on the side of the Allies. America will yet go all the way. This I have for a long time foreseen. I have looked forward to this development not only for the sake of our victory but also for the sake of the peace that is to follow. I cannot see a real fruitful peace without America right in it. I cannot see America participating in the peace, unless she has been through the crucible of war with us."

Whereupon Dr. Malan shouted: "The worst thing we have to guard against is the possibility that after the war South Africa should become part of a new combination of English-speaking people with America as the principal. We will fight any such move tooth and nail, and we will keep on fighting even if it takes a hundred years."

The fight for the soul of South Africa was closely aligned with the ups and downs of the war. Allied successes were a tonic to morale on the home front, but when Rommel came into the picture the sabotage wave, the treason cases, and the provocative insolence of the O. B. increased tremendously. The fence sitters came to regard the whole war in Africa as a duel between Smuts and Rommel. This duel had its humorous aspect, too. On May 24, 1941, on Smuts' seventy-first birthday, King George VI appointed him Field Marshal of the British Army. It was only the second appointment to this high rank during the present war. Gratefully, the Old Master accepted the insignia of his new dignity: the crossed batons in a laurel wreath, with the crown above, to be worn on the shoulder epaulettes. The baton itself would follow later. Smuts said: "While officially I have to rank as a Field Marshal as from today, I trust that my friends and those who have known me as General Smuts during the last forty years will not hesitate to use my old title. I am still General Smuts to my friends in South Africa, and I hope that the continuity of many years will not be broken by the new appointment. I am too old now to change names."

Even as an Imperial Field Marshal he wanted to remain the Boer General. But this expression of fidelity did not satisfy the opposition. "We are very pleased," wrote the leading Nationalist paper. "From now on it will be impossible to mistake the British Field Marshal for the General Smuts of the Boer War." Boonzaier, the creator of "Hoggenheimer," expressed his congratulations in a cartoon depicting Smuts as a sentry, standing guard on the South African shores. "Who goes there?" he asks a shadowy stranger. "Enemy of Afrikanerdom!" comes the answer. "Pass, my friend!" says the sentry Smuts.

Herr Adolf Hitler, however, seemed seriously perturbed over Smuts' promotion. His own Erwin Rommel was still a simple Lieutenant-General. Moreover, Rommel was at that moment hiding in some foxhole, so that he could not come to Potsdam, where, since time eternal, conquering German war lords have received the marshal's baton. Herr Hitler broke another precedent. Posthaste he sent a marshal's baton to Africa, where Rommel snatched it with little ceremony. "Field Marshal Rommel!" Zeesen blared triumphantly on the same evening. The South African station continued, modestly, to refer to the Old Master as "General Smuts."

The Springboks entered Sidi Barrani and Sollum. *Ouma* and seven of her grandchildren had a bird's-eye view of Pretoria, flying above the capital in a captured three-engine Caproni bomber. Lord Croft, British Under Secretary for War, eulogized the South African troops: "They are the spearhead of the later operations in East Africa," he said. "Their advances in the race against the long rains were amazing. To the Union troops, under the umbrella of their airmen who have flown an immense mileage with amazing immunity from losses, fell the great honor of that remarkable uphill advance from the Awash River, and when they entered Addis Ababa, instead of taking a well-earned rest, they started in further pursuit of the enemy. Already their advance from Kenya to Jyiga was surely a world record of distance made in astonishingly short time. To that record must be added the exploit at Ambi Alagi, 1,400 miles from the Kenya border, and 1,731 from their original railhead. These achievements can never, I think, be equalled for time."

The Springboks, in fact, conquered within five months an area larger than the whole German East Africa, from which, during the First World War, Germany was ejected only after three years' fighting. The subjugation of Abyssinia and Italian Somaliland was achieved within one-seventh of that time. It was, of course, the conquest of a less pestiferous, swampy and malaria-ridden territory than German East Africa. But the main reason for the success was the highly organized efficiency of the services. Mechanical transports replaced the huge armies of native porters. Food was better in quality and more varied than in any previous campaign. The medical service under Brigadier Dr. Orenstein was exemplary. Moreover, Italy had not produced a Lettow-Vorbeck. In close comradeship with the R.A.F. the South African Air Force had given the enemy a terrible grueling. Italian fighters were swept from the skies. The morale of Il Duce's ground forces, particularly of their black contingents, was destroyed. Excellence of staff work, fine qualities of leadership, the fighting spirit of all ranks, and streamlined equipment scored. Above all the success of the campaign was due to the inspiring guidance and long-range vision of General Smuts, who from the outset had laid out the plans for crushing Mussolini.

Now even the Dutch Churches paid eloquent tribute to the valor, endurance, and "finishing power" of the South African troops. The slime-flood of Nazism in the Union was beginning to recede when the German invasion of Greece, the conquest of Crete, and the ensuing British reverses in North Africa revived the furor. As always, the South African airmen had valiantly done their share. They had protected British warships and merchantmen evacuating the Imperial troops from Crete. Smuts appealed for new volunteers. He predicted heavy fighting. "The Italian menace has been eliminated," he said, "but now we will have to meet a more formidable threat: German forces in North Africa. South Africa calls on every man and woman to do his and her duty."

In response, the united opposition met at a rubber-stamp congress at Bloemfontein. Twelve hundred delegates crowded town hall. All the stale grievances were repeated, the *Vierkleur* was waved, Nationalist anthems were sung. The foreign situation was not mentioned by a single word, and the war only to be ferociously condemned. Dr. Malan moved a motion: "The Congress rejects Smuts' war policy with determination and in its entity, and demands the immediate withdrawal of South Africa from the war." But while he sputtered his venomous words, his voice sounded broken. He was the dictaphone, no longer the dictator. He was the leader under the lash of the O. B. *sjambok*. Behind him stood Pirow, the self-styled man of destiny, who emphatically warned President Roosevelt to keep out of the tangle, and grinning van Rensburg. All three, van Rensburg, Pirow, and Dr. Malan, a poor third, were in the race for Hitler's favor. All that was left was for Adolf to win the war.

America's entry would prevent it, Smuts repeated incessantly, once even at the opening of a new and splendid Johannesburg movie theater with a Hollywood picture. Before boy met girl, General Smuts appeared on the stage, and smiled: "They say that the United States is a country of hustle. If hustle means what I think it does, then, I trust, America will live up to it in the near future. I am sometimes a prophet, often a false one, but occasionally a true one, and I feel tonight I can venture on a prophecy. If you read hustle and the United States of America in terms of the present world crisis, I think you will not be far wrong!"

"General Smuts has suggested that the United States shall inherit South Africa," Dr. Malan replied in Senekal, a sleepy small town in the Free State. "We will oppose America just as we have struggled against foreign domination during the past one hundred fifty years. We will not shirk the battle. It is clear that the United States is only concerned with her own interests. She wants a say in the peace conference and wishes to be heir to the British estate. The Royal Navy is Britain's movable property, and the United States wants to hold a mortgage in case Britain should lose her fleet." Hitler, on the other hand, Dr. Malan assured, had none but honorable ambitions as far as South Africa was concerned. As a token of his trust in the great man he, Dr. Malan himself, was now ready to accept the title *volksleier*, Afrikaans for Fuehrer. He frankly offered himself as Quisling: "Germany wants a government in South Africa which would be amiably disposed to her. We can provide a government of men who have already shown that they have no hostility toward Germany."

Pirow thought the same thing. The difference was only that the *gauleiter* wanted nothing of a *volksleier*. "The program of the *Herenigde* Party is good, but still diluted by too much milk and water," he carped. To emphasize that *he* was the right man, and no one else, he promised: "I will continue to advocate African National-Socialism and changes upside down!"

Dr. Malan took up the gauntlet. To beat Pirow at the game, his first action as *volksleier* was to overhaul his party, and re-establish it on the Nazi cell system. The *platteland*, deeply impressed by the latest German successes, liked the change. But shrewd peasants as they were, they preferred the whole hog to half a hog. They deserted both Malan and Pirow, and streamed in masses to *sjambok*-wielding O. B. Commandant-General van Rensburg, whose very looks identified him as the real thing: a genuine Nazi.

"Russia becomes ally against Hitler. The Allies are fighting the war on behalf of Jewish Imperial Capitalism!" shouted *Die Burger's* flaming headlines across eight columns. Since the Pact of Moscow the *Nasionale Pers*, the powerful Afrikaans press combine with *Die Burger* as its most important mouthpiece, had never attacked Soviet Russia. For two years Dr. Malan had not mentioned Stalin's name. Now he issued a statement: "Churchill and Smuts are dragging us with open eyes into the abyss. Britain, and through Britain, we, now stand in alliance with Russia. If it had not been for Germany, the tidal wave of

Bolshevism long would have swept the world. Now Mr. Churchill, with his arm around Stalin's neck, and with Field Marshal
Smuts at his coat tails, has decreed the total destruction of the
only bulwark against Bolshevism, which, for a long time, has
had its eyes on South Africa. We have always been against
participation in this war, but if we ever had good reason to
demand that South Africa should withdraw, then we have a
hundred times more reason today."

Once again Smuts proved his visionary foresight. He understood that Russia's entry into the war, although tremendously
important in itself, was the harbinger of a real world war.
Quietly he conferred with Mr. Wilfred J. Kennedy, the President of the Johannesburg Chamber of Commerce. The outcome was the decision to restrict severely Japanese imports,
and all trade with Japan. Then he broadcast a message to his
people, which, indeed, anticipated the Allied invasion of North
Africa by a year and a half. Predicting heavy fighting on the
Russian front, he foretold on July 14, 1941: "But the final
knock-out blow will come elsewhere. The definite turn of the
tide will probably begin in North Africa, and the Springboks
will have their share in the crowning glory just as they have
had in the first successes of the war."

On the next day Winston Churchill, in the House of Commons, quoted another passage from Smuts' broadcast. "With
his usual commanding wisdom General Smuts has made a comment which, as it entirely represents the view of His Majesty's
Government, I should like now to repeat: 'Nobody,' said General Smuts, 'can say we are now in league with the Communists
and are fighting the battle of Communism. More fitly can the
neutralists and fence sitters be charged with fighting the battle
of Nazism. If Hitler and his insane megalomania has driven
Russia to fight in self-defense, we bless her arms and wish her
all success without for a moment identifying ourselves with her
Communistic creed. Hitler has made Russia his enemy, and not
us friendly to her creed.'"

The Nationalist press raged against Smuts. It proved that
Hitler's attack on Russia, on June 22, 1941, had unloosed the

final stage of the life-and-death struggle between two diametrically opposed philosophies. Now the papers of the *Nasionale Pers* formally embraced the creed with which their country was officially at war. Their entire propaganda was concentrated on the fight against Communism, next to the "black danger" the peril most easy to exploit among the Church-loving farmers. In this respect Hitler's invasion of Russia was a godsend to the Boer Republicans.

Into the struggle over Bolshevism crashed the battle over V. Smuts was quick to grasp that the coming general election might go to him who fought it under the V sign. On July 23, he started the V campaign in South Africa with a broadcast: "We adopt the V sign as our own. It stands not only for Victory, but in our country also for *vryheid*—freedom. It is therefore to us a symbol of the two things for which we are now making the greatest national effort in our history. The V sign will be the symbol of protest of all good South Africans against disloyal and often treasonable talk, against the subversive propaganda of certain sections. Let the whole world see our colors—this V symbol of our faith in our cause. This common symbol will thus become a source of unity, strength and inspiration to us in the trials and difficulties which may still face us before the final victory."

His appeal found a tremendous echo among the Loyalist section of the population. An onrush to the colors ensued. Young and old volunteered. The youngest recruit was a lad of, he insisted, seventeen, who gave his name as Smuts and did not deny a distant kinship with the Prime Minister. The recruiting officers scrutinized him suspiciously. He seemed a little underdeveloped for his age. *Ouma* was sent for. Smiling, she took her thirteen-year-old grandson home. "He shall first get his matriculation certificate," she decided. "Then he will go up North."

Among the oldsters Colonel Creswell emerged out of oblivion. His prestige with labor was unimpaired, although he had already been living in political retirement for many years. The lifelong socialist spoke about British tradition, ending—it was an unmistakable warning to the Quislings—with Kipling's words: "When he stands stock-still in the furrow, his stupid ox-eyes on your own, and grumbles 'This isn't fair dealing!' My son, leave the Saxon alone!"

The Cape, the mother colony, usually kept aloof from the struggles of the day. But the V campaign swept the peninsula like bush fire. The august *Cape Times* repeatedly appeared with an enormous crimson V on its masthead. Business houses with a V in their name used the felicitous letter for patriotic advertising. When even the imperturbable Cape bestirred itself, the battle over V was won.

Vituperatively the Republican leaders accused one another of the responsibility for their failure. Why did Dr. Malan not appropriate V for Victimization, *Vierkleur, Voortrekker, Vervolging* (persecution)? Why did Pirow, for his part, deride the V in mass gatherings if his party wanted to utilize it? Finally Dr. Malan, in his holy fury, even served an ultimatum to the O. B. Van Rensburg laughed it off. But the United Republican Front cracked. The isolated groups spent most of their rage fighting one another. Their hatred against the existing world order did not weaken. Hitler remained their idol. But many of their followers walked out, bored, or even disgusted. Rightly, Smuts could tell an interviewer from the *Daily Telegraph:* "When the war began, South Africa was divided in her soul as regards fighting. That passed. Hitler proved my case for me. Today we have a strong political opposition, and a small, subversive element underground. I can handle both of them."

"Things are well in hand. I'll keep South Africa right!" the Old Master repeated. This time he addressed his soldiers in Egypt. Mrs. Smuts stood at his side. She smiled.

Oubaas and *Ouma* arrived in Cairo on August 12, in an American-built Lockheed, to visit the Springboks. They toured the camps. In each one the two main arteries were called *Oubaasweg* (road) and *Oumalaan* (lane). The main road, running through the entire South African encampment, was named Smuts Avenue. True to his habits, the soldiers' father flew to the forwardmost trenches, where he picked up his son Lieutenant Jan to accompany him, and meet *Ouma* in Cairo. He took breakfast in a dugout many feet below the surface. He told the soldiers: "Your friends and families are always thinking of you."

The Second Division had just arrived. The men were still busy digging themselves in, many stripped to the waist. While digging they came upon the ruins of a temple full of relics. They were stunned to see their Commander in Chief recognizing and explaining every piece.

Opening the South African Officers' Club in Cairo, Smuts told his officers that the opposition elements in the Union who had been thwarting the war effort were weakening. Ominous clouds still loomed. But the people realized ever more clearly that the government had been right in not remaining neutral. "The Mediterranean may well become the greatest battlefield in human history," he told his men on another occasion. "This is the testing ground. You'll get all the fighting you want. You'll be in it up to the neck!" The Springboks cheered.

Smuts spent three days in Egypt. He had a long talk with Churchill. He conferred with Sir Alan Cunningham, then General Officer commanding in East Africa, and his brother Admiral Sir Andrew Cunningham, with Air Marshal A. W. Tedder, Sir Claude Auchinleck, Lieutenant-General Sir Thomas Blamey, Commander in Chief of the Australian Force and then second in command in North Africa, and finally with Mr. Oliver Lyttleton, British Minister of State in the Middle East. Throughout his talks he emphasized his belief in the supremacy of the air force over all other weapons. Ever since he had witnessed the first German air raids on London in 1917, he recollected, he had no doubt that air force would be the decisive instrument in any struggle of the future. Perhaps his vision led him a bit too far. The septuagenarian air-enthusiast ventured to predict that Air Force alone would defeat Germany, the South African Air Force, of course, participating powerfully. An invasion of the continent would not be necessary. His prediction was respectfully listened to. But "the Auk" begged to disagree. In his opinion an invasion of Europe would be inevitable. And a strong American Expeditionary Force would have to be in it.

Mrs. Smuts had an equally busy program of engagement. Visiting hospitals, she said to a wounded Springbok: "You are not only fighting for South Africa. You are also helping Great Britain to save western civilization." The former Isie Krige of Stellenbosch had come a long way.

With her sweet grandmotherly smile *Ouma* visited the quarters of the *Mossies,* the South African *Wrens.* She complimented the "army of girls" upon the important part they were playing in the war. She gave a tea on the Lotus Houseboat on the Nile where the women in uniform spent their time off. She shook hands with hundreds of South African soldiers, noted their home addresses so that she might inform their families that their sons were well, and formally opened the Springbok Club.

At the opening, the Old Master related that the idea of the air commando had really been his wife's. After her tour over Pretoria in the captured Caproni—a propaganda stunt to aid the Gifts and Comforts Fund—she had broached the question. "As a good husband I followed my wife's advice," Smuts confessed. "We broadened the idea to become the air command that is now flying over the length and breadth of the Union."

A high-ranking observer, watching Smuts' unforced intimacy with his men, smiled: "The Smuts rule is, indeed, a patriarchy."

It is, to be exact, at once a patriarchy and a matriarchy.

As if an epilogue to Smuts' conferences in Cairo, the late Sir Patrick Duncan, Governor-General of the Union, on behalf of the King, handed Smuts his Field Marshal's baton on October 1. "My dear Field Marshal," read the royal message, "I was hoping to present your Field Marshal's baton to you personally in England, but I well understand the reasons why you do not want to be away from South Africa for so long at the present time . . . I should like you to know how proud my field marshals are to count you among their number. . . ."

This was all the formal part of the ceremony. The Governor-General's tribute sounded rather like recollections from an old friendship that had weathered many a storm. Tactfully and persistently, he called the new Field Marshal by his old title. Sir Patrick, indeed, had spent most of his political life in close association with Oom Jannie. Their old antagonism at the time when the then Mr. Duncan acted as Milner's chief secretary and Advocate Smuts was hell-bent on ousting the proconsul with his kindergarten, had given way to decades of co-operation and alliance in the service of a common cause. Now both old men stood in the mellow light of the evening sun.

"The baton is an emblem of military dignity, but it would be quite inadequate to suppose that General Smuts' services have been purely of a military kind," Sir Patrick said. "I can tell you from my own experience that there is no one inside or outside South Africa who has to make decisions, whether on military strategy or state policy, who would not seek and follow the advice and counsel of the General. He is a great rock in a weary land. On the one side General Smuts met flattery and approval, on the other the breezes and blasts of enmity. But he has been neither softened by the one, nor hardened by the other. He has pursued his own way. I have never seen General Smuts more cheerful, more the center of jokes and laughter, than when he was going out to confront some critical occasion where his own personal safety was very much involved. It is not only in the spheres of war and statesmanship that our general is consulted and listened to. In high centers of philosophy and science his name is respected. So this friend of ours is a man of many parts and of great distinction, a prophet not without honor in his own country. . . ."

Thus far Smuts had listened with his habitual composure. But the Old Master flushed with pleasure at his friend's last sentence: "In spite of many adverse blasts there are few South Africans today who are not in the depths of their hearts proud to acknowledge General Smuts as a son of South Africa."

This was all that the universal genius wanted for himself.

PEARL HARBOR SHOCKED THE UNION OF SOUTH AFRICA AS MUCH
as it did the United States. In point of fact, the Japanese peril
was considerably nearer to South Africa, whose east coast is
washed by the Indian Ocean. Smuts had certainly sensed the
danger. Ten days before Pearl Harbor he had opened a conference "to improve the protection and increase the working
capacity of South African harbors." Since Italy seemed practically out, at least out of Africa, and German U-boats could
endanger the shipping lanes but not the harbor fortifications,
it was easy to guess against which potential aggressor the new
defense measures were directed.

The very instant the news of the barbaric assault came, an
official statement assured the public that South African gunners
and the airmen of the costal command were ready for any
emergency which might result from Japan's entry into the war.
Heavy guns, manned by excellently trained gunners, guarded
the coastal approaches day and night. Long-range bombers constantly swept the sea routes. Anti-submarine patrols and mine
sweepers ensured safe passage to Allied shipping. On Sunday
night Cape Town had its first blackout.

The Union Cabinet met on Monday morning. After the session Smuts received Mr. Keena, then United States Minister to
the Union. The American diplomat was told that the declaration of war against Japan must await certain formalities, but
that the decision had already been taken. On the next day a
Gazette Extraordinary published in Pretoria declared that the
Union of South Africa and Japan were at war. In the evening
Smuts spoke to a party meeting in Cape Town. He began by
welcoming a group of American visitors: "We have known for
a long time that our American friends were with us. We have,
however, waited a long time for them. The longer they stayed

away, the greater was our anxiety." And he concluded, after a sharp indictment of Japan's "black record" with a comparison: "In America, too, there was bitter division on the war issue, just as in South Africa. Yet today the most bitter opponents of the President are supporting him. Is that not the pattern of a truly great nation? If there is any love of our country here, let us copy the example of the great American Republic!"

The Nationalists answered Smuts' call to unity by unloosing another wave of sabotage along the Witwatersrand and terrorism in town and country. Dr. Malan was busy telling them that America, now fully occupied in the Pacific, would no longer be able to supply Britain with implements of war. Hitler's victory was absolutely assured. The sinking of the *Prince of Wales* and the *Repulse* clearly indicated the end of the Empire.

But most South Africans felt that the war menaced their own doorsteps since Japan was in it. A number of by-elections shattered the opposition, although Smuts was still the target of insane hatred. "Stalin's comrade" was one of the milder epithets hurled at him. But more and more Boers came to recognize that the country could not do without him. Major P. V. G. van der Byl put it in this way: "General Smuts has not shirked, or complained of the appalling load of responsibility that his people laid on his shoulders at a time when our country was shaken to its foundations, and he, he alone had the courage, the brain, the leadership, the strength, and the ability to carry it. . . . A man is as old as his physical strength, his nerve, his courage, and his brain make him. Measured by this yardstick General Smuts is hardly middle-aged. He draws his strength from the confidence his people have in him. He has only one urge: to serve his great love—the people and the country."

To this eulogy by a follower and Cabinet colleague a leading Nationalist answered: "Damn Smuts! We want a Republic! But who shall be President? Dr. Malan? That *papbroek* (weakling)—no, thank you! Herr Pirow? He shall go to—Germany. . . . I think we'll have to elect Jannie Smuts!"

"Be up and doing!" was Smuts' New Year's message to his people. "Double your efforts!"

Like a voice from the grave came the echo from Hertzog's farm: Afrikanderdom should call him back, was the gist of his address. Only if he returned as Caesar would South Africa be free and her participation in the war end.

The war up North went excellently. The Springboks were hotly engaged in Libya. Together with British and New Zealand troops they had taken part in severe hand-to-hand fighting near Sidi Rezegh, the keypoint of the whole Libyan offensive. They helped raise the siege of Tobruk. Bardia surrendered after an assault by South African and British troops lasting sixty hours. They had an important part in the capture of Sollum. Springboks under Major General de Villiers defended a sector of the Halfaya—hellfire—Pass against a powerful Axis force.

The war, into which South Africa had entered with a scant majority of thirteen votes in Parliament, and which a large section of the population had just endured, became popular. Hertzogite stalwarts came over to Smuts. Mr. Quinlan, M.P., one of the oldest Nationalists, could no longer stomach the subservience to Hitler shown by Dr. Malan and Pirow. "I made a mistake about the war," he announced. "I am a Nationalist. To me patriotism means love for South Africa, not hatred for England. Now that democracy is in danger, lip service is no longer sufficient. It is necessary to support the government. Since my efforts to persuade my own party failed, I have only one alternative left: personally to support General Smuts." Mr. Havenga, since the days of the Boer War Hertzog's *fidelis achatus*, did not go as far as to announce his support of the government. But, protesting his unending love for Hertzog, "the only true *volksleier*"—which was a quip against Dr. Malan—he formally parted with the idol of his life, who now was a blunted tool of Hitler. Finally, Professor Cilliers of Stellenbosch, for many years Hertzog's political tutor, dropped "the advocate of Nazism."

These conversions deeply impressed the country. But the

irreconcilables were driven into a fury. They tried to make up in increased terror what they were losing in popular appeal. A new sabotage wave swept the Rand. The Johannesburg police seemed unable to check it. This was the moment for which Smuts had waited so long and so patiently, and so little understood by his own most faithful followers.

A parade of the police and detective corps was arranged on Marshall Square. The police were lined up on one side, the National Volunteer Brigade on the other. Four hundred known *Brandwagter* among the police and detectives were called out, man by man, while the National Volunteers held their rifles ready. The guilty men were put under arrest. Military trucks took them to the fort in Johannesburg. The whole affair had been planned so secretly that neither the police nor the National Volunteers had been informed why they were paraded on this particular afternoon of January 20, 1942. Police from other parts of the Union were drafted. Two days after the purge the Johannesburg police force was again at full strength. The pest of sabotage was not yet under control, but at least crime was no longer aided and abetted by accomplices within the forces. Quiet, calm, imperturbable as ever, Smuts told Parliament: "For the moment the government has gone far enough in stamping out sabotage. But we will certainly take stronger measures if things go further."

Things did go further, and not for the better. The Japanese conquests stunned the world. Rommel began to assert himself in Libya. Again a wave of half-heartedness swept the country. And again Smuts was at his post. Paternally he scolded his people for their lukewarm attitude, for behaving as if they were not part of the war. "Some people still look to maintaining conditions as they were before the war. They seem not to realize that we are all engaged in a life-and-death struggle, in a global war in which South Africa has a vital stake. Yet some people feel the little deprivations. When we have to pay more for this and that, or find that things previously common are difficult to obtain, we should remember that bearing this patiently is only a very small contribution. We must make our contribution without criticism or grumbling. Our fate is at stake in a way never before experienced in history. Let us cultivate the spirit of gravity." Life, in South Africa, alas, had been too sweet and bountiful to foster much spirit of gravity.

In addition to all his strenuous duties the Old Master had now to deliver his daily pep talk. "The time will come when the Japanese will run the other way . . ." he said, and, "certainly the Allies are passing through difficult times, but war is like that." The first German setbacks in Russia filled him with great expectations. "After losing a million of men, a great mass of war material, and the richest part of their country the Russians have made a grand recovery. It all reads like a miracle." He rarely spoke about conditions in his own country. Only once, on one of the most critical days of 1942, he put his finger on the sore spot: "South Africa is not a country where conscription can be applied. But although the burden falls only on a portion of the people, there is no country in the world where war service is conducted with so much earnestness and devotion. The tragedy is that this war burden is being carried by the few, and is not an all-out effort. The few are carrying on their backs the unwilling ones."

All decent people in the country thought that Smuts himself was carrying too heavy a burden. Some old friends in the Senate voiced this fear openly. But how could the Old Master take a rest while Australia was training guerrillas in preparation for an attack, Rangoon had fallen, followed by Singapore, while the Indian ocean seethed with enemy raiders, and the hideous outrages at Hong Kong aroused the world? Even South Africa awaited a Japanese attack by air and sea.

Smuts made a momentous declaration: "Before the Japanese take this country, I will see to it that every colored man and every native who can be armed, will be armed. It will help us to know that if the struggle comes to our coasts and frontiers, we will not be alone. I will train and arm any non-European prepared to help defend South Africa. I have not the slightest doubt whatsoever that the bulk of our people agree with me in this attitude."

With his habitual courtesy Smuts called the natives: "non-Europeans." But to the racialists they were *kleurlinge* and *slepsels,* just creatures, less than human. Nationalist members in the Senate, where Smuts had made his announcement, shouted and yelled. Smuts had his famous steel-rod glance in his eyes when he quietly took the opposition to task. "For a considerable time members of the opposition have said that they were going to remain aloof at all costs and that they would not even participate in the defense of our soil. But the natives and the colored porters and drivers have voluntarily come forward to make their contribution, notwithstanding the restrictions placed upon them. There are sixty thousand non-Europeans in the army, all in non-combatant services. But they want to be armed. They do not want to be regarded as inferiors, but as citizens. If we grant their demand they will come forward to fight in great numbers. I am very sorry to say that the attitude of the native population is in many respects more praiseworthy than that of some honorable senators opposite. There is no doubt that those sixty thousand non-Europeans who have voluntarily taken part in the struggle, even if they were only permitted to serve in a limited capacity, are an example to many of the white people who stand aside at this grave crisis."

The battle of the Middle East was interrupted by a lull. Smuts grew restless. With the old warrior, as in war itself, motion was everything. He went up North again. He covered another two thousand miles by car and by plane to inspect Egypt and Cyrenaica. He repeated his already customary tour of bases, hospitals, aerodromes, and trenches. Yet he set up a new record: he was the oldest soldier and the only Field Marshal ever to venture out into the first line of battle, where he spent three days. At the headquarters of the Eighth Army, as the Army of the Nile had been rechristened, he met representatives of all the South African units in the field. They were weary of months of comparative inactivity. The sight of *Oubaas* cheered them up. Smuts acquired another nickname among the Springboks: Old Tonic.

Between audiences with the Kings of Egypt and Greece, respectively, Smuts traveled along bumpy, dusty desert tracks, made most uncomfortable by the hot, dust-laden *khamseen* that cut men's faces like sharp blades. Untiring, the Old Master braved the blazing sun for hours. He could no longer climb Table Mountain, although it was strictly forbidden to mention this fact. But here at the front he proved that he could perfectly well climb escarpments to watch points of specific interest. He visited the Springboks' proud battlefields at Bardia and Sollum. He took his meals with his men, unless General Sir Claude Auchinleck or Mr. Casey got hold of him for dinner. With a group of Springboks he went bathing in the sea. Healthy and bronzed, he stood for a few minutes on the beach of a little cove between Tobruk and Bardia. Then he plunged into the water. "I am going to swim in the Mediterranean, and I am not going to ask Mussolini's permission, either," he decided. He could only stay a few minutes in the water. A wildly gesticulating man stood on the beach, signaling the Field Marshal to return. Lieutenant-General Ritchie, then commander of the Eighth Army, had been hunting Smuts for several days.

At a press conference he reaffirmed his unshakable belief in the strategic importance of this very theater of war. During this dangerous lull, which everyone knew was exactly what Rommel, the desert fox, needed to prepare for the leap, the Old Master predicted: "Just as Wellington held on to an apparently worthless strip of Portugal, until Napoleon was broken, so we must hold this Middle East block, and we will hold it. There is a possibility that it will become the base for a great offensive. I have come to the conclusion that we will see a great trial of strength. You may see it here in North Africa, which, I have always felt, is destined to become one of the great battlefields of this war." The day was May 22, 1942. The young man, who had been Smuts' inseparable companion during his tour of the front, nodded respectfully.

This mystery man was Mr. S. F. Waterson, then Union High Commissioner in London, now Minister of Commerce in Smuts' government, and, many believe, one of the coming men of

South Africa. Smuts used every free moment—they were rare enough—for whispered conversations with him. Obviously, a grand strategic plan was in the making. Smuts' trustee should convey it to Churchill. So much was clear. But no one could guess as to the facts and merits of the Old Master's grand strategy. It remained an anxiously guarded military secret. On his return to Pretoria, Smuts disclosed that he had discussed with Mr. Waterson the important matter of South African wool prices and the general rise in the production costs of South African agriculture. Mr. Waterson had been instructed to approach the British Government with the request that an increase in the wool price should be considered at an early date.

Another result of his inspection was that Smuts, early in June, announced he had decided on a complete reorganization of the South African army. Both Springbok divisions in North Africa should be turned into tank divisions, which would "enormously increase the Union's contribution to the general war effort." Simultaneously Smuts formed two new home commandos, a Coastal Command, and an Inland Command, under Major General J. P. de Villiers, the victor of Halfaya, Bardia, and Sollum, consisting of full-time forces, fully trained, perfectly equipped, and highly mobile. This latter commando boded ill for the future of the *Ossewa Brandwag,* whose seditious, already revolutionary, activities had reached an all-time peak while Rommel was lurking around the corner.

"We are back in the Boer War days," the Old Master exclaimed joyfully. "Our ancient traditions fit splendidly into the most recent developments in tactics. The days of stationary warfare are past. The experience of the First World War has largely been negatived by what has happened today. We are once more launched upon a warfare of mobility, of surprises, tricks, ruses, and all the sort of things we practised and knew so well in the Boer War. Then there were no textbooks, no red tape. We kept our eyes open and moved fast by night and day, surprising the enemy."

Oubaas was in his twenties again. The King's field marshal was the general by the grace of a defunct republic and by the choice of three hundred comrades on stolen horses who trusted him blindly.

"If you go to Libya today and look at what is happening," Smuts continued, "you will see that there is no front. It is a wild war dance between the armies. They are here, there, and everywhere. Tanks, almost as mobile as motorcars, have made all the difference in the world. The mounted forces of the Boer War repeat their tactics in the age of steel. Here in this war we do not sit in fortifications and pillboxes. There is room for maneuver!" Did the old warrior hear his stallion neighing from the grave, one of the dozen horses the English had shot from under the raider of the Cape, the man with the charmed life? He heard, it appeared, two voices, and both at the same time: the undying melody of the past, and the clarion call of the future. It is this complex faculty that makes Jan Christian Smuts.

He is a prophet, even in disaster. Less than three weeks after he had announced his intention to mechanize the entire Springbok force, Tobruk fell. An entire South African division was captured. When the terrible news came through, Smuts, according to reliable reports, asked only two words: "How many?" Fifteen thousand, he was told. Again two words: "So many?" It later proved that the number was less than thirteen thousand. Major-General Dan Pienaar reported that the troops had been condemned to a passive role by lack of tanks, "although they had only Italian opposition against them. When they at last had an opportunity of attacking, it was too late."

It was, his friends, insist, the heaviest blow General Smuts had sustained, not only since the beginning of the war, but for a great many years. His sudden pallor frightened his entourage. To lose fifteen thousand young men, each of whom the Old Master loved like a son. . . .

It was time for a scheduled broadcast. Without a break in his voice he sent a message of hail and good cheer to a meeting of the Friends of Soviet Russia.

On the next day he made his famous Tobruk statement. He

spoke crisply, accurately, to the point: "The fall of Tobruk has involved the capture by the enemy of substantial numbers of the South African forces in Egypt. The exact composition of the South African Forces which formed part of the Tobruk garrison is not yet known. The general situation is confused as a result of the withdrawal of the Eighth Army. While we should not minimize the seriousness of the losses, there remains in the field a strong, well-equipped and experienced fighting force, the larger part of the total South African forces sent to Egypt. These units together with reinforcements which South Africa will now provide will play a vital part in the defense of Egypt and in the ultimate wresting of Libya from the Axis. South Africa can take it, and South Africa will seek retribution."

The General spoke of Egypt and Libya. But he meant Italy. The Springboks took a valiant part in the epic of the Eighth Army. When the last Italians were driven into the sea, they shouted: "We are coming, Musso!"

Chapter 34   SOUTH AFRICA FIGHTS

"AVENGE TOBRUK!" SMUTS EXCLAIMED. HIS WORDS BECAME SOUTH Africa's battle cry. He had carefully worked out his new recruiting campaign, the biggest and most successful, as was soon proved. The provinces vied with one another to replace their losses. Proud regiments with a century-old tradition were fully restored. The Western Province of the Cape established a new Cape Field Artillery Regiment. The Eastern Province rebuilt the Kaffrarian Rifles, and Natal the Mounted Rifles. At the same time Smuts pressed the conversion of the Union's fighting divisions to armored and mechanized troops. On August 1,

425

1942, he announced that the Seaward Defence Force would henceforth be known as the Royal South African Navy. The "tin-can fleet" of converted trawlers and improvised mine sweepers was now a formidable naval force of sixty-four units. South African ships convoyed Allied merchantmen through the Mediterranean, then known as the "alley of death." At the end of July the Admiralty in London congratulated the new sister fleet upon the exploits of the *Protea* and the *Southern Maid* which, between them, had destroyed a pack of German U-boats and captured the survivors. Nevertheless, the U-boat menace off the South African shores was increasing. The sea lanes, along which the Allies had to send practically all their supplies for the Eighth Army, were infested with German submarines. Smuts later confessed that he had many a sleepless hour while pondering the U-boat problem. Soon events proved that his brain is most fertile when he cannot sleep, which, incidentally, happens rarely.

All loyal sections assisted in recruiting. The Rand industry decided to keep staffs necessary only to maintain production, but not to expand business, despite the alluring possibilities of the war boom. Smuts appointed advisers from the trade-unions to sift labor in search of new volunteers. A committee under a Cabinet minister—Colonel Deneys Reitz—transferred civil servants to the army. Transport was restricted in order to free employees for the forces. Cape Town, Johannesburg, and Durban, the three biggest English-speaking towns, achieved a record in recruiting. But also the Dutch-speaking *platteland* contributed its fair share. Colonel Werdmuller, Director of Recruiting, toured the country as the special emissary of General Smuts. His meetings, he reported, were "crowded and spirited." But the young Dutchmen from the *veld* could not volunteer without exposing themselves to being called *"Hanskhakis"* (substitute Englishmen) or, politely, *"Rooi-luise"* (red lice) by their Nationalist neighbors.

"Many people sneered and jeered at the Avenge Tobruk campaign," Smuts said over the radio. "But we help each other. The Defense organization of South Africa is a circle of friend-

426

ship. We do our best to meet our difficulties and misunderstandings. To me, of course, the recruiting work comes first and foremost. And I can say, I am getting my men."

While the fight with Rommel still hung in the balance, South Africa's contribution to the Allied war effort advanced in mighty strides. At a particularly critical moment Major-General Dan Pienaar, commanding the First Springbok Division, said cheerfully: "Rommel will never enter the Nile Valley, or occupy Alexandria, or dine on Shepheard's Terrace, unless he goes there as a tourist after the war."

The Springboks were as good as their commander's word. The Royal Natal Carabineers, the senior volunteer regiment of the British Empire, attacked on the El Alamein front. At 8:30 p.m. the troops advanced on a path through the enemy mine fields English sappers had cleared. Hundreds of guns followed them. At 9:20 the troops were in battle position. Intelligence officers briefed them where to take prisoners. At ten forty the Germans started a diversion in the south. But there the Australians countered instantly. While the Aussies fiercely engaged the enemy, the South Africans moved forward, unnoticed by the Germans. The sky began to light up before midnight. At five to twelve the South African guns opened fire to silence the heavy German mortars sending barrage after barrage into the Aussie's lines. The German mortars replied, and the Springboks started their bayonet attack through a hail of German 88 mm. shells bursting all around. At twelve thirty the Brigadier reported: "Our boys have now penetrated the wire into the mine field." Six minutes later came a report from the Natal Carabineers: "Having a thin time with shells and heavy machine-gun fire." At one o'clock, however, they were inside the mine field. At one ten they had advanced seven hundred yards, and were just in front of the German pillboxes. At one fifty British units marched through the gap into the mine fields. A hurricane of gunfire received them. It was a desperate attempt to stave off a bayonet attack, which Jerry fears most of all. The attempt miscarried. Soon Jerry evacuated most of his pillboxes.

Yet the Afrika Korps continued its furious resistance. At
2:00 A.M. the Carabineers reported heavy losses. "Go right in,"
replied the Brigadier, "stick them with your bayonets, and revenge yourselves!" At two thirty in the morning British tanks
moved forward straight into a heavy German barrage. More
tanks followed a quarter of an hour later. The German opposition continued until four thirty. Then Rommel's men retreated.
The first German prisoners, including officers, were brought
in. But the men did not care. Digger, Springbok, and Tommie
slept until bright daylight.

The first encounter in the battle of El Alamein was won. The
German flood receded. The way to victory was opened.

Another feat of arms stirred the Union. British and Free
French forces invaded and occupied Madagascar, lest the big
island off the African coast should become a second Indo-
China, another jumping-off place for Japanese expansion. Smuts
was heart and soul for the Madagascar venture. He sent a
strong contingent to participate in the operation. Every student of warfare recognized the Old Master's fine Italian hand
in the strategic plan. It was again a simultaneous attack from
different sides. The Springboks operated in three columns. The
main party landed on the west coast, and marched upon Diego
Suarez. The second column captured the strategic island of
Nosi Be. The third took Ambya. On September 24, the Springboks, supported by South African armored cars, marched
through the streets of Antananarivo, the capital of Madagascar.

Smuts congratulated General Platt, the British commander of
the campaign upon having captured, within a month, all the
principal centers of the huge island. "The South Africans are
proud to have had their share in this notable exploit," his message ended.

The South Africans, indeed, were so proud of their fighting
men that Dr. Malan thought it politic to state that the Nationalists had no grievance whatever against the soldiers. "We only
ask one thing from you. Though you may give your bodies, do
not sell your Afrikaans souls. Don't forget that some day the

army will be reorganized on Republican foundations. . . ." The inevitable, spiteful smear on Smuts followed: "Smuts wants to make South Africa a base for British and American ambitions. It was he who has declared the war, not the people of South Africa. He has broken his promise not to send troops overseas, his promise not to arm natives and colored people, his promise not to exercise pressure on people who would not enlist. After the elections, he might well break his promise not to introduce conscription. Or, if he loses at the polls, he might take all the powers in his own hands, to fight the war to the bitter end. If he does so, I can only say that greater men have climbed the scaffold for lesser wrongs, or have swung from the gallows."

It was the all-out assault. The tide of the war was turning. The racialists and Nationalists were well aware that the opportunity to establish their dictatorship—over Smuts' dead body—was irretrievably waning. Van Rensburg, of the half-defunct *Ossewa Brandwag*, admitted frankly that a Hitler victory was the essential supposition for severing the British relation and establishing a dictatorial system in South Africa. But even in the moment of the panic the ringleaders could not agree on who should become the country's Quisling.

Dr. Malan had a shrewd idea. Let's stop the struggle about who should be fuehrer, and let us first choose a South African Hindenburg, he suggested. With the blessing of all the opposition leaders he visited, on September 18, Hertzog at his farm. Graciously the stalking ghost received the old henchman, who had betrayed him and driven him out of politics. All was forgiven. Hertzog was perfectly willing to accept "honorary leadership" of the country. It would be the crowning triumph of his life. The joy of expectation, it appeared, overwhelmed him. He felt a little dizzy after Dr. Malan had left his house. Immediately he was taken to the Pretoria General Hospital. An abdominal operation was necessary, the doctors said. Because of the advanced age of the patient such an operation would demand prolonged preparatory treatment. Persistent even in the face of death, Hertzog lingered another two months. Then he was gathered to Hindenburg in Valhalla.

Rommel was retreating, and, for all practical purposes, the enemy within was beaten. When Smuts had the whole directorate of the *Ossewa Brandwag* arrested and interned, "Commander General" van Rensburg whined that he was only an appointed officer, not responsible for shaping the policies of the organization. Suddenly Dr. Malan spoke about the long and tiresome path of the polling booth which would, some distant day, lead to the Republic. He speculated on the political setback that follows every war.

Now Smuts could carry out a plan he had cherished for ten years. He availed himself of Winston Churchill's repeated invitation. In a new Lockheed Ventura, piloted by Lieutenant-Colonel Piet Nel, he flew to England. He arrived in London on October 13, two days ahead of schedule. As always, his decisions and actions were swift. He had been so impatient that he did not permit his plane to interrupt the journey at the regular stops. He came, he said, for consultations and discussions; not with preconceived ideas, but as a champion of a definite settlement of the campaign in North Africa.

With an audible sigh of relief the Old Master said on arrival: "And so I am back in London after an interval of many years. That I have not come earlier is due to circumstances largely beyond my control. Like other Dominion Prime Ministers, I had frequent and pressing invitations from Mr. Churchill. But unlike them I was peculiarly tied down to my duties in South Africa and to a political situation very different from that in other Dominions. The position in that respect, has, however, considerably eased. My talks with Mr. Churchill last August in Egypt made it clear to me that there might be some advantage in further talks in London."

Mr. Churchill whisked him right from the aerodrome to attend a meeting of the War Cabinet at Downing Street starting at ten o'clock in the evening.

Throughout his stay in London Smuts moved in with all his old speed and urgency. He had come—in Churchill's words—at a stern and somber moment. Nearly all his numerous conferences were directly concerned with the immediate purpose of his self-imposed mission: acceleration of the general conduct of the war. Yet he proceeded in London just as informally and simply as he was in the habit of performing his routine duties at home.

Frequently he visited South Africa House. Crowds were gathered outside to cheer the Old Master when he showed himself—despite the London October chill—without an overcoat. Again he met the members of the War Cabinet. He lunched with the King at Buckingham Palace. The Old Master had brought a little gift: a complete collection of current issues of the stamps of the Union and South West Africa. He knew that George VI would appreciate it. The times had changed since the Edwardian era. It was no longer the biggest diamond in the world a grateful Dominion had to present its sovereign. The present King, a keen philatelist, enjoyed the collection of stamps probably more than his grandfather had relished the Cullinan. To keep the balance, another high-ranking philatelist was on the same day presented with another set of the collection: President Roosevelt, it is said, was much pleased at this attention.

After lunch Smuts attended a meeting of the Defence Committee—the chiefs of staff—presided over by Mr. Churchill. Then the Old Master issued his first public statement. Emphasizing South Africa's dominant strategic position, he declared that the war was entering upon a new phase: from defensive warfare to the offensive. With victory in sight, if only at a distance, he could not refrain from making a reference to the peace to come. "This is a man-made war," he said, "and the peace to follow it should not prove beyond human capacity—beyond the untapped sources of wisdom and planning, of forethought and good will."

To the Cabinet he delivered what one of its members called a "masterly exposé of the war situation." He was confident of Russia's staying-power, and viewed the future with cautious optimism. He had lunch with King Haakon of Norway, interviews with Ambassadors Winant and Maisky, and a long talk with Vincent Massey, the Canadian High Commissioner. For the week end he retired to a country house to prepare his great speech. Throughout his ride to the countryside his dark blue limousine was everywhere recognized and cheered.

He spoke on Wednesday. The scene was unique in the history of Parliament. A thousand members of both the Houses were gathered, the Lords occupying the front seats, behind them the faithful Commons. On the platform sat Smuts in his field marshal's uniform, between Churchill and Lloyd George. On the left was a small tribune for the lady guests, including Mrs. Churchill and Mrs. Eden. The brilliant assembly chatted for half an hour. Then three cheers were given: Lloyd George, the father of the House, rose. He looked frail, thin and worn in his simple navy-blue suit. Yet his magnificent voice had lost nothing of its resonance. Lloyd George said only a few words: "Smuts is one of the foremost statesmen of my generation." That was about all. Winston Churchill jumped up from his seat of honor to help the old man into his overcoat.

Now Smuts took the floor. Every point he made was quickly seized by the audience. "My small country" brought an outburst of laughter. Stating the great issues at stake, he was listened to with the closest attention. A solemn hush reigned as he quoted Scripture. It was followed by general hilarity when he dealt with Hitler's blunders. He more than hinted that Pearl Harbor was a blessing in disguise. He evoked a storm of applause with the statement: "This is Trafalgar Day!"

Smuts predicted the war would last until 1944. The Allies had had to cope with an exceptional run of bad luck. Russia was doing more than her share. The German Army was bleeding to death on the Russian front, while Stalin's army would certainly hold out. The unloosing of the yellow flood and the Allied reverses in the East were largely caused by the tragic fall of France through the treacherous surrender of Indo-China by Vichy.

In the silence that followed, Smuts said with raised voice: "Once the time has come to take the offensive and to strike while the iron is hot, it would be folly to delay, to overprepare, and perhaps to miss our opportunity. Nor are we likely to do so. Of that I am satisfied."

The speech rose to a noble, generous tribute to all that England had endured, and a eulogy of the Commonwealth of British Nations. "This is its glory," he said with deep emotion. "To have stood in the breach, and to have kept open the way to man's vast future. This is the glory of the spirit which sees and knows no defeat or loss, but increasingly nerves, nourishes, and sustains the world to final victory."

Smuts ended in his best manner by pointing to the future: "This is at bottom a war of the spirit—of man's soul. Hitler has tried to kill this spirit and to substitute for it some *ersatz*-thing, something which is really its negation. His faith is a revival of the pagan past and a denial of the spiritual forces which have carried us forward in the Christian advance, the essence of civilization. Hitler has trampled on the cross, and substituted for it the crooked cross. He has started a new era of martyrdom, an era of persecution such as mankind has not known since it emerged from the Dark Ages. At the bottom, therefore, this war is a new crusade, a new fight to the death for man's rights and liberties, and for the personal ideals of man's ethical and spiritual life.

"We cannot hope to establish a new heaven and a new earth in the bleak world which will follow this most destructive conflict of history. But certain patent social and economic evils could be tackled on modest, practical lines on an international scale almost at once. In sober resolution, in modest hope and strong faith, we move forward to the unknown future. There is no reason why we should not hopefully and sincerely attempt to carry out for the world the task which now confronts us. Health, housing, education, decent social amenities, provisions against avoidable insecurities, all these simple goods and much more can be provided for all, and thus a common higher level of life can be achieved for all.

"As between nations, a new spirit of human solidarity can be cultivated, and economic conditions can be built up which will strike at the root causes of war, and thus lay deeper foundations for world peace. With honesty and sincerity on our part it is possible to make basic reforms, both for national and international life, which will give mankind a new chance for survival and for progress. Let this program, by no means too ambitious, be our task, and let us now already, even in the midst of war, begin to prepare for it."

Fifteen million people in the United Kingdom alone, according to the BBC estimates, had heard his speech. Immediately afterward Smuts hastened to Downing Street to take part in the deliberations of the Pacific War Council which lasted all night. Everyone was amazed at the Old Master's vitality and stamina. In the company of Winston Churchill and two American friends, Messieurs Henry Morgenthau, Secretary of the United States Treasury, and Averill Harriman, President Roosevelt's personal envoy, he went to inspect the Dover defenses. He addressed a parade of the Civil Defence Workers: "I have very unpleasant memories of Dover from the last war, when I came across the channel and left in a small destroyer. I thought these unpleasant memories of 1917 would be the only ones of Dover I should carry into the future when I read reports of blitzes on Dover, singled out by the enemy for special punishment. We really thought that Dover was gone. But now I come here, and find Dover's men and women smiling, happy—and still alive. There'll always be a Dover!"

A couple of sentimental visits followed. Smuts called upon Lloyd George at his farm at Churt, in the most beautiful part of Surrey. The father of Parliament showed some of the results of his experiments in fruit growing. The Old Master, in turn, gave accurate data about his prize bull, Doornkloof's acquisition from America. The war was forgotten. The veterans were exceedingly happy. On Sunday Smuts took his son, Captain Japie Smuts, on a motor trip to Cambridge to see his old college, Christ's. The students interrupted dinner to give the doyen of the alumni a rousing cheer. Smuts joined them. Seated at the right of Professor Raven, the master of the college, he displayed a most healthy appetite.

His every hour was crowded. On a single day—Wednesday—
he had an audience with Queen Wilhelmina, whereupon he
broadcast in the Dutch language to Holland and Belgium. An
engagement with Mr. Harriman followed; the outcome was
that President Roosevelt sent a group of lend-lease administrators to South Africa. Lord Leathers, British Minister of Transport, was his next caller. Smuts saw General de Gaulle, had
dinner with Mr. Eden, and attended another night session of
the War Cabinet after having put in a short appearance at a
reception at the South African Club.

One event stood out: on October 31, three thousand Welsh
coal miners were assembled in Central Hall, Westminster.
Churchill and Smuts addressed them. What the two leaders
had to say was so serious that their speeches were not released
until half a year later. They asked the miners to increase production because England was faced with the very great danger
of fuel shortage. The time of peril was not yet over, both speakers emphasized. The U-boat menace was becoming worse; the
danger of invasion was still real, and Hitler was hell-bent on
achieving a stalemate, his last, desperate hope. He was trying
to turn Europe into a fortress that would be able to hold out
for years, waiting for the Allies to grow weary of war, fall out
among themselves and agree to a compromise peace. Under
such conditions no internal disturbances could be tolerated.
Coal miners and operators must get together. The ensuing Coal
Conference brought them, indeed, together, and removed for
good the danger of serious disturbances in the mines of Wales.
Churchill had again proved his intuition in calling in Smuts,
the peacemaker *par excellence* to help in bringing about a
reconciliation.

During his entire stay in London Smuts was in constant contact with South Africa. The news was good. Two by-elections
went to his followers. But the U-boat peril had reached South
African waters in earnest. During the second half of October,
U-boats struck for the first time west of the Cape to interrupt
the stream of supplies and reinforcements to the Allied armies
in the Middle East. A few weeks later German U-boats were

sighted off South Africa's east coast. Obviously they were the same packs. This meant that they had already been at sea eight or nine weeks, and would take another three weeks to return to their nearest bases in the Bay of Biscay. They must have been furnished with fuel, fresh water, and torpedoes by German supply ships, probably anchored somewhere along the coast of the Portuguese colonies. There was another possibility, too. A few small islands in the "Roaring Forties," south of the Cape, Gough, Bouvet, Prince Edward, Marion, and the Twin Islands, had, in peacetime, been used by whaling fleets as temporary bases. Smuts decided to have these almost inaccessible rocks cleared up. But this was only a local expediency. The Old Master joined in establishing a supreme anti-U-boat staff to supervise the campaign to stamp out the menace. Churchill himself presided.

Again, as in the First World War, Smuts had an important part in shaping the Allied grand strategy. He was recognized as a man of outstanding intellect, of profound experience in war and peace over half a century, and, above all, as a man, for reasons of race and geography, able to take a broader view of events and development than that generally prevailing. His work in London re-established him as one of the acknowledged leaders of the United Nations, more particularly of the British Commonwealth of Nations, somewhat aloof, but passionately in the center of things, sharing in the making of history.

In conferring the freedom of Plymouth upon him, Lord Astor acknowledged his peculiar position: "The South African Prime Minister exemplifies all that is best in the traditions and ideas of the British Commonwealth of Free Nations." Addressing Smuts directly, he continued: "You are not of British blood. At one period you actually fought against this country. But you are the answer to the critics of the British Commonwealth."

Smuts' last speech in England summed up what he had come to urge: the acceleration of the pace of the war. "The issue of a second western front takes new shape," he said, "and several new fronts against vulnerable areas should now become possible. All western and southern Europe lies exposed not only to attacks from Britain, but also across the Mediterranean. Our lines of movement are multiplied. Possibilities become tremendous. The offensive should continue without rest or pause, and attacks on enemy countries should make it most difficult for them to regain their lost offensive. We have already wrested air supremacy from the enemy. There remains the sea offensive. By this I mean the U-boat campaign, the most serious menace against us. It is evidently the last hope of Germany, so it should be our foremost task to tackle it. For this purpose we command unrivalled skill and experience. We have the air supremacy to demolish U-boat building bases in enemy and occupied countries, and to hunt U-boat marauders from the high seas. We have, besides, the finest scientific genius in the world, consisting not only of the foremost British physicists of the age, but also of brilliant sons of Germany, now refugees here and in Allied countries." Then he smiled: "I speak, of course, with all due modesty. I am only a landsman from Africa. Others would know much better how to proceed about this job."

All England smiled in return, gratefully and affectionately, when the Old Master stepped into his Lockheed to return to his old home, but ever to new destinies.

"General Smuts' presence in London was sinister evidence of the weakness of Allied arms and the darkness of Allied prospects!" *Die Burger* received the homecoming Prime Minister. It sounded like a cry in the dark. Dr. Malan knew that the game was up. While his great opponent had made history, he himself had been sidling from *dorp* to *dorp,* endlessly dissecting the barnyard squabbles of his *volk.* Frustrated and bitter, wrapped in archaic flags, making safe threats of "going to jail," he failed even in the leadership of a handful of Afrikaners. Now he was to pay the penalty of basing his whole policy on nothing more substantial than impotent rage and obsolete prejudices. Although the opposition Afrikaners, even in the judgment of their progressive fellow Boers, were the most stupid isolationists in the world, they reacted more quickly to events in the world than any other section of the population. Their own fate, after embracing Hitlerism, was even more dependent on what happened abroad.

A short time before Dr. Malan had still used a secret transmitter to discuss with Zeesen the conditions a victorious Hitler was willing to grant to a subservient, dictatorially run South Africa. Now his retreat from Nazism coincided with Rommel's retreat, but it was considerably faster. He directed all his attacks toward van Rensburg and Pirow. Those two were hopelessly compromised. They were doomed, the moment Hitler should fall.

The Old Master no longer deigned his opponents a single word. He was above the squabble. His lifelong austerity was mellowed by the serenity of active, purposeful, highly successful age. Nothing could affect him.

Nothing?

Dan Pienaar was killed in an airplane crash. Smuts' face went white, when the news came. "It is as bad as Tobruk!" he murmured. But instantly he pulled himself together. He ordered done everything necessary for Dan's widow and the families of the other airmen who had perished with their general. He suggested that the news of the tragedy should be held back until Sunday morning. He did not want to ruin the big rally in Johannesburg in his honor. In the late afternoon he wrote a personal tribute to the memory of his young friend who had died just as he was on the way to greatness. Dan Pienaar's position was sure to increase while the Axis would have been blasted out of Africa and the battle would roll to the south of Europe. Moreover, Dan Pienaar was scheduled to become commander of the South African Army after the war, succeeding Smuts, and perhaps also to make a great contribution to the political reconstruction of the country.

Smuts looked tired, when a crowd of twenty thousand cheered him in Johannesburg. But he recovered as he spoke, and he spoke much more personally than usual. Reporting on his journey to England, he summed up, as it were, the experience of his life: "I wish to express to my British friends, known and unknown, my deep gratitude for the reception they have so warmly and spontaneously given me. In my person as a South African and as a Boer the British system of today stands vindicated before history. Promises have been kept, freedom granted in fullest measure, and a generosity has been shown, unprecedented in history, which in turn has evoked the most moving response on the part of the British people, both in the last war and in this. The critics of the British Empire have their answer. At the same time it is a reminder to the British people that the Empire is no mean thing, but something to be proud of, and worth serving and dying for. My visit in the Empire's historic setting was a symbol and a reminder of what was deepest and best in this vast system of ours, which will endure beyond this war, and point the way to mankind towards the future commonwealth of the world.

"In all practical matters I have found single-mindedness and open-mindedness in the Prime Minister, and a fanatic inflexibility in his only objective of winning the war. To him, above all, the success—whatever it may be—of my visit has been due, and my deepest thanks are due to him, my old enemy and later comrade of a lifetime. Forty-three years ago I had to sit in judgment on him and condemn him to internment as a combatant passing under the guise of a press correspondent. I was right then. Ever since he has continued as a fighter, as a combatant, in spite of the aliases of politics and literature. What else can one expect from a member of the tribe of *Malbrouk?* To me the most comforting sign of all I saw was the solid and enthusiastic support of the whole nation behind Churchill. So forward to victory behind the leader!"

Now he devoted most of his energy to the training of the new Sprinkbok recruits to which he applied the scientific Smuts touch. The men were schooled in the fine art of mechanic warfare to become, as tank crews, the spearhead of the fighting forces. Special courses were given to the assault troops. Potential officers and non-coms received instruction to develop the quality of leadership. The secret of fighting, the Old Master repeated, was initiative. The Springboks were born desert fighters, crafty and experienced in the trickiness this particular sort of warfare demands. Some of their regiments soon proved outstanding qualities. The Transvaal Scottish were an example. Many were awarded the Military Cross or the Military Medal for particular bravery, extreme gallantry, initiative and good leadership in patrol activities, cutting enemy wires, crossing German mine fields, hand-to-hand fighting, raiding, night reconnaissance, taking individual patrols, and harassing the veterans of the Afrika Korps. As commander of the First South African Armoured Division, Dan Pienaar was replaced by Major-General W. H. Evered Poole, an officer who had received the D.S.O. for "great gallantry and devotion to duty" at the start of the Alamein offensive.

The support the conquering Eighth Army received in South African war supplies was no less magnificent than the contribution of the South African soldiers. The Union's new industry delivered the goods while the Axis was being driven out of Africa. Tens of thousands of heavy aerial bombs, of shells, grenades, land mines, scores of millions of rounds of small arms, ammunition, hundreds of guns, mortars, tanks, as well as clothing, boots, transport vehicles, and highly specialized technical gear such as gun sights, radio sets, carbide, wire ropes, and structural steel flowed from South African workshops. More than five hundred thousand replacement parts for tanks and guns were delivered to the Eighth Army. Captured enemy guns were reconditioned and many special steels, including armor-plates produced in the National Steel Works in Pretoria. All this was new for South Africa. Also the drastic taxation Smuts demanded was new to a country famous for having the lowest taxes in the world.

The country did not grumble. Slowly but steadily the population fell into step with the Old Master. He did not promise them early relief. After the Axis had been driven out of Africa, he said: "We are very far from the end of the war. Only the first long phase of defensive warfare has been successfully concluded. A second phase is beginning. The great danger is that the people might tire of the war, and slacken in their effort.

That is the peril to be avoided." And again he insisted: "Don't forget that Hitler is still holding more of Europe than Napoleon at the peak of his triumphs."

In Standerton, his old constituency, he opened his electoral campaign. Standerton, which he has represented, so far, for fifteen years, is the place where he makes his most important and most personal speeches. "During the past years I was like a captain guiding a ship through a rocky sea. But things have improved, and I am grateful for that. The political squabbles in South Africa today leave me ice-cold, more than ice-cold. I am not interested in them, because I am too busy with my work. I have had repeated invitations from President Roosevelt to go to the United States. But I was afraid that if I stayed away too long you would forget me. Perhaps I shall go to America later. If it is in the interests of South Africa I shall certainly go. I have been told that I should not fly so much, and not take so many risks. But we are fighting for a very great cause, and if anyone can do anything to help in the attainment of victory it is his duty to take risks and make sacrifices. For South Africa I will go to England, to America, I almost said to Moscow, I will go to the gates of hell!"

This was the old soldier's bugle call, opening the electoral campaign. Meekly Dr. Malan replied: "Let no one place all his hopes on the outcome of the war. The outcome may make it more difficult for us to achieve our object."

The campaign gathered momentum as Smuts asked, and received, parliamentary authorization to send South African troops anywhere in the world. Other good auguries followed. The Legislative Assembly of the former Germany Colony of South West Africa, ever the trouble center of the continent, decided to seek admission to the British Empire by incorporation with the Union of South Africa. A week before the elections South African gold shares boomed in the city of London. The cause for buoyancy was the general confidence that Smuts would obtain an overwhelming majority.

The most spectacular feature of the campaign was the competition for the soldiers' vote. It was an utterly fair competition. *The Springbok,* the newspaper of the Defence Force, divided its space equally between pro-government propaganda and opposition manifestoes. More than 90 per cent of the men in the South African citizen army voted. They voted in hospitals, between fighter sorties, in one case interrupted by an enemy bombing raid. Electoral officers under Major W. G. Geach traveled thousands of miles by air and car. Soldiers in outlying areas and forlorn desert posts marched long distances to mail their ballot papers. Bags bulging with ballots came in from New Delhi and London. The men of the Sixth Armoured Division left tanks and guns to queue up in long lines before the voting booths. Special arrangements had been made for ships plying the seas. A general had been sent to the Mediterranean to arrange the voting among the great number of South Africans serving in the Royal Navy.

Smuts scored. One hundred and seven of his supporters were returned or newly elected, as against forty-three Nationalists. Never since the first Union Parliament had a majority been as strong and as decisive. Pirow's "New Order" with sixteen followers in the old House of Assembly, as well as the Afrikaner Party, consisting of eight stalwart Hertzogites, under Klaasie Havenga's leadership, disappeared completely. Choosing prudence, the better part of valor, the boisterous *Ossewa Brandwag* had "boycotted" democratic elections. Dr. Malan's mouthpiece, the Bloemfontein *Volksblad,* took the defeat of aggressive nationalism stoically. "When General Smuts retires," the paper wrote, "we will have to deal with worse jingoes whose aim will be complete annihilation of the spiritual possession of Afrikanerdom."

South Africa was jubilant. From all over the world came messages of congratulation. Smuts answered a telegram from Colonel Deneys Reitz with an expression of warmth which he rarely permits himself: "Thank you, my life's comrade. We now begin to gather the fruits of long labor." Then, ever true to style, he found a few kind words for his enemies: "It was a clean fight. All sides, even our opponents, fought decently and well, and they were decently and well beaten. Perhaps this was my last struggle. If so, then I will say that the last was the best."

A few days later he condensed this judgment to the phrase: "The last race of the old horse."

Chapter 35 AT THE HELM

THE OLD MASTER HAD REACHED THE PEAK OF HIS DOMESTIC CA-reer. But he showed no signs of elation. Serious-minded he gazed into the time to come. The next five years, the span of life of his new Parliament and by the same token his own last lustrum in public life, would be the most difficult ones. He summed up: Undoubtedly there was a strong upsurge of liberal thought throughout the country. There was social progress. At least among the intellectuals a vigorous movement for English Afrikaans fellowship had set in. But against this advance stood racial bitterness, deeper than ever before, an immovable block of intolerance against the colored people, seeds of discontent among many sections of society, and a certain political lassitude among his own following. The balance seemed not unfavorable, but by no means reassuring. Yet Smuts was not disheartened. He profoundly believes in the good sense of his people. Constant compromises, he is convinced, will lead his nation to a higher level of life.

He started his march into the new world by reshuffling his cabinet. A Ministry of Transportation replaced the old Ministry of Railways and Harbours; the new office is also in charge of the administration of road transport, a post-war South African merchant marine, and civil aviation which shall greatly expand. A new Ministry for Welfare and Demobilisation was established to co-ordinate all social security activities. A Ministry of Economic Development, uniting the old Departments of Commerce and Industry, will pay special attention to opening up the so far unused economic resources of South Africa. At the same time Smuts created a National Supplies Council and a new Cabinet Committee on Reconstruction. The Old Master reserved the chairmanship of both these organizations for himself.

Even his most faithful followers grumbled. They recognized that the two more important new ministries—Welfare and Economic Development—were entrusted to the two youngest members of the government, Messieurs Lawrence and Waterson, respectively. Yet, they insisted, the rejuvenation did not go far enough. Moreover, they protested against Oom Jannie adding new duties to his already superhuman burden. Their objections were of no avail. Smuts remains his own jack-of-all-trades. He trusts his personal friends, but there is no one whom he would credit with his own supreme wisdom of moderation.

The great reformer has more and more learned to proceed gradually. He is well aware that the economic and social system is changing all over the world. The septuagenarian hails the change. But he is determined to keep it under control. He wants prosperity without a boom, industrial expansion without a mushroom growth of industry, neither state socialism nor laissez faire. "The structure and activities of society are undergoing extensive alterations," he explained. "An increasing amount of State interference with privately conducted business is in evidence in all countries. We in South Africa want to preserve the system of private enterprise. Yet there must be certain economic controls to bridge the transition period to peacetime economy. The wider problems of State's responsibility will remain, and the government will have to find out by experience how extensive the controls should be and what form they should take."

Post-war planning, however, works both ways. While Smuts was all set for his march into the new world the danger he had anticipated actually arose: almost unconsciously South Africa was slipping out of the war. Her shores were no longer threatened by a Japanese attack. The enemy had been driven out from the black continent. Smuts' "Clear Africa first!" policy was triumphantly vindicated. Mussolini was done for, and Italy had unconditionally surrendered. Both events justified Smuts' long range vision. But now the people at home relaxed. With their own country out of imminent danger, victory seemed in the bag. Recruiting declined so steadily that only young men reaching military age volunteered. Complacency and optimism began to work for Hitler. When Major-General George Brink, C.B., D.S.O., was appointed Director General for Demobilisation, thousands of people simply forgot their war duties. General Brink had to emphasize that his job was only to prepare for the return of the soldiers after the war. His department, he stressed, was concerned with problems which would become acute a year or two hence.

Smuts himself had to bring his people back to reality. He outlined the actual war situation: "We are now rapidly approaching that great moment which will open the final phase of the war in Europe. From now on we possess full freedom of strategic movements across the oceans, and our vastly superior airpowers enable us to exert decisive air-superiority on all fronts. With our increasing tempo of bombing most of the great centers of Germany will, in another twelve months, be in ruins or nonexistent," he predicted on the fourth anniversary of the war. "The Fortress of Europe will disappear physically before this air onslaught by night and day. Its effect on civilian morale will be more devastating than its physical effects. But there is even more than the air blitz to point out the doom of Festung Europe. Hitler is already falling back upon and using his reserves of manpower and material resources. The limits of physical exhaustion are not so far off. Occupied and satellite countries are being pumped dry for manpower, raw material, and food. The suffering subject peoples are writhing and seething with suppressed or open revolt. The German fighting forces do not remain unaffected. German U-boat crews and airmen are no longer fighting up to their old standards. In Germany Himm-

ler with his Gestapo and S.S. forces had to be put in charge—a
sure sign of internal heaving and cracking. Apathy, disillusion,
and despair are beginning to grip the people who see victory
and its conquests going, who have seen Mussolini and Fascism
go, who now see the immense forces of East and West marching toward the Fortress of Europe. The internal agitation is
growing and is all the more dangerous because it is suppressed
and driven underground. Faith in the Fuehrer and belief in the
New Order are vanishing."

In a mass rally in the City Hall of Johannesburg he added,
three weeks later: "This time there will be no less than unconditional surrender, though the German armies will fight bitterly
and hard. There is no question of Germany winning this war or
of a stalemate. The war has to be won, and it has to be won on
German soil. There must be nothing like what happened in the
last war, when Germany made an armistice and secured peace
without the foot of a single Allied soldier being set on German
soil. This time it must be unconditional surrender, dictated in
the enemy's capitals, in Berlin—and elsewhere."

Is this bitter-ender still the Smuts of Versailles? Certainly he
is. He wants to castigate the Germans, but only in order to forgive them once more. His great diatribe against Nazism was
coupled with the German people's apology: "The Germans are
a great people. For centuries they have taken a leading part in
most of the lines of European advance. They are not all Nazi
monsters, moral perverts, or devil worshippers infected with the
satanic virus of Hitler. Deep in the heart of that great people
slumbers something which is very precious to our race. What
has happened inside Germany, what has been done to innocent
neighboring people in recent years had sunk deeply, scorch-
ingly into millions of German minds. There is another and a
better Germany that must have passed through hell in witness-
ing the brutal and lawless inhumanity of their people. The
degradation of their people under Hitler and his fellow gangsters must be more than decent human nature can stand or bear
for long. A deep revolt is brewing inside Germany which must
be more catastrophic for Hitler and Nazidom than even the

terror of the air by night. Of all the vast forces gathering for the doom of Hitler not the least will be the fifth column, representing the revolt in the German soul itself."

It must be truthfully stated that there is so far no evidence of any revolt in the German soul itself, nor have Smuts' millions of scorched German minds in any recognizable way protested against what was happening inside Germany and what has been done to innocent neighboring people. In fact, the "decent, human nature" of the Germans *did* stand and bear the "degradation" of their people long enough, precisely ten years, without bursting out. But such trifling objections would not occur to the old warrior without hatred.

His house-cleaning most efficiently done, Smuts went on leave, and once more plunged into history. His private airplane, a four-engined American machine, took him to Cairo, the halfway house. He spent two busy days in conferences with military and political leaders, and witnessed a parade by an armored division. While the tanks rolled slowly past, he himself stood on the turret of a General Sherman, with one foot resting on the 75 mm. gun. Gravely he saluted each unit. To the Springboks and the Rhodesian troops of the Sixth South African Armoured Division he said: "I am convinced that the hardest, the bloodiest battles of the war still lie ahead. You must return not only with victory, but with peace in your hands!"

Another scene: the harbor of Alexandria. Smuts, flanked by Admiral Sir John Cunningham and General Sir Henry Maitland Wilson, standing on the bridge of a captured Italian battleship. Silently, with tight lips, the deeply furrowed face blank and without discernible expression, the Old Master surveys the long rows of surrendered Italian vessels. The fall of Fascist Italy, so impressively demonstrated in this show, was the reward of his long exertions, his personal triumph. He does not care to speak about it.

An airplane of the R.A.F. Transport Command, escorted by ten Spitfires, picked up Field Marshal Smuts in Cairo, and brought him to an airfield in the Home Counties. His reception was quick and informal. There was no time to exchange speeches. Smuts did not even stop at the brownstone mansion which serves him as his London quarters. The War Cabinet was already in session. This time he joined the Inner War Cabinet not, as during his previous visit in London, as a guest of honor, but as a full-fledged member. Mr. Churchill explained that he and Mr. Eden would be much abroad in the weeks and months to come. Would Field Marshal Smuts preside over the Council? And so the self-styled "simple landman from South Africa" stepped, temporarily, into Winston Churchill's shoes.

He is occupied with grand strategy and post-war reconstruction. Most of his work must be kept secret. Only one of his off-the-record activities during his stay in London may safely be revealed. While planning a new world Smuts did not forget his old friends, the Jews. Dr. Chaim Weizman, chemist of world fame and leader of the Zionist movement, had for months been anxiously waiting for a meeting with Mr. Churchill. It did not take the Old Master more than two or three days to bring about this palaver. The three participants left it in high, good spirits.

Returning to Cape Town, to open the new House of Assembly, Smuts made his habitual stop in Cairo. By one of those coincidences which great men rarely escape, the historic Cairo conference had just begun. The Old Master was not of the conference, but very much in it. Mr. Churchill consulted his veteran adviser between almost every pourparler. Less spectacular, but no less significant was the first personal meeting between President Roosevelt and Field Marshal Smuts. The two statesmen had frequently talked over the transatlantic telephone. Now they met face to face.

"We two old Dutchmen got along splendidly!" Smuts chuckled afterwards. Embracing his new, old friend with a positively tender look, the President remarked to the press: "No comment!" In fact, Oom Jannie had used the opportunity to drive home his point once more. He had pressed for an equitable solution of the Palestine problem.

Smuts has the privilege of speaking with frankness opinions

no other responsible statesman could possibly utter. On October 19, 1943, Smuts delivered his already historic speech in the battered, blackened and blitzed Guildhall. Surrounded by the most eminent men of the Empire, he stood in his familiar attitude: his right hand pressed against his hip, his left turning the pages of his carefully prepared manuscript, his eyes, behind horn-rimmed spectacles, fixed upon his text. He spoke of the second front in the making.

Suddenly he turned from the manuscript, took off his glasses, waved them, and declared, laying stress on every word: "In the assault upon Hitler's Europe the United States will undoubtedly take a leading part—perhaps *the* leading part. In spite of her already great contribution her role in the war has been principally what it was originally intended to be: the arsenal of democracy. Her industrial effort has been prodigious, and is still moving to an almost incredible peak. But in view of the intense and prolonged strain and the excessive demands upon the British Commonwealth, American manpower has been rightly looked upon as our grand strategic reserve in the West for the final moves in this war. While, therefore, every ally will go all out to bring about the final climax, the United States, latest and freshest and most potent newcomer into the field, may have to play the decisive part in the concluding act of the great war drama."

A month later Smuts addressed the British Empire Society. His theme was the state of the world immediately after the end of the war. "There will still be dark days ahead," he predicted. "Humanity will be disrupted, and the world milling round in suffering and disruption such as it has never known before. We will see greater changes than have happened in hundreds of years. We will see a temper in the world which is entirely new and very dangerous. There is today more hatred running through the actions of the aggressors, more human ill will and ill feeling than probably has been the case for hundreds of years." After this gloomy introduction, however, Smuts expressed his staunch confidence that the United Nations would win the peace as well as the war. "In this task," he ended, "the

British Empire and its system of democracy will play an outstanding role. Our unwritten way of life, this common understanding which is the soul of our group, has seen us through. I think, in that way, perhaps, we can make an enormous contribution to the future of the world."

In the evening of his life the evolution of the once fiery Boer guerrilla fighter to the father of the British Commonwealth is fulfilled. He cares for and worries over the future of Britain. "She will emerge from the war with a glory and an honor and a prestige such as perhaps no nation enjoyed," he told the Empire Parliamentary Association in an off-the-record speech which was only belatedly published. "But economically she will be impoverished. This country has held nothing back. There is nothing left in the till."

Smuts foresees that ultimate peace will come very slowly, perhaps so slowly as never to make possible any general peace conference at all, but only a comprehensive armistice that would permit a long process of working out solutions. For this long time, at least, America, Britain and Russia will hold world power, and must retain leadership. Significantly the Old Master has omitted China in speaking of the "trinity" of world powers. He believed, although he never said so in plain words, that nothing in China's record put her on equal basis with America, Britain, and Russia. But he recently changed his mind on this point, deciding to recognize China's inherent importance, her heroic resistance against Japan, and her new leadership in Asia. Moreover, it appears to be Smuts' conviction that France has disappeared as a great power in Europe. "If she ever returns, it will be a hard pull for her to emerge again. A nation that has been overtaken by a catastrophe such as France has suffered, reaching to the roots of her nationhood, will not easily resume her old place again. We may talk about her as a great power, but talking won't help her much. France has gone and will be gone in our day, and perhaps for many a day."

Thus three of Europe's five big powers are done for: France at least for any predictable time, Germany, and Italy. "The Japanese Empire will also go the way of all flesh. Therefore any check or balance restraining Russia in the East will have disappeared. Russia will be dominant in Asia, and she will be the mistress of the European continent. She will be in a position of power unique in European history. Then you have the United States, the other great world power, with enormous assets, with resources and potentialities beyond measure. Against the vast resources of the Soviet Union and the United States Britain may find herself in a position of unequal partnership, I am afraid. And I should not like to see an unequal partnership."

His advice was that Britain should "cease to be an island. Should we not work together intimately," he continued, "with these small democracies in Western Europe which by themselves may be lost as they are lost today and may become lost again? Surely they must feel that their place is with the British member of the great trinity. Their way of life is with Great Britain, their outlook and their future is with Great Britain and the world-wide British system. . . . I utter no dogmatic conclusions," Smuts added with his habitual caution. "I have no set ideas. I am simply giving you the lines of thought that run in my mind when I survey the new situation facing us in the world."

Once more Smuts had expressed what the average Englishman thought, but the average British statesman is not supposed to say. Wholeheartedly, the most directly concerned parties agreed with him. The Minister for Colonies of the exiled Belgian Government immediately took up the cue. His country would certainly welcome such a proposition. Dr. Van Kleffens, Dutch Foreign Minister, also expressed his approval. He only attached one demand: Great Britain should not disarm immediately after the war.

Some critics accused Smuts of reviving the balance-of-power bogey. He did not shirk the accusation. The old philosopher, the stargazer and humanist, concluded with the pregnant words: "The greatest lesson to come out of this war is the value of power. Peace not backed by power remains a dream."

STILL IN THE THICK OF THE FIGHT, AND YET ALREADY A MYTH, Jan Christian Smuts knows well that the trouble will begin when the war ends. "What worries me is not what is going to happen during this war, but what will happen after the war when we have to live together in this country," he told a deputation of Loyalist women in Pretoria. "We must build up the spirit of reconciliation," he tried to stifle his own worries. "Keep quiet, keep the peace, and do not try to down those who do not agree with you."

It is his keynote. He applies it to his own divided South Africa, to the relations between color and race, this central problem of Africa and, ever more, one of the central problems of the world, and to the links between nations, groups of nations, continents, and hemispheres.

Unity, or Holism, as he calls it, was his lifelong aim. The lesson of the war, particularly the gruelling lessons South Africa has had to learn, has only confirmed his belief in co-operation, patience, and tolerance. "My government has exercised the greatest tolerance in the face of almost unbearable provocation, yet the country achieved a war effort practically unsurpassed in the world," he insists, looking back on the hard and stony road he has had to tread in these last years. "We have a complex and difficult country. There is no young country in the world where the problem of government is more difficult. We have a divided people. But it will not always remain so. The time is coming—although I shall not see it—when this will be a united people, and there will be a united national will. We have not yet reached that stage. All our work has been done not by a united people—we have not had that gracious blessing here in South Africa. It had to be done with a hopelessly divided people, against an opposition which did not merely dissent passively, but was violently active. It has been done through patience and tolerance, mostly on the part of the government. The provocation was sometimes almost more than human nature could bear—but we bore it. We have been patient, forbearing, long-suffering, trying, like a wise doctor, to probe into the disease. Personally, I have always been filled with love for my own people. If they have sometimes talked too strongly, and looked upon me as an enemy—I have not done the same.

"Political life in South Africa is a lesson in patience. I myself have been impatient, and most of my life I have hustled and pushed on to secure what I thought was the good of the country. But more and more in the long vista that lies behind I have learned that you must be patient. Tolerance and patience are the things we have to learn. We have an obstinate and wrong-headed people fighting for their own obstinate wrong-headedness as if it were the law of heaven. I am sure that the tolerance the government has shown to those who differed so violently will have its effects in the future—that the people of South Africa will be prepared to make much more allowance for the other man's point of view than they have done in the past."

The visionary Smuts never forgets his realism. He knows what human nature wants: good jobs and profitable business. "Our ultimate aim is to provide fruitful employment, housing, and the necessities of life, including food and clothing, for our whole community of all races and colors. We are now taking the longest stride ever taken toward that greater industrial future that surely awaits the country. At last we have learned the lesson that we cannot afford to waste our human resources, and that there is no place in this young country with its rich assets for unemployment and similar uneconomic waste. And when this greater industrial South Africa arises after the war we may also hope to see many of our present political slogans and war cries fall into a merciful oblivion.

"We have a human situation as difficult and complex as anywhere in the world. We shall only progress and make a success out of this country if we can succeed in establishing harmony and balance. I am sometimes afraid that conditions are working up for a clash if we are not careful. Our human society is stratified in various racial and cultural layers, and there is more and more a feeling of strain that fills me with some anxiety for the future. I see growing indications of it from day to day, from year to year. It is today worse than it was a generation ago; and so I am afraid it is worsening all the time. And yet all our human material is so good.

"I am very much afraid that we are not handling our colored population, especially our natives, in the best and most sympathetic way. A temper and outlook is arising among them which in the end may lead not to co-operation between us all, but just to the contrary."

It is one of the greater proofs of Smuts' courage that he frankly speaks about the native question, taboo in South Africa. His own record concerning his country's central problem is chequered, a fact not speaking against his consistency but demonstrating the intellectual and ethical development of a long and rich life. Although since his early youth on excellent personal terms with natives, still in his middle age he believed in strict segregation of white and black. He did not propound white superiority, though frequently stating that he was determined to keep South Africa a white man's country, but he was convinced that the natives were happier in their reservations and *kraals*, under their own tribal chiefs, living their own way of life, than as an urban proletariat, which was, indeed, their only alternative. On the other hand, the rise of the individual native should not be hampered. "Equality for all civilized people!" had been Cecil Rhodes' prescription for Africa's headache number one, and, like many of the colossus' "thoughts," Smuts accepted this one, too, as gospel truth.

Rhodes was long resting in peace, when Smuts recognized that the issue of the contacts between various colors and civilizations was destined to become a dominant problem of the twentieth century. The Native Representation Act and the Native Lands Act of 1936 were largely based on Smuts' ideas. "What is wanted in Africa," he said, introducing the bills, "is a wise, farsighted native policy. For there is much that is good in the African, and which ought to be preserved and developed. The negro and the negroid Bantu form a distinct human type which the world would be poorer without. This type has some wonderful characteristics. It has largely remained a child-type, with a child's psychology and outlook. A child-like human cannot be a bad human. Perhaps as a direct result of this temperament the African is the only happy human I have come across. No other race is so easily satisfied, so good-tempered, so carefree. A race which could survive the immemorial practice of the witch doctor and the slave trader, and yet preserve its inherent simplicity and sweetness of disposition must have some very fine moral qualities. The African easily forgets past troubles, and does not anticipate future troubles. This happy-go-lucky disposition is a great asset, but it also has its drawbacks."

Smuts' native policy consisted in carrying out a scheme of gradual development, the establishment of schools and even colleges, with a large measure of co-operation by the natives themselves, but always maintaining a superior, if friendly, attitude. He called it trusteeship, and believed that it was the only basis on which a happy relation between Afrikaners and Africans could be obtained. "It has far-reaching implications in regard to education, health, and housing of the natives, which call for much greater efforts than hitherto," he explained during the present war. "Good relations between South African troops and natives from various parts of the country whom the war had brought together, are a happy augury." Yet he recognized the almost insurmountable difficulties of the problem. "Always, since the dawn of history, the race relation was the most difficult field in the whole range of human activities. Here in South Africa this old, primordial race feeling is complicated by another strong factor: fear. The whites are a small minority —in regard to the dimensions of this continent an insignificant minority—actuated by motives of fear. In the twentieth century the race feeling became strongly intensified. Nazism was held to be the apotheosis of race. In Central Europe race has become not only an idea, but a creed. In the Nazi ideology race is God. The preaching of that doctrine has spread all over the world. We in South Africa felt the effects of it particularly strongly. The idea of the master race appealed to the fear motive. Some Afrikaners believe if they do not retain complete mastery over Africans, they would be endangered.

"We tried to go round this fear by adopting segregation, by keeping whites and Africans apart. The results have been disappointing," he criticized his own policy of a few years before. "Our hopes that whites and blacks would live happily together were not realized. But now isolation has gone, and I am afraid segregation, too, has fallen on evil days."

In January 1942, Smuts took the last step forward: "Segregation is dead," he proclaimed. Instantly he introduced administrative recognition of Native Trade-Unions. He demanded higher wages and better opportunities for natives. Bantus should share in old-age pensions, and the fact should be recognized that natives were now permanent urban dwellers. They needed better housing, and particularly better food. "I cannot allow the health of the Bantu people to deteriorate because maize (corn) remains their staple diet," he told the Senate. "In our own interest it is essential to raise the standards of living among natives. Increased wages will do the trick; they would also stimulate the consumption of our own products."

Smuts' volte-face in the native question is not quite complete. South African natives have not yet the vote. In Parliament they are represented by three white members appointed by the government. This measure of precaution seemed necessary due to the Communist agitation which strongly appealed to at least the urbanized colored people of South Africa. Whether Stalin's dissolution of the Comintern will stop red propaganda in the bush and in the mines is a matter of conjecture. Smuts, for his part, does not trust anyone but himself. He makes his own radio propaganda among the natives. Three times a week man and beast in the bush are startled by an invisible voice. "This is Lukasa calling. You will now hear the news in Bemba, Chinyanja, Lozi, and Tonga. . . . The Bwana

Mkubwa's (great masters, the term the Germans applied to themselves in their colonial days) forces have received another beating. Their sea-alligators and fire-spitting crocodiles are rapidly being destroyed." As soon as the bush negroes have learned their lessons the sea-alligators and fire-spitting crocodiles will be called U-boats, and "the Bwana Mkubwa's forces" Jerries.

The color problem in South Africa is by no means confined to the natives. There is the huge colony of Indians, most of whom sabotage the war effort. Smuts has no love for them. When a number of rich Indian merchants complained that they were unable to purchase real estate in Durban—where they already form half the population—the Old Master advised them instead to invest their surplus cash in war bonds.

Finally there remain five thousand Chinese, sons and grandsons of the indentured labor on the Rand. Fighting them, Smuts had come into power. He never forgets a debt of gratitude. He recognizes that their descendants form an exceptionally law-abiding, frugal, industrial community, who do not even complain about a series of restrictive laws restraining their economic rights.

Ever since his speech in Kimberley, delivered in 1895, which had been his true baptism of fire in politics, Smuts dreamed Cecil Rhodes' plan "from Cape to Cairo." He greatly enlarged it. Smuts means the real thing: the whole black continent.

For almost four decades his English friends did not see eye to eye with him. The native question stood between them. A White Paper, issued in London in 1923, and still valid, declared paramountcy of the Africans'—natives'—interest the bedrock of British policy in Africa. The official policy of the Union, however, clung to the color bar and "trusteeship." In later years, and primarily through the war, in which English and South African troops have fought in exemplary comradeship with colored and colonial units, both policies have moved closer toward each other.

Smuts repeatedly assured that his plan of the United States of Africa was a matter of economic interest and concern, not a question of jingoism or African Imperialism, and in no way affecting the different sovereignties, the European loyalties or relationships of the several communities. Yet pan-Africa, as he interpreted it, should be much more than merely an economic scheme to favor the removal of trade barriers wherever possible, and coupled with greatest freedom of economic intercourse between the African states and colonies. The destiny of the Union depends on Africa moving closer together, Smuts insists.

The final regulation of the color problem shall be attempted by regular conferences to achieve the greatest measure of coordination within the African territories; if not today, so over a period of years. Administratively Smuts favors—as within the British Commonwealth—the growth of local autonomy. But practical problems, pertinent to all parts of Africa, communications, scientific and medical research, fight against plagues, diseases and soil erosion, should be solved by pan-African collaboration.

The foremost aim of Smuts' great conception is, in his own words, "the ultimate control of defense." It was practically achieved in this war when British, Union, Free French and Belgian troops, both white and black, co-operated without regard for the inter-Allied borders they were crossing. The Portuguese alone stood aside. But Smuts, with his strongly developed understanding of human frailties, refuses to leave the Portuguese in the lurch. In many conferences with Portuguese statesmen and colonial administrators, he stressed the community of interests between neighbors. To him it is all Africa, with no exceptions.

Unfortunately, all Africa is a very large portion, and with the wisdom of his age the Old Master understands it. Lately, he speaks less of a dogmatic pan-Africa, and more of a federation of its four great regions: first, the Mediterranean region, which is indivisibly linked to southern Europe; second, the rich western coastal region, including the Belgian Congo; third, the North East with Somaliland, Eritrea, and Ethiopia; and finally, the Union of South Africa and the British colonies and mandates including Kenya.

If this conception no longer represents the United States of Africa, it does embody his idea of greater federations to replace and amalgamate the small nation-states which, to Smuts, are today an anachronism.

And this is not only true for Africa, but for the world. The world Smuts looks forward to can only emerge from an out-and-out victory of the United Nations. It can no longer be a world of small independent sovereign states. The future belongs to larger human groupings. The pressure of the times has already welded the free democracies, representing western civilization, into one group. Similar pressure, Smuts believes, will bring all together into one great world organization.

This association will not be a mere repetition of the League of Nations. There will be various degrees of affinity. The inner circle will be built by the United States and the Commonwealth of British Nations, which, Smuts believes, have the same ethics of life and the same political philosophy. They have, in addition, the strong links of a common language and literary culture. Thus the United States and Great Britain should form a very natural group. But he warns lest the natural group should develop into an Anglo-American political Axis. To him it would be a lopsided world if these two powers attempted to rule the rest of the world. It would be a union of interests, and sure to arouse opposition.

Smuts' holistic order embraces more than an Anglo-American alliance, or even an alliance of the Trinity. To him all the victims of Hitler and Japan represent the outer circle of free democracies; a few other states, neutrals, would also fall into this group. When peace comes they will quite naturally form themselves into a world society which will provide for effective action in all important matters affecting future security and reform. In this way an efficiently functioning organization of the world community will arise, capable of tying even nations competing with each other to the paths of peace and ordered progress, and arranging its relations with the defeated Axis states, who should, at first, not be members of the association.

This new world society would follow positive and constructive policies for the future, and not concern itself particularly with penal or revengeful action toward old enemies. And in this way, Smuts hopes, the world may forget its bitter wrongs. "First and foremost we shall be called upon to put our own house in our own democratic circle in order," Smuts concludes his vision of the new world, "and ensure as far as possible against the sort of dangers which have now twice overwhelmed us in one generation. Leave the rest to time, to the workings of ordinary prudence and sympathy and reviving generosity. Do not let us attempt more than is wisely possible for the immediate future after the war. Time is a great force, a great healer, and a great builder. Let us leave it its place and its function in our vision of the future."

The Old Master will certainly occupy a seat of honor at the peace conference. He has rendered the cause of humanity tremendous service during the war. Perhaps he will have an opportunity of rendering even greater service when the war is over. When there will be deep, almost mortal wounds to heal, and gigantic tasks of reconstruction to fulfill, the world will need his wise, tolerant, farseeing statesmanship, his philosophic understanding of human nature, his unparalleled experience, and his dauntless faith.

The Old Master does not advertise his faith. But once, in the worst crisis of the war, he told his people: "I do not see the man of Munich. I see the man of Galilee." And throughout his blessed life, he has lived the Lord's word: "Love thine enemy."

BIBLIOGRAPHY

Bell, F. W., "General Hertzog," *Fortnightly Review,* New York, 1924.

Benson, A. C., *The Happy Warrior,* Cambridge University Press, 1917.

Buchan, John, *The African Colony,* W. Blackwood and Sons, Edinburgh, 1903.

——, *The Pilgrim's Way,* Houghton Mifflin & Co., 1940.

Churchill, Winston, *From London to Ladysmith via Pretoria,* Longmans, Green & Co.

Colvin, Ian Duncan, *The Life of Jameson,* E. Arnold & Co., London, 1922.

De Wet, Christiaan R., *Three Years' War,* Charles Scribner's Sons, 1902.

Doke, J. J., *An Indian Patriot in South Africa,* G. A. Natesan & Co., Madras.

Doyle, Sir Arthur Conan, *The Great Boer War,* New York, McClure, Phillips & Co., 1900.

Engelenburg, F. V., *General Louis Botha,* London, G. G. Harrap & Co., 1929.

Fitzpatrick, Sir Percy, *The Transvaal from Within,* W. Heinemann & Co., London, 1899.

Garvin, J. L., *The Life of Joseph Chamberlain,* Macmillan & Co., London.

Headlam, Cecil ed., *The Milner Papers,* Cassell, 1931.

House, E. M., Seymour, C., *What Really Happened in Paris,* Charles Scribner's Sons, 1921.

Iwan-Mueller, E. B., *Lord Milner and South Africa,* W. Heinemann & Co., London, 1902.

Levi, N., *Jan Smuts,* Longmans, Green & Co., 1917.

Millin, Sarah G., *Cecil Rhodes*, Harper & Brothers, 1933.

——, *General Smuts*, Little Brown & Co., 1936.

——, *The South Africans*, Boni & Liveright, 1927.

Neame, L. E., *General Hertzog*, Hurst, London, 1930.

——, *Some South African Politicians*, Capetown, Maskew Miller Ltd.

Nicolson, Harold, *Peacemaking 1919*, Houghton Mifflin Co., 1933.

Phillips, Sir Lionel, *Some Reminiscences*, London, Hutchinson & Co., 1924.

Reitz, F. W., *A Century of Wrong*, Transvaal Government Publication, Pretoria, 1899.

Sampson, P. J., *The Capture of De Wet*, E. Arnold & Co., London, 1915.

Simpson, J. S. M., *South Africa Fights*, Hodder & Stoughton Ltd., London, 1941.

Smuts, Jan Christian, *Holism and Evolution*, The Macmillan Co., 1926.

——, *Plans for a Better World*, Hodder & Stoughton Ltd., London.

Trollope, Anthony ed., P. Haworth, *South Africa*, Longmans, Green & Co., 1939.

The Cape *Times, Forum (South African Newsmagazine)*.

INDEX

INDEX

INDEX

INDEX

469

INDEX